THE NEW GERMAN COOKBOOK

THE NEW GERMAN COOKBOOK

More Than 230 Contemporary and Traditional Recipes

Jean Anderson
and Hedy Würz

HarperCollins*Publishers*

Portions of this book originally appeared in slightly different form in *Bon Appétit* and *Family Circle* magazines.

Recipes for Cod with Sauerkraut and Tarragon Sauce (p. 212), Cauliflower Custard with Spinach Sauce (p. 257), Gratin of Porcini (p. 274), Potato Salad in Light Chervil Dressing (p. 293), Pumpernickel Bavarian Cream with Raspberry Purée (p. 348), and Poppy Seed Ice Cream (p. 353) adapted and reprinted from *essen & trinken Die Schönsten Rezepte der Deutschen Küche* courtesy of *essen & trinken*.

HarperCollins books may be purchased for educational, business, or sales promotional use. For information please write Special Markets Department, HarperCollins Publishers, Inc., 10 East 53rd Street, New York, NY 10022.

FIRST EDITION

Designed by Paula Scher and Ron Louie, Pentagram, NY

Library of Congress Cataloging-in-Publication Data

Anderson, Jean
    The new German cookbook/Jean Anderson, Hedy Würz. Wines and beers of Germany by Lamar Elmore.—1st ed.
       p.   cm.
    Includes bibliographical references and index.
    ISBN 0-06-016202-3
    1. Cookery, German. 2. Food Habits—Germany. 3. Food—Terminology. 4. German language—Glossaries, vocabularies etc. 5. English language—Glossaries, vocabularies, etc. I. Würz, Hedy. II. Elmore, Lamar. Wines and beers of Germany. 1993. III. Title.
TX721.A62 1993
641.5943—dc20   92-56211

      03 04 05 RRD   15 16 17 18 19 20

Dedication

To the memory of our mothers, Marian March Johnson Anderson and Rosa Honold Würz, who not only taught us to cook but also passed along their love of good food.

Also to our editor, Susan Friedland, who believed in this book from the start, went to bat for it, and then gave us the time we needed to get the job done.

A Special Acknowledgment

First and foremost, profuse thanks to ever-willing, ever-professional Georgia Chan Downard for yeoman service in testing many of these recipes and adapting them so skillfully for American cooks and kitchens, often under ferocious deadline pressure.

Special thanks go, too, to our wonderful agent, Barney Karpfinger, who fought for this book and found it just the right home.

So many other people lent a hand in one way or another in the shaping of this book that we would like to say at the outset, *Vielen Dank!* to one and all. These are colleagues, friends, acquaintances, even perfect strangers from all parts of Germany who took time to track down favorite recipes and send them to us, people who shared their particular knowledge of regional food and drink.

For the names of those both in Germany and the United States who have been particularly helpful, please see the more detailed acknowledgments at the end of the book.

CONTENTS

German cooking may be the most misunderstood—the most *underrated*—of western cuisines. Any mention of it calls to mind fatty wursts, "cannonball" dumplings, pigs' knuckles, sauerkraut, black bread—the old-fashioned, rib-sticking recipes we all associate with Germany.

9

Such dishes still exist, a few are firmly fixed in the repertoire of German classics. For the most part, however, the weighty war-horses are served in country homes, the small-town *Gasthaus,* or in traditional restaurants where old ways die hard. Elsewhere, in the big towns and cities, and especially among modern cooks, be they young or simply of a youthful turn of mind, there's an interest in fitness, driven perhaps by Germany's two tennis superstars, Boris Becker and Steffi Graf. Whatever the reason, many Germans are beginning to lighten up, both in what they cook at home and in what they choose to eat in restaurants.

This break with tradition began fifteen, maybe twenty years ago, when a new band of young German chefs took up the tasting spoons—chefs who roamed far and wide, then came home to reinterpret and refine the dishes with which they grew up. In addition, talented chefs from neighboring countries—notably Austria—landed in Germany because of the appreciative audiences there as well as an increasing supply of top-quality produce.

You've only to wander the back roads of Bavaria or the Black Forest, for example, pausing at some of the romantic little inns and castle-hotels to see what today's German chefs are up to. Or spend an evening at such celebrated restaurants as Munich's Aubergine or Tantris. Or try such distinguished hotel dining rooms as Brenner's Park in Baden-Baden, the Vier Jahreszeiten Kempinski in Munich, Hotel-Restaurant Ritter in Durbach, the Nassauer Hof in Wiesbaden, or Pflaum's Posthotel in Pegnitz.

What you're likely to find here is *not* a weighty Schnitzel à la Holstein with a fried egg plopped on top or a killer farmer's lunch of pumpernickel, ham, bacon, and half a dozen different wursts. No, the menu choices are more apt to include a delicate tartare of smoked salmon, feathery pike dumplings veiled with Riesling sauce, and a lebkuchen soufflé so light it all but levitates. Not bad for a country often called "the Capital of Cabbage."

German cooking today has clearly emerged from—merged with—the old. Sauerkraut remains a staple, as do wursts. But the cooking is subtler, lighter, and often far more sophisticated. That old standby, potato salad, may be barely glossed with dressing, then greened with fresh chervil. Wurst may be sliced thin and marinated in tart dressing for a quick summer lunch, or it might be bubbled with leeks into a savory winter stew. Cauliflower may be steamed, then stirred into a smooth egg custard, or leeks may be sautéed and slipped into a quichelike tart. And sauerkraut might be teamed with, of all things, cod. Or simmered with smoked turkey breast into an unexpectedly delicate soup. Or tossed with shredded beets into a side dish that's as lovely as it is low calorie.

The imagination of Germany's contemporary cooks—both the hobby cooks and the pros—knows no bounds. And no traditional German food is too mundane for them to metamorphose into something quite extraordinary. In the hands of one gifted chef, for example, sweet-sour black pumpernickel has been reduced to crumbs, then folded into an airy Bavarian cream. Delicious!

There are French overtones here and there, to be sure. And Oriental and Italian. But at heart German cooking today is distinctly, proudly German, compounded of the ingredients that made Germany famous: asparagus, cabbage in all its permutations, mushrooms, potatoes, beef, pork, veal, poultry, game and game birds, a huge repertoire of fish and shellfish, and, not least, orchards full of fresh fruits. Europe's finest strawberries grow in the warm flatlands around the tiny half-timbered town of Oberkirch near the Rhine, and the specimens here, nestled in little wooden baskets, are so perfect they appear to be molded of marzipan. So do the raspberries and cherries.

German cooking today is a felicitous mix of fruits from farm, forest, and sea, of recipes new and old. And it lures the French across the border more often than they care to admit. No small compliment.

Given all that's happened in the contemporary German kitchen, we felt it was time for a book on German cooking today, not only as practiced by some of the country's innovative young chefs, but also by a whole new generation of amateurs—housewives, yes, but also the men and women for whom cooking has become a passionate indoor sport.

To research *German Cooking Today*, we crisscrossed the country from the North Sea to the Swiss and Austrian borders, and from the Rhine and Moselle to Poland and the

Czech Republic, lifting the lids of kettles in romantic little inns, historic castle-hotels, restaurants both sung and unsung. We've seen what's cooking in the famous delicatessens, bakeries, and *Konditoreien,* and yes, in private homes, too.

From our travels, from conversations with friends and relatives, from interviews with chefs and devout hobby cooks, we've assembled this sampler of the German recipes popular today. The tried-and-true is here as well as the brand new, but it's this mix, after all, that constitutes German cooking today. There are more than 230 recipes in all. And although each remains faithful to the original, it has been carefully tested—and retested as often as necessary—to adapt it to American measures, ovens, and equipment.

We don't claim to have written "the definitive new German cookbook." Nor was that our intent. Our aim was simply to introduce German cooking today and include a broad sampling of it. The best of the classic, you might say, and the best of the contemporary.

We think you're in for a surprise.

Caution

We'd like to alert our readers to the fact that some half dozen of our recipes contain raw egg. We are well aware of the problems of salmonella in the American poultry industry and do not include these recipes irresponsibly.

We worked long and hard to find safe substitutes for each and every recipe containing raw egg that did not compromise the taste, texture, and authenticity of the German original. And we were successful more than 98 percent of the time. A few recipes, however, most of them desserts, stumped us. They didn't take kindly to tampering and defied our best efforts.

Because they broaden our view of German cooking today, we opted to include them for cookbook *readers.* To those who'd like to prepare these few recipes, we offer this general caveat, plus additional warnings in every recipe headnote.

It is, of course, possible to buy salmonella-free eggs today. *But you most know your source.* It is also possible that poultry scientists will one day rid all chickens and eggs of salmonella.

May our book live to see that day.

PART 1

North Sea

Baltic Sea

DEN.

SCHLESWIG-
HOLSTEIN • Kiel
Lübeck • • Rostock
MECKLENBURG-
WESTERN POMERANIA
• Hamburg
• Schwerin

NETH.

• Bremen
LOWER SAXONY

Elbe

POLAND

BRANDENBURG

• Hannover

Weser

★ Berlin
• Potsdam

Oder

• Munster

• Hamm

Dusseldorf •

• Göttingen

• Magdeburg

SAXONY-
ANHALT

• Halle

Rhine

NORTH RHINE-
WESTPHALIA

• Cologne

• Leipzig

• Dresden

HESSE

• Erfurt
THURINGIA

SAXONY
• Zwickau

LG.

Koblenz •

• Frankfurt

Prague ★

CZECHOSLOVAKIA

Moselle

LUX.

• Mainz
RHINELAND-
PALATINATE
SAARLAND

• Nuremberg

FRANCE

• Heilbronn

BAVARIA

• Stuttgart

Danube

BADEN-
WÜRTTEMBERG

• Munich

AUSTRIA

• Freiburg

Bern
★

SWITZERLAND

LIECHTENSTEIN

0   50 miles

0   50   100 Km

Germany

ITALY

Deutschland Heute

A Broad Overview of the Land and Its People
Überblick über Land und Leute

Whatever your images of Germany, they are probably wrong. Or at least incomplete, for few countries offer greater contradiction.

Half-timbered Hansel and Gretel houses, forests primeval, castles on the Rhine, cuckoo clocks, lederhosen, sausages and sauerkraut. All belong to Germany.

But so do skyscrapers of glass and steel, Porsches and Mercedeses barreling down Autobahns at near orbital speed, computerized smart-trains streaking from one modern metropolis to another. Germany is a land of high tech, high fashion, and haute cuisine.

What few non-Germans realize is that there was a United States of America before there was a united Germany. Although the area's recorded history dates back more than two thousand years and includes such occupants and aggressors, rulers and reformers, as the Romans, Charlemagne, Frederick the Great, Martin Luther, and Napoleon, what could be called a single unified country didn't emerge until the nineteenth century.

Germany's first real unification took place in 1871 under the Prussian Chancellor Otto von Bismarck and lasted through Kaisers Wilhelm I and II until World War I. Next came the Weimar Republic, the Third Reich, World War II, and once again, a divided Germany, not reunited until October 3, 1990.

Before 1871, Germany had been a mosaic of duchies, principalities, bishoprics, and kingdoms: by the mid-seventeenth century there was an all-time high of around 350 of them—all in an area smaller than Texas. Each of these German states or microstates had its own ruler, its own castles, churches, and abbeys, and sometimes its own language and currency as well.

15

This explains the extraordinary number of walled towns, palaces, castles, cathedrals, and monasteries scattered across Germany today (there are literally thousands), not to mention the regional differences in architecture (everything from Baroque to Bauhaus), culture, cooking, and not least, attitude and personality. Bavarians, by nature, are outgoing and gregarious, Prussians disciplined and formal, Westphalians persistent (but with an often salty sense of humor). The country people of the north are reserved to the point of withdrawal and the residents of Hamburg, Germany's largest northern city, conservative, aloof, or as someone once said, "more British than the British themselves." Indeed, Germans joke that when it rains in London, umbrellas go up in Hamburg.

Regional pride lives throughout Germany. Local fairs and festivals are more popular than ever: the *Winzerfeste* (wine festivals) of the Rhine, Moselle, and other winegrowing regions, the *Salatkirmes* held every spring in the Hessian town of Schwalmstadt to commemorate the arrival of the potato, the Corpus Christi processions of the Black Forest, with women in native costume parading across marguerite-spattered meadows, the anything-goes pre-Lenten carnivals of Cologne, Düsseldorf, and Mainz with celebrants in outlandish garb, the colorful Christmas markets of Cologne, Lübeck, Nuremberg, Berlin, Rothenburg, Frankfurt, and Munich; and the granddaddy of them all, Munich's Oktoberfest, a rollicking two-week-long beer bust that begins each year in mid-September. Food is, of course, integral to every festival, visitors are welcome, and there's no better way to get a fix on the rib-sticking regional recipes of old.

The landscapes of Germany vary dramatically, too, particularly as you move from north to south. The Frisians, a dot-dash string of North Sea islands; Lower Saxony, which fronts them; Schleswig-Holstein next door to Denmark; and the Baltic-washed upper reaches of Mecklenburg-Vorpommern (until recently part of East Germany), are for the most part flat coastal stretches. Beyond the dunes they're alternately bluffy/marshy and splodged here and there by glacial lakes.

The broad sandy beaches along Germany's ragged loops of Baltic and North Sea shore are all popular bathing resorts, but the season, alas, is short. This is the land of the shipbuilder, the fisherman, and the farmer who still lives in the thatched cottage of his ancestors. The great seaports of Bremen and Hamburg ("Germany's eye on the world") are here, together with two other important members of the old Hanseatic League—Lübeck and, farther inland, Lüneburg. Both grew rich in the salt trade and, with their step-gabled red brick warehouses still intact, they look very much as they did in their Hanseatic heyday.

Here, too, is the vast somber sprawl of Lüneburg Heath, snarled and heathery, grazed by clouds of curly-horned *Heidschnucken*, a breed of sheep unique to these parts. Agribusiness is encroaching on this great moor, however, so today, in addition to sheep farms, there are also apiaries and carp and trout hatcheries.

Germany's midriff, cleaved by four great rivers—the Rhine, Weser, Main, and Elbe—and several lesser ones, is hilly, mountainous even, along the heavily forested Harz range on the east and the Siebengebirge on the west. Its flatter reaches are agricultural, especially in Westphalia, a place of exquisitely smoky hams and dozens of moated castles.

Many of the Rhine and Moselle towns were Roman. Relics and ruins remain here and there, although nowhere more impressively than at Cologne and Trier. That skein of Rhine between Mainz and Koblenz is the river's most romantic stretch, eddying, snaking through mountains of slate. Here, it seems, every other crag is crowned by a castle or keep. The place brims with legend. It is home to the Lorelei, a siren whose singing lured fishermen onto dangerous shoals. Home, too, to Siegfried and Brunhild, stars of Wagner's *Ring des Nibelungen,* as well as to the Rhine Maidens, who guarded the pot of gold at the bottom of the river. The brothers Grimm lived east of the Rhine in the forests of Hesse and here wrote tales of Snow White, Sleeping Beauty, and Little Red Riding Hood.

But the cauldrons of industry belong to the Rhineland, too, plus big and bustling Frankfurt am Main, that twentieth-century center of high finance, all futuristic towers strafing the clouds. Cynics call it "Bankfurt." Or "Mainhattan."

The Black Forest (Schwarzwald) lies farther south, beyond the Student Prince castle-and-college town of Heidelberg. Tucked into the southwest corner of Germany, it begins just north of the elegant spa town of Baden-Baden (a speedy hour and a half south of Frankfurt by Autobahn) and sweeps 106 miles south to the Swiss border. It fronts France on the west and vaults mountains of nearly five thousand feet on its forty-mile march east from the Rhine Plain toward Stuttgart and Lake Constance.

The Black Forest is not, as some believe, a part of Bavaria. It belongs to Baden-Württemberg. Nor is it a vast unbroken forest, or for that matter even *black,* except on gray days when mists silhouette one furry ridge against another. The Black Forest is a rumpled piece of real estate, part woodland (with fat and flavorful mushrooms), part vineyard, part orchard (with apples and plums, but especially cherries, from which comes the famous kirschwasser). There are high meadows here and small family farms that produce, as they have for centuries, the foods that made the Black Forest famous—none more important than the sweet-meated hogs that will emerge in due time as smoky Black Forest hams.

And then there is Bavaria, largest of Germany's sixteen *Länder* (states and city-states). It is "the belly of the country" and, for the traveler, one of its most rewarding areas because there is more majestic scenery here per square mile than anywhere else in Germany. This is the land of Ludwig II, that mad or maybe not-so-mad king who built the fantasy castle of Neuschwanstein against a backdrop of Alps.

The Alps—icebergs in the sky—parade right across Bavaria's southern border, separating it from Austria and, to the delight of skiers, reaching heights of nine thousand feet. The Bavarian Alps rise, almost without preliminary foothills, from rolling green uplands south of Munich. There are immense lakes here—Ammersee, Starnberger See, and Chiemsee, the biggest, where King Ludwig II built his own Versailles on the lake island of Herrenchiemsee. His third dream castle, Linderhof, lies in solitary splendor deep in the forest near Oberammergau of Passion Play fame (clearly Ludwig wasn't crazy when it came to picking castle sites). Linderhof may be smaller than Neuschwanstein, but it outglitters Versailles and includes a knockoff of Capri's Blue Grotto, fake stalactites and all. After touring Linderhof, Liberace, never one to dress down, announced that there was all too much gold and glitz for him.

Bavaria's capital is Munich, a city of unexpected sophistication, cultural largess, and a greater constellation of Michelin-starred restaurants than any other German city (among these is Eckhart Witzigmann's trend-setting Aubergine, which Michelin critics blessed with three stars shortly after it opened some fifteen years ago). Munich's shopping streets are a match for the snazziest of Paris, New York, and Beverly Hills. All the boutiques with eminently droppable names are here—Armani, Chanel, Hermès, Tiffany, Yves Saint Laurent, even Ralph Lauren and Calvin Klein.

Munich can also claim two stellar food boutiques, Dallmayr (caterer to kaisers, kings, and counts) and Käfer, where rich Munichers lay in their provisions. Then there's the extraordinary open-air *Viktualienmarkt,* where every baker, butcher, and greengrocer has his own little kiosk. Munich may be Germany's nicest city, certainly it is where most Germans would love to live—if they could afford to. A Parisian even once admitted that he'd move to Munich in a minute—if only he could speak the language.

Germany's five new eastern states (Mecklenburg-Vorpommern, Saxony-Anhalt, Saxony, Thuringia, and Brandenburg) are all struggling to catch up with the high standards of western Germany. None lacks attractions—scenic, historic, architectural, cultural—but after years of Communist domination, few can provide the accommodations westerners demand.

Three cities must be mentioned, however, because of their historic and artistic significance. First, Dresden, the birthplace of German opera and the repository (at the Zwinger Pavilions) of an extraordinary cache of Old Masters by German, Dutch, French, Italian, and Spanish painters. Nearly fire-bombed off the map in 1945, Dresden is now being painstakingly reconstructed. Next, there's Bach's town, Leipzig. It was while he was choir director at Leipzig's Gothic St. Thomas church that the great Baroque musician composed many of his most profound works. The third important eastern city is Weimar, cradle of the Weimar Republic and a center of learning that attracted such poets as Goethe and Schiller (their homes are now museums).

Finally, there is Berlin, reunited after forty years. Ironically, Berlin began as a divided city—two trading posts on opposite banks of the River Spree. What is now

Germany's biggest city (with a population pushing 3¼ million) is also one of its newer cities. Seven hundred and fifty years ago, when Cologne, Nuremberg, and Munich were already full-blown towns, Berlin was little more than a wide place in the road. Its place in the history books was assured when it became the capital of the Kingdom of Prussia (1701), then, successively, the capital of the German kaisers, the Weimar Republic, and Hitler's Third Reich. Things have at last come full circle with the naming of Berlin as capital of the newly united Germany—the Federal Republic.

Berlin's most explosive growth took place in the 1920s when eight satellite cities and dozens of small towns were fused into Greater Berlin. The city's spread today is positively Los Angelean—in fact you could dump Munich, Frankfurt, and Stuttgart inside the city limits and still have room to spare. More than a third of Berlin, however, is still wooded—or plowed. And here's another irony: Germany's biggest agricultural fair—the *Grüne Woche*—takes place every year in Germany's biggest city.

Though landlocked, Berlin doesn't lack for water. Two rivers—the Spree and the Havel—course through the city. And three lakes—the Müggelsee, Tegelersee, and Wannsee—further soften any hard edges. According to John Dornberg in the *Berlitz Travellers Guide to Germany 1992*, in Berlin "there are 113 miles of rivers and canals and about 1,000 bridges—more than Venice…The *Weisse Flotte*, or white fleet, of excursion steamers and ferries plies the waterways, and some 75,000 pleasure boats are registered in Berlin."

Always known for their independence and swagger, Berliners take their pleasure seriously. The city's golden years were the 1920s. In that decade, Berlin was so kinetic, so exciting, so open that it was where Europe's top talent wanted to be: Greta Garbo, Marlene Dietrich, Paul Klee, Mies van der Rohe, W. H. Auden, Vladimir Nabokov, and Christopher Isherwood. Isherwood's *Berlin Stories* were the genesis of *I Am a Camera*, the play that spawned the musical *Cabaret*. Its portrait of Berlin as a wicked, wide-open city is how most Americans view it today. And the image is not altogether wrong.

With the infamous wall reduced to rubble, Berlin is more wide open than ever, a city of round-the-clock action. The numbers quickly explain why. Berlin has sixty theaters, fifty museums, fourteen palaces and castles, eight symphony orchestras, three opera houses, hundreds of shops (including the toney KaDeWe department store and its immense sixth-floor food bazaar), not to mention eight thousand restaurants, pubs, and nightclubs.

Berlin, however, is no more representative of Germany today than Munich, Hamburg, Frankfurt, Düsseldorf, or any other big city. It is a part of the whole but not the big picture.

Germany today is cosmopolitan, but it is also rustic. It is modern and medieval, opulent and understated, sacred and secular, big and little, high and low, fast and slow. A complex but captivating mix.

The Language of German Food, Drink, and Dining

Deutsche Umgangssprache für Essen und Trinken

20

Englisch may be a Germanic language, but any English-speaking person unversed in German will be bewildered by the culinary words and phrases he or she encounters while traveling about Germany. Lunch and dinner menus, moreover, are often indecipherable, written as they are in angular German script. And as if to muddle things even further, different dishes are often known by different names in different parts of the country. In the north of Germany, for example, dumplings are *Klösse*. But in Bavaria they are *Knödel*. And in northern Germany, hard rolls are *Brötchen*, whereas in Bavaria they are *Semmeln*.

Strangers to Germany will also be puzzled by the number of French words in the German culinary lexicon. There are two easy explanations for this. First, French became the fashionable language at the German courts during the days of Napoleon. And second, French is the language of cooking.

This glossary is designed to introduce you to common German foods, drinks, and menu and culinary terms, "to get your ear and eye in." We have not included those German words that are identical or similar to those used in the United States (Beefsteak, for example, Karamel, Alkohol, or Aspik) unless there is something unusual or interesting to say about them.

Aal: Eel. In the old days, eels were taken from the Elbe, Hamburg's river, which may explain why eel is so popular in that city. However, most of the eels served in Germany now come from the Baltic or North Sea and, according to connoisseurs, the choicest are those caught just as they set out on the two-thousand-mile swim to their spawning grounds in the Sargasso Sea south of Bermuda. Such eels are fat, firm, and lobster-tender. Some say they taste as much like meat as fish, which prompted one Hamburg chef to remark, "Nobody even knows if an eel is a land animal or a fish." Although most north Germans relish fresh eel, smoked eel (*geräucherter Aal*) is their favorite snack. The way to eat it is cold, with tart pickles to cut the richness. In the U.S., where eel is nearly nonexistent, mackerel makes an acceptable substitute. We've used it in place of eel in the two German eel recipes included in this book. The results, let us be the first to admit, aren't the same. But they *are* good.

Aalsuppe: Eel soup. A sweet-sour Hamburg classic made of the oddest mix of ingredients: ham broth, eel, dried apricots and prunes, fresh apples and pears, plus a garden full of vegetables (see Eel Soup from Hamburg, page 114).

Abendbrot: Light supper; literally, "evening bread." But broadly speaking, it is simply the evening meal—bread and cold cuts, warm food—whatever you eat.

Abendessen: Dinner. In Germany, the dinner hours extend from about 6:30 to 8:30, and the more cosmopolitan the city, the later the hour. In Berlin, Hamburg, and Munich, for example, the pricey restaurants don't begin to fill up until around 7:30.

Allgäu Emmentaler: Ivory-hued Allgäu Emmentaler is Germany's most famous hard cheese, the one with the big holes, and it is every bit as delicious as the more famous Emmentaler made next door in Switzerland. Allgäu Emmentaler is made of cow's milk, molded in wheels or blocks, and depending upon how long it has aged, ranges from mild to moderately strong. Known for its nutty, pleasantly salty-sweet flavor, Emmentaler is a high-protein cheese that averages about 45 percent butterfat. It shreds and slices neatly (one reason Germans slip it into salads and sandwiches). It melts smoothly, too, and is integral to that glorious German quiche called *Lauchkuchen* (page 269).

Alse: Shad. Shad is extremely rare in northern Europe because it doesn't swim in the Baltic. It is being imported to Germany more and more often, however, and young German chefs are beginning to improvise with it.

Ananas: Pineapple. One of the French food words used widely in Germany today, and one of the lush tropical fruits Germans adore. "We stir pineapple into lots of things," Hedy says. "Bavarian creams, tortes, even meat and poultry recipes; then we call them 'Hawaiian.'" This fondness for pineapple developed during the American occupation after World War II, when shipments of canned pineapple suddenly became available. Germans even began cooking sauerkraut with pineapple—using approximately equal amounts of each. "Hawaiian" sauerkraut remains popular to this day.

Anis: Anise. The licorice flavor of these tiny tan seeds is reserved for sweet breads, cakes, and cookies. To heighten the rich, sweet-spicy taste of anise, grind the seeds in a little coffee grinder just before you use them. The difference in flavor between freshly ground aniseeds and commercially packed powders is incredible.

Anschovis: Anchovies. They are also known in Germany as **Sardellen.** They are not as popular as other fish, but are integral to such classic recipes as Schnitzel à la Holstein (browned veal cutlets topped with a fried egg and a crisscross of anchovy

21

fillets) and Steak Tartare.

Apfel: Apple. Among the more popular varieties today are James Grieve (an uncommonly juicy apple that's only medium-sweet), Cox's Orange Pippin (succulently sweet and full of rich apple taste), Gravensteiner, Boskop (a pleasantly sour apple used in cooking), Jonathan, and even Granny Smiths and Golden Delicious. **Bratapfel** is a baked apple and **Apfelstrudel** is just what it seems—apple strudel. There's none better than Bavarian Apple Strudel, page 331), which is baked in a casserole with cream.

Apfelmus: Applesauce. A must with potato pancakes, also integral to a creamy horseradish sauce that's delicious with baked ham, boiled tongue, assorted wursts, and cold cuts. See Apple-Horseradish Sauce (page 390).

Apfelsaft: Apple juice. German apple juice is clarified, a lovely rich amber color, and its flavor captures the very essence of the apple. **Apfelmost:** is more like our apple cider, but isn't readily available. Indeed, it's considered something of a specialty (one of the driest and best is *Viez*, produced along the Moselle). **Apfelwein** is a sour drink of low alcoholic content that's drunk mostly in and around Frankfurt. Then there's **Apfelschnaps,** a sweet golden liqueur, savored at meal's end like a fine brandy.

Apfelsine: Orange. *Apfelsine* is the old German word; **Orange** (see below) is more widely used today.

Aprikose: Apricot. Apricots grow well only in the Rhineland, Rhineland Palatinate, and Baden areas, where the climate is temperate. During the summer apricot season, Germans like to eat these sun-ripened fruits out of hand or simmer them into a compote (*Kompott*) or a voluptuous sauce to ladle over chocolate cake. Germans are particularly fond of apricot marmalade, which they not only spread on bread, but

also use in making layer cakes (the marmalade is smoothed on the layers before the final frosting to seal in the crumbs).

Aubergine: Eggplant. Although not a vegetable we usually associate with Germany, eggplant is very popular across the country today. Open-air food markets like Munich's sprawling *Viktualienmarkt* sell big, glossy purple eggplants, round white ones the size of grapefruits, lavender specimens as long and slim as bananas, and even egg-size aubergines. And thanks to Germany's major food magazines—*essen & trinken, Feinschmecker, Kochen & Geniessen, Schöner Essen,* and *Rezepte mit Pfiff,* to name a few—home cooks are learning to cook eggplant just as the French, Italians, Greeks, Turks, and Americans do.

Auflauf: Casserole. It can be sweet or savory, a dessert or a main dish.

Austern: Oysters. A delicacy found only in top restaurants and fish markets. What Germans eat is the European oyster (*Ostrea edulis*), found in offshore waters from Morocco to Norway. French oysters are choicest and these, together with Dutch oysters, are exported to Germany. They are best in the "R" months, which in Germany means from September right through April. Germans rarely cook oysters, preferring to eat them on the half shell with a squeeze of lemon—nothing more—at the start of an elegant meal. German hostesses usually put out special oyster forks, but it is perfectly acceptable to pick them up and slurp them out of their shells.

Bachforelle: Brook trout. Because this European trout can survive only in high, clear mountain streams, it is becoming scarce. The rivers around Triberg, in the Black Forest, used to jump with trout and no less an angler than Ernest Hemingway once went there to fish.

Bachkrebs (also **Krebs**): Crayfish. Freshwater or river crayfish are growing scarcer and scarcer in Germany and are now a luxury. Even though they're being farmed in Bavarian lakes, their price isn't likely to drop anytime soon. Home cooks consider them the province of the professional chef, and most chefs treat *Krebse* with respect and agree that the best way to cook them is to boil them 3 to 4 minutes—often with bundles of chervil, parsley, or dill. Once cooked, the *Krebse* are piled on platters and sent forth. An experienced diner knows just how to attack the scarlet mound. Holding a crayfish in his left hand, he breaks off the tail with the right. He then cracks the back so its meat can be gotten at, and twists off the claws. Next, with a special crayfish knife, he slits the tail open, lifts out the vein, and twists out the meat with a special crayfish fork. Most crayfish fans save the best till last—the claw meat. Depending on the formality of the occasion, they either suck the meat out or go after it with the crayfish fork.

Bäckerei: Bakery. The varieties of breads, pastries, cakes, and cookies is staggering, particularly at Christmastime when bakers pull out all the stops and fill their windows with *Zimtsterne* (cinnamon stars), *Stollen,* and *Lebkuchen* (gingerbread) houses trimmed in stunning detail.

Backpflaume: Prune. German cooks are far more imaginative about cooking with prunes than Americans, who use them mostly for breads and desserts. Northern German cooks like to pair prunes with meat, poultry, and fish. No recipe proves how freewheeling they are more than Eel Soup from Hamburg (page 114), an awesome combination of eel, prunes, apples, pears, celery root, leek, kohlrabi, carrot, green peas, and asparagus. Another odd pairing—also a classic from the north of Germany—is a porridge made of prunes, barley, and bacon.

Banane: Banana. Germans are more likely to slice bananas into fruit salads or to peel and eat them rather than to cook with them.

Barsch: Lake perch. A lean white freshwater fish, very good but not as popular as *Zander* (pike-perch).

Basilikum: Basil. Fresh basil is a comparative newcomer to German kitchens, just as it is here. And German cooks use this aromatic, sun-loving member of the mint family very much as we do—to enhance the flavor of tomatoes. In soups and stews, crumbled dried basil is an acceptable substitute.

Bauer: Farmer. **Bauernomelett** is a farmer's omelet, also sometimes called **Bauernfrühstück,** or farmer's breakfast. It's a hearty one-dish meal that begins with potatoes and diced bacon or ham being browned in a skillet, and is then finished off with beaten eggs cooked just until set.

Baumkuchen: Tree cakes. *Konditoreien* that specialize in making these tall, stately tree cakes often forest their windows with them. The original *Baumkuchen* recipe comes from Berlin, and even today only professional bakers can make it because it requires a spit with an iron tip shaped like a fir tree. While the hot iron spins slowly, the baker pours a thin stream of yellow cake batter evenly over the iron, a little bit at a time so each layer browns before the next is applied. *Baumkuchen* are hollow and, when sliced crosswise (the correct way), their dozens of thin layers resemble the annual rings of a tree. Some *Baumkuchen* are glazed with white icing, others with chocolate. Most are sealed in tins or clear plastic tubes and travel well. We've brought many of them home to the United States and found them as fresh, moist, and beautiful as the day they were baked.

Bayern: Bavaria. Something that comes from Bavaria—and that includes recipes—would be **bayerisch.**

Beeren: Berries.

Beilagen: Side dishes. The ones Ger-

23

mans dote on are potatoes, dumplings, and spaetzle, but *Beilagen* is an umbrella term that also includes rice, vegetables, even condiments—anything served as an accompaniment to the main dish.

Bier: Beer. See German Beer, page 77.

Bierhalle: Beer hall. But if Germans want to go out for beer, they don't say, "Let's go to a *Bierhalle*." They say, "Let's go for a beer," or, "Let's go to *Augustiner*," or, "Let's go to the *Hofbräuhaus*," the name of the specific *Bierhalle*. On the other hand, if they're headed for one of the big brewery-owned **Biergärten** (beer gardens), they *would* say, "Let's go the beer garden." As soon as the spring sun appears and it's warm enough to sit outdoors, people flock to *Biergärten,* most of which are in Bavaria. Many *Biergärten* are shaded by enormous chestnut trees and, as Germans sit drinking their steins of beer and chatting with friends, they usually eat soft pretzels and a big white radish, maybe even some cold cuts they've brought along (perfectly proper).

Bierkeller: Beer cellar. Smaller than a *Bierhalle* but larger than a *Bierstube.* Today a *Bierkeller* may or may not be in a cellar. In the old days it always was—the place, in fact, where the barrels of beer were stored.

Bierstube: Beer tavern. A small and cozy spot, usually without music. In a *Bierhalle* there's often an oom-pah-pah band.

Bierwurst: Beer sausage. This bologna-sized wurst is not made with beer; it does go well *with* it—as a cold cut. A Bavarian favorite, *Bierwurst* is pink, coarsely textured, and heavily flecked with smoked pork and fat.

Birne: Pear. Pears grow best in the temperate lower reaches of the Black Forest, especially around Freiburg. The favorite German varieties are the juicy Clapps Liebling, the sweet and fleshy Alexander Lucas, the buttery but not so perishable Gellerts Butterbirne, and the spicy but sugary Köstliche von Charneux. The most pop-

ular of all, however, is the elegant Williams Christbirne. Germans use pears in eel soup (see Eel Soup from Hamburg, page 114), teamed with green beans and bacon (see Green Beans, Pears, and Bacon, page 242), and not least, in a variety of fruit breads (see Dried Fruit Bread, page 319). In Bavaria, where dried pears are known as *Kletzen,* women also bake a dark, heavy, dried pear bread called *Kletzenbrot* for the Christmas holidays.

Birnenschnaps: Pear eau-de-vie. A colorless, potent pear brandy much like Poire William that is both drunk at meal's end and used in cooking. Some of the best comes from the Black Forest (*Schwarzwald*).

Blattspinat: Leaf spinach. See *Spinat.*

Blaubeeren (also **Heidelbeeren**): Blueberries. What grows in Germany is the Bilberry, a first cousin to the blueberry so familiar to Americans. It's a wild berry, smaller and tarter than our commercially cultivated berries (these are now available in Germany, too). *Blaubeeren* thrive in evergreen forests and in peak season (July and August), whole families take to the woods and fill their baskets. These wild blueberries may be eaten out of hand, mixed with quark and honey, tossed into a fresh fruit salad, or simmered into a *Kompott* or jam.

Blaukraut (also **Rotkohl** and **Rotkraut**): Red or purple cabbage. The difference in terminology is mostly regional. In northern Germany, for example, it is *Rotkohl* or *Rotkraut* (red cabbage). And in the south, it is *Blaukraut* (blue cabbage). German cooks, who cook red cabbage better than anyone in the world, know that adding acid intensifies the rich red color (see Braised Red Cabbage with Onions and Apples in Red Wine Sauce, page 250). Omitting vinegar and/or red wine gives cooked red cabbage a bluish cast.

Blauschimmelkäse: Blue cheese. There are two types of German blues, the sharp and crumbly Edelpilz Blue (available in slimmed-down varieties with 26 percent butterfat) and the blander but richer (70 percent butterfat) Creamy Blue, best described, perhaps, as a cross between a blue and a Brie (it has the same white rind and melt-on-the-tongue texture). Both are superb snacking cheeses, delicious, too, at meal's end with fresh fruit.

Blumenkohl: Cauliflower. The connoisseur's cabbage, the most elegant family member, or as Mark Twain once joked, "It's nothing but cabbage with a college education." As its German name suggests, cauliflower is a "cabbage flower." Although a Württemberg paper included it among a list of new vegetables at the end of the sixteenth century, cauliflower wasn't firmly established in Germany until the next century. It was an immediate hit, and its buttery richness made it a Lenten favorite. The peak season for cauliflower is between December and April, but in most parts of Germany it is available year-round.

Blutig: Undercooked. If meat is too rare, it is *blutig*, or "bloody."

Blutwurst: Blood sausage. A dark, almost black sausage made of fresh hog's blood, diced pork and pork fat, salt, pepper, and assorted seasonings. It's cooked and smoked, then sold as links (about two inches in diameter and six inches long). The classic way to serve *Blutwurst* is whole, after a brief warming in hot water, with fried potatoes and onions on the side. Sometimes, the *Blutwurst* is coarsely chopped and fried in lard or butter right along with onions and potatoes (in olden days, when money was tight, this made a frugal but filling meal). There are also blood sausages that fall into the cold-cut category, mostly coarsely textured, bologna-size links studded with bits of pork fat.

Bockwurst: *Bockwurst* is a short, chunky frankfurter type of sausage, delicately seasoned and always served hot. Originally, *Bockwurst* was made only in

spring—at *Bockbier* time, usually May when Germany's strong, dark bock beer was available, hence its name. Today *Bockwurst* is available year-round.

Bohnen: Beans. A generic term that includes a large variety of fresh, canned, and dried beans. To get down to specifics, *grüne Bohnen* are green beans; *weisse Bohnen*, white or navy beans; *gelbe Bohnen*, wax beans, *Puffbohnen*, limas, and *Kaffeebohnen*, coffee beans. In haute German cuisine, green beans are used more than the other varieties, particularly the young, exquisitely tender *Prinzessbohnen* (princess beans), carefully selected so they are all the same slim size. These fragile green beans are available from July to November and must be cooked quickly because they're extremely perishable.

Bohnenkraut: Summer savory. Not so long ago, Germans used savory almost exclusively to flavor beans—green beans, broad beans, dried beans, every kind of bean—which explains why they call it *Bohnenkraut* (bean herb). Did they know that the Greeks and Romans used it as an antiflatulent thousands of years ago?

Bowle: Cold wine punch. A *Bowle* always has additional ingredients—berries or other fruit, for example, or woodruff (*Waldmeister*). Germany's *Bowlen* season traditionally begins in May (with the woodruff-infused May Bowl) and then lasts through the summer as long as the weather is warm and fresh fruits are available. Most *Bowlen* are made in large glass punch bowls, then kept cool with little sealed containers of ice. This way the ice doesn't water down the punch.

Bratapfel: See **Apfel**.

Braten: Roast. This may be a roast or pot roast, it may be pork (the most popular), beef (almost as popular), or veal (the most expensive and elegant), but it may also be goose or duck—anything, in fact, that is roasted. To non-Germans, the most famous

Braten is probably *Sauerbraten,* a pot roast of beef that's sliced and smothered with spicy, brown, sweet-sour gravy. See Rhineland-Style Sauerbraten with Raisin Gravy (page 143).

Bratwurst: "Frying" sausage. Sometimes partially cooked, sometimes raw, this spicy pork sausage link is always browned before it's served—either in a skillet or on a grill. It is a coarsely textured wurst, traditionally seasoned with caraway, marjoram, and nutmeg.

Braun: Brown. Germans love *braune Butter* (browned butter), also called *Nussbutter* (nut butter). This is nothing more than clarified butter that has been heated until it takes on a pale amber color and delicate nut flavor. Once the browned butter is put through a fine sieve, it's used to brown meats, poured over mashed potatoes, or tossed with dry bread crumbs and strewn over a steamed head of cauliflower or sweet fruit dumplings.

Brei: Purée or porridge. A *Brei,* something like baby food, is usually fed to infants and invalids. In Bavaria, however, mashed potatoes are called *Kartoffelbrei,* not *Kartoffelpüree.*

Brezel: Pretzel. Pretzels are more popular in the south of Germany than in the north and they're quite unlike the crunchy ones familiar to most Americans. German *Brezeln* are soft (except those served during the wine festivals), usually about four inches across, and they're eaten as often as we eat bread. Germans nibble pretzels with a glass of beer, for example, they eat them with *Weisswurst*—a must—and they eat them for lunch, dinner, even breakfast. Hedy says there's nothing better for breakfast than a fresh pretzel, split and spread with sweet butter and liverwurst.

Brokkoli: Broccoli. A relative newcomer, despite the fact that Italy has been growing broccoli for years. Although German chefs are adventurous about preparing broccoli, most home cooks prefer to boil it and butter it.

Brombeeren: Blackberries. They're native to northern Europe as well as to the northeastern United States, thanks to the Ice Age's massive glaciers. *Brombeeren* still grow wild in Germany, and in summer Germans go after them, carefully dodging the briers. The sweetest, plumpest blackberries come from Baden-Württemberg, the Rhineland-Palatinate, and Rhinegau. As with most berries, the blackberry season is all too short—from July until September. Although wild blackberries are sometimes eaten out of hand, they are more often boiled into jams and jellies.

Brot: Bread. When did man first learn to make bread? Probably before he left the cave. But primitive man's bread was…well, primitive. A thick gruel of crushed grains either baked on hot stones or left to harden in the sun. Historians tell us that the Swiss Lake Dwellers (very near to present-day Germany) were harvesting wheat, barley, rye, millet, and oats by about 8000 B.C. They were also combining some of these crude flours in coarse, unleavened ash cakes and seasoning them with caraway seeds.

The Romans glorified bread, designed mills that could be powered by animals or water, and established commercial bakeries, which by the time of Christ were sometimes producing, 500,000 loaves a day.

As the Roman Empire spread northward into Germany and elsewhere, so did the technology of milling grains and baking bread. Throughout the Middle Ages, coarse, dark, nutritious breads sustained the peasantry while finer, paler loaves embellished the feasts of the privileged.

To this day, Germans prefer dark, compact loaves—usually made with rye flour—almost all of them store-bought. German bakeries are so superior that only recently have hobby cooks even begun to bake bread—and then mostly for fun, not because they think home-baked breads out-class the mass-produced. The variety of breads produced in Germany today runs into the hundreds (see also specific popular breads—**Pumpernickel, Roggenbrot, Schrotbrot, Weizenbrot,** etc.—else-where herein).

Brötchen: Rolls. These yeast rolls are usually made of refined white flour and are also called **Semmeln.**

Brotzeit: A Bavarian term for a between-meal snack, often eaten about 11 o'clock in the morning or 4 o'clock in the afternoon. A *Brotzeit,* never hot food, usually consists of bread and cold cuts, or pretzels or hard rolls, often taken with beer.

Brühe: Broth. A popular first course made with beef, veal, chicken, even vegetables. German broths are dressed up or down with a variety of herbs and carefully cut garnishes, even plumped into the main-course category with slivered pancakes (page 99) or tiny liver dumplings (see Rosa's Liver Spaetzle Soup, page 105). *Brühe* is also used to make a variety of sauces, gravies, and other soups.

Brunnenkresse: Watercress. Much of it is now commercially grown and two types are available: the large-leaf variety familiar to us, which used to thrive in stream beds, and the tiny-leaf pepper grass, or **Kresse** (see below).

Brust: Breast. **Hühnerbrust** is chick-en breast, **Entenbrust** is breast of duck, **Kalbsbrust** is breast of veal.

Butter: Butter. Germans prefer unsalted (sweet) butter. Most German markets now also sell little tubs or plastic-wrapped links of *Kräuterbutter* (herb butter), all ready to spread on bread or slice and plop on top of steaks, chops, fish, fowl, and vegetables. Most blends contain onion, garlic, parsley, chives, and salt.

German butters are divided into three categories: *Markenbutter* (brand-name but-ter, strictly top quality), *Molkereibutter* (dairy butter, the next best), and *Kochbutter* (cooking butter, the lowest quality). Finally, there is something called *Butterschmalz,* an almost white, top-quality butter from which the water and milk solids have been extracted. It can take much higher heat than regular butter without burning or spit-ting, and is thus used for frying, panbroil-ing, and braising.

Butterkäse: Butter cheese. This mild golden cheese contains no butter, but it tastes as if it does. Its extraordinary creami-ness hints of butter, too, and yet its fat con-tent is lower than you might think—about 45 percent. *Butterkäse* is loaf-shaped, shot through with small holes, and melts like a dream. Eat it as is, cube it into salads, or melt it on toast.

Buttermilch: Buttermilk. Germans love to drink buttermilk but they also use it in baking, in soups, and to marinate (and tenderize) venison.

Café: A German *Café* can be cozy and old-fashioned, but it can also be unabashedly elegant with crystal chande-liers, gilded mirrors, and marble tables. *Cafés* are friendly places to gather for coffee and cake, to relax, read the paper, and chat. As someone once said of Berlin's celebrated Café Kranzler, it's known for "the best cof-fee, the best pastries, and the worst gossip."

Cervelat: (also **Zervelat**): Cervelat. A hard, dry link similar to but smaller and finer-grained than salami. Cervelats may be made of pork or a combination of beef and pork. Most are heavily smoked and highly spiced, but do not contain garlic. In nearly every German butcher shop, you see great lengths of *cervelat* swinging from the ceiling; kept in a cool place, they last for months.

Champignon: Mushroom. A mushroom much like our everyday cultivated variety that's grown year-round on *Plantagen* (plantations). Whenever wild woodland mushrooms aren't available (or within financial reach), German cooks rely on the *Champignon*. There are three different types: the white, the pink *Egerling*, and the beige to brown *Steinpilzchampignon*, a woodsier species that's a little more expensive.

Chicorée: Belgian endive. Used primarily as a salad green. Whole endives are sometimes braised, often in beef or chicken broth, then sprinkled with crumbs and grated cheese and quickly gratinéed in the oven.

Christstollen: Christmas stollen. Germany's most famous Christmas loaf, a long, flat, oval yeast bread strewn with raisins and minced candied fruits and heavily dusted with confectioners' sugar. Stollen recipes vary by region and the most famous one is the rum-and-raisin-rich *Dresdner Stollen* (from the city of Dresden). We prefer Hedy's mother's marvelous Bavarian recipe, which is more delicate. See Rosa's Christmas Stollen (page 310).

Creme: Cream. *Creme* is always a finished recipe, a cream sauce or soup, a cream pudding or mousse—*Zitronencreme*, for example, which is a fluffy lemon cream. Whenever *creme* appears in a recipe title—*Tomatencremesuppe*—it is a richer version made with cream.

Datteln: Dates. Strictly a winter specialty, dates are usually eaten like candy or incorporated into fruit platters along with oranges, dried figs, and nuts. On St. Nikolaus Day (December 6), it's traditional for Germany's "Santa Claus" to leave a plate of dates, dried figs, oranges, and nuts for children who have been especially good during the year. German cooks don't often cook or bake with dates.

Deutsches Beefsteak: Hamburger. This is actually a "steak" made out of a half-and-half mixture of ground beef and pork with a bit of melted butter, salt, and pepper kneaded in. The meat is patted into steak shapes, bigger and thicker than our hamburgers, not necessarily round, and never served on buns. The classic *Deutsches Beefsteak* is quickly browned in hot butter or margarine along with plenty of sliced onions. The pan drippings are made into a rich brown gravy. The traditional accompaniments are pickled vegetables and mashed potatoes for getting up every last drop of gravy. German cooks counting their Deutschmarks often stretch the *Deutsches Beefsteak* mixture by working in some bread crumbs, or a hard roll that has been soaked in cold water, then squeezed as dry as possible. Also see **Frikadelle.**

Dicke Bohnen: Broad beans. A great favorite in the flat, fertile farmlands of central and northern Germany, where for years they nourished those who couldn't afford meat. Westphalian women boil broad beans with bacon much as American southerners do green beans. They also simmer *Dicke Bohnen* into sustaining soups, or bubble them in casseroles with bits of pork—the very sorts of dishes that drove one Westphalian to verse. "Oh, holy broad bean time," he wrote, "Oh, stomach of mine, be twice as big." His couplet doesn't rhyme in English, but the message is clear. *Dicke Bohnen* (also called *Puff-*, *Acker-*, or *Pferdebohnen*) are pods with very plump white or brown inner beans. The inner beans are what every Westphalian loves—and the younger (whiter) the bean the better. In season from June to September, *dicke Bohnen* are perishable and must be cooked as soon after they're gathered as possible.

Dill: Dill. The Romans carried dill to England and, it seems safe to assume, to Germany as well. It was an important medicinal in cloister gardens—a digestif, diuretic, and antispasmodic. Strong infusions of it were even said to induce sleep. In Germany today, dill is integral to the making of pickles and cucumber salads. But it is not nearly as important a kitchen herb as it is in Scandinavia—except in the northern reaches of Germany that abut Denmark, where it is used in hot and cold fish sauces and to season certain herring salads.

Dorsch: Cod. This is Baltic cod, smaller than those that swim the North Atlantic. Its flesh, however, is equally white, lean, and delicate.

Dunkel: Dark. Usually used to describe beer (see next entry). The word would also be used to describe a dark roux—*dunkle Einbrenne.*

Dunkles Bier: Dark beer. See German Beer (page 77).

Durchgebraten: Well done. Most Germans like their meats well done, although if the young chefs now cooking in the country's one-, two-, and three-star restaurants have their way, this will soon change. The roasts and chops they send forth are often very rare. Even fish comes to table after only a few minutes in the pan.

Eier: Eggs. Like us, Germans differentiate between the yolks and whites. *Eigelb* (egg yellow) is the more acceptable word for yolk, the one used in cookbooks and magazine recipes; *Eidotter* also means egg yolk, but is colloquial and confined to southern Germany. All Germans, however, say *Eiweiss* (egg white).

As for the different types of cooked eggs, fried eggs are *Spiegeleier* (always sunny-side up in Germany), *Eier mit Speck* (bacon and eggs, an American breakfast innovation available mostly at large hotels), poached eggs (*pochierte Eier;* less likely to be served at breakfast than as the main course of a vegetarian supper, usually with a tomato sauce), *gefüllte Eier* (stuffed or deviled eggs), and, the breakfast favorite, *gekochte Eier* (eggs boiled in the shell), either *weiche Eier* (soft-boiled) or *hartgekochte Eier* (hard-boiled). Hard-boiled eggs also show up on most cold-cut platters,

in many salads, and as popular picnic fare.

Salmonella hasn't yet become a major problem in Germany as it has here, and Germans continue to use raw eggs in many of their recipes to impart singular richness and creaminess. At Christmas time, they still make honest-to-goodness *Eierlikör* (eggnog), which few Americans would dare do today.

Eingemacht: Canned food. In the old days, every housewife had a pantry full of *Eingemachtes,* fruits and vegetables she'd put up herself; farm women even preserved meat. Few modern German women have the time or inclination to do so.

Eintopf: One-dish dinner. Very much like our boiled dinner, an *Eintopf* always contains potatoes, other vegetables, and meat.

Eis: Ice, also ice cream. Italians are credited with introducing ice cream to Germany. Most German restaurants and *Konditoreien* feature a special *Eiskarte* with dozens of ice creams, toppings, cordials, whipped creams, and fruits. You can choose from a variety of inventive or classic combinations, most of which arrive in gorgeous big glasses, fancily decorated, and sprigged sometimes with little paper umbrellas.

Eiskaffee: Not iced coffee but coffee poured over a couple of scoops of vanilla ice cream in a tall glass. Topped with whipped cream, *Eiskaffee* can be taken as a dessert or midafternoon break. It is always sipped through a straw, although spoons are provided for scooping out the ice cream that doesn't melt.

Elisenlebkuchen: The most famous version of these spicy cookies comes from Nuremberg, where they are baked by the millions, shipped all over Germany, and also exported abroad, often in decorative tins. *Elisenlebkuchen* are available year-round but the peak season is Christmas. See Rosa Würz's Cinnamon-Hazelnut Lebkuchen with Candied Orange Rind (page 379).

Ente: Duck. Duck is the finest poultry available in Germany. You can buy *junge Ente* (young duck only six months old and no more than four pounds), *Ente* (a sexually mature duck of four pounds or slightly more), and the new leaner, tastier *Flugente* (flying duck that has been allowed to forage for seeds and corn kernels). Germany's choicest ducks come from Vierlande, a huge swatch of farmland southeast of Hamburg. Here the feeding and finishing of ducks has been raised to high art. German ducks, unlike their American counterparts, are lean and tender, so they needn't be pricked constantly as they roast to rid them of excess fat.

Entenbrust: Duck breast. Like their French colleagues, many modern young German chefs are cooking duck breasts quite rare, slicing them thin, and fanning them out on plates with colorful clusters of baby vegetables.

Erbsen: Peas. The general term for the whole family of peas. The finest *grüne Erbsen* (green peas) are *Kaiserschoten* or *Zuckererbsen* (sugar peas), eaten pods and all like our sugar snaps. When the more common green peas are young, fresh, and tender, German cooks may just shell them and sauté them in butter. Or they may cook them with diced carrots—a popular duo. As for dried peas, most German cooks boil them in husky soups. But Berliners like to purée them and serve them with boiled pig's knuckles and sauerkraut.

Erbsensuppe: Pea soup. A porridge-like split pea soup, often studded with frankfurters (*Erbsensuppe mit Würstchen*) or cubed double-smoked bacon (*Erbsensuppe mit Speck*), even potatoes (*Erbsensuppe mit Kartoffeln*). Whenever the soup contains meat, it is the main course of the meal. Skiers and winter hikers look forward to nothing so much as a steaming bowl of *dicke Erbsensuppe*, an especially thick split pea soup. Sometimes—especially if the soup contains some meat—it's called *Erbseneintopf* because it's more stew than soup.

Erdapfel: Potato. Hedy says that her father always used the old-fashioned German word for potato, *Erdapfel* (earth apple), instead of the more widely accepted **Kartoffel** (see below).

Erdbeeren: Strawberries. In the Black Forest town of Oberkirch, there's a medieval square cleaved by a fast-flowing stream and rimmed with tall, half-timbered houses. Shopkeepers here nestle the famous local strawberries in rosettes of tissue as carefully as if they were truffles. These strawberries (the intensely aromatic *Senga sengana*) are plump, sugary, and perfectly shaped. Unlike the pithy, mass-produced fruits of America, they burst with flavor. Strawberries have been cultivated in Germany for centuries (by the end of the sixteenth century there were two crops a year). And hothouse specimens today, available from March through autumn, are almost as rich and red as the sun-ripened field berries of June, July, August, and September. Still, *Feinschmecker*, like gourmets elsewhere, insist that nothing can match wild woodland strawberries, or *fraises des bois*. As Waverley Root so aptly noted in *Food*, "The chief gains of cultivation for strawberries in general have been the increase in yields, the lengthening of the season, and the production of bigger (not necessarily better) berries."

Erdnüsse: Literally "earth nuts." We call them peanuts.

Esrom: You might call this cheese the German Port-Salut. Made partly of skim milk, Esrom is the color of country cream and is strewn with tiny holes. Although mild when young, it gathers strength as it ages. It's a perfect table cheese, best served with apples and pears, pumpernickel or *Bauernbrot*, robust red wines or good German beer.

Essen und Trinken: (Food and drink). The general term for eating and drinking.

An old German proverb goes thus: "Eating and drinking keeps body and soul together." *essen & trinken* is also the name of an important German food magazine, a glossy, four-color journal published every month in Hamburg.

Essig: Vinegar. The vinegars most commonly used in Germany today are apple cider vinegar, wine vinegar (red, white, and sherry), herb vinegars, and garlic vinegars. Chefs are fond of berry vinegars, too, especially the fruity red raspberry vinegar.

Esskastanien (also **Maronen**): Chestnuts. Chestnuts figure prominently in German cooking, although perhaps not so prominently as they do in French cuisine. In his encyclopedic history, *Food,* Waverley Root writes: "The chestnut passed into western Europe via Castan, a town of eastern Thessaly, hence its generic name *Castanea*" (from which the German *Esskastanie* clearly descends). Root further says that the Romans were fond of chestnuts and often tempered the bitterness of wild greens by boiling them with chestnuts. Today German cooks use them in stuffings, as an accompaniment to venison, or puréed as a potato substitute. They even braise kale with chestnuts—an inspired pairing. See Kale with Chestnuts and Glazed Potatoes (page 264).

Esslöffel: Tablespoon. In cookbooks and food magazines this is often written simply *Essl*, but with the German double S (*beta S*) that looks somewhat like the dollar sign or a fancy script *B*. Sometimes tablespoon is even more abbreviated and written *El*.

Estragon: Tarragon. Germans have never been as passionate as the French about this summery herb with the delicate licorice taste. Even today it is more likely to be used by chefs than home cooks. Tarragon is essential to béarnaise, the French sauce that Germans like to ladle over stalks of ivory asparagus. Mostly, however, it's stirred into ethereal fish sauces or used to infuse wine vinegars.

Fasan: Pheasant. These are mostly wild birds, still brought down by hunters. They must be hung—with the feathers—before they're cooked.

Feigen: Figs. Until recently, the only figs available were dried. They would appear in winter on a fruit platter along with dates, oranges, and nuts. Today, fresh imported figs show up in season in fancy big-city markets, also on the menus of restaurants specializing in "new German cooking." Sometimes the combinations are predictable—fresh figs with tissues of Westphalian ham. But at other times they're more off-the-wall—figs with chicken, for example, or figs with chocolate mousse.

Feinschmecker: Gourmet; also the name of one of Germany's major gastronomic magazines.

Felchen: Lake trout. It is better known as **Renke** (see below).

Feldsalat: Field salad. Germans prize mâche for its slightly nutty flavor and it is mostly eaten by itself or tossed into green salads. Usually it is dressed with a cool creamy dressing or a hot bacon one, then strewn with crisp brown bacon bits. In addition, trendy young chefs like to garnish their plates with tiny rosettes of field salad.

Fenchel: Fennel. Also known in the United States by its Italian name, *finocchio*, this licorice-sweet bulb is sliced raw into German salads or braised as a vegetable .

Fett: Fat. An umbrella term that refers to all kinds of fat butter, lard, margarine, even goose, duck, and chicken fat.

Feuerzangenbowle: Firetong bowl. The traditional New Year's toast. But Hedy remembers her family serving *Feuerzangenbowle* both on Christmas and New Year's Eves. "It's a very convivial drink," she says. "But to prepare it, you need a sugar cone about six inches high and special sugar cone tongs." Here's how the *Feuerzangenbowle* is made: Slowly heat freshly squeezed orange juice, whole cloves, and dry red wine (preferably a German red such as a Spätburgunder or a Trollinger) in a big copper pot or chafing dish just until the mixture steams. Center on a large table and ask everybody to gather round. Next, pour dark rum over a large sugar cone, place it in its metal holder, and lay across the chafing dish. Turn off all the lights and blaze the rum-soaked cone with a match so it melts and drips down into the bowl. "You keep pouring rum over the sugar cone, using about a pint in all," Hedy adds, "until all the sugar has dissolved. It's quite a show."

Fisch: Fish.

Fischbrühe: Fish broth or stock.

Flädle: Thin pancake strips. *Fladen* is the Swabian word for pancake, *Pfannkuchen* the broad German one. When either is applied to soup, it's understood that the pancake is cut into strips. Frugal German cooks let nothing go to waste. Any cold leftover pancakes are slivered, then floated in clear broth (usually beef) and sprinkled with freshly snipped chives. In Swabia (Baden-Württemberg), it's called *Flädlesuppe,* elsewhere, *Pfannkuchensuppe* (page 99).

Flambiert: Flambéed. Like the French, from whom they learned the art, Germans are fond of flaming dishes—dessert pancakes, for instance, and also meats and fruits. But they are just as likely to blaze their alcoholic drinks.

Flasche: Bottle. If it's a bottle of beer you want, you should ask for a *Flaschenbier.*

Fleisch: Meat. A broad term that refers to all kinds of meat—beef, veal, and pork but not ham, which is **Schinken** (see below).

Fleischbrühe: Meat broth. Usually this is made of beef or a combination of beef and veal.

Fleischklösschen: Meatballs. These are also called **Klopse** in the north of Germany. *Fleischklösschen,* made of ground beef and/or pork, are often cooked and served in clear broth. Germany's lightest meatballs come from the Rhineland and none are more beloved than "Pälzer Fleschknepp," made with ground pork, veal, and beef (see Rheinpfalz Meatballs Poached, page 172).

Flunder: Flounder. Germans are partial to the whole family of flatfish to which flounder belongs. They can be quickly filleted and cooked, they are supremely sweet and tender, and not least, they are uncommonly versatile.

Forelle: Trout. Much of the trout swimming in German rivers and streams is rainbow trout, introduced from America many years ago. It's able to survive in high-tech times far better than **Bachforelle** (see above).

Frankfurter: Frankfurter. The wurst that started it all, the wurst that Germans—from the North Sea to the Bavarian Alps—have made their preferred snack. They like it hot, usually with a slice of bread, a good German mustard, and beer. True *Frankfurters* must be made in the Frankfurt am Main region and adhere to strict quality controls laid down by court order in 1929. They must be 100 percent pork (the best are made from the leg meat of well-fattened hogs). The meat must be devoid of fat, tendons, and chemical additives, then minced in special machines according to prescribed recipes. There's more: The *Frankfurter* mix must be stuffed into natural sheep casings, smoked according to traditional methods, then sold in pairs attached at one end. Despite all the restrictions, genuine *Frankfurters* are mass-produced, with some factories turning out as many as fifty thousand pairs of them a day.

Frankfurter Kranz: Frankfurt wreath. A light and airy butter cake baked in a ring mold, split two to four times, then sandwiched together with a rich rum-flavored buttercream and apricot marmalade. The finished cake is frosted with more of the buttercream, then sprinkled with a mixture of finely chopped ground almonds (or other nuts) that have been browned in butter with a little sugar.

Frikadelle: Meat patty. The generic term for a meat patty that's not only smaller than *Deutsches Beefsteak* (they average 2½ to 3 inches across and an inch thick) but also more complex and highly seasoned. Called *Fleischpfanzel* in southern Germany and *Buletten* in Berlin, these beef-pork or all-beef patties (sometimes made of left-overs) also contain a hard roll wrung out in cold water, chopped onion, egg, salt, pepper, and possibly a little nutmeg or other seasoning, too. Usually they're fried and served hot—traditionally with mashed potatoes, and often a pan-drippings gravy as well. But *Frikadellen* are also eaten cold. They're perfect for picnics because they can be made ahead and are eminently portable. In Berlin, they're popular bar food. *Bierstuben* there often set bowls of cold *Buletten* on the bar for customers to eat out of hand with beer (they're not free, how-ever—someone keeps tabs and you're assessed for each one you eat).

Frisch: Fresh. Given a choice, Germans will choose fresh food over frozen or canned. They certainly use much more of it than we do.

Frischkäse: Fresh cheese. An umbrella term that includes a variety of fresh cheeses: quark, ricotta, and cream cheese, to name three.

Früchte (also **Obst**): Fruit. *Obst*, the all-inclusive term for fruit, includes the fresh, the preserved, and the dried. *Früchte* is also generic but only a German knows the subtle difference.

Fruchtsaft (also **Obstsaft**): Fruit juice. This is a broad term that refers to all fruit juices. Specific juices have specific names—*Apfelsaft* (apple juice), for example, and *Orangensaft* (orange juice).

Frühstück: Breakfast. In Germany, breakfast is served between 6 and 10. And what a meal it is! There are platters of cold cuts and cheese, fresh fruit or juice, an assortment of breads and rolls (even soft pretzels in southern Germany), a variety of marmalades and honeys, and often soft-boiled eggs, cereal, and yogurt, along with plenty of freshly brewed coffee. The break-fast buffets laid on by Germany's big-city hotels are guaranteed to convert the most devout breakfast-hater.

Füllung: Stuffing. A *Füllung* can be savory or sweet, and it's used to stuff every-thing from poultry to *Rouladen* (meat rolls) to dumplings to scooped-out fruits and vegetables.

Gabel: Fork.

Gans: Goose. During the 1980s, goose was out and turkey in because Germans were concerned with health. Today, goose is reappearing on restaurant menus, par-ticularly at Christmastime. Usually it is baby goose (*Frühmastgans*, 6 to 8 pounds and no more than 5 months old) or young goose (*junge Gans*, 8 to 12 pounds and from 5 to 9 months). Older birds rarely make it to market.

Gänsebraten: Roast goose. The tradi-tional winter holiday bird throughout Ger-many. Goose is served first on St. Martin's Day in November, and then again as the centerpiece of the midday Christmas feast (see Christmas Goose, page 191). On Christmas Eve, it's carp.

Gänseleber: Goose liver. Like the French, Germans are fond of *Gänseleber-pastete* (goose liver pâté). Theirs, however, is usually softer, spicier, and devoid of black truffles.

Garnelen (also **Krevetten**): Shrimp. These are what we call "brown shrimp," sweet-meated little crustaceans averaging one and a half to two inches in length. They're netted from Norway south to the Mediterranean. Germans like shrimp cock-tail almost as much as we do, but are more likely to accompany it with a creamy fresh horseradish sauce than a ketchup-based one. They also grill shrimp, toss cold shrimp into salads, garnish fish platters with hot boiled or steamed shrimp, and even scatter them on pizza.

Garniert: Garnished. This may mean more than garnished, however, and include the artful arrangement of vegetables on the plate with the meat. In Germany's better restaurants, chefs send no plate out that isn't colorfully garnished. And some of them, like Eckhart Witzigmann of Munich's Aubergine Restaurant (a Michelin three-star), have ennobled the art.

Gasthaus (also **Gasthof** and **Gaststätte**). Rustic inn specializing in the regional food. Usually they are where the locals hang out, eat and/or drink beer, and discuss the ways of the world. The only difference is that a *Gasthaus* and *Gasthof* may have rooms to rent. The *Gaststätte* just serves meals.

Gebäck: Baked goods. *Feingebäck* are fine cakes and pastries, *Weihnachtsgebäck*, Christmas cookies.

Gebacken: Baked. Anything baked—a savory as well as a sweet.

Gebraten: Roasted. More accurately, perhaps, "browned." *Gebratene Ente* is indeed a roast duck, but *gebraten* can also refer to *Schnitzel* or, for that matter, to any steaks, chops, fish, even mushrooms or potatoes browned in a skillet on top of the stove.

Gedeck: Prix fixe. A meal—usually three courses—listed at a fixed rate. Cocktails, wine, and beer are extra.

Gedünstet: Braised.

Geflügel: Poultry. All farm-raised fowl—chickens, turkeys, ducks, geese, guinea hens—but not wild game birds, which are called *Wildgeflügel*.

Gefüllt: Stuffed. See **Füllung.**

Gehackt: Minced. Also finely chopped or diced, but the word applies primarily to meat and nuts.

Gekocht: Cooked. *Kochen* means "to cook" and *gekocht* means anything that *is* cooked, whether hot (as in *gekochte Kartoffeln*, or boiled potatoes) or cold (as in *gekochter Schinken*, or boiled ham).

Gemischt: Mixed. An adjective used almost exclusively to describe salads, which may be a mixture of greens, or greens plus tomatoes, radishes, carrots, or other vegetables.

Gemüse: Vegetables. The umbrella term that includes them all.

Geräuchert: Smoked. As in *geräucherter Lachs* (smoked salmon) or *geräucherter Schinken* (smoked ham).

Gerieben: Finely ground or grated.

Gerste: Barley. Germans are fond of vitamin-B-rich whole grains and use them in a variety of whole grain breads, soups, and porridges. A particular favorite in the north of Germany is a mush made with barley, prunes, and bacon.

Gesalzen: Salted.

Geschlossen: Closed. Whenever you see this posted on a door, it means the shop, restaurant, bakery, bank, or whatever is not open for business.

Getränke: Drinks. This one word embraces the whole spectrum of beverages, including coffees, teas, and soft drinks (*Alkoholfreie Getränke*), plus all beers, wines, brandies, liqueurs, schnapps, cocktails, and highballs made with spirits (*Alkoholische Getränke*).

Gewürze: Spices. Cinnamon, cloves, nutmeg, curry, and ginger are all *Gewürze*. A *Gewürzkuchen* is a spice cake. And the popular German white wine, Gewürztraminer, is so named because of the spiciness of the grape from which it's made.

Glas: Glass. *Glas* is the material itself, also the collective word for all drinking glasses. To get down to specifics, a wineglass is a *Weinglas*, a champagne glass, *Sektglas*, and a juice glass, *Saftglas*.

Glasiert: Glazed, iced, or frosted.

Glasiert can mean glazed meats or candied or crystallized fruits. But it is used most often to describe cakes, cookies, or other baked goods.

Glühwein: Mulled wine. The classic winter punch. Anytime it's cold, Germans drink Mulled wine.

Granat: Prawn. Bigger, sweeter, and more tender than shrimp, prawns are scarcer, too. They're a luxury found mostly on pricey restaurant menus.

Gratiniert (also **überbacken**): Gratinéed. Whenever a dish is *gratiniert*, it is topped with crumbs and/or shredded cheese and quickly browned in the oven.

Griess: Semolina. Known in the United States as couscous, this is a fine meal ground from the hard, golden heart of durum wheat. In Germany, there are two types of *Griess*, one made of wheat, and another of corn (what Italians call *polenta*). Germans prefer wheat semolina and can buy it in three different grinds: coarse, medium, and fine. *Griess* makes splendid dumplings (see **Griessnockerl**, below) as every good German cook knows.

Griessnockerl: Semolina dumplings. In southern Germany, these dumplings are floated in clear, rich beef broth. They are served exactly the same way in the north of Germany, where they are called *Griessklösschen* (see Beef Broth with Semolina Dumplings, page 98).

Gross: Big.

Grün: Green. Germans are quite precise about food names. Green beans, for example, are *grüne Bohnen*, and the green sauce for which Frankfurt is famous is *Frankfurter Grüne Sauce* (page 388), a creamy sauce thickened with a garden of chopped greens (sorrel, watercress, chives, chervil, parsley—and more, too, if the cook has it). It's the traditional accompaniment to boiled beef and pâtés.

Grünkohl: Kale. The original cabbage, according to most food historians. This dark green, nonheading variety may not be fancy, but it is a nutritional powerhouse (just one cup of cooked kale provides more than the USDA Recommended Dietary Allowance for both vitamins A and C, and plenty of iron, too). Kale thrives in the cool German climate and, as cooks and farmers there both know, it shouldn't be gathered until after the first frost. As for cooking kale, Germans are the masters. There's Kale with Bacon, or Christmas Kale (page 263), for example, and Kale with Chestnuts and Glazed Potatoes (page 264), even Kale Soup (page 128), which our very American taste-testers proclaimed the best soup they'd ever eaten.

Gugelhupf: Bundt cake. This is not just any Bundt cake. It's a tall gold cake dotted with dried raisins and/or dried currants (see *Gugelhupf*, page 365). Sometimes, however, it may even be made with fresh red currants (see Red Currant Cake, page 367).

Gulasch: Stew. Although we tend to associate *Gulasch* with Hungary (where it's spelled *Gulyás*), it is equally popular in Germany. What distinguishes it from the average stew is the quantity of paprika stirred into it—enough to redden both meat and gravy, also the fact that it contains no vegetables other than onions and, maybe, green peppers. Hungarian *Gulyás* may be made with different kinds of meat—beef, pork, even sausage. But in Germany, beef and veal are preferred.

Gulaschsuppe: Goulash soup. Nothing more than a watered-down *Gulasch*. Don't misinterpret "watered-down" to mean insipid. German goulash soups don't lack for flavor. They are simply thinner than stews and usually contain fewer chunks of meat but more vegetables. With a cool, tall glass of beer, they make a filling but frugal lunch. After a night on the town, Germans often stop by a *Bierkeller* for a bowl of *Gulaschsuppe*.

Gut durchgebraten: Well done. If meat

35

is *gut durchgebraten,* no trace of pink shows.

Guten Appetit! Good appetite! Bon appétit! Have a good meal!

Hackbraten: Meat loaf. This is the meat loaf German cooks make at home for an economical meal, also the one family-style restaurants often offer on their menus. *Hackbraten* can be made of ground beef or a mixture of beef and pork, but it almost always contains hard rolls wrung out in cold water, chopped browned bacon, onion, eggs, and either paprika or pepper. Once the loaf is shaped, it's rolled in dry bread crumbs, then baked so its crust is nice and brown and crunchy; the pan drippings are made into gravy. Whenever a German cook wants a little fancier *Hackbraten,* he'll bury hard-cooked eggs in the middle of the loaf so that when it's cut, the slices of egg show clearly.

Hackfleisch: Ground meat. If you buy *Hackfleisch* at a butcher shop, you get a ready-made, half-and-half mixture of beef and lean pork. If you want lean ground beef, you ask for *Rinderhack.*

Hähnchen: Broiler-fryer. A small, tender spring chicken that can be fried, broiled, grilled, spit-roasted, or roasted in the oven.

Hähnchenbrust: Chicken breast. These are available both fresh and frozen.

Halb durchgebraten: Medium rare. Translated literally, this means "half roasted." In any event, *halb durchgebraten* meat will be juicily pink, not red, not brown.

Hammel: Mutton. Not a popular meat among Germans.

Hartgekocht: Hard-cooked. As in a hard-boiled egg (*hartgekochtes Ei*).

Hase: Hare. Hunters still go after hares in fields and forests during the autumn hunting season, and cooks prize them for their rich, woodsy flavor. There are many ways to prepare hare, but none is more beloved than *Hasenpfeffer* (page 181), an ancient German recipe that originally

meant *Hase in Pfeffer* (hare in pepper).

Haselnüsse: Hazelnuts, or filberts. If Germans were asked to name their favorite nut, it would be a toss-up between the hazelnut and the almond. For most recipes, they do not blanch hazelnuts because they like the color the brown skins add.

Hauptgericht: Entrée. The main course of the meal.

Hausgemacht: Homemade. A homemade broth (*hausgemachte Brühe,* for example) as opposed to a canned one.

Haxe: Shank or knuckle. Germans love to tackle a giant veal shank that's been roasted or grilled to succulence. Or pig's knuckles served with sauerkraut and potato salad or dumplings.

Hecht: Pike. Pike like crystalline ponds, lakes, and broad slow-moving rivers. And the colder the water, the bigger and better the fish. The best pike are lean, white, sweet, and firm-fleshed. Their biggest shortcoming is their multitude of bones, which makes them pesky to eat. Canny German cooks eliminate the problem by turning pike into boneless dumplings.

Hefe: Yeast. It's available both in cake form and as active dry yeast.

Hefeteig: Yeast dough. Most German breads are leavened with yeast, although busy working women are now beginning to make the sorts of quick soda or baking powder breads Americans love.

Heidelbeeren: Blueberries. Also called **Blaubeeren** (see above).

Heilbutt: Halibut. This giant North Atlantic flatfish can reach awesome dimensions and may weigh as much as 600 pounds. The choicer specimens are smaller. For German cooks, halibut is a good all-around fish, easily adapted to a variety of cooking methods. Its flesh is lean, white, and delicate, and bones aren't a problem. Best of all, halibut is readily available and the price is usually right.

Heiss: Hot. Just the way Germans like their coffee.

Hering: Herring. Bremen, Hamburg, and Lübeck all grew rich in the herring trade back in the age of the Hanseatic League (thirteenth to seventeenth centuries). And to this day this small oily fish remains king, a staple throughout the Baltic. Usually it is salted, cured and/or pickled, then eaten cold—as an appetizer or in salads. And, Germans swear, nothing can touch it as a hangover remedy. **Matjeshering,** the choicest of all, are younger, fatter, tenderer herring that haven't yet spawned (no other herring can be called matjes), and when properly brined or cured, they melt in your mouth.

June is matjes month in the north of Germany, a time to celebrate, to feast, and no more so than in the Elbe River town of Glückstadt, where matjes, caught off the coasts of Denmark and Holland, are still cured according to age-old methods.

Among the classic ways to serve whole matjes: in a sandwich with bacon, in a cream sauce with apples and onions, in a sauce greened with herbs, and best of all, *natur*—just as they come from the brine or cure. Hedy says she never ate finer matjes than at Schiffergesellschaft, an old Lübeck restaurant with darkly paneled walls and model ships hanging from the ceiling. "These were just the cured matjes fillets," she says, "accompanied by steamed potatoes and green beans. Nothing more."

Most of the matjes herring brined in Germany today is considerably less salty than it once was. It averages about 16 percent salt and needs only the briefest rinse, or better yet, quick milk bath, before it's eaten.

Fine German *Matjeshering* is available in the United States at specialty food shops and better supermarkets.

Herz: Heart. One of the innards Germans like, their particular favorites being beef or veal heart. Usually it is stuffed (one recipe calls for cubed apples and dried prunes), then braised with bacon, onions, mushrooms, red wine, bay leaves, and allspice.

Himbeeren: Raspberries. There's an interesting story as to how the *Himbeere* got its name. When raspberries grew wild, there was a particular doe—the *Hirschkuh* or *Hinde*—that liked to hide behind raspberry bushes. *Himbeere*, it's said, descends from *Hindebeere*, meaning "deer berry." Although raspberries were known to Romans, only in the Middle Ages did German monks begin to plant them in cloister gardens. Not, however, as a food. In those days, raspberries were believed to heal the bites of snakes and scorpions, to break high fevers, and to ease nausea. Today, of course, raspberries are esteemed as food. They are commercially farmed in Germany and bear fruit from the end of June until September. Raspberry vinegar, the favorite of faddish chefs today, was known a hundred years ago. Recipes for it can be found in turn-of-the-century cookbooks, which recommended its use in the preparation of duck and venison.

Himbeergeist: Raspberry eau-de-vie. A colorless "firewater" fermented from raspberries, very much like the French framboise.

Hirsch: Stag. Deer do still roam the forests of Germany and hunters do bring them down. In autumn and winter, restaurants all over Germany—but especially those in Bavaria and the Black Forest—feature venison. If the venison is tough and sinewy, you can be sure the chef will cook it as **Hirschragout,** or venison stew. We offer a very good one (see Ragout of Venison with Chestnuts and Mushrooms, page 178).

Holsteiner Schnitzel: A breaded pork cutlet browned in butter and served with a fried egg on top and an anchovy for decoration.

Honig: Honey. German honey is wonderful, and in the old days before sugar was readily available, bakers used it to sweeten cakes and cookies. Standouts in Germany's modern repertoire of honeys (most of them available here) include the intensely fragrant, molasses-dark Black Forest honey, the pale amber acacia honey (delicate), and the opaque yellow linden honey (mellow), which resembles nothing so much as lemon curd. There's none finer, however, than pine honey (*Tannenhonig*), which has a woodsy freshness.

Huhn: Hen. Tough old birds that thrifty German cooks simmer into broth or stock (*Hühnerbrühe*). The meat is usually diced and slipped into chicken soup (*Hühnersuppe*) or fricassees.

Hummer: Lobster. Both the American lobster (an import) and its smaller cousin, the European lobster, are available in Germany. Supplies have dwindled, however, and prices skyrocketed.

Imbiss: Snack. An *Imbiss-Stube* is a little fast-food place and an *Imbiss* can be anything from a sausage to soup to a sandwich. You can have an *Imbiss* in the morning, in the afternoon, or in the evening. If you're in Bavaria, however, it's a *Brotzeit* you have, not an *Imbiss*.

Ingwer: Ginger. The Romans found ginger such a good substitute for pepper they never left home without it, and ultimately carried it all the way to Britain. Gingerbread emerged from the medieval pharmacopoeia of England, but it was German bakers who brought it out of the pharmacy and into the kitchen. They also elevated the making of gingerbread to high art by shaping it into everything from cottages to castles. Strangely, not all *Lebkuchen* (gingerbread) made today contains ginger, although our recipe for it does (see page 377).

Jakobsmuscheln: Scallops. The Jacob's or Pilgrim's mussel is a rarity in Germany, but does appear now and then on snazzy restaurant menus. This is the *Pecten jacobaeus*

species of the Mediterranean, not the exquisite little bay scallops so beloved by Americans. In Germany, scallops are never breaded and fried as they are here. More often they are poached—coddled—in a gentle court bouillon or wine broth in the company of chervil, tarragon, or dill, then finished off with a delicate sauce such as *beurre blanc.*

Joghurt: Yogurt. A popular breakfast item, between-meals snack, and when mixed with fresh fruit, dessert. Health-conscious cooks also use yogurt as a fat-and-calorie-cutting substitute for cream and mayonnaise.

Johannisbeeren: Currant. Three kinds grow in Germany—the red, the black, and the white. The taste of fresh currants varies not only from one variety to another, but even among berries of the same color and species. Some might be aromatic and mildly sweet, others tart almost to the point of astringency. Highly perishable, fresh currants are in season only between June and September. They are used in jams, jellies, compotes, puddings, even cakes (see Red Currant Cake, page 367).

Jung: Young. Precise about most things, Germans classify many of their foods according to age—or lack of it. *Junge grüne Bohnen*, for example, are "young green beans."

Kabeljau: Cod. Called "the fish that filled the belly of the world," cod swim the North Atlantic, although not so profusely as in centuries past. France, Norway, and Portugal are the countries we tend to associate with cod. And yet it is important to Germany, too. During the Middle Ages, dried salt cod (*Stockfisch*) sustained the poor and became the "beef" of the endless Catholic fast days. Even today, Germans count on cod. It is lean, white, sweet-meated, economical. And its endless versatility has inspired a number of German chefs to reach beyond the more predictable ways of preparing it (see Cod with Sauerkraut and Tarragon Sauce, page 212).

Kaffee: Coffee. Every second cup of coffee drunk in Germany comes from beans that were roasted, ground, and tinned in the northern seaport of Bremen. And very good it is, too. Elsewhere, fancy food emporiums (like Dallmayr in Munich) devote whole sections to exotic coffees, stock their shelves with the finest beans imported from around the world, and grind them to order. The aroma is irresistible.

Kaffeesahne: Coffee cream. What we would call light or single cream, what Germans usually stir into their coffee.

Kakao: Cocoa. No one prepares better cocoa or hot chocolate than the Germans— it is rich, dark, and thick. The better cafés and *Konditoreien* often serve it in dainty porcelain cups with a float of whipped cream. *Kakao* is also the chocolate powder used in baking.

Kalb, Kalbfleisch: Veal. Veal is the meat Germans prize the most, but it is also one of the most expensive. This is true veal, mind you, the pale, fine flesh of calves that have never gone off mother's milk. Once calves begin to graze, their meat reddens, and until recently much of the veal sold in America was actually baby beef. When you try the recipes in this book, we urge you to use the fine, European-style veal now sold by better butchers across the country. This is "nature," "special-fed," "fancy quality" meat from bull Holstein calves no more than sixteen weeks old that have been penned, pampered, and fattened on a ration of milk solids, vitamins, and milk. Wisconsin produces most of America's good veal, scarcely surprising when you consider that it is our leading dairy state and that veal is a by-product of the dairy industry, not of the beef industry. Holsteins, from which our best veal comes, are abundant milk producers. Female calves ultimately join the dairy herd, but the males become veal.

Kalbsbraten: Roast veal.
Kalbsbries: Sweetbreads.
Kalbsbrust: Breast of veal. One of the tougher, cheaper cuts of veal that Germans cook to perfection, often with an herb-oniony stuffing that can be made of anything from rice to potatoes to hard rolls and mushrooms.

Kalbshaxen: Veal shanks. When cooked long and slow, these sinewy, bony cuts become supremely succulent. In country inns—big-city restaurants, too—you often see people tackling veal shanks so whopping they overhang the plate. Our recipe is somewhat daintier (see Veal Shanks Northern German Style, page 154).

Kalbsleber: Calf's liver. German cooks treat calf's liver with as much respect as they do caviar, understanding full well that to overcook it is to ruin it. So they may brown it zip-quick over a high flame, then season with a squeeze of lemon and sprinkle of sugar. Or they may sliver it and cream it. But they like it best of all Berlin style— sautéed with apples and onions (see Calf's Liver Berlin Style, page 157).

Kalbsnieren: Veal kidneys.
Kalt: Cold. For a people who must battle cold weather much of the year, Germans are inordinately fond of cold food. Their snacks run more to pickled herring, smoked eel, cold cuts, cheese, and bread than to a burger or cup of soup. And their restaurant menus often include such headings as *Kalte Speisen* (cold dishes) or *Kalte Gerichte* (small cold courses).

Kaninchen: Rabbit. Buying a rabbit in the United States is a snap because the animal is cleaned, dressed, disjointed, and packaged in plastic like chicken parts. To visit some German butchers, however, is to confront the whole rabbit—head, tail, legs, fur (the better to determine age and quality). The butcher then prepares the rabbit according to how it will be cooked. Although Germans make a great distinction

39

between rabbit (mostly farm-raised, white of flesh and tender) and wild and gamy hare (*Hase*) they tend to cook them both *en casserole* (see Jugged Rabbit or Hare, page 180).

Kapern: Capers. These tiny pickled buds of the spiny Mediterranean caper bush (*Capparis spinosa*) have just the tartness Germans relish, which may explain why they're mixed into steak tartare and assorted salads.

Karotte: Carrot. The carrot is known in Germany by at least four different names—*Möhre, Mohrrübe,* and *Gelbe Rübe,* in addition to *Karotte*—hardly helpful to the non-German. The differences in terminology are primarily those of region: *Gelbe Rübe* is southern; *Möhre, Mohrrübe,* and *Karotte* are more used in the middle and north of Germany.

Karpfen: Carp. An Asian freshwater fish, carp has been important in the German diet for at least four centuries. Indeed, it is listed in an Augsburg inventory dated 1558—and at a price quadruple that of beef. Food historians believe the popularity of carp can be traced to the Middle Ages, specifically to the monks, whose vast carp ponds provided a ready supply of "meat" at a time when fast days outnumbered feast days. In Germany today, carp is eaten mostly in winter (its flavor goes musky in summer), but it is served most of all on festive occasions. The traditional Christmas Eve dinner is carp cooked in beer, and on Silvester or New Year's Eve, all of Germany celebrates by eating carp poached in red wine. For some reason, carp has never gained favor in the United States—perhaps we relate it to our pet goldfish, which is also carp. Carp can grow to immense size—the largest ever recorded was a 154-pounder caught in the Ukraine nearly three hundred years ago. Southern Germans like their carp small—in the two-pound range—but northerners prefer them a bit larger.

Kartoffel: Potato. Given the Germans'

fondness for potatoes today, it's difficult to understand why they were so slow to accept them. Like other Europeans, many considered *Erdäpfel,* or "earth apples," as they were also called, dangerous; some even believed potatoes caused leprosy. Frederick the Great knew better. To encourage Prussians to eat the starchy tubers, he distributed seed potatoes to the poor, then stationed guards round their fields to ensure that they were planted, harvested, and eaten. When the peasants continued to resist, Frederick finally won them over by standing on the balcony of his palace and publicly eating a potato. The types of potatoes Germans use today are varieties well known to us—all-purpose, bakers, the firm and waxy (Germans call them "salad potatoes"), and the nut-sweet little new potatoes (*neue Kartoffeln*). These are harvested in May when they're about the size of Brussels sprouts.

Kartoffelpuffer: Potato pancakes. Butter-browned and crunchy, these can become an addiction (see Potato Pancakes I, page 224, which contain no egg, and Potato Pancakes II, page 225, which do). In the north, these are also called *Reibekuchen* (grated cake).

Kartoffelpüree, Kartoffelbrei: Mashed Potatoes.

Kartoffelsalat: Potato salad. Germans like it hot, Germans like it cold—or at least at room temperature. In the south, potato salads are made with browned cubes of bacon, then dressed with bacon drippings plus oil and vinegar; in the north, they are mixed with mayonnaise. When making potato salad, Germans choose a firm potato of the waxy type that won't disintegrate when cooked or tossed with the other salad ingredients. A particular favorite is the *Mäuschen,* which grows in abundance around Mannheim and Mainz.

Käse: Cheese. Soft fresh cheeses… piquant golden semisofts…biting blues…

40

buttery French-style Bries and Camemberts…Dutch-style Edams and Goudas…Emmentalers as highly prized as those of Switzerland. Germany makes them all and exports many of their best to the United States. Cheese making is not new to Germany. Indeed, cheese was being made in Bavaria two-thousand years ago, and some 75 percent of the country's finest still come from that area. These are, for the most part, cheeses made from cow's milk or cream, cheeses with a butterfat content that ranges from a low of 20 percent to a high of about 70. (See also the classic German cheeses—**Allgäu Emmentaler, Blauschimmelkäse, Butterkäse, Esrom, Münster, Steppenkäse,** and **Tilsiter**—elsewhere in this glossary.)

Käsekuchen: Cheesecake. Only Germans would make it with **Quark** (see below).

Käseplatte: Cheese plate. A platter of cheeses, usually thinly sliced and accompanied by bread, which may be served at breakfast, lunch, supper, or even as a mid-morning or afternoon snack.

Kassler Rippchen: Smoked pork chops. There's still plenty of argument about where these rosy loin chops originated. The Hessian town of Kassel claims them as its own. But Berliners say, "Nonsense!" Everyone knows they came from a Berlin butcher named Kassel. Originally the specialty of both Berlin and Frankfurt, *Kassler Rippchen* are now served all over Germany—boiled, boned, cut thick, then nestled in a bed of sauerkraut. Mashed potatoes are the traditional accompaniment.

Kerbel: Chervil. Fresh chervil is all the rage just now in Germany. It looks like a fragile parsley—frilly, the loveliest of spring greens—but it tastes like tarragon. More subtle, definitely, but like licorice all the same. Chervil dates to Biblical lands and times. Maybe even farther. In *A Book of Herbs & Spices*, Gail Duff writes: "It is

thought to be one of the warming spices that was used to make the oil with which Moses blessed the vessels of the Tabernacle." As contemporary German cooks have learned, chervil is a versatile kitchen herb, complementary to most fish, to poultry, salad greens, even potatoes (see Potato Salad in Light Chervil Dressing, page 293) and soup (see Fresh Chervil Soup, page 131). Unfortunately, chervil is not easily come by in this country, so if you're determined to try it, you may have to grow your own (any sunny windowsill will do). Or, you can do as we've done on occasion and counterfeit it out of a mix of tarragon and parsley.

Kieler Sprotten: Smoked sprats. The old Hanseatic port of Kiel, now one of Germany's busiest ports-of-call for Scandinavia-bound cruise ships and ferries, is famous for its golden, smoked, and salted sprats (small herring).

Kirschen: Cherries. Cherry orchards flourish along the east bank of the upper Rhine and much of the crop is distilled into kirschwasser, a crystalline eau-de-vie. Kirschwasser is sipped at the end of a fine dinner as a digestif, but it's also integral to many classic German recipes; no decent Black Forest Cake can be made without it (see Black Forest Cherry Torte, page 357). Germany's beloved sweet cherries, the *Herzkirschen* (heart cherries), are so sugary they can be eaten out of hand. The favorite sour or "cooking" cherries are the *Schatten-morellen.* Germany's cherry season begins in the middle of May and continues through the summer until early September.

Klar: Clear. As in *klare Suppe* (a clear soup or broth).

Klein: Small. Because Germans are great snackers, many German menus include *kleine Gerichte*, little snacks or "fillers" that often include such things as hot potpies.

Klopse: Meatballs. See **Fleischklösschen.**

41

Klösse: Dumplings. To northern Germans (anyone living north of the Danube, according to Bavarians), dumplings are *Klösse* and little dumplings, **Klösschen.** South of the Danube, they are *Knödel* and *Nockerl,* respectively. Bavarians, by the way, make dumplings out of almost everything—bread, vegetables, ham, pretzels. See Potatoes, Dumplings, Spaetzle, Rice, and Other Side Dishes, page 216.

Knackwurst: Knackwurst. These plump little links are crisp of skin and, when cooked, *knack* (crunch or crackle) and spurt juices as you bite into them. "Just like an apple," one German friend said. They taste somewhat like frankfurters, except that they're garlickier, spicier, and compounded of a mix of beef and pork (franks are 100 percent pork). *Knackwurst* are often warmed in hot water, then split and grilled. Country cooks also like to slice them into split pea soup or steam them whole with sauerkraut. See also **Regensburger.**

Knoblauch: Garlic. Except in the making of sausage, Germans were never intrepid about garlic. But times change, tastes change, and today's young cooks have become quite daring.

Knödel: Dumpling. See **Klösse.**

Kohl (also **Kraut**): Cabbage. The generic words for cabbage vary from north (*Kohl*) to south (*Kraut*). German lore tells us that the man in the moon was put there for stealing cabbages on Christmas Eve. Aside from the many legends that have attached themselves to the cabbage family, there are practical reasons for its popularity. Not the least of them is that these cruciferous vegetables are highly nutritious, supplying impressive amounts of vitamin C, and in the case of kale and broccoli, of beta carotene as well. German peasants discovered early on that cabbages were easy to grow and that they tolerated their country's wild fluctuations of temperature. The different types of cabbage (except for broccoli, which comes mainly from Italy) all grow across the country, but in the farms around Stuttgart, the growing of **Weisskraut** (white cabbage) is big business (most of it goes into **Sauerkraut;** see below). If German peasants soon perceived how easy it was to grow cabbage, savvy German cooks were equally quick to learn that all members of the cabbage family can be prepared in numerous ways that are nourishing, delicious, and inexpensive.

Kohlrabi: Kohlrabi. Charlemagne, that zealous medieval promoter of agriculture, ordered that kohlrabi be planted throughout his empire, which at its height stretched from the Ebro (in Spain) to the Elbe (Germany/Czechoslovakia). Could Karl der Grosse, as Germans call Charlemagne, have had any notion of the kohlrabi's nutritional power (it's loaded with vitamin C)? Probably not. Kohlrabi is a German word. It means "turnip-cabbage," an apt description for this member of the cabbage family that looks like a turnip. Raw kohlrabi is unpleasantly bitter and tough, but as every good German cook knows, careful cooking works miracles (see Shredded Kohlrabi in Onion-Parsley Sauce, page 266, and Stuffed Kohlrabi, page 267).

Kokosnuss: Coconut. Not very popular in Germany, except for making Christmas cookies, especially *Kokosnuss-Plätzchen* (coconut meringues).

Kompott: Compote. This always means stewed fruits.

Konditorei: Pastry shop. *Konditoreien* are fancier than *Bäckereien* (bakeries), and unlike bakeries, never sell bread (other than fancy sweet breads like *Stollen*). Most *Konditoreien,* like Kreutzkamm in Munich, König in Baden-Baden, and Krönner in Garmisch-Partenkirchen, serve coffee, hot chocolate, tea, a celestial assortment of tortes and pastries, and sometimes light savory snacks as well.

Konfitüre: Jam.

Kopfsalat: Boston lettuce.

Korinthen: Small raisins: What we call

"dried currants," Germans call *Korinthen*. They are used strictly in baking.

Kotelett: Chop. As in *Schweinekotelett*, or pork chop.

Krabben: Small Baltic shrimp. Much more readily available than the larger *Garnelen*, because they're scooped from the cold waters of the Baltic and North Sea. They are almost always served shelled, and German food magazines are filled with jazzy new ways to serve *Krabben*—in a radish, red onion, and avocado salad, for example, or creamed and ladled atop farmer's bread.

Krapfen: Cruller. A jam-filled, deep-fried, yeast-raised, doughnut-like pastry—minus the hole. It is also sometimes called a *Berliner* after the city where it was invented. Here's how *Krapfen* came to be. More than 100 years ago at the time of Prussian Berlin, a bakery apprentice yearned to join the artillery. He was rejected, but with sense of humor intact, he created these little round fritters. "I may not be able to join the artillery," he said, "but at least I can make cannonballs."

Kraut: Cabbage. Also called **Kohl** (see above).

Kräuter: Herbs.

Kräuterbutter: Herb butter. German cooks can buy packages of it at almost every grocery.

Krautsalat: Coleslaw. In Bavaria, *Krautsalat* is always made with white cabbage and dressed with bacon drippings and caraway. In the north, it's called *Weisskohlsalat*, and it's a different recipe altogether. The shredded cabbage may be raw or lightly braised, mixed with chopped apples, dressed with vinaigrette, and sprinkled with walnuts.

Krebs: Crayfish. Short for **Bachkrebs** (see above).

Kren: Horseradish. See **Meerrettich.**

Kresse: Pepper grass. Tiny, peppery sprouts that are tossed into salads or used as a garnish.

Krevetten: Shrimp. Also called **Garnelen** (see above)

Kuchen: Cake. This is something of a misnomer because German *Kuchen* are savory as well as sweet and include such classics as the quichelike onion tarts so popular along the Rhine (see Onion Cake from the Rheinpfalz, page 270).

Kümmel: Caraway. You might as well handcuff a German cook as take away his caraway. Native to Europe and western Asia, caraway is now grown commercially throughout northern Europe for its intensely aromatic, small brown seeds. German cooks knead them into rye breads, then for good measure grind a few more and work them into the dough, too. The flavor of these small crescent-shaped seeds is a little bit sweet, a little bit sour. There are hints of carrot and parsley, too, but these three belong to the same big family. Nailing down the exact flavor of caraway seeds, however, is not nearly so important as knowing that they're simply marvelous with beets, sauerkraut, and fresh cabbage. *Kümmel* is also a vodka-clear schnapps infused with caraway.

Kürbis: Pumpkin. Not many Germans cook pumpkin, or even winter squash, which fall into the same family.

Kutteln (also **Kuttelfleck**): Tripe. Germans have none of the American squeamishness about animal innards and put all of them to good use. Much of their offal goes into wursts. But honeycomb tripe is too precious to grind to paste, so it's reserved for special recipes. One of the best tripe dishes we've ever eaten is Peter Wehlauer's surprisingly delicate Tripe Soup with Morels (page 106), which we enjoyed ten years ago at Burg Windeck, a small Black Forest castle-hotel near Baden-Baden, then owned and operated by Wehlauer.

Labskaus: Sailor's hash. Once made aboard ship, this salty mix of pickled pork or corned beef, potatoes, onions, and

43

anchovies remains popular in Hamburg, Bremen, Lübeck, and Kiel—port cities all.

Lachs: Salmon. Rhine salmon was always what Germans prized most, but this great stream, once the richest salmon river of Europe, has succumbed to industrial advance. Dwindling supplies have driven the price of salmon so high that this "staple of the poor" is now a luxury. Today, few fish possess greater cachet in Germany than salmon—except, perhaps, the even scarcer brook trout. Salmon falls into the oily fish category, that is, instead of its essential oils being concentrated in the liver (the case with cod), they are distributed evenly throughout its flesh. This accounts for the almost buttery texture of salmon, its rich flavor, and its ability to hold its own with zippier sauces and seasonings. See Terrine of Sole and Salmon with Lobster and Sorrel Sauce (page 198). Of course, smoked salmon is equally popular and pricey, the darling of resourceful chefs (see Smoked Salmon Tartare with Black Caviar, page 82).

Lachsforelle: Salmon Trout. This isn't a single fish but three close relatives—brown trout, which swim the rivers of Germany, lake trout, and sea trout. They are smallish (the best freshwater salmon-trout weigh only a pound or two apiece; the sea trout runs somewhat more), their flesh is firm, and depending on diet, can range from pale pink to bright orange (for crayfish eaters).

Lamm, Lammfleisch: Lamb. Except for the lambs that graze the salt grasses of the North Sea dunes, which have a cachet like that of the *agneau pré salé* of Normandy, lamb has never approached the popularity of pork, veal, and beef in Germany. Until recently. Today, it's not unusual to see lamb on a restaurant menu or even a family dinner table. This new acceptance of lamb can be traced to the waves of Turks who immigrated to Germany in the 1970s and 1980s to perform the menial jobs

Germans no longer would perform. Butcher shops began carrying lamb for their Turkish customers, and then curious Germans began to buy it, too. They found it delicate, succulent, and tender and began adding lamb recipes to their repertoires.

Languste: Spiny lobster. The North Sea is the northern limit of these clawless creatures, which are happier in warmer waters (though found in the Mediterranean, they're at their best off the coast of France). *Langusten* are as available in Germany as the European lobster (*Hummer*) and they are equally revered.

Lauch (also **Porree**): Leek. Essential to many good soups, leeks are also used in dozens of inventive ways by good German cooks. There's none more inspired than Leek Tart (page 269), a phyllo-crusted leek and Emmentaler tart spiked with kirschwasser.

Leber: Liver. Beef and pork livers usually go into wursts, beef liver also into dumplings, but delicate, fragile calf's liver is usually reserved for such special recipes as Calf's Liver in Horseradish-Mustard Cream Sauce (page 155) and Calf's Liver Berlin Style (page 157).

Leberkäse: Liver cheese. This Bavarian classic never contains cheese and rarely contains liver. It's a spicy, compact, pink meat loaf made of the butcher's odds and ends, and each butcher has his secret recipe. Germans buy *Leberkäse* fresh from the butcher's oven, all crusty and hot. Or they buy it cold and eat it that way. It reminds us of a very upscale American Spam.

Leberwurst: Liverwurst. There are dozens of different liverwursts, some of them lightly smoked, most of them cooked before they are sold, and most of them eaten cold. The big exception is *frische Leberwurst* (fresh liverwurst), which is boiled, then eaten hot with boiled or fried potatoes. A particular favorite all over Germany is a combination platter—fresh liverwurst plus fresh bloodwurst, both of them steaming hot and accompanied by sauerkraut and boiled potatoes. German liverwurst recipes vary hugely. Some liverwursts are made of pork and pork liver, then stuffed into pork casings (among them the famous *Braunschweiger*). Others are compounded of a mixture of beef and pork livers, some have even had browned onions added (*Zwiebelwurst*). In most parts of Germany, liverwursts are categorized according to texture and quality: *grobe Leberwurst* (coarse), *Landleberwurst* (also coarse, the farmer's liverwurst), *Kalbsleberwurst* (liverwurst made of calf's liver), *feine Kalbsleberwurst* (an even finer calf's liver liverwurst that is as rich and silky as pâté), and *Kalbsleberwurst mit Trüffeln* (an extravagant calf's liver liverwurst studded with minced black truffles).

Lebkuchen: Gingerbread. What's odd about German gingerbread is that it sometimes contains no ginger. Ground cinnamon, yes, and freshly grated nutmeg, too. These are the spices that flavor this dark brown dough, which is shaped, come Christmas, into gingerbread men and women, rocking horses, stars, bells, trees. In a Garmisch-Partenkirchen *Konditorei* window one December, we even saw a miniature Bavarian village intricately worked out in *Lebkuchen*.

Lende: Loin. As in loin of pork, beef, or veal.

Lendenstück: Tenderloin. The choicest, costliest, tenderest cut of any animal, be it venison, beef, veal, pork, or lamb.

Limone: Lime. Until recently, limes were unknown in Germany. But you see them today piled up in the groceries and outdoor markets (most are imported from the warm Mediterranean countries). You also learn unusual new ways to use limes by leafing through German food magazines. See Shredded Carrots with Lime and Rosemary (page 256).

Linsen: Lentils. Germans are fond of dried legumes—peas, beans, and lentils—and like to bubble them into nourishing winter soups.

Löffel: Spoon. A tablespoon is *Esslöffel*, a teaspoon *Teelöffel*.

Lorbeerblätter: Bay leaves. The evergreen leaves of the bay laurel (used by Greeks to crown their champions) have been indispensable to the German kitchen for years. They add lemony savor to soups and stews of all sorts, to carrots, cabbage, and sauerkraut, as well as to the *Eintopf* (one-dish dinner) every German adores.

Lunge: Lung. One of the innards Germans put to good use.

Mager: Lean. *Magerer Speck* is lean bacon; *Mager-Quark,* low-fat quark.

Maibowle: May bowl. A sparkling white wine punch infused with sweet woodruff, which blooms in German meadows and woodlands during the month of May.

Mais: Maize. Germans used to consider corn fit only for hogs. Recently, however, cooks are more aware of it as a vegetable and actually look forward to summer's corn season when fresh ears (*Maiskolben*) show up in local markets. In addition, whole-kernel corn is now often incorporated into salad platters. Cornmeal, moreover, is integral to certain German breads.

Majoran: Marjoram. A popular medieval monastery medicinal believed to cure (or at least relieve) a variety of digestive ailments, marjoram arrived in the kitchens of western Europe during the eighteenth century from balmy Mediterranean lands. In modern-day Germany, marjoram is more available dried than fresh; still, it's one of the sweet herbs cooks count on to season soups, stews, stuffings, gravies, sauces, vegetables, and salads. German chefs, like their American colleagues, often pluck fragrant sprigs of marjoram from their own herb gardens and use them both to garnish and season.

Makrele: Mackerel. Mackerel is a close relative of the herring and, like it, very fatty. In Germany, it's seldom available fresh, only smoked, marinated, or canned.

Mandeln: Almonds. What *would* Germans do without almonds? No marzipan, no *Mandelstollen* (page 312), no *Pfeffernüsse* (page 381). Unlike Americans, Germans rarely blanch or toast almonds before chopping or grinding them in cakes and cookies, believing the brown skins add flavor, color, vitamins, and minerals. They're right.

Mariniert: Marinated. Because they relish the tougher cuts of meat, Germans learned early on that marinating them in buttermilk, wine, and/or vinegar makes them tender. They know, too, that wine and vinegar can "cook" raw herring (see Rollmops, page 90, and Pickled Herring, page 91).

Maronen: Chestnuts. See **Esskastanien.**

Marzipan: Marzipan. Few people work marzipan into more enchanting shapes than the Germans, who learned the art early on. History tells us that almond paste originated in the Middle East among the Moslems, who doted upon all things sweet. As early as the fifteenth century, however, Germans were making their own marzipan, flavoring it with rose or orange flower water, and sculpting it into figures and flowers of exquisite detail. During its Hanseatic heyday, the Baltic seaport of Lübeck became Germany's center for the manufacture of marzipan, and it remains the Marzipan Capital today, although the candy is now also made in Aachen, Adendorf, and elsewhere. At New Year's, *Konditoreien* all over Germany are filled with beautifully wrapped red marzipan mushrooms, polka-dotted in white, and plump pink pigs, both symbols of good luck.

Matjeshering: Herring. See **Hering.**

Maultaschen: Filled pasta. You might call these the ravioli of Germany. They are a Swabian specialty, not sauced as a rule, but floated in broth (see Swabian Broth with Spinach-and-Meat-Stuffed "Ravioli," page 100).

Meeresfrüchte: Seafood. Translated literally, this means "fruit of the sea" and includes raw fish and shellfish. Seafood is also known as *Früchte des Meeres* and *Fischgerichte* (a menu term that refers to cooked seafood only).

Meerrettich (also **Kren**): Horseradish. Many dedicated German cooks not only grate their own horseradish, but also grow it. Fresh horseradish is more peppery than the bottled, but it's sweeter, too, and that sweet-hot pungency is what Germans like in their sauces. *Kren* is the word used in southern Germany, and at Munich's *Viktualienmarkt* you occasionally still see old women in folkloric dress selling big baskets of fresh *Kren*. They're called *Krenweiberl* (little horseradish women).

Messer: Knife.

Mettwurst (also **Teewurst**): Tea sausage. Although as soft and buttery as liverwurst, *Mettwurst* contains no liver. It's a lightly smoked, paprika-reddened paste made of beef, pork, and pork fat. Too soft to slice, it is always spread on bread. However, there are exceptions. *Rügenwalder Mettwurst*, for example, is small and salami-hard. Then there's *Hamburger Mettwurst,* which, after a second cooking, is also firm enough to slice.

Milch: Milk. In Germany, whole milk must contain 3.5 percent butterfat—the dairy cannot alter the composition. Nor can it change low-fat milk (1.5 to 1.8 percent butterfat) or skim milk (*Magermilch*). The German dairy industry has now developed something called *H-Milch*, a super-pasteurized type that stays fresh—outside the refrigerator—for about six weeks. In addition, there is the even less perishable "sterilized" milk, which keeps at room temperature for as long as a year. *Vorzugsmilch* (raw milk) is available in Germany, but it cannot be sold unless it has been produced under rigid standards of hygiene.

Mineralwasser: Mineral water. Springs bubble all over Germany and dozens of these spa waters are bottled. Among the most famous sparkling waters: Apollinaris, Gerolsteiner, and Peters Val (all available in this country); also Brohler and St. Gero. Gerolsteiner is available as a nonbubbly, too, but an even better known still mineral water is Fachinger. It's available all over Germany.

Mischbrot: Mixed bread. Meaning a mixture of grains, invariably a hearty blend of wheat and rye. The proportions and fineness of the flours may vary from region to region, but all mixed breads fall into one of two categories: wheat-mixed bread (at least 51 percent wheat flour) or rye-mixed bread (at least 51 percent rye). They are leavened with sourdough starters and/or yeast and are so popular they might be considered Germany's "daily bread." The obvious advantage of mixed breads is their broad spectrum of tastes and textures. Rye-heavy breads are spicy, wheat-heavy ones bland. Germany's best known mixed bread is probably the crusty-chewy, spicy, brown *Bauernbrot* (farmer's bread), now available in the United States in little airtight plastic boxes and well worth seeking out.

Among Germany's other popular *Mischbrot* are: *Paderborner Landbrot* (sturdy long loaves that look like our sandwich bread), *Doppelt gebackenes Bauernbrot* (crusty round loaves with shiny, caramel-brown crusts), *Gerstenbrot* (a bland, fairly soft rectangular bread), *Eifelerbrot* (plump long loaves with glossy brown crusts), *Schwarzwälder Brot* (the husky, floury round loaves for which the Black Forest is famous), *Krustenbrot* (a jawbuster similar to Black Forest bread), *Kasselerbrot* (a long, plump, mild and nutty loaf slashed across the top), *Mischbrot halb und halb* (a chewy elongated oval with a near fifty-fifty ratio of wheat and rye flours).

Mittagessen: Lunch. In Germany the midday meal is usually served between noon and 2 o'clock.

Mohn: Poppy seeds. Almost as popular as caraway seeds. Germans sprinkle poppy seeds over rolls, stir them into cakes, and grind them to paste and roll them up in strudel and stollen (see Poppy Seed Stollen, page 315).

Möhre, Mohrrübe: Carrot. See **Karotte.**

Morchel: Morel. This tan to brown little mushroom with the tall, honeycombed cap is prized for its deep earthy flavor. It thrives in humus-rich soil, especially underneath bushes, and the Black Forest is one of the morel gatherers' happier hunting grounds. The morel season in Germany is desperately short. Those who don't get out in May or June to pick their own must either buy them (not cheap) or settle for the dried.

Most: Cider. See **Apfelsaft.** *Most* is also what Germans call grape must.

Münster: Munster cheese. A well-aged German Münster makes our domestic versions about as exciting as porridge. It is intensely sharp, biting, buttery (45 to 50 percent fat), glorious. Unfortunately, it is rarely available here.

Mürbteig: Pastry. This is the short, buttery pastry Germans use for tarts, both sweet and savory. (See recipe, page 398.)

Mus: Purée. Especially a purée of fruit such as applesauce (*Apfelmus*).

Muscheln (also **Miesmuscheln** and **Pfahlmuscheln**): Mussels. Germans call these briny blue-black bivalves "the oysters of the simple man." They are harvested from the North Sea—mostly off the coast of Holland—and compared to other mollusks, they are cheap. Germans eat mussels only in months that end with R—September through February—when they come from waters nearby. The best of all are December mussels, taken from German waters (connoisseurs consider the mussels of February already

47

pallid). In season, German taverns often feature mussels cooked in a peppery broth. Steaming bowls of them are brought to table, together with chunks of black bread, steins of beer, and extra bowls to catch the shells. As every aficionado knows, the way to eat mussels is with the fingers. The German technique is this: The first mussel is picked up and its meat slurped out. The empty mussel shell then becomes a pair of tongs with which the meat of each succeeding mussel is plucked. Bowls of mussel cooking broth are usually served separately and the broth is eaten with a spoon.

Muskatnuss: Nutmeg. Next to cinnamon, nutmeg is probably the most widely used spice in Germany. It is the seed of the fruit of the nutmeg tree, and over time it made its way from the Spice Islands of the East Indies to Asia, then westward along the old trade routes to Constantinople. By the thirteenth century, this sweet, lemony spice was in great demand throughout western Europe with first the Portuguese, then the Dutch, controlling the trade. Almost from the beginning, nutmeg was as important in the kitchen as it was in the apothecary. German cooks have always been imaginative in their use of nutmeg, mixing it into soups, stews, sauces, gravies, stuffings, and vegetables, as well as into an eye-popping battery of cakes and cookies.

Nachspeisen (also **Nachtisch**) (and, most common of all today, **Desserts**): Desserts. Sweets are where Germany's master bakers, confectioners, and dessert makers can pull out all the stops and construct architectural confections of astonishing intricacy. Even though the fitness craze has hit Germany (albeit less resoundingly than here), most Germans would rather trim their calories and cholesterol from courses other than dessert. What *is* happening, however, is the reinterpretation of classic desserts in new and unusual ways. In the hands of Eck-

hart Witzigmann of Munich's celebrated Aubergine Restaurant, for example, *Lebkuchen* (gingerbread) becomes Lebkuchen Soufflé with Dark Beer Sabayon (page 327). And Josef Viehhauser, the gifted young chef at Hamburg's Le Canard Restaurant, takes pumpernickel, of all things, and churns it into a stellar Pumpernickel Bavarian Cream with Raspberry Purée (page 348).

Nelken: Cloves. The history of cloves, like that of nutmeg and cinnamon, is filled with scheming, skulduggery, and full-scale war. All because Europeans, from Roman times onward, used this rare, costly East Indian flower bud as medicine. In the early sixteenth century, only the Portuguese knew where cloves grew (the Moluccas). And, lest they lose the lucrative clove trade, they actually faked sea charts that sent many a competitor's ship to the bottom of the South Pacific. Early on, the disinfectant qualities of cloves were appreciated as well as their spicy taste (no small consideration in the days before refrigerators). Cloves have long been indispensable to the confectioner, the baker, and of course, the home cook. That said, let us add that German cooks are more sparing in their use of cloves than they are of either nutmeg or cinnamon. But they are no less imaginative. Whole cloves, for example, are often slipped into stews and marinades (especially those used for game). Ground cloves, however, are reserved for the spiciest German baked goods.

Neu: New. *Neue Kartoffeln*, for example, are new potatoes.

Niere: Kidney. Veal kidneys are the most delicate, the ones Germans prize the most, and the ones they are most likely to focus their culinary talents on.

Nockerl: Small dumplings. This is the Bavarian or southern German word for a little dumpling that goes into soup. In the north, they are **Klösschen.**

Nudeln: Noodles. The golden German pasta that purist cooks still make at home. *Nudeln*, whether eggless or made with egg (*Eiernudeln*), are almost always served with meats that have gravy. Sometimes, however, they're just turned in melted butter. The new fad: *Nudeln* with meat sauce, Italian style.

Nüsse: Nuts. The indispensables are hazelnuts (see **Haselnüsse**), almonds (**Mandeln**), and walnuts (**Walnüsse**). But pistachios (**Pistazien**) are popular, too.

Obst: Fruit. See **Früchte.**

Obstler: Fruit brandy. A crystal-clear spirit distilled from a mix of fruits—usually apples and pears, but sometimes plums and cherries, too. *Obstler* is cheaper and less refined than kirschwasser.

Obstsalat: Fruit salad. Delicious when made with fresh seasonal fruits and spiked, perhaps, with a little liqueur.

Ochsenfleisch: Ox. Germans are partial to the tougher cuts, **Ochsenschwanz** (oxtail), to name one, which they simmer into husky soups and stews (see Oxtail Ragout, page 145).

Öl: Oil. Corn oil, sunflower oil, and blended vegetable oils are what most home cooks use, but chefs—and the younger generation of hobby cooks—stock their kitchens with fine olive oil (*Olivenöl*) and such aromatic nut oils as *Haselnussöl* and *Walnussöl*.

Orange (also **Apfelsine**): Orange. *Orange* is what most modern Germans use, not the old-fashioned word, *Apfelsine*. And orange juice is **Orangensaft,** not the **Apfelsinensaft** of times past.

Pampelmuse (also **Grapefruit**): Grapefruit. Grapefruit is in fact the preferred word today. White and pink varieties, both widely available, are either halved and eaten, sectioned, or squeezed into juice (*Grapefruitsaft*).

Paniert: Breaded. *Wiener Schnitzel* (page 151) is a perfect example of how

exquisitely Germans bread and brown food.

Paprika: Paprika. A staple among Hungarian peasants at the turn of the seventeenth century, paprika did not gain nobility in western Europe until nearly two hundred years later when Escoffier served *Poulet au Paprika* and *Gulyás Hongrois* in Monte Carlo. The year was 1879, and it's thought that the German love of paprika began at about that time. Or possibly a few decades earlier because Empress Elizabeth of Austria, the daughter of Duke Maximilian Joseph of Bavaria who also became the queen of Hungary, was mad for *Paprikás Chicken*. Today, German cooks use paprika judiciously—to blush soups and stews and impart a sweet, faintly musky flavor. The paprika is stirred in, cooked, not just sprinkled on top, so that its flavor is released. Sweet paprika is their preference, and in this book's recipes we specify Hungarian sweet rose paprika, now available in better supermarkets across the country. What few people realize is the nutritive value of paprika. It's loaded with beta carotene and, ounce for ounce, fresh paprika peppers contain more vitamin C than any citrus fruit. Albert Szent-Györgi, a twentieth-century Hungarian-American biochemist who discovered their vitamin C content, won the Nobel prize.

Paprikaschote: Sweet pepper. Bell peppers—the green, red, and yellow—are available in German groceries, supermarkets, and open-air markets just as they are here.

Pastete: Filled pastry. These are always savory and include such things as liver pâté wrapped in pastry.

Perlhuhn: Guinea hen. These broad-breasted, tender-meated birds are popular among the new young generation of German chefs.

Perzwiebel: Pearl onion. Used in cooking as well as in dry martinis.

Petersilie: Parsley. As late as World War I, parsley tea was being drunk to treat kidney disorders. Today, however, its uses are strictly culinary. In Germany, flat-leaf parsley is preferred because of its intense flavor (see Fresh Parsley Soup, page 130). Germans are even more partial, however, to parsley root, which looks like a small parsnip. It's meatier, mellower, and sweeter than leaf parsley and imparts its special flavor to scores of German soups and stews. Fortunately, it's becoming more available these days in American supermarkets.

Pfannkuchen: Pancake. In Germany, most pancakes are thin and as big as a skillet bottom (see Apple Pancakes, page 334).

Pfeffer: Pepper. Germans use white pepper almost as frequently as they do the black, and are particularly meticulous about using it to season white or light dishes. A peppermill is a *Pfeffermühle.*

Pfefferminze: Peppermint. Used mostly as a garnish.

Pfeffernüsse: Peppernuts. Spicy Christmas cookies about the size and shape of walnuts (see Pfeffernüsse, page 381).

Pfifferlinge: Chanterelles. The flavor of these ruffly little flat-top mushrooms has been likened to everything from toasted hazelnuts to freshly ground nutmeg. The *Pfifferlinge* that flourish in German forests between June and November are the yellow variety, and experienced hunters know that the smaller they are, the better. Experienced cooks know, too, that *Pfifferlinge* must be salted only after cooking. Otherwise, they become watery.

Pfirsich: Peach. Peaches are very nearly as popular in Germany as apples and pears, but unlike them, are rarely stirred into savory recipes. Mostly they are eaten out of hand, sliced into fruit salads, or used to top cakes.

Pflaume: Plum. Germans use plums in cakes, compotes, marmalades, little pastries, even dumplings.

Pils: A type of beer. See German Beer (page 77).

Pilze: Mushrooms. The generic term that includes all varieties, both the cultivated and the wild, with which Germany is singularly blessed. Most Germans are skillful mushroomers and know at a glance which ones are safe to eat. Whole families take to the woods in May to gather the first specimens pushing up through the forest floor. Their outings continue until October and in those few months they manage to pick hundreds of tons of wild mushrooms. The Germans consider themselves not only the world champion mushroom gatherers, but also the world champion mushroom eaters. They've even invented a special brush for cleaning mushrooms called a *Pilzputzpinsel.* The most prized German woodland mushrooms are the **Morchel, Pfifferling, Steinpilz,** and **Waldegerling.**

Pistazien: Pistachio nuts. Germans use them not only to garnish dinner and dessert plates, but also to brighten meat terrines, breads, and cakes.

Platte: Platter. *Platte* can refer to the dish and to what's arranged on it. *Käseplatte,* for example, is a cheese plate.

Porree: Leek. See **Lauch.**

Preiselbeeren: Cranberries, Lingonberries. The German cranberry is small, red, and tart—the lingonberry, in fact, of Sweden. American cranberries, a close relative, are now exported to Germany, and during November and December you see plastic bags of them piled up in grocery counters just as you do here (*grosse Moosbeeren,* "large moss berries," the Germans call them). *Preiselbeeren* are grown in Poland, Holland, and in small amounts in northern Germany, where they are also known as *rote Heidelbeeren* ("red blueberries"). Like our cranberries, *Preiselbeeren* are plenty tart and for this reason are always cooked and sweetened. Germans find them the perfect accompaniment to goose and venison (see Baked Wine-Glazed Apples Stuffed with Marzipan, Cranberries, and Raisins, page 395).

Prise: Pinch. As in a pinch of *Salz* (salt) or *Pfeffer* (pepper).

Prosit or **Prost:** The German toast, meaning "Cheers," "To your health!"

Pumpernickel: True German pumpernickel is black—or very nearly so. It owes its color to a high percentage of dark rye flour and to prolonged baking at low temperatures during which the starches in the flour caramelize. Professional bakers use steam ovens and may leave their loaves of pumpernickel in for twenty-four hours. This slow, moist baking also gives pumpernickel its density. Westphalians claim pumpernickel as their own, and certainly there's nothing more Westphalian than a thin slice of pumpernickel topped by a thin slice of mahogany-hued Westphalian ham.

But they get an argument from the citizens of Osnabrück, an industrial city in the neighbor state of Niedersachsen, who point to their Pumpernickel Tower and swear that the first loaf was baked there in 1400 during a famine. "*Bonum paniculum*," it was called. Does *pumpernickel* derive from *paniculum*?

Perhaps. But there are other theories. Some say the miller who mixed and milled the grains for these early black breads was named Pumper Nickel. But we prefer the story (probably also apocryphal) passed along by our Munich friend Gertrud Schaller. She says that when Napoleon led his armies into the north of Germany and tasted the leaden, local black bread, he spat it out and said, "Pour Nicole!" Then directed his aides to feed the stuff to his horse.

Punsch: Punch. Specifically the spicy red wine punch served hot at Christmastime all over Germany.

Pute (also **Truthahn**): Turkey. Not served in Germany as often as goose, duck, or chicken, although given the frequency with which German food magazines are beginning to feature **Putenbraten** (roast turkey) and turkey parts, this may soon change.

Quark: Quark. Germans are passionate about a thick milk product called quark, and those living abroad where it's unavailable feel deeply deprived. The most acceptable substitute seems to be whole-milk ricotta or finely curded cottage cheese puréed or sieved with a little crème fraîche, Devon cream, sour cream, cream cheese, even yogurt, buttermilk, or acidophilus milk. The texture of quark is a cross between cream cheese and ricotta. Its flavor is like ricotta, too, but tarter and saltier. Some American health food stores now sell locally produced quark, as do fancy food stores and vendors at some of the upscale big-city greenmarkets. If you're unable to find it, use one of the substitutes suggested in the recipes that call for quark.

Quitte: Quince. To many Germans, the best thing about a quince is that it can be boiled into gorgeous sweet-sour jams and jellies.

Ragout: Stew. Germans are master stew makers and almost any animal can land in their stew pots: venison, hare and rabbit, of course, but also beef.

Rahm (also **Sahne**): Cream. *Rahm* is more commonly used in the south of Germany, *Sahne* in the north, but they are one and the same. *Rahmschnitzel* (page 152) is nothing more than a butter-browned veal cutlet sauced with pure cream, *Rahmkartoffeln* are creamed potatoes. German creams, like those of the United States, vary as to butterfat content. Coffee cream (*Kaffeesahne*) or "drinking cream" (*Trinksahne*) must contain at least 10 percent butterfat. It is not drunk, by the way, but poured into something that *is* drunk—like coffee or tea. *Süsse Sahne* or *Schlagsahne* (the equivalent of our whipping cream) must weigh in at 30 percent butterfat or more. There are differences in sour cream, too. *Saure Sahne* (at least 10 percent fat) is more liquid than our sour

51

cream. *Schmand,* on the other hand, is very thick, very fat. The two other types of sour cream sold in Germany are crème fraîche and crème double (soured double cream).

Raststätte: Rest-stop restaurant. You see these fast-food restaurants all along Germany's Autobahns, usually in pull-offs that also include picnic tables, gas pumps, and rest rooms.

Ratskeller: City hall restaurant. In Germany, city halls are often architectural landmarks and the restaurants in their basements serve excellent food at reasonable prices. You can count on well-prepared schnitzels, sauerbraten, spaetzle, potato dumplings, wursts, and sauerkraut. And plenty of good wine or beer on tap.

Rechnung: Bill. The restaurant check. In Germany, taxes and service are included in the bill; still, it's customary to round the total out—upward to the nearest round number. In pricey expense-account restaurants like Munich's Aubergine and Tantris, customers often tip 10 to 15 percent.

Regensburger: Knackwurst. The Bavarian town of Regensburg has its own famous recipe for knackwurst, and these chunky little wursts are not only spicier than the classic version but also speckled with bits of fat.

Reh: Deer, venison. Very nearly a national passion. To be completely accurate, *Reh* is the roe deer. Roe deer and red deer (*Rotwild*) roam Germany's forests and hunters are allowed to shoot them in season. In fall and winter, venison appears on restaurant menus all over Germany. And nowhere is it more inventively prepared (see Chestnut-Wrapped Tenderloin of Venison, page 177, and Roast Saddle of Venison with Spiced Vegetable Gravy, page 175).

Reis: Rice. Rice is not usually associated with a people so committed to potatoes, dumplings, and noodles. And yet modern German cooks are discovering the beauty and versatility of rice. And that

includes American wild rice, in Germany very nearly worth its weight in gold.

Renke (also **Felchen**): Freshwater whitefish. Like many fresh-water fish in Germany, *Renke* is known by more than one name. It's delicate and lean-meated, a fish so prized by chefs it's now being farmed in Alpine lakes. Most German cooks agree that the best way to cook *Renke* is to pan-fry it quickly at intense heat so its skin crisps and browns.

Rettich: Radish. The beloved big white radish of Bavaria. Bavarians, who call it a *Radi,* eat it with beer and soft pretzels. It is thinly spiraled, with salt sprinkled between the layers so it goes a bit limp. A *Radi* may also be grated, drizzled with a tart dressing, and served as part of a salad platter.

Rezept: Recipe. In German cookbooks, the style is often to begin with a **Grundrezept,** or basic recipe, then to offer dozens of quick variations.

Rind, Rindfleisch: Beef. *Rindfleisch* is the general word for meat of oxen, cows, young steers, and steers. The most oft-bought is oxen meat, which is well marbled, then heifer meat, then the lean meat of young steers. Cow and bull meat is nearly always ground into sausage. Strangely, steaks and prime ribs have never been as popular in Germany as pot roasts, shanks, and oxtail, which demand more ingenuity on the part of the cook. These tough cuts never lack the rich brown gravy Germans love to ladle over mashed potatoes, spaetzle, and dumplings.

Roggen: Rye. For bread making, rye flour, not wheat, is the German staple, perhaps because it produces satisfactory crops in frigid regions, even where the soil is less than adequate. Northern Europe, and this includes Germany, grows about 90 percent of the world's rye. Consumes it, too. Germans, in particular, like the dark, slightly sour breads rye flour produces. Rye flour may be light, medium, or dark; it may be whole-grain, partially or fully refined. Many German breads are made entirely of rye flour, but their rye flour is quite different from ours and contains enough gluten to produce good chewy loaves.

Roggenbrot: Rye bread. Although made wholly of rye flour, the grinds may differ, which explains why these loaves vary in color, texture, and flavor. As for the nonuniformity of shapes, this is mainly a matter of regional traditions and preferences. In the north, for example, breads tend to be long, in the south, round or oval. Most German rye breads are slightly sour, compact, and dense (some are unleavened or barely leavened). They are moist, too, and excellent keepers. Rye flour is rich in B vitamins and minerals and the darker the bread—a *Berliner Landbrot,* for example—the more nourishing it is.

Rollmöpse: Pickled herring rolls. These herring rolls stuffed with dill pickles and onions are a popular snack and hangover remedy all across Germany, but nowhere more so than in Baltic and North Sea ports, where herring arrive almost daily by the boatload. See Rollmops (page 90).

Rosenkohl: Brussels sprouts. *Rosenkohl* means "rose cabbage," and these baby cabbages, lined up and down a tall chunky stem, do indeed resemble roses. No one knows for sure where Brussels sprouts originated or even when, for that matter. But it was a long time ago—maybe in Belgium, maybe in Germany—in a cold climate for sure because Brussels sprouts can't stand heat. On the contrary, they are improved by frost, growing sweeter and tenderer as temperatures plummet. In Germany, the Brussels sprouts season extends from September until March. Because of the long season, German cooks have devised many unusual ways to prepare them (see Quark Tart with Brussels Sprouts, page 244).

Rosinen: Raisins. **Sultaninen** are seedless raisins. Both dark and golden raisins figure prominently in German cooking. They're used in a variety of breads and also stirred into such savory dishes as the sauerbratens of the Rhine area (see Rhineland-Style Sauerbraten with Raisin Gravy, page 143).

Rosmarin: Rosemary. When the Romans brought rosemary over the Alps into Swabia, it was used as a medicine (to calm the nerves), as a good-luck charm (sprigs of it were scattered about at weddings and funerals), and as a seasoning, too. Although twentieth-century German cooks do not use rosemary as often as they do chervil, marjoram, or thyme, they agree that it improves the flavor of beef and lamb, also that it's singularly compatible with green peas and carrots.

Rot: Red. Germans are often quite specific when it comes to naming fruits, vegetables, even wine. For example, *Rote Grütze* (page 350) is a pudding made out of red berries; *rote Bete* (also *rote Rübe*) is a beet.

Rotkohl (also **Rotkraut** and **Blaukraut**): Red or purple cabbage. See **Blaukraut.**

Rouladen: Meat rolls. The classic *Rouladen* are little beef scallops twirled up around dill pickles (see Roulades of Beef, page 137), but modern German cooks are experimenting with other meats and fillings.

Rumtopf: Rum pot. A tall glass or ceramic pot into which fruits are layered as they come into season, each layer being topped off by a hefty slug of dark rum. The fruits are left to macerate for half the year, then used in dozens of ways, though mostly as a dessert topping (see Gertrud Schaller's Rum Pot, page 396).

Saft: Juice. Usually tacked onto the name of a specific fruit or vegetable— *Apfelsaft* (apple juice), for example, or *Tomatensaft* (tomato juice).

Sahne: Cream. See also **Rahm.**

53

Saibling, Bachsaibling: Arctic char, freshwater char. A polar fish of the salmon family, which some connoisseurs consider even better eating. *Saibling* meat, like that of salmon, is firm but buttery and can range in color from white to orange. *Saibling*, also like salmon, has a landlocked cousin— *Bachsaibling* (brook char). Caught mostly in cool Alpine lakes, *Bachsaibling* is such a favorite it is now being farmed commercially. Germans consider its firm, easily flaked pale pink flesh a great delicacy.

Salami: Salami. Unlike their Italian counterparts, which are air-cured, German salamis are nearly always smoked. They consist of roughly three parts beef to one part pork, and they are garlicky, peppery, heavily flecked with fat.

Salbei: Sage. Not a must, although young cooks are using it more freely than their predecessors.

Salz: Salt. From A.D. 956 right up until 1980, salt was mined around the old Hanseatic town of Lüneburg in the north of Germany, then shipped farther north along the "Old Salt Road" to the Baltic port of Lübeck. There, tons of salt were stored in six- and seven-story, step-gabled, red brick warehouses (still standing today) before being shipped abroad. Tons more of the Lüneburg salt was used to preserve the local herring catch. To this day, Germans salt their food more heavily than most other people (except maybe the Japanese and Chinese). This appetite for brined, cured, and salted foods, some food historians believe, dates to the mid-eighteenth century and Frederick the Great, whose Salt Monopoly forced Prussians to buy more salt than they needed. Today Germans use a lot of sea salt (*Meersalz*).

Sardellen: Anchovies. See **Anschovis.**

Sauer: Sour. The taste dear to every German.

Sauerampfer: Sorrel. Given their craving for all things sour, it's scarcely surprising that Germans relish sour grass, or sorrel. In rural areas, it grows wild, so cooks can gather their own. Sorrel is cultivated, too, harvested just when the tongue-shaped leaves are about the size of a teaspoon, and this is what shows up in big-city markets. Germans use sorrel in many ways—in green sauces and dressings, for example. Also in soups.

Sauerbraten: Sour pot roast. This might be called the German National Dish (see Rhineland-Style Sauerbraten with Raisin Gravy, page 143).

Sauerkraut: Strange as it may seem, sauerkraut is a Chinese invention, not a German one. During the building of the Great Wall in the third century B.C., laborers discovered that their supply of cabbage was spoiling. In an attempt to preserve it, they shredded what cabbage they could salvage, mixed it with rice wine, and barreled it. Much to their surprise, the mixture began to bubble and froth, and presto! Sauerkraut. They tasted it and liked it, and sauerkraut soon became the staple of the poor.

Nearly a thousand years later, Genghis Khan's armies traveled with rations of sauerkraut, but theirs had been packed in salt, not rice wine, and lasted even longer. The Mongols brought this briny fermented cabbage to the Middle East and the Turks introduced it to western Europe.

Nowhere was it more appreciated, however, than in Germany, where today the bulk of each cabbage crop is transformed into sauerkraut. It all begins in late autumn when whole families go into the fields to cut the cabbage from the stalk. The heads, some of them weighing an awesome forty pounds, are lined up in the fields, pitchforked onto trucks, then transported to kraut factories. Here they are shredded by the ton, mixed with salt, barreled, and pressed to extract the juice and expel all air. For only then can fermentation begin. Some farm families, mostly in Bavaria and

Swabia, still make their own sauerkraut, zealously guarding secret recipes handed down from one generation to the next.

The fresh sauerkraut of Germany is crisp, slightly saltly, and far more delicate than the canned variety familiar to Americans. Fortunately, many specialty groceries here now sell fresh sauerkraut by the pound or pint. And better supermarkets stock one-pound plastic bags of it in their meat or dairy counters.

Realizing the extraordinary nutritional value of sauerkraut (measure for measure, it contains as much vitamin C as oranges) and its almost total lack of calories (¼ pound adds up to a mere 16), contemporary German chefs have created a new repertoire of sauerkraut dishes that are light, easy, and elegant. The recipes included in our vegetable chapter prove the point.

Sauerrahm: Sour cream. See **Rahm.**

Schalentiere: Shellfish.

Scheibe (also **Schnitte**): Slice or piece. *Schnitte* refers only to bread, meaning either a slice or an open-face sandwich. *Scheibe* is a slice of anything—cucumber, cheese, meat, and, just to confuse things, bread, too.

Schellfisch: Haddock. Not, as you might suspect, shellfish. This small member of the cod family is one of the most commonly used fish in Germany. Its lean white meat is tenderer than that of cod, but unlike cod, doesn't take well to salting. Fortunately, there is no shortage of fresh *Schellfisch*. German fish markets sell it whole, sliced, and filleted, all at reasonable prices. See Haddock in Mustard Sauce (page 204).

Schinken: Ham. The three major categories of German hams are: *roher* (raw), *gekochter* (boiled), and *geräucherter* (smoked). Its two best-known smoked hams (*geräucherter Schinken*) are the mahogany-hued, air-cured hams of Westphalia (made from hogs fattened on acorns) and the

sweeter, smokier, rosier, Black Forest hams. Both are exported to the United States and can be bought at better delicatessens, butcher shops, and specialty food stores across the country. True *Schinken* comes from pork, but thanks to "the new German cuisine," the meat of other animals is being cured and/or smoked into *Schinken.* There is now *Hirschschinken* (venison ham), for example, also *Wildschweinschinken* (wild boar ham).

Schnaps: Schnapps. Distilled spirits, often colorless, often made with caraway, juniper, or fruit, and always potent.

Schnecken: Snails. Germans, especially those living along the Rhine, relish snails almost as much as the French just across the river. (See Black Forest Snail Soup, page 117.)

Schnittlauch: Chives. How German cooks love this daintiest member of the onion family! Chefs and serious home cooks often grow their own—on the windowsill if not in a kitchen garden—lest they run short. Among the traditional ways to use chives are to snip them into clear broths and liver dumpling soup (see Rosa's Liver Spaetzle Soup, page 105), to scatter them over buttered vegetables or into omelets and salads. Then, too, chives are one of the green herbs essential to the classic Frankfurt Green Sauce (page 388).

Schnitzel: Cutlets. Since veal has become so expensive, many of the classic German schnitzels are now made with pork.

Schokolade: Chocolate. How the Germans love it—in cookies, cakes, confections, and, let's not forget, in **Schokoladeneis** (chocolate ice cream).

Scholle: Plaice. A highly regarded member of the flatfish family that's more abundant in Germany than sole (*Seezunge*) or turbot (*Steinbutt*)—and less expensive. Fresh *Scholle* is available almost everywhere, either whole or as fillets, which, because of their ease of preparation, are a

55

particular favorite (see Plaice with Bacon in the Style of Finkenwerder, page 202). In the Lübeck area, smoked *Scholle* is a specialty.

Schrotbrot or **Vollkornbrot:** Whole wheat bread. German whole wheat breads, like our own, contain the vitamin-and-mineral-rich bran and germ. But German breads tend to be coarser than ours and there's greater variety, too. They may even contain rye flour, but the proportion of wheat is higher and the breads are lighter colored and textured than classic ryes. They are also milder and nuttier and lack the characteristic spicy-sourness of rye bread. Two of Germany's best known whole wheat breads are *Rheinisches Schrotbrot* and *Holsteiner Schwarzbrot.*

Schwarz: Black. But, make a note, the *Schwarzbrot* (black bread) beloved by all Germans isn't black. It's tan, or at the very most, brown.

Schwein: Hog, pork. The preferred meat of Germany. And among the preferred cuts? *Schweinebraten* (pork roast), *Schweinekoteletten* (pork chops) and *Schweinshaxen* (pig's knuckles).

Seelachs: Pollack. First cousin to cod, and in Germany very nearly as plentiful. *Seelachs* has firm, lean, grayish meat that whitens in the cooking. Home cooks like *Seelachs* fillets (the most popular market form) because they don't fall apart and are easy to handle. Just how did a fish so lean and white come to be called "sea salmon?" In *North Atlantic Seafood*, Alan Davidson suggests that the German practice of salting and smoking slices of *Seelachs* may be responsible. "During the process," he writes, "a salmon-like colour is imparted to the flesh, which is normally grey."

Seezunge: Dover sole. The queen of flatfish and always expensive. It swims the eastern Atlantic from the Mediterranean to Norway, but the choicest are taken from the North Sea. In Germany, as elsewhere, Dover sole is the chef's darling because its lean, white, firm flesh has an almost meaty flavor that lends itself to countless variations. See Terrine of Sole and Salmon with Lobster and Sorrel Sauce (page 198).

Sekt: Germany's sparkling wine. See German Wine (page 65).

Sellerie, Knollensellerie, Stangensellerie (also known as **Bleichsellerie**): Celery, celery root, stick celery. When a German menu or recipe mentions *Sellerie*, celery root is what's meant. Stick celery is always specified—*Stangensellerie.* Of the two, celery root is more widely used. It's available year-round and a chunk of it is always included in the "German soup green" (a little packet of vegetables ready to drop into soups). Stick celery is available only between September and March.

Semmel: Roll. See **Brötchen.**

Senf: Mustard. Marvelous mustards are made in Germany in three basic strengths—mild, medium-hot, and hot. The two best-known exports are the mild, sweet, brown Bavarian mustard (sometimes made with whole grains), the traditional accompaniment to *Weisswurst* (but terrific, too, on hamburgers), and the smooth, golden Düsseldorf mustard, which is authoritative without being incendiary. There are specialty mustards, too, among them horseradish-mustard blends, and *Mostrich*, in which young wine or grape must is used in place of vinegar. In addition, German cooks use plenty of Dijon mustard, imported from France.

Serviette: Napkin.

Sosse (also **Sauce**): Sauce.

Spargel: Asparagus. "Quicker than you can cook asparagus!" That's what the Emperor Augustus, Julius Caesar's nephew, used to say whenever he wanted something done in a hurry—proving that first-century Romans knew how to cook asparagus.

But then it was the Romans who learned to cultivate the spindly wild stalks of *asparagos* (or *aspharagos*) that grew each spring in the hills above Athens and were beloved by the Greeks. No pencil-slim stalks for the Romans, however. They lavished so much time, attention, and fertilizer on their asparagus beds the stalks sometimes weighed three pounds apiece. And even these giants, Augustus decreed, could be given only a few minutes in the kettle.

The Roman passion for asparagus grew so intense at the height of the Empire that the plant's feathery green fronds could be seen billowing from the balconies and rooftops of Rome.

It was the Romans who planted the first asparagus in Germany. That was two thousand years ago and the vegetable has thrived ever since in those areas where the soil is loose, sandy, and mineral-rich.

To most Germans today, the only asparagus worth eating is *white*, not a special variety, mind you, but green asparagus grown underground. The stalks, deprived of sunlight, remain as pale as ivory. Their flavor never develops fully and they are softer than their green counterpart. "Buttery" is how connoisseurs describe the texture of white asparagus.

In Germany, white asparagus is the aristocrat of vegetables. And when the *Spargel* season begins early in May, these normally sane, logical people go quite berserk, particularly in the country's five major asparagus-growing areas: Finthen, near Mainz; Lampertheim, halfway between Worms and Mannheim; Schrobenhausen, in southern Bavaria; Schwetzingen, near Heidelberg; and Tettnang, in the vicinity of Lake Constance. These last two towns both claim to be "The Asparagus Capital of Germany."

Indeed, they are where asparagus addicts converge at the height of the season. The town of Schwetzingen stages a classical music festival while local restaurant chefs cook asparagus every way imaginable—and a few unimaginable. Tettnang chefs, not to be outdone, lay on an equally impressive *Spargel-Karte*, or Asparagus

Menu, the nearest thing to Mecca being the Hotel Rad dining room, which features sixty different asparagus dishes. In *The Cooking of Germany*, Nika Standen Hazelton writes that the best asparagus she ever ate was during the season at Tettnang: "It was one of the simplest," she continued, "a bowl of asparagus covered with a tart, thin hollandaise sauce, with which I ate a *Speckpfannkuchen*, a plate-sized egg pancake with bits of bacon in the batter." Luckily, fresh white asparagus is now coming to American supermarkets, meaning we no longer have to settle for the mushy canned stalks—an unacceptable substitute.

Spätzle: Spaetzle. You might call these the German gnocchi. They are little squiggles of egg batter either scraped off wooden paddles into cauldrons of steaming water or pushed through a spaetzle-maker, which looks something like a potato ricer. Germans serve spaetzle in place of potatoes and they are perfect for sopping up every drop of gravy (see Spaetzle, page 229).

Speck: Bacon. A generic term that refers both to bacon and lard. When it comes to bacon, Germans prefer *geräucherter Speck* (the double-smoked) because of its mellowness and intense taste of wood smoke.

Speisekarte: Menu.

Spezialbrote: Specialty breads. The list is long and includes everything from raisin to linseed bread. Among the better known specialty breads are:

1) *Grahambrot:* Graham bread. A rich brown loaf much like our whole wheat bread except that it's coarser, chewier, and nuttier in flavor.

2) *Schlüterbrot:* Schlüter bread. A rye-and-oat-bran bread made according to a process patented by a man named Schlüter. The bread is faintly sweet and, when just baked, wonderfully aromatic.

3) *Simonsbrot:* Simon's bread. A sweet-sour brown loaf made of rye or whole wheat flour. The bread owes its uncommon moist-

57

ness and density to the fact that the whole rye or wheat kernels are tested for viability, then sprouted in water and ground to paste. The dough is leavened with yeast or sourdough starters, put into square pans, then baked slowly in steam ovens so the loaves never develop a crust.

4) *Steinmetzbrot:* Steinmetz bread. A fairly spicy bread made of rye and/or wheat. The whole grains are soaked, husked while wet, then coarsely ground. The dough is baked long and slow in tins of different shapes until some of the starches caramelize, giving the bread its characteristic dark color and strong flavor.

5) *Toastbrot:* Toast bread. The white bread of Germany and a dead ringer for our standard sandwich loaf. It contains some fat and is called toast bread because it toasts beautifully.

6) *Zwiebelbrot:* Onion bread. A newcomer that's wildly popular. The dough, made of wheat, rye, and crisply fried onions, is rolled and shaped into crescents or spirals, then baked until richly golden.

7) *Knäckebrot:* Crisp flatbread. These rectangular flatbreads are made from rye or wheat or a mix of grains, but they are always baked fast at high temperatures, then left to dry so they're good and crisp. As for flavor, *Knäckebrot* ranges from bland to spicy.

Spinat: Spinach. Germans adore spinach, particularly the tender young *Blattspinat* (leaf spinach) of spring.

Sprotte: Sprat. See **Kieler Sprotte.**

Stachelbeeren: Gooseberries. Few berries are more surrounded by superstition than the gooseberry. In medieval Germany, it was said to keep witches and poisons out of the garden. It was also said that St. Christopher was crowned with the thorns of a gooseberry bush to keep evil spirits away. With all this humbug, it's surprising the gooseberry found its way into the German kitchen. In Germany today, gooseberries come in three colors:

green (unripe and so tart it can turn your mouth inside out), red and yellow (ripe berries sweet enough to eat raw). Gooseberries thrive in the rainy, wet, mild climate of northern Europe, and modern-day Germans are almost as inventive about preparing them as the British. They candy them in sugar syrup, then use them to top tortes; they simmer them into a variety of compotes, sauces, and preserves, even bake them into pies.

Steckrüben: Turnips. See **Weisse Rübchen.**

Steinbutt: Turbot. If a German chef cannot obtain good sole, he won't do himself in with a bacon slicer as the renowned Vatel of France did 300-odd years ago. He will simply substitute *Steinbutt*, a lookalike of the same big flatfish family. Although equally lean and white-fleshed, turbot lacks the texture and flavor of Dover sole. Still, it can double nicely in any recipe that calls for sole.

Steinhäger: The most popular juniper schnapps. As clear and lethal as gin.

Steinpilz: Yellow boletus. Called *cèpe* by the French and *porcini* by the Italians, this big, beefy mushroom has a club-shaped stem, a beige to brown cap that's clearly convex, and a flavor reminiscent of pine. *Steinpilze* favor evergreen forests and are in season only in July and August. Hedy says that when she was growing up in the foothills of the Bavarian Alps, her family had its own secret *Steinpilzwald.* "It was a pine forest near our home and I knew just where to look for the *Steinpilze.* I was the champion *Steinpilz* picker in my family." Today, alas, many of Germany's forests have been overpicked and, as a result, the wild mushrooms Germans prize above all others are becoming a luxury.

Steppenkäse: This low-fat, high-protein, yellow loaf cheese is both bland and nutty. Cube it to eat out of hand, or slice thin and serve on crisp crackers. In either case, accompany with a Riesling, Spätburgunder (pinot noir), Portugieser, or Trollinger.

Suppe: Soup.

Süss: Sweet.

Süssigkeiten: Sweets. A broad term that includes candy, cookies, almost anything that's sweet.

Tagesgericht: Daily Special. A special or seasonal dish, not always listed on the menu.

Tagessuppe: The soup of the day.

Taube: Squab. A farm-raised bird, the best of which are only a few weeks old; older birds are usually reserved for soups and stews. For a delicious new way to prepare these small, young doves, see Squab, Green Bean, and Red Lettuce Salad with Warm Gravy Dressing (page 281).

Tee: Tea. Not as popular in Germany as coffee, although all cafés and *Konditoreien* serve tea as well as coffee.

Teegebäck: Tea cakes. These are the little cookies, pastries, and *petits fours* often served in Germany as an accompaniment to coffee or tea.

Teelöffel: Teaspoon.

Teller: Plate.

Thunfisch: Tuna. Fresh tuna is not often seen in Germany, except in some of the fancier restaurants. But tins of tuna are available everywhere and German cooks use it much as we do—in salads and casseroles.

Thüringer: Thüringer. A smoky cervelat from the state of Thuringia in the eastern part of Germany.

Thymian: Thyme. Pliny once wrote that when burned, thyme put all venomous creatures to flight. And indeed, it seems to have been used as a bug bomb not only in Greece, but also in medieval Europe. It was a tonic, too, prescribed for everything from indigestion to whooping cough. But its uses were not confined to the chemist. Cooks, early on, treasured the lemony taste of thyme. They still do

. In Germany today, thyme (mostly the dried variety, although chefs insist upon fresh sprigs) is used to flavor beef, pork, wursts, poultry, game and game birds, stuffings, soups, sauces, and such vegetables as asparagus, green beans, carrots, and cauliflower.

Tilsiter: Tilsit cheese. Small of eye, ivory of hue, and depending upon age, mild to robust, this semisoft loaf is a good all-around cheese. Good for cooking, good for nibbling, good on a slice of pumpernickel with a tall glass of dark beer. Tilsiter comes plain, also studded with caraway seeds or peppercorns. Its butterfat content ranges from 30 to 60 percent.

Topf: Pot. An *Eintopf* is the German one-dish dinner, and a *Rumtopf* is a medley of rum-drenched berries that soak for the better part of the year before they are ladled onto ice creams, puddings, and cakes.

Topfen: Another word for **Quark** (see above), more often used in southern Germany than elsewhere.

Touristenwurst: Tourist sausage. A salami-style ring sausage popular among hikers and picknickers.

Trauben: Grapes. German wine grapes—both the white and the red—are used for wines and rarely eaten. Eating, or table, grapes are imported—mostly from Mediterranean countries—and include such varieties as *Muskateller, Alicante,* and *Almeria.*

Trocken: Dry. As in a fine German wine. See German Wine, page 65.

Trüffel: Truffle. As rare as diamonds and almost as expensive, truffles are unearthed once in a great while in Germany—in fact, a man found a grapefruit-size one recently in the Black Forest and the papers were full of the news. No commercial truffling exists in Germany, however, as it does in France and Italy.

Truthahn: Turkey. See **Pute.**

Überbacken: Gratinéed. See **Gratiniert.**

59

Ungezuckert: Unsweetened.

Vanille: Vanilla. Whenever they want a vanilla flavor, German cooks do one of two things. They either slip a vanilla bean (or its seeds) into whatever it is they're preparing or—and this is usually the technique for baked goods—they use vanilla sugar, which they can buy in little packets much the way we do gelatin or yeast.

Vanillezucker: Vanilla sugar. In the United States, vanilla sugar is confectioners' sugar flavored with vanilla. But to Germans, it is granulated sugar. They use vanilla-flavored confectioners' sugar, too (*Vanillepuderzucker*), although not so frequently.

Vom Fass: On tap. *Bier vom Fass* means "beer on tap."

Vorspeisen: Appetizers or hors d'oeuvre.

Wacholderbeeren: Juniper berries. Germans, perhaps more than any other people, cherish the evergreen flavor of these dark purple berries and use them to season everything from sauerkraut to venison.

Wachtel: Quail. The Common European quail is what sportsmen go after every autumn. These small meaty birds should be dry-plucked—gently lest their fragile skin tear—and eaten within a day of shooting. Quail are lighter meated than many game birds, less gamy, too. In Germany, they are often braised in the company of onions, juniper, and a healthy splash of wine. Quail eggs (*Wachteleier*), small and speckled, are the rage just now among trendy German chefs, who can dream up more ways to prepare and present them than seems possible.

Waldegerling: Wild brown champignon. A little mushroom that looks for all the world like our white cultivated mushroom except that it's brown. The *Waldegerling* grows abundantly in German fields as well as forests, which explains why it's also called *Wiesenchampignon*, or "meadow champignon."

Waldmeister: Sweet woodruff. This low, shade-loving creeper grows wild in Germany and is also used in garden borders. Its small white flowers open in May. In Germany you can buy little tins of dried woodruff leaves much as we do herbal teas. Dried woodruff is also an effective insect repellent and some *Hausfrauen* sprinkle it into cupboards and drawers rather than use modern bug bombs.

Waller: Catfish. This big freshwater catfish used to be taken from the Danube. Today it is farm-raised, much the way our own catfish are. And as with our own "cats," the best-tasting *Waller* are young ones weighing four to six pounds. They are supremely tender, too, and not very bony.

Walnüsse: Walnuts. Next to almonds and hazelnuts, these are the nuts Germans like best. The fresh harvest of walnuts comes on the market in late fall, and "green" walnuts are excellent with young wine. Dried walnuts (the walnuts we know best), can be bought year-round. They come from the wine-growing areas of Germany because walnut trees and vines both demand the same temperate climate.

Warm: Warm. Or to be more accurate, *hot. Warme Getränke* are hot drinks, *Warme Speisen* and *Warme Gerichte*, hot items on the menu.

Wasser: Water. It's safe to drink throughout Germany; still most Germans prefer **Mineralwasser** (see above).

Wein: Wine. German wines are far less known in this country than those of France and Italy. People tend to think them sweet—quite wrongly. To set the record straight, see German Wine, page 65.

Weinkarte: Wine list. When you travel in Germany, we urge you to try the local wines and also to ask the wine steward for his recommendations.

Weinstube: Wine tavern. These cozy little restaurants are where Germans go

60

when they want to join friends for a simple meal and a good bottle of wine.

Weiss: White. *Weissbier* is a pale, spicy beer made partly of wheat (Berliner Kindl Weisse is imported here). *Weisskäse* is, of course, white cheese, but more specifically, it is what northern Germans sometimes call **Quark** (see above).

Weisse Rübchen (also **Steckrüben**): Turnips. These pungent white roots have never been as popular in Germany as kohlrabi, but tender young specimens are appearing in open-air markets like Munich's several-block-square *Viktualienmarkt*. In the proper German hands, they can be superb (see Glazed Turnips, page 280).

Weisskohl (also **Weisskraut**): White cabbage. To Americans, this is "green" cabbage. In Germany, *Weisskohl* (as they say north of Frankfurt) or *Weisskraut* (the southern term) is the lowliest cabbage, the one that's shredded into sauerkraut and coleslaw (see Warm Coleslaw with Bacon and Caraway, page 288). The major cabbage harvest may take place in autumn, but these compact green heads store well and are available right around the calendar.

Weisswurst: White sausage. In 1986, Munich celebrated the 130th anniversary of *Weisswurst,* the bland white sausage developed there quite by accident. It all began one winter morning in 1857 when a Munich butcher named Sepp Moser set out to make *Bratwurst.* Lacking some of the crucial ingredients, he decided to improvise with what he had at hand—sausage meat, boiled veal, a little onion, grated lemon rind, and chopped parsley. The rest is history.

In Munich today, *Weisswurst* is the only excuse any Municher needs to take a break at a favorite pub—and this includes film stars, politicos, and journalists as well as secretaries. *Weisswurst* is what everyone eats when it's too late for coffee and too early for lunch.

There is only one correct way to eat

Weisswurst. It comes to table in its own little ceramic pot of simmering water (it must never boil lest it rupture or toughen). The steaming *Weisswurst* is lifted to a heated plate, its casing slit from end to end and peeled away. Then the wurst is cut, piece by piece, as it's eaten. The traditional accompaniments: Bavarian sweet mustard, *Weissbier* ("white" beer brewed from wheat), and a soft pretzel or roll. Nothing more.

Weizen: Wheat. Rye is the number one grain in Germany, but wheat is important, too. Some hobby bakers are now trying their hand at baking *Weizenbrot* (wheat bread).

Weizenbrot: Wheat bread. Refined wheat flours are made into a variety of breads and *Brötchen* or *Semmeln* (rolls). They are yeast-leavened and lighter than rye breads in color and texture. Wheat breads are popular throughout Germany because of their mild, slightly nutty flavor—a refreshing change of pace from rye. These are the breads Germans choose to accompany hearty dishes or to spread with jam, jelly, and preserves. Wheat breads stale fast and not so long ago village bakers delivered *Weizenbrot* door-to-door just as American dairies once delivered milk.

Wiener Schnitzel: Breaded veal cutlet. This actually originated in Milan at the time of the Austrian Empire. The story goes that when the Austrian emperor was served *Scaloppini à la Milanese,* he liked them so much he took the chef back to his court in Vienna so he could have them whenever he liked. From there, *Wiener Schnitzel* became famous throughout the German-speaking countries, and they're now as popular in Germany as they are in Austria.

Wild: Game. Venison is the hands-down favorite. But Germans are also partial to wild hare (*Wildhase*) and boar (*Wildschwein*).

Wildgeflügel: Game birds. Ducks lead the list, but pheasant and quail rate high, too.

Winzerfeste: Wine festivals. These are

61

held wherever wines are made, usually in early autumn. They're lively outdoor affairs with street bands, dozens of food booths, and, needless to say, new wine flowing like water. A particularly exhuberant *Winzerfest* is the one held every September in the Rhine Valley town of Bad Dürkheim. Visitors welcome!

Wirsing: Savoy cabbage. This is the cabbage Germans single out for special attention. It's nuttier and sweeter than *Weisskohl*, and its crinkly yellow-green leaves make dandy wrappers for all kinds of fillings. The whole head can be stuffed, too, then steamed or braised. Fortunately for *Wirsing*-loving Germans, it comes to market in June and is readily available until March of the following year. We specify savoy cabbage in many of our recipes (see Savoy Cabbage and Onion Cake with Bacon, page 248, and Sweet-Sour Savoy Cabbage, page 247). If it is unavailable, substitute green cabbage.

Wurst: Sausage. "The name of our city has achieved worldwide fame—thanks not to Goethe, but to our sausages." A Frankfurt newspaper, 1938.

When did the German passion for sausages begin? No one can say for sure, but the first mention of a "Frankfurter" was in 1487 when a town historian described this specialty of the old "Sausage Quarter."

Even native son Goethe wrote of sausages being distributed to the crowds at the coronation of Joseph II. But that was three hundred years later—in 1764.

Today, wursts are so much a part of everyday German life they figure as prominently in that country's proverbs, folksayings, and slang as apples do here. A devil-may-care attitude, for example, is *Wurstigkeit*, the clown of German puppet theaters is *Hanswurst*, and whenever there's a crucial decision to be made, Germans often say "The wurst is at stake!" ("*Es geht um die Wurst!*")

Well, what can you expect of a country that produces 1,500 different kinds of sausage? It's impossible to keep them straight—the chunky links and the skinny, the smoked and the unsmoked, the fresh and the cured. We'll confine ourselves here to a few of the best known.

To simplify things, Germans group their sausages into three broad categories: *Kochwurst* (boiled sausages, which include liverwursts, mettwursts, blood and tongue sausages), *Brühwurst* (parboiled or scalded sausages like frankfurters, bockwurst, bratwurst, knackwurst, and weisswurst, which need to be heated before they're eaten), and, finally, *Hartwurst* or *Rohwurst* (hard, dry, preserved sausages such as salami and cervelat—"summer sausages" that are sliced and eaten cold).

By law, all sausages made in Germany, whether for export or domestic use, must be 100 percent pure meat with no fillers, colorings, or other additives.

Wurstplatte: Sausage platter. To be more accurate, a platter of cold cuts served with rye bread, sweet butter, and pickles.

Würze: Spice. Which explains why the spicy Traminer grape that produces the gingery white wine is called Gewürztraminer (see German Wine, page 65).

Würzig: Spicy. The very word to describe many German dishes, both the sweet and the savory.

Zander: Pike-perch: *Zander* is a freshwater white fish of uncommon delicacy that's enhanced by fresh chervil (a favorite herb in Germany), lemon thyme, basil, even parsley. Once upon a time, fishermen pulled them from Germany's clear, cold lakes, but the *Zander* showing up in markets and restaurants today are more likely to have been pond-raised. The choicest *Zander* weigh between one and two pounds. They spawn in spring and are unavailable between March and May.

Zervelat: Sausage. Also spelled **Cervelat** (see above).

Zimt: Cinnamon. Once worth its weight in gold, cinnamon became affordable only after a few slips of the cinnamon tree were smuggled out of the East Indies and planted in the French colonies. That was in the late eighteenth century and one can only wonder what direction German cooking would have taken without it because cinnamon is Germany's favorite spice today. For starters, there would be no cinnamony fruit breads or nut wreaths, no *Lebkuchen* (page 377), *Pfeffernüsse* (page 381), and least of all, no *Zimtsterne* (page 376), the beloved Cinnamon Stars of Christmas.

Zitrone: Lemon. Many German recipes owe their sourness to lemon, and others, of course, to vinegar.

Zucker: Sugar. Confectioners' sugar is **Puderzucker.**

Zunge: Tongue. Germans are fond of tongue—the fresh, the cured, and the smoked. Veal tongue is considered a great delicacy. Usually it's poached, sliced, and served with a cream sauce, sometimes with capers added. Beef or pork tongue is more likely to be diced and mixed into sausage.

Zungenwurst: Tongue sausage. Blood sausage (see **Blutwurst**) to which cubes of cooked tongue are added.

Zwetschgen: Plums. These are very special plums—small, blue-black, oval, and sweet. In this country they are sold as Italian plums.

Zwetschgenwasser: Plum brandy. Not so much a brandy as a clear, colorless firewater distilled from *Zwetschgen* that is usually sipped at the end of the meal as a digestif. A shot of it may be taken at any time of the day, however. *Zwetschgenwasser*, like kirschwasser, is also occasionally used in recipes.

Zwiebel: Onion. In the old days, onions were prescribed for insomnia, but today they are the vegetable Germans use most as a seasoning—summer onions, winter onions, pearl onions, shallots, the lot. Experienced cooks who "know their onions" realize that the rounder the onion, the sweeter it will be. Elongated ones—like *Frühlingszwiebeln* (spring onions)—are sharper and should be used with restraint.

WINES AND BEERS OF GERMANY

Deutschlands Wein und Bier

Lamar Elmore, Ph.D.,
Former Executive Director of the German Wine Information Bureau

German Wine: A Unique Style

Germany's reputation for producing some of the world's finest wines is not based on quantity, for Germany produces less than 3 percent of the world's wines. The area devoted to wine production in the thirteen approved German winegrowing regions adds up to just 250,000 acres. That's one seventh of the vineyard acreage in California, or about one third the size of Rhode Island.

It is the quality of German wines, their unique style and taste, that gives them their international reputation. Although the same grape varieties are planted in many countries and vintners produce what they call "German-style" wines, only in Germany do nature, geography, and the winemaker's art combine to produce such uniquely refreshing, delicate, and aromatic wines.

German wines burst with flavor and bouquet; they are full on the palate. And yet they are light. With an alcohol content ranging from 7 to 11 percent, German wines are a fifth to a third lower, on average, than the wines of other countries. Which means they are lower in calories, too.

Another characteristic of German wines is that their taste, thanks to a minimum of manipulation and handling, is true to the grape. The wines are fresh with refined nuances of fruit and bouquets that literally spring from the glass.

Tension is the word that best describes the unique quality of German wines. The best of them vibrate with a nervous interplay of fruit and acidity—the result of a cool northern climate that permits German grapes to ripen slowly without losing their crisp acidity. Thus a Riesling from Germany will have far more verve and focus than Rieslings from warmer climates where the heat of the sun lowers the essential acidity of the wine.

Light yet full-bodied German wines range in taste from bone dry to lusciously sweet. They are the world's most adaptable apéritif wines—wonderful by themselves or with hors d'oeuvre. They are also supremely flexible, complementing not only the dishes that made Germany famous, but also today's lighter cuisine.

A Quick History of German Winemaking

The making of wine in what is now Germany goes back more than two thousand years, before the Romans, when Celtic tribes roamed the great forests and valleys of the Rhine and its tributaries. Artifacts in the museums of the region show that these tribes did make wines from wild grapes, but the wines were certainly very different from the wines we know today.

Systematic cultivation of grape vines to produce wines—specifically *Vitis vinifera*, a species that includes all of Europe's great winemaking grapes—was introduced into Germany by the Romans, probably in the first century A.D. The Romans conquered most of Gaul, establishing settlements throughout what is now France and Germany up to the west bank of the Rhine. Wherever the Roman army went, wine was sure to follow. Part of the reason was that ample wines were needed to supply the Roman troops, who were allotted daily rations of wine rather than the often contaminated water.

Following the decline of the Roman Empire and the establishment of Christianity through the region, the Catholic Church played a decisive role in the development and direction of winemaking in Germany. Not only did the Church acquire extensive properties over the years, but during the Middle Ages the monastic orders—especially the Cistercians and Benedictines—actually established some of the finest vineyards in both France and Germany. Monks were exemplary record keepers. The industrious brothers introduced systematic annual evaluation of grape varieties and vineyard sites, which over the centuries, would help identify the best growing areas and vineyards as well as the grapes most suited to the particular site or microclimate.

In the nineteenth century, Napoleon conquered the Rhine valley. To the great joy of many and the dismay of others, he imposed the Napoleonic Code of law throughout the region, secularized most church property, and abolished primogeniture. Former ecclesiastical vineyards were auctioned to the highest bidders; some vineyards were awarded as prizes to Napoleon's supporters and others went to the German states. The face of winemaking changed. It became privatized and remains so today.

German Grape Varieties

Riesling is king in Germany. Although Riesling accounts for only 21 percent of plantings, it is the grape most responsible for Germany's international reputation. Riesling is one of the world's noble grape varieties (others include Chardonnay, Cabernet Sauvignon, and Sauvignon Blanc). It is slow to ripen, reaching an acceptable level of ripeness later than Chardonnay or the pinot family; it is a hardy variety, flourishing in difficult terrain and requiring minimal moisture; it is frost resistant—important in this far northern climate; and, finally, it is consistent. Although Riesling is grown throughout the world, Germany's Rieslings are the benchmark by which all others are judged.

Another important traditional variety in Germany is the *Silvaner*, which, in earlier times, accounted for most of the plantings in Germany. Today only 8 percent of vineyard acreage is devoted to Silvaner, having been replaced by more prolific, earlier ripening varieties. Silvaner can produce wines of undeniable character, fragrance, and substance, often exhibiting a nutty aroma, particularly in Franken and parts of Rheinhessen.

Commercially, the most important grape variety in Germany, with 24 percent of the plantings, is the *Müller-Thurgau*. A crossing between Riesling and Silvaner, the Müller-Thurgau ripens earlier than Riesling or Silvaner—usually in September. It is named after Professor Hermann Müller of Thurgau, Switzerland, who developed the variety in 1882. The wines are clearly related to Riesling in style, but lack its finesse and invigorating acidity. There is often a pronounced muscat flavor and these are the major blending wines in Germany today.

Other traditional varieties that enjoy a strong reputation:

- *Gewürztraminer*, or spicy Traminer, is famous for its gingery, highly aromatic bouquet and flavor of roses and litchi nuts.
- *Weissburgunder* (*pinot blanc* in France) produces dry, full-bodied white wines that are exceptionally good with food.
- *Ruländer* (*pinot gris* in France and *pinot grigio* in Italy) produces full-bodied wines that are often rich and darker in color, characterized by intense flavor, low acidity, and some spiciness.
- *Gutedel* (*chasselas* in France and *fendant* in Switzerland) is planted primarily in Baden and makes a mild quaffing wine low in acidity.

Like the Müller-Thurgau, many of Germany's grape varieties are crossings, the results of Germany's scientific viticultural research aimed at creating varieties that will ripen earlier than Riesling and be even hardier, more frost-resistant, less prone to diseases. Some of the more promising newer crossings are *Kerner, Scheurebe, Optima, Morio-Muskat, Ortega, Bacchus,* and *Faber*. Of these, the Kerner is most Riesling-like, producing clean wines with good acidity and often a mild grapefruit bouquet and taste.

Many popular wines from Germany are blends. If no grape variety is mentioned on the label, the wine is probably a blend of different varieties to ensure consistent and balanced taste.

Red Wines

Although production of German red wines is small and their export significance minuscule, Germans are very fond of their light, fruity red wines and are devoting

67

increasing acreage to their production. As with German white wines, the hallmark of German reds is the fresh fruit taste, good acidity, and fragrant bouquet. Some wine experts compare German red wines to Beaujolais.

Ironically, red wines are a specialty in the tiny, far-northern region of the Ahr and in the Rheingau around the village of Assmannshausen. The Württemberg, Baden, and Rheinpfalz regions are also known for quality red wines.

The most important red grape varieties are *Spätburgunder* (*pinot noir*), *Portugieser*, and *Trollinger*.

The Winegrowing Regions

The German winegrowing area lies along the northern limit of the grape, parallel in latitude (50 degrees) to Newfoundland and Labrador. North of this line grapes will not ripen in quantities suitable for commerce. Indeed, were it not for the mitigating influence of the Rhine and its tributaries, wines could not be produced here at all.

A map of the German winegrowing regions is a map of the Rhine and its tributaries, particularly the Moselle, the Main, the Nahe, and the Neckar. Wine grapes are planted only on or near rivers. The river tempers the climate, acting as a heat reflector, helping to maintain a mild temperature both day and night. Contributing to milder microclimates, the rivers allow the growing season to extend into late September, October, and even November, long after harvests are finished in other parts of Europe.

In this far-northern climate, every ray of sunshine counts. Throughout the winegrowing area, you will find vineyards planted on south-facing slopes, often very steep slopes, positioned to benefit from every possible hour of sunlight. The vineyards themselves are frequently surrounded by mountains and forests that shield them from chill northern winds.

It's said that in Germany the vines need 100 hours of sunlight between May and October to produce an average vintage, and 120 hours to produce an outstanding one. Germany gets the requisite 100 hours almost every year, it is blessed with the 120 hours needed for an outstanding vintage only two to three times in a decade. Recent years have been an exception, with good to outstanding vintages in 1983, 1985, 1988, 1989, and 1990.

Although there is a distinct family resemblance among all German wines, there are thirteen German quality wine regions (approved by the German government and the European Economic Community) and each produces individualistic wines.

An important rule of thumb to follow is that the wines from the more northerly regions are lighter, lower in alcohol, and usually display a pronounced, crisp acidity. Wines from the southern regions are generally bigger, rounder, and softer with slightly higher levels of alcohol.

The most important wine regions with regard to export to the United States are

Germany's Winegrowing Regions

the Mosel-Saar-Ruwer, the Rheingau, Rheinhessen, Rheinpfalz, the Nahe, Baden, and Franken.

Mosel-Saar-Ruwer: Flanked by extremely steep slate soil vineyards, the Mosel is joined by its two tiny tributaries, the Saar and the Ruwer, to define one of the world's most beloved winegrowing regions. Situated on the river at the base of vine-covered slopes are such famous wine villages as Bernkastel, Piesport, Wehlen, Trittenheim, Zeltingen, Brauneberg, Zell, and Ockfen. The Riesling wines from this region are noted for their fresh spice and citric or applelike acidity. They can range from austere to delicate and charming, often exhibiting a hint of effervescence.

Rheingau: The entire Rheingau is one south-facing slope overlooking the Rhine, which, blocked by the Taunus mountains in its race to the North Sea from Lake Constance in the south, flows east to west for the twenty-six miles between Mainz and Bingen. The vineyards here enjoy the wide breadth of the Rhine—almost a lake at this juncture—and produce some of Germany's noblest and most famous wines, displaying rich aromas of ripe pears, apples, apricots, peaches, and spices. The Rheingau includes such celebrated wine towns as Rüdesheim, Johannisberg, Eltville, Erbach, Hattenheim, Rauenthal, Kiedrich, and Hochheim (from whence "hock" comes, the word the British use to identify all German wines).

Rheinhessen: Rheinhessen lies among rolling hills in a valley between the Rhine and Nahe Rivers. It is noted for the many grape varieties that flourish in the exceptionally rich and hospitable climate. The wines often reveal less acidity than their neighbors to the north, but make up for it with a ripeness and round succulence that can be very appealing. The Riesling vines from the *Rheinterrasse* or *Rheinfront*, the vineyards directly along the Rhine between Nierstein and Oppenheim, produce some of the most fragrant, ripe, and luscious wines in Germany. The city of Worms in Rheinhessen is also the source of the original Liebfraumilch.

Nahe: Between the Rheingau, Rheinhessen, and the Mosel-Saar-Ruwer is the Nahe region, which bears strong resemblances to all its neighbors. The mineral-rich soil of the Nahe adds its own indelible tone and makes this fertile ground for the wine lover interested in sampling different varieties of grapes and styles of wines.

Rheinpfalz: Located to the south of Rheinhessen and just northeast of Alsace in France, the Rheinpfalz is Germany's second largest winegrowing region and it produces some extraordinary wines. The word *Pfalz* derives from the Latin *palatium,* or palace, referring to the palaces built here by the Romans and then later by Carolingians and Franks who conquered the area. The English word *Palatinate* is also used to denote the Rheinpfalz. Rheinpfalz wines are exotic. Sheltered by the Haardt Mountains, the climate is surprisingly warm. Indeed, figs, apricots, and even almonds grow here. The wines are full-bodied and attractively balanced, showing nuances of citrus and apples as well as bolder flavors of more exotic fruits like mango, kiwi, fig, and passion fruit. Particularly noteworthy are the wines from the Mittelhaardt towns of Deidesheim, Forst, Wachenheim, and Ruppertsberg.

Baden: Baden is the southernmost of Germany's wine regions, extending from just north of Baden-Baden south to Lake Constance. This long, slim strip is also Germany's third largest winegrowing area. Its wines range from fragrant and light in the north to full-bodied and even fiery in the volcanic soils of the Kaiserstuhl-Tuniberg. Nearly 90 percent of the Baden wines are produced and bottled by cooperatives.

Franken: Located on the gentle slopes of the Main River in northern Bavaria, the vineyards of the Franken region have always been known for producing dry, assertive wines. Franken produces both excellent Riesling and Silvaner wines, often referred to as *Steinwein* because of the famous Stein vineyard near the capital city of Würzburg.

The remaining wine-producing regions, whose output is rarely imported into the United States, are the Ahr, Hessische Bergstrasse, Mittelrhein, and Württemberg. Two regions have recently been added as a result of the reunification of Germany: the Saale-Unstrut near Leipzig and the Elbe at Dresden.

Other Important Geographical Divisions

In addition to the thirteen recognized quality winegrowing regions in Germany, there are further divisions, each defining smaller areas approved for cultivation, each yielding more distinctive wines. Most regions are divided into one or more *Bereiche,* or subregions. A *Bereich* contains many wine villages and usually takes its name from the most prominent—*Bereich Bernkastel,* for example, or *Bereich Johannisberg.* A wine identified on the label as a *Bereich* wine can best be described as a regional wine, blended from grapes harvested within the *Bereich.*

Each *Bereich* is further subdivided into *Grosslagen* (large collections of vineyards that share similar characteristics) and *Einzellagen* (individual small vineyards).

The Classification System and Terminology

In Germany there is no official ranking of vineyards as in France. Unofficially, of course, experts recognize that certain vineyard sites consistently outperform others. But this is not the basis for classifying German wines. Ripeness is everything. Indeed, the entire German wine classification system is based on how ripe the grapes are at harvest. Germany is the only major wine country in the world to classify its wines this way.

There are nine categories, each denoting a higher degree of ripeness. It is a simple and straightforward system. There is, however, a major caveat. The categories are called *Qualitätsstufen,* or quality levels, suggesting that the higher up the ripeness scale one goes, the better the wine. This is misleading. There are outstanding wines at all levels, from the bottom to the top. The best way to make sure you are getting the quality you want is to experiment, asking the advice of your wine merchant and identifying those producers, estates, and shippers that consistently please you.

Levels of Ripeness: Under the current German Wine Law, there are two overall categories of ripeness and quality: *Tafelwein* (table wine, the equivalent of the French *vin du table*) and *Qualitätswein* (quality wine).

Tafelwein: Very little *Tafelwein* (or its subcategory, *Landwein*) is exported to the United States. It is the lowest designation given to wine grown in Germany. It has reached a minimal level of ripeness so that when beet or cane sugar is added before fermentation, it can reach the minimum alcohol level required by law. It is drunk young and usually sold as bulk wine or in liter or two-liter bottles at the supermarket.

Qualitätswein: Most of the German wines imported into the United States are *Qualitätswein,* or quality wine. Before they can be approved for sale, quality wines must be analytically tested by experts and tasted by panels of government authorities. There are two divisions of *Qualitätswein:*

Qualitätswein bestimmter Anbaugebiete (QbA): These are quality wines from one of the thirteen approved German quality winegrowing regions and include the largest quantity of German wine. The wines must be made of approved grape varieties, which have reached the requisite level of ripeness and will offer the style and traditional taste of their appellation. Just as in the great estates of Bordeaux, in most years QbA wines may be *chaptalized,* that is, beet or cane sugar may be added before fermentation to boost the alcohol to a desired level. All of this sugar is fermented into alcohol and does not affect the sweetness of the wine. QbA wines are produced in both dry and medium-dry styles in every vintage.

Qualitätswein mit Prädikat (QmP): Fulfilling all the requirements for QbA wines as to origin and legal approvals, these are quality wines with special attributes and they include most of Germany's finest bottles. QmP wines may *never* be chaptalized.

The six *Prädikats,* or levels of special distinction, in ascending order of ripeness at the time of harvest are:

- *Kabinett:* The world's naturally lightest wines. Made from fully ripened grapes, *Kabinetts,* with their extremely low alcohol content yet fully ripe taste and bouquet, are unique in the world of wines. *Kabinett* wines may be produced in dry and medium-dry styles and occur in most vintages.
- *Spätlese:* Literally "late harvest" wines made from grapes harvested at least one week after the normal harvest that have reached a higher level of ripeness. They make a more substantial wine, exhibiting intense concentration of flavor. *Spätlese* wines are available in dry, medium-dry, and sweet styles and are produced, on the average, in every other vintage (year) in most regions. In other words, *Spätlese*

can be produced only in vintages when nature cooperates to produce this higher level of ripeness.

- *Auslese:* Wines made from selected bunches of overripe grapes. In exceptional years *Auslese* wines may be affected by *Botrytis cinerea,* the noble mold that helps produce the world's best dessert wines. These are elegant wines with intense flavor, usually sweet, although dry *Ausleses* can be found. *Auslese* wines rarely occur in significant quantity more than three to four times in a decade.
- *Beerenauslese* (BA): A lusciously rich, sweet dessert wine made from individually selected grapes that are overripe and often affected by *Botrytis cinerea.* Each individual overripe grape must be cut separately by hand from the bunches. Although the wines are sweet, the sweetness is balanced by a lively acidity. *Beerenauslesen* are rare wines, occurring only two to three times every ten years.
- *Eiswein:* Literally "ice wine," is the very essence of the grape—sweet and concentrated. It is made from fully ripened, non-*Botrytis* grapes that were intentionally left on the vine until the first severe frost. The grapes are picked while frozen (at temperatures of about −8 degrees Celsius) and pressed before they can thaw. The water in the grape remains behind as a solid block of ice, while the concentrated grape juice at the ripeness level of *Beerenauslese* flows out of the pressing to be made into some of the most memorable wine in the world. *Eisweins* are characterized by extremely high acidity that brings a mouth-puckering tartness to balance their luscious sweetness. *Eiswein* can be made in many regions about every third year, but the annual production remains low—and the price high—because of the risks and intensive labor involved in their production.
- *Trockenbeerenauslese* (TBA): The rarest of German wines, made from dried, raisined, Botrytised, individually hand-picked grapes. They remain low in alcohol and retain a high acidity, distinguishing them from the other noble dessert wines of the world. This is the richest, most intensely honeyed wine in existence. TBAs can be made only once or twice in a decade.

How Dry Is the Wine?

QbAs, Kabinetts, Spätlesen, and *Auslesen* can all range in levels of dryness. If you want an absolutely dry wine with no perceptible residual sweetness (fewer than 9 grams per liter of unfermented sugar, or 0.9 percent) look for the word *trocken* (dry) on the label. The term *halbtrocken* denotes a wine that is also dry to the taste, with very slight residual sweetness (fewer than 18 grams per liter, or 1.8 percent). If no taste description appears on the label, the wine will usually have some perceptible sweetness, depending on the style preferred by the winemaker. Remember, German wines are high in acidity and you may actually prefer a little sweetness for balance.

What is the Optimum Age to Enjoy the Wine?

German wines are very long lived because of their high acidity, extract, and, where applicable, residual sweetness. Most QbAs and Kabinetts are ready to be drunk as soon as they appear on the shelves. Select recent vintages and drink them within five years for their fullest flavor. You may also drink *Spätlese* wines young, but they improve considerably with a little age and will continue to be enjoyable five to ten years after bottling. *Auslese* wines are best with at least two to three years of age and will continue to develop new and subtle flavors for a decade or more.

BAs, TBAs, and *Eiswein* should be put down for several years to reap maximum benefit from the maturation of these rare wines. They may peak seven to ten years after bottling and, with good storage at a constant temperature, can remain remarkably fresh and enjoyable for decades.

The German Wine Label

Once you have mastered the basic label information format, you should know a great deal about the origin, style, and taste of the wine in the bottle. All quality wine labels provide the following information: geographic origin, the wine's vintage, its quality category (the level of ripeness of the grapes at harvest), the name of the producer, and, if at least 85 percent of the wine is one variety, the label will usually give that information, too.

1. The winegrowing region, one of the thirteen approved regions in Germany, in this case the *Mosel-Saar-Ruwer.*
2. The quality level of the wine, indicating the ripeness of the grape. This is a *QmP* wine and the particular *Prädikat* is *Spätlese.*
3. The vintage, the year the grapes were harvested—1990, for this wine.
4. The name of the village where the vineyard is located—*Zeltingen.*
5. The name of the particular vineyard, *Schlossberg,* where the grapes were grown, either an individual vineyard (*Einzellage,* as here) or a collective vineyard (*Grosslage*).
6. The grape variety (*Riesling*), used only if 85 percent of the grapes are of that variety.
7. The *Prädikat* level of the wine, how ripe the grapes were at harvest, in this case, a late-harvested wine, or *Spätlese.*
8. The taste style of the wine, in this case, *trocken* (dry). *Halbtrocken* would also indicate a wine that is dry to taste, but less austere than *trocken.* If no style designation appears on the label, you can assume that it will display some sweetness.
9. The name of the wine estate, here *Weingut Selbach-Oster.*
10. A wine grown, produced, and bottled by the producer may be labeled as an *Erzeugerabfüllung.*
11. The *A.P.* number (*Amtliche Prüfungsnummer*), the official testing number indicating that the wine has passed analytical and sensory testing required for all German quality wines. It allows authorities to trace a particular bottle of wine should there be a question about it.

What's in a Name?

Most German wines derive their names from geography, the town and vineyard where the grapes were grown. If a wine is labeled *Wehlener Sonnenuhr,* it comes from the village of Wehlen and the specific vineyard of Sonnenuhr. This is the nomenclature system for most German wines today.

Wines may also be named simply after the region. For example, a wine that is blended from Riesling grapes harvested in portions of the Rheingau may be named simply *Rheingau Riesling.* Similarly, *Baden Pinot Gris* is produced from pinot gris grapes harvested in Baden.

If a wine is produced from grapes of a particular *Bereich* (subregion), such as Bernkastel or Nierstein, it may be named *Bereich Bernkastel* or *Bereich Nierstein.*

Because many foreign consumers find the German geographic nomenclature difficult and confusing, some producers are simplifying their labels. A producer may elect, for instance, to give the wine a simple but appealing brand name such as "Bishop of Riesling" or "Blue Nun."

And finally, a producer may wish to simplify his label by emphasizing his estate in the name of the wine. Thus you will find such labels as *Deinhard Riesling Dry* from the Deinhard estate, or *Sichel Riesling* from the Sichel firm. Additional information on the label will tell you the geographic origin of the wine.

Other Important Terminology

Abfüller: The bottler.

Botrytis cinerea: "Noble rot." A fungus that is responsible for the world's best sweet wines. It punctures the grapes and the moisture inside escapes, leaving behind the intense, sweet essence of the grape.

Liebfrauenmilch/Liebfraumilch: A popular medium-dry German quality wine of the QbA category, usually blended from several grape varieties from one of four regions—Rheinhessen, Rheinpfalz, Rheingau, or the Nahe—to provide consistency year after year. The overwhelming majority of popularly priced German wine exports are Liebfraumilch.

Sekt: German sparkling wine that ranges in taste from bone dry to pleasingly sweet.

Weingut: A wine estate that produces and bottles wines from its own vineyards. In Germany, the vineyards are rarely clustered around the estate itself, as in Bordeaux. Indeed, a *Weingut* may possess holdings in vineyards scattered over a large area.

Weinkellerei: A winery that purchases base wines and grape juice from several growers, then produces and bottles the finished wine.

Weissherbst: Rosé wine.

Matching German Wine and Food

The most important rule to remember in food and wine pairings is that there are no longer any rules. If you experiment, you will discover enjoyable combinations that enhance your meal. However, a few guidelines may be helpful:

First, try to balance the intensity of flavor of the dish with the intensity of flavor of the wine. A delicate dish calls for a light and subtle wine; robust recipes call for more vigorous wines.

Second, there are two basic ways to match wine with food—either to serve as a complementary flavor or to serve as a contrast. The fruitiness of all German wines harmonizes perfectly with many popular dishes. For example, mildly sweet sauces and vegetables call for a fruity wine that is not austerely dry.

In terms of contrast, think of our love for counterpoints in flavors; salt enhances sweet; spice and heat can be played off against fresh fruity flavors. You, of course, must be the arbiter. Serve all German white wines well chilled and German reds slightly chilled.

For Hors d'Oeuvres: German *QbAs* and *Kabinetts*—whether dry or slightly sweet— make wonderful apéritifs. Low in alcohol, they are superb with a wide range of cold cuts, cheeses, canapés, and smoked fish. Rich pâtés call for the ripe intensity of sweeter *Spätlese* or *Auslese* wines.

For Main Courses: Dry *Kabinetts* offer an excellent complement to most grilled, broiled, and sautéed seafood. If a cream sauce is served with the fish, a slightly sweeter *QbA* or *Kabinett* may be in order. Lobster has an underlying sweetness that partners well with wines containing a bit of residual sugar.

Best with poultry, pork, and veal are either a dry or traditionally styled *Kabinett* or *Spätlese*. And dry white German *Spätlese* and *Auslese* wines are the perfect match for most game, particularly when prepared with pungent sauces. If you are grilling red meat, however, select a red wine such as *Spätburgunder* or *Trollinger*.

For Desserts and Cheeses: *Auslese* and *BA* wines can often serve as desserts themselves. They also excel with desserts that are not overpoweringly sweet, particularly desserts with some tartness made from apricots, oranges, peaches, pears, apples, plums, even exotic fruits like mango and passion fruit. Rare *TBAs* and *Eisweins* should be savored by themselves without competition from dessert.

German *QbA* and *Kabinett* wines with their low alcohol and pronounced fruit flavor are superb with most neutral and hard cheeses. Softer cheeses call for richer wines of *Spätlese* ripeness. Blue-veined cheeses are marvelous with *Auslese* and *BA* wines.

German Beer:
A Quick History of German Brewing

Beer is so closely associated with Germany it's natural to assume that it was invented there.

Actually, beer has a much longer history, going back more than five thousand years to the Fertile Crescent, the cradle of civilization, where the Sumerians discovered that their bread dough was fermenting. From this happy accident, they developed the brewer's art, which spread, in time, throughout the world. It reached Germany about 800 B.C., and nowhere did brewing make a greater impact. Some nine hundred years later, the Roman chronicler Tacitus refers with more than a little awe—to the German's love of fermented beverages.

In German cloisters, the bibulous brothers played a key role in refining the brewer's art. Hops, they discovered, added zest, spiciness, and longevity to the brew. Although monks are famous in history and legend for their love of beer, they did not brew merely for their own pleasure. Beer, like wine, contributed to a very lucrative cloister economy.

Secular entrepreneurs were quick to discover the commercial value of beer, and breweries sprang up in cities, towns, and hamlets throughout Germany. Over the years, scientific research introduced new processes, including select, pure yeast strains and temperature control, which help assure quality and consistency keg after keg and year after year.

German beers today are so superior they're the standard by which all others are judged. One of the milestones in their journey toward perfection is the famous *Reinheitsgebot* (purity law), proclaimed in 1516 by Duke Wilhelm IV of Bavaria. It prescribed that beer could be brewed only from barley malt, hops, and water. (The essential role of yeasts was, as yet, undiscovered, and therefore unmentioned in the law.) This is recognized as the world's first consumer protection law for foodstuffs and it still applies to beers made in Germany.

Germany has more than 1,250 breweries—about 40 percent of the world total—whose combined production amounts to 100 million barrels each year. In general, beers from the north of Germany are slightly bitter and somewhat higher in alcohol than the softer beers of the south. The average German drinks 147 liters of beer each year—the highest per capita consumption in the world. By contrast, American beer lovers manage to down only 91 liters per person per year.

The Brewer's Art

To make good beer requires expert knowledge, skill, and technology. The process is as follows. First, under the watchful eye of a skilled mallster, barley is converted into sugar-rich brewing malts. Next, the malts are dried or kilned. Hops are mixed in (to give the beer a bit of bitterness), then the mixture is boiled with minimal exposure to oxygen so the flavor is preserved. The mixture is clarified and then chilled quickly before a pure strain of yeast (always a carefully guarded company secret) is added to jump-start the fermentation.

There are two basic types of fermentation, each requiring different kinds of yeast and producing a different style of beverage. *Top fermentation* takes place at higher temperatures (15 to 19 degrees Celsius) and requires less time. *Bottom fermentation,* responsible for 83 percent of German beers, occurs at cool temperatures (between 4 and 10 degrees Celsius) and lasts about ten days. In both cases, the end products are alcohol and carbon dioxide.

All German lagers are bottom fermented, a more expensive process. After fermentation, the "young" beer is transferred into tanks where it is *lagered* (or stored) for several weeks of further development. This development takes place under pressure so that the carbon dioxide is evenly dispersed and becomes an integral part of the beer, giving it its bubbles. Before bottling, the finished beer is filtered for absolute clarity. A typical premium beer averages between 4 and 5 percent alcohol by volume.

Stronger beers are made by using more malt per liter of water, and dark beers by drying the barley at higher temperatures.

Some Helpful Beer Terminology

Bock: Strong beer, usually having more than 6 percent alcohol by volume. It may be light gold or dark brown. These beers are popular in the autumn, winter, and spring.

Doppelbock: Even stronger, at least 7.5 percent alcohol by volume.

Dunkel: The German word for *dark*, hence a dark beer is called *"ein Dunkles."*

Export: A term used to describe a pale, bottom-fermented beer that is higher in alcohol and body than the average pilsner.

Hell: The German word for *light*, hence a pale, golden beer is often referred to as *"ein Helles."*

Kölsch: A top-fermented beer with relatively low level of alcohol (4.3 to 5 percent by volume) made in the region around Cologne.

Lager: *Lagern* means *to store*, hence beer that has been *gelagert* or stored for development. It is a generic term today for bottom-fermented beer. Alcohol levels range from 4 to 5 percent for most premium lagers.

Maibock: A high-quality bock beer, usually pale, available in late April and early May, and popular at spring festivals.

Märzen: From the German word for the month of March, when the beer is produced. It is a medium-strong beer.

Pilsner/Pils: The generic term for bottom-fermented, pale golden lager beer. The term comes from the Czech town of Pilsen, where this style of beer was developed.

Rauchbier: German for *smoked beer*. This is a dark, bottom-fermented beer made from smoked malts that is particularly popular around Bamberg. As its name implies, it tastes of smoke.

Weissbier/Weizenbier: From the German *Weizen,* meaning *wheat*, hence beer made from the addition of wheat to the mash. Particularly popular in summer (with a slice of lemon), this is a tart and spicy, top-fermented beer with normal to relatively low alcohol.

German Beer and Food

Because they are so thirst-quenching, German beers go with a wide variety of foods. The popular golden lagers and pilsners are the most versatile, pairing superbly with everything from cold cuts to salads to stews. Unlike wine, they can also hold their own with the sweet-and-sour dishes adored by Germans.

The rich dark beers are best with smoked foods, sausages, and strong cheeses. The delicate wheat beer, or Weissbier, is a standard, between-meals, hot-weather refresher. And in Berlin, a favorite way to serve it is with a dash of raspberry syrup.

PART 2

APPETIZERS AND SNACKS
Vorspeisen und Snacks

SMOKED SALMON TARTARE WITH BLACK CAVIAR
Lachs-Tartar mit schwarzem Kaviar

Salmon swim German rivers and the smoking of them has long been a German tradition. Usually the smoked salmon is sliced tissue thin and served on dark bread spread with sweet butter. In the hands of a gifted chef, however, salmon becomes something special. This recipe was inspired by the salmon tartare Chef Heinz Winkler once served as an appetizer at Tantris in Munich (he now presides over the stylish new Residenz Heinz Winkler in Aschau, southeast of Munich). For all its showiness, this tartare couldn't be easier to prepare. If you don't want to arrange individual appetizer plates, mound the tartare in a bowl, put out a plate of thinly sliced black bread, and let guests help themselves. No watercress, caviar, or lemon slices needed.

1 pound lightly smoked salmon, finely chopped

2 extra-large hard-cooked eggs, peeled and finely chopped

2 tablespoons finely minced shallots

¼ teaspoon freshly ground black pepper

56 watercress leaves of uniform size, wilted in hot water

4 teaspoons black caviar, preferably beluga

8 thin lemon slices

Makes 8 servings

Beat the salmon, eggs, shallots, and pepper in an electric mixer at high speed until flecks of egg are no longer visible. Cover and chill until ready to use.

Meanwhile, wreathe 7 watercress leaves around the rim of each of 8 salad plates, pressing them to flatten. Pack a scoop of the salmon mixture into a ¼ cup measure and invert in the center of the plate. Repeat until there is a mound on each plate. Make a small depression in the center of each mound and spoon in ½ teaspoon caviar. Garnish each portion with a lemon slice and serve with thinly sliced black bread.

TINY POTATO PANCAKES WITH SMOKED SALMON

Kleine Kartoffelpuffer mit geräuchertem Lachs

You can make the pancakes about an hour before assembling the canapés and keep them crisp and hot in a very slow oven. You can also cut the rounds of salmon well ahead, cover them, and refrigerate until serving time. With these two jobs done in advance, these fancy little German appetizers go together zip-quick.

1 pound baking potatoes, peeled and coarsely shredded

2 tablespoons finely minced shallots

3 tablespoons all-purpose flour

⅛ teaspoon salt

Pinch of freshly ground black pepper

Pinch of freshly grated nutmeg

¼ cup clarified butter

6 ounces thinly sliced smoked salmon, cut into 2-inch rounds with a cookie cutter

½ cup (approximately) sour cream

½ pint (approximately) watercress or peppergrass sprouts

Makes about 20 bite-size canapés

83

Preheat the oven to 150° to 200° F.

Place the potatoes, shallots, flour, salt, pepper, and nutmeg in a large mixing bowl. Using your hands, mix well until the ingredients hold together nicely.

Heat the clarified butter in a heavy 12-inch skillet over moderate heat for 1½ to 2 minutes, just until a shred of potato will sputter vigorously when dropped into the skillet. Scoop up the potato mixture by level tablespoonfuls and drop into the skillet. With an oiled pancake turner, flatten into cakes about 2 inches in diameter and ¼ inch thick. Don't try to cook more than half the pancakes at a time. Brown them for 2½ to 3 minutes on each side, until crisp and brown. Lift the browned pancakes to a baking sheet lined with several thicknesses of paper toweling and set, uncovered, in the warm oven.

When ready to serve, center a round of smoked salmon on each potato pancake, top with a scant teaspoon of sour cream and a few watercress sprouts. Serve at once.

PARFAIT OF SMOKED SALMON AND TROUT

Parfait aus geräuchertem Lachs und Forelle

If you use a food processor to grind the fish and mix the parfaits, you'll find this gossamer spread a breeze to prepare. It's one of the signature dishes of Harald Schmitt, chef at the Orangerie in Wiesbaden's Hotel Nassauer Hof. Accompany with thin slices of homemade melba toast.

Smoked Trout Parfait:

½ cup fish stock or bottled clam juice

½ cup Riesling or other dry white wine

1 tablespoon dry vermouth blended with 1 teaspoon cornstarch

1 envelope plain gelatin softened in ¼ cup cold water

½ pound skinned, smoked trout fillets, cut into 1-inch chunks

1 tablespoon freshly squeezed lemon juice

½ teaspoon salt

¼ teaspoon ground hot red pepper

¾ cup heavy cream, stiffly whipped

Smoked Salmon Parfait:

½ cup rich fish stock or bottled clam juice

½ cup Riesling or other dry white wine

1 tablespoon dry vermouth blended with 1 teaspoon cornstarch

1 envelope plain gelatin softened in ¼ cup cold water

½ pound boned and skinned smoked salmon, cut into 1-inch chunks

¾ cup heavy cream, stiffly whipped

Garnish:

6 small watercress sprigs

Makes 12 servings

For the smoked trout parfait: Bring the stock and Riesling to a boil in a small heavy saucepan over high heat. Blend

**PARFAIT OF SMOKED
SALMON AND TROUT**

a little of the hot liquid into the cornstarch mixture, stir back into the pan, and cook, stirring constantly, until the liquid thickens, bubbles up, and clears – 2 to 3 minutes. Remove from the heat, add the softened gelatin, and stir until dissolved; set aside. Place the trout, lemon juice, salt, and pepper in a food processor fitted with the metal chopping blade and process 10 to 15 seconds, until fine and feathery. Add the gelatin mixture and process 10 to 15 seconds longer, until smooth. Transfer to a large mixing bowl and, by hand, fold in the whipped cream; set aside.

For the smoked salmon parfait: Bring the stock and Riesling to a boil in a small heavy saucepan over high heat. Blend a little of the hot liquid into the cornstarch mixture, stir back into the pan, and cook, stirring constantly, until the liquid thickens, bubbles up, and clears – 2 to 3 minutes. Remove from the heat, add the softened gelatin, and stir until dissolved; set aside. Place the salmon in the food processor, still fitted with the metal chopping blade, and process 10 to 15 seconds, until fine and feathery. Add the gelatin mixture and process 10 to 15 seconds longer, until smooth. Transfer to a large mixing bowl and, by hand, fold in the whipped cream; set aside.

To assemble the parfait: Rinse a 6½-cup ring mold with cold water and fill it by spooning in the two fish mixtures alternately. Then marbelize by drawing the tines of a kitchen fork through the mixture in two concentric rings. Cover with plastic wrap and chill overnight. To unmold, dip the mold briefly in hot water, then turn out on a round platter. Sprig with watercress and serve.

85

SMOKED MACKEREL PÂTÉ

Geräuchertes Makrelen Pâté

Judith Schäfer of Weingut Michael Schäfer, in Burg Layen in the Nahe Valley of the Rhineland-Palatinate, recommends serving this prize family recipe with Weisser Burgunder Spätlese trocken, Riesling Qualitätswein, or Spätlese trocken. If none of these fine German wines is available to you, you might substitute a full-bodied Sauterne, even a gingery Gewürztraminer. Like most pâtés, this one should be made one day and served the next. Accompany with crisp melba toast, preferably homemade.

¾ pound skinned smoked mackerel fillets, cut into 1-inch chunks

½ cup sour cream

5 tablespoons unsalted butter

2 tablespoons freshly squeezed lemon juice

1 tablespoon Cognac

2 tablespoons minced flat-leaf parsley

½ teaspoon salt

½ teaspoon freshly ground black pepper

½ cup heavy cream, whipped to stiff peaks

Optional Garnishes:

1 medium-size lemon, cut into slim wedges

1 parsley sprig

Makes about 3 ½ cups

Place the mackerel in a food processor fitted with the metal chopping blade. Add the sour cream, butter, lemon juice, Cognac, parsley, salt, and pepper and process 1 minute. Scrape down the sides of the workbowl and process 1 minute longer, until smooth and fluffy. Add the whipped cream and pulse lightly to incorporate.

Scoop the pâté into a medium-size serving bowl, cover with plastic wrap, and refrigerate overnight. Next day, garnish, if you like, with lemon wedges and sprig with parsley, then serve as a cocktail spread.

GREEN POT FROM MAINAU

Mainauer Grüner Topf

Mainau, an island in Bodensee *(Lake Constance), is known as "the flower paradise of Germany." The lake region, which sits astride the German-Swiss border, is a popular summer resort and its hotels and restaurants serve fish so fresh it practically swims into the dining room. This unusual island appetizer is a kind of escabeche, that is, raw fish "cooked" in a vinegar marinade. There all similarity to the classic escabeche ends, however, because this fish marinates twice, the second time in a creamy sauce greened with fresh dill, chives, and parsley. Serve as an appetizer with crisp rounds of freshly made melba toast.*

Marinated Fish:

1¼ pounds skinned fillets of ocean perch or red snapper

2 teaspoons salt

1⅔ cups water

⅓ cup white vinegar

⅓ cup sugar

Green Sauce:

1 cup mayonnaise (preferably homemade)

1 cup sour cream

2 tablespoons moderately finely chopped flat-leaf parsley

2 tablespoons moderately finely snipped fresh dill

2 tablespoons moderately finely snipped fresh chives

3 tablespoons finely chopped shallots

2 large garlic cloves, peeled and finely chopped

1 teaspoon sugar

¼ teaspoon salt

¼ teaspoon freshly ground black pepper

Makes 8 to 10 servings

For the marinated fish: Sprinkle both sides of each perch fillet with salt, using 1 teaspoon in all. Arrange the fish in a 13 x 9 x 2-inch glass or ceramic baking dish. Combine the water, vinegar, sugar, and remaining salt and pour evenly over the perch fillets. Cover with plastic wrap and refrigerate 24 hours, turning the perch in the marinade several times. Drain off all marinade and cut the perch into bite-size pieces.

For the green sauce: Place all ingredients in a small bowl

continued on next page

87

GREEN POT FROM
MAINAU (cont.)

and whisk until creamy and well blended. Or, if you prefer, pulse all ingredients 8 to 10 times in a food processor fitted with the metal chopping blade.

To assemble the green pot: Spread ⅓ cup of the sauce evenly over the bottom of a 1-quart casserole. Top with a layer of perch, using one third of the total amount, then spread with another ⅓ cup sauce. Add two more layers of perch, topping the first with ⅓ cup sauce and the final layer with all remaining sauce. Cover with plastic wrap and marinate in the refrigerator for 6 to 8 hours before serving.

HERRING SALAD WITH APPLES, DILL PICKLES, AND HORSERADISH
Heringssalat

The best herring to use for this recipe is the red-fleshed young matjes, which can be bought in most good delicatessens and specialty food shops. This salad is a popular first course throughout much of northern Germany. Unlike the herring salad that follows, this one contains no mayonnaise, meat, potatoes, or hard-cooked eggs, thus it's considerably lighter. And its flavor is heightened with horseradish and lemon.
The herring must marinate overnight in the buttermilk, so plan accordingly.

8 large matjes herring fillets (about 1 pound)

1 cup buttermilk

1 cup sour cream (use "light" sour cream, if you like)

⅓ cup plain yogurt (use low-fat or nonfat yogurt, if you like)

1 medium-size yellow onion, peeled and finely chopped

2 medium-size tart apples, peeled, cored, and coarsely chopped

2 medium-size dill pickles, minced

1 tablespoon prepared horseradish

1 tablespoon (approximately) freshly squeezed lemon juice

1 tablespoon (approximately) sugar

Salt and freshly ground black pepper to taste

Makes 4 to 6 servings

Lay the herring fillets in a shallow baking dish. Add the buttermilk, cover, and marinate in the refrigerator overnight. Next day, drain and rinse the herring fillets well, then cut into bite-size pieces. Place the herring in a shallow glass or porcelain baking dish.

88

HERRING SALAD WITH
APPLES, DILL PICKLES,
AND HORSERADISH

Combine the sour cream, yogurt, onion, apples, pickles, horseradish, lemon juice, and sugar. Taste for lemon juice and sugar and add a bit more of each, if needed – there should be a light lemon flavor and just enough sugar to mellow the tartness. Season the sauce to taste with salt and pepper. Spoon over the herring, cover, and marinate several hours in the refrigerator before serving.

ROSA'S HERRING SALAD
Rosas Heringssalat

Like her mother, whose recipe this is, Hedy serves herring salad as either an appetizer or main-dish buffet salad. "In our house it's traditional for Christmas Eve," she says. "We eat it when we come home from midnight Mass." Now that she's living in New York, Hedy finds her mother's herring salad perfect for a post-theater meal and accompanies it with French bread or hard rolls. It's heartier than the previous herring salad, which contains no meat or potatoes.

3 large baking potatoes, boiled or steamed in their skins until tender, then peeled and cut into ¼-inch cubes

2 medium-size Golden Delicious apples, peeled, cored, and cut into ¼-inch cubes

5 extra-large hard-cooked eggs, shelled and cut into ¼-inch cubes

3 medium-size dill pickles (not too tart), cut into ¼-inch cubes

1 large yellow onion, peeled and coarsely chopped

¾ pound boiled ham or leftover roast beef, cut into ¼-inch cubes

4 large matjes herring fillets (about ½ pound), cut into ¼-inch cubes

1 cup mayonnaise (preferably homemade)

1 cup plain low-fat yogurt

1 teaspoon salt

½ teaspoon freshly ground black pepper

Makes 10 to 12 servings

Mix all ingredients together in a large glass or ceramic bowl, cover with plastic wrap, and refrigerate 24 hours. Let stand at room temperature ½ hour before serving as an appetizer or main-dish salad.

89

ROLLMOPS

Rollmöpse

A classic German snack that remains as popular as ever. In northern Germany, rollmops are also a popular hang-over remedy. "They really work," Hedy says, "because they're so sour." Rollmops make an excellent appetizer, too.

8 herring in brine (about 1¾ pounds)

4 small dill pickles, quartered lengthwise

4 small yellow onions, peeled, thinly sliced, and separated into rings

1⅓ cups cider vinegar

1⅓ cups cold water

10 peppercorns

2 medium-size whole bay leaves

2 medium-size garlic cloves, peeled and halved lengthwise

5 whole cloves

¼ teaspoon red pepper flakes

Makes 6 to 8 servings

Soak the herring in several changes of cold water in the refrigerator for 24 hours. Remove and discard the herring heads, then fillet each herring. Lay the herring fillets skin side down on the counter, place a piece of pickle crosswise on top of each, then add several onion rings. Roll up and anchor with toothpicks. Arrange the rollmops seam side down in a large heatproof glass bowl and set aside.

Bring the vinegar, water, peppercorns, bay leaves, garlic, cloves, and red pepper flakes to a boil in an uncovered, large heavy saucepan over moderate heat. Cool 10 minutes and pour evenly over the herring. Scatter any remaining onion rings evenly on top, cover with plastic wrap, and marinate 3 to 4 days in the refrigerator before serving.

PICKLED HERRING

Marinierter Hering

Particularly popular in northern Germany, where herring is king. Serve as an appetizer or snack.

8 herring in brine (about 1¾ pounds)

4 small yellow onions, peeled, thinly sliced, and separated into rings

1½ large lemons, thinly sliced and seeded

2 cups cider vinegar

1 medium-size bay leaf, finely crumbled

1 medium-size garlic clove, peeled and quartered lengthwise

1½ teaspoons mustard seeds

1½ teaspoons mixed pickling spices

2 teaspoons sugar

Makes 6 to 8 servings

Soak the herring in several changes of cold water in the refrigerator for 24 hours. Remove and discard the herring heads, then fillet each herring, and, if you like, skin the fillets. Cut the herring into 1-inch squares and place half in a large heatproof glass bowl, top with half the onion rings and lemon slices. Add the remaining herring, onion rings, and lemon slices and set aside.

Bring the vinegar, bay leaf, garlic, mustard seeds, pickling spices, and sugar to a boil in an uncovered, large heavy saucepan over moderate heat. Cool 10 minutes and pour evenly over the herring. Cover with plastic wrap and marinate 3 to 4 days in the refrigerator before serving.

91

HERRING IN SOUR CREAM
Hering in Sahnesauce

Here's a third herring appetizer that's served in homes and restaurants throughout Germany.

6 herring in brine (about 1¼ pounds)

2 small Italian (red) onions, peeled, thinly sliced, and separated into rings

2 medium-size Golden Delicious apples, peeled, cored, cut into eighths, then each eighth thinly sliced

1 cup sour cream

2 tablespoons dry white wine (preferably German)

1 tablespoon cider vinegar

1 teaspoon Dijon mustard, or ¼ teaspoon dry mustard

½ teaspoon sugar

¼ teaspoon ground hot red pepper

Makes 8 to 10 servings

Soak the herring in several changes of cold water in the refrigerator for 24 hours. Remove and discard the herring heads, then fillet and skin each herring. Cut the herring into 1-inch squares, place in a large mixing bowl, and top with the onions and apples. In a small bowl, combine all remaining ingredients, pour over the herring, and toss lightly to mix. Transfer to a 1-quart jar or glass bowl, cover with plastic wrap, and chill 24 hours or, better yet, 48 hours before serving.

HUSUM SHRIMP SALAD

Husumer Krabbensalat

In the North Sea town of Husum (and indeed throughout Germany), shrimp salad is served as an appetizer, not as a salad or main course. If the salad is to be properly flavorful, you must use fresh herbs. The dressing is equally delicious ladled over cold cooked salmon, lobster, or crab.

Salad:

½ pound shelled and deveined cooked small shrimp

2 extra-large hard-cooked eggs, peeled and coarsely chopped

1 cup drained, cooked green peas

1 tablespoon finely snipped fresh chives

2 tablespoons finely snipped fresh dill

2 tablespoons minced parsley

Dressing:

½ cup mayonnaise (preferably homemade)

1 tablespoon Dijon mustard

¼ cup heavy cream, whipped to stiff peaks

1 tablespoon freshly squeezed lemon juice

⅛ teaspoon salt

⅛ teaspoon freshly ground black pepper

Makes 6 servings

Lightly toss all salad ingredients together in a medium-size bowl.

Combine all dressing ingredients in a 2-cup measure, pour half over the salad, cover, and refrigerate for at least 1 hour. Cover and refrigerate the remaining dressing.

Just before serving, toss the salad well, adding a little more dressing, if necessary. Also taste for salt and pepper and adjust as needed. Pass the extra dressing separately.

93

LIVER-ALMOND PÂTÉ

Leber-Mandel-Pastete

Erika Wedell of Frank-furt often serves this pâté of hers with a classic Cumberland sauce, but we think it's marvelous as is with nothing more to accompany than thin slices of melba toast or Wheat (White) Bread (page 295). Although Erika has lived and worked in Frankfurt for years, she was born in eastern Germany. If you have a food processor, you'll find this pâté a snap to make. If not, you'll have to put the meats through a meat grinder. Messy work!

10 slices double-smoked bacon

⅔ cup cold water

1 kaiser roll (2 ounces)

3 tablespoons unsalted butter or margarine

1 medium-size yellow onion, peeled and moderately finely chopped

1 teaspoon dried leaf marjoram, crumbled

½ teaspoon dried leaf thyme, crumbled

¼ teaspoon freshly grated nutmeg

½ pound calf's liver, cut into 1-inch cubes

6 ounces sweet Italian sausages, removed from their casings and cut into 1-inch chunks

6 ounces lean ground round

1 tablespoon sweet paprika

1 tablespoon minced flat-leaf parsley

¼ cup Malmsey or Bual (sweet Madeira wine)

1 extra-large egg

¾ teaspoon salt

¼ teaspoon freshly ground black pepper

¼ pound blanched almonds, moderately finely ground

Makes 10 to 12 servings

Preheat the oven to 350°F.

Lightly butter an 8½ x 4¼ x 3-inch loaf pan, then line the sides and bottom with 7 slices of the bacon. The easiest way is to lay a strip in the bottom of the pan, crosswise and centered, so it can be smoothed up the sides of the pan.

LIVER-ALMOND PÂTÉ

Keep adding strips the same way, each overlapping the previous one slightly until both the pan bottom and sides are lined. Set the pan aside; reserve the remaining 3 bacon strips – they'll be laid on top of the pâté.

Pour the water into a small bowl, crumble in the kaiser roll, cover, and let stand at room temperature while you proceed with the recipe.

Melt the butter in a heavy 8-inch skillet over moderate heat. Add the onion, reduce the heat to moderately low, and sauté 8 to 10 minutes, stirring often, until limp and touched with brown. Blend in the marjoram, thyme, and nutmeg and mellow over moderately low heat for 1 minute. Remove from the heat and set aside to cool.

Meanwhile, place the liver in a food processor fitted with the metal chopping blade and pulse 10 to 12 times, until moderately coarsely chopped; transfer to a large bowl. Pulse the sausages 10 to 12 times, until moderately coarsely chopped, and add to the liver. (If you have no food processor, first put the liver, then the sausage, through the coarse blade of a meat grinder. Add the ground round to the processor workbowl, along with the paprika, parsley, wine, egg, salt, pepper, water-soaked roll, and onion mixture and pulse about 15 minutes to combine. Return the liver and sausages to the workbowl, add the almonds, and pulse 8 to 10 times more. (If you are not using a food processor, simply mix all ingredients together with your hands.)

Pack the mixture into the bacon-lined pan, smooth the surface, then lay the 3 remaining bacon strips on top, lengthwise and not overlapping. Bake the pâté, uncovered, 1 hour. Remove from the oven, set upright on a wire rack, and cool for 1 hour. Wrap the pan of pâté snugly in foil and refrigerate 12 hours, or overnight.

Carefully loosen the pâté around the edge with a small spatula, then set the pan upright in a sink containing about 2 inches of hot water and let stand 2 to 3 minutes. To unmold, rap the sides of the pan sharply once or twice

95

continued on next page

LIVER-ALMOND PÂTÉ
(cont.)

against the edge of the counter, then invert on a small rectangular platter and turn the pâté out. To serve, slice the pâté about ¼ inch thick using a very sharp knife. Serve as is or accompany with thin slices of firm-textured white bread or crisp slices of melba toast.

HEDY'S LIPTAUER
Hedys Liptauer

This biting cheese spread originated in Lipto, at the time a Hungarian county but now a part of Slovakia. In the beginning Liptoi, as it is still known in Hungary, was made with a soft, sour goat's cheese, flavored with paprika, caraway, mustard, capers, chives, and beer, then packed into goats' bladders. The German Liptauer, a somewhat more robust version, is made with approximately equal parts cream cheese and runny-ripe Camembert. Germans would use the Camembert made in their own country, but the French original is superb, too.

1 medium-size yellow onion, peeled and cubed

3 tablespoons unsalted butter

2 (3-ounce) packages cream cheese, at room temperature, cubed

8½ ounces very ripe Camembert, at room temperature, cubed (do not remove white rind)

1 tablespoon sour cream

1 tablespoon plain yogurt

1½ teaspoons Hungarian sweet rose paprika

½ teaspoon salt

½ teaspoon white pepper

Makes about 2 ½ cups

Process all ingredients for 1 minute in a food processor fitted with the metal chopping blade. Scrape down the sides of the workbowl and process 1 minute more.

Pack the Liptauer in a 1-quart plastic container, snap on the lid, and refrigerate at least 24 hours. Serve as a cocktail spread with crisp melba toast.

MÜNSTER CHEESE SPREAD WITH FRESH CHIVES

Angemachter Münsterkäse mit schnittlauch

Originally German – and still beloved by Germans living along the Rhine – Münster is now categorized as a French cheese. Most of it comes from Alsace, a fertile stretch of Rhine bottomland over which the French and Germans have squabbled for centuries. If this cheese spread is to be properly biting, you must use a nicely ripened imported Münster. The bland domestic varieties just won't do. If you can't find imported Münster, substitute a runny-ripe Pont l'Evêque, Camembert, or Brie. You must also use freshly snipped chives, not frozen or freeze-dried, which taste more like grass than a fragrant member of the onion family. In the old days, German cooks would sieve the Münster to make a smooth spread. A tedious job. The food processor is faster and more effective.

10 ounces ripe imported Münster cheese, trimmed of rind and cubed

8 tablespoons (1 stick) unsalted butter or margarine

¼ pound cream cheese, at room temperature

½ teaspoon freshly ground black pepper

⅓ cup freshly snipped chives

Makes about 2 ½ cups

Place all ingredients in a food processor fitted with the metal chopping blade and process 15 seconds. Scrape down the sides of the workbowl and process 10 seconds longer. Scoop the cheese mixture into a small pretty bowl and serve as a spread for Black Bread (page 300), melba toast, or crackers.

97

SOUPS
Suppen

BEEF BROTH WITH SEMOLINA DUMPLINGS
Hausgemachte Fleischbrühe mit Griessnockerl

98

Dumplings are known by different names in different parts of Germany. In the north, for example, semolina dumplings are Griessklösschen, *but in Bavaria, Swabia, and other regions south of Frankfurt, they're* Griessnockerl, *and that's where this soup is particularly popular. Most semolina sold in American supermarkets is a flavored couscous mix – not appropriate for this recipe. For the real thing, go to a specialty grocery or market specializing in Middle Eastern foods. The dumpling dough must chill for at least two hours before it's shaped. You can even make it a day ahead. The most effective way to mix the dough is in a food processor because you can knead it zip-quick to the proper stiffness and resilience. You can also use an electric mixer, but you'll have to double the mixing time.*

5 tablespoons unsalted butter or margarine

1 extra-large egg

¾ cup unsifted semolina flour or couscous (not a mix)

1 tablespoon all-purpose flour

½ teaspoon salt

¼ teaspoon freshly grated nutmeg

3½ quarts rich beef broth (preferably homemade)

½ cup freshly snipped chives

Makes 8 servings

Cream the butter and egg in a food processor until light by processing about 30 seconds. Add the semolina and all-purpose flours, the salt, and nutmeg and process about 2 minutes, stopping midway to scrape down the sides of the workbowl. The dough should form a ball that rides up on the central spindle. Transfer the dough to a small bowl, cover snugly with plastic wrap, and refrigerate for at least 2 hours, or until stiff enough to shape.

When ready to proceed, bring the broth to a simmer over high heat in an uncovered large heavy kettle. Adjust the heat so the broth bubbles gently. Take up the semolina dough by rounded tablespoons, roll into ovals, and drop into the broth. When all the dumplings are in the broth, cover and simmer 18 to 20 minutes – without peeking – until the dumplings are puffed and light. Ladle the broth and dumplings into large soup bowls, sprinkle liberally with the chives, and serve.

PANCAKE SOUP
Pfannkuchensuppe

A recipe clearly invented to accommodate leftovers. All you need are a couple of leftover German pancakes, 5 cups of rich beef broth, and a handful of fresh chives to snip into the broth at the last minute.

⅓ recipe Basic German Pancakes (page 325), or
   2 leftover pancakes

5 cups rich beef broth (preferably homemade)

1 teaspoon freshly squeezed lemon juice

1 teaspoon sugar

⅛ teaspoon freshly grated nutmeg

⅛ teaspoon salt

⅛ teaspoon freshly ground black pepper

¼ cup moderately finely snipped fresh chives

Makes 4 servings

Prepare the pancakes, then stack between sheets of wax paper on a large plate; cool to room temperature.

Heat the broth, lemon juice, sugar, nutmeg, salt, and pepper in an uncovered medium-size heavy saucepan over moderate heat for 4 to 5 minutes, just until the mixture begins to boil. Taste for nutmeg, salt, and pepper and adjust as needed.

Quickly roll each pancake into a cigar shape and, with a sharp knife, slice ¼ inch thick. Unroll the strips of pancake and drop into the broth. Stir in the chives, ladle into shallow soup plates, and serve.

Note: If the pancakes are to slice cleanly, you should spray the knife with nonstick vegetable cooking spray.

SWABIAN BROTH WITH SPINACH-AND-MEAT-STUFFED "RAVIOLI"

Maultaschen

Originally a Lenten specialty in the Baden-Württemberg area of Germany, these spinach-filled pasta pillows are now often fortified with ground veal, pork, bacon, and salami. The trick is to roll the pasta dough as thin as possible, incorporating minimal flour. (Too much flour will toughen the dough, as will over-working it.) The food processor makes short work of both the dough and filling.

Pasta Dough:

1 extra-large egg

2 tablespoons vegetable oil

2 tablespoons cold water

2 cups minus 2 tablespoons sifted all-purpose flour

¼ teaspoon salt

Filling:

2 ounces slab bacon, cut into ½-inch cubes (about ½ cup bacon cubes)

1 tablespoon unsalted butter or margarine

1 medium-size yellow onion, peeled and finely chopped

¼ pound finely ground veal shoulder

¼ pound finely ground lean pork shoulder

2 ounces salami, finely ground

1 (10-ounce) package frozen chopped spinach, thawed, drained, and squeezed as dry as possible

2 tablespoons fine soft white bread crumbs

5 tablespoons heavy cream

1 extra-large egg yolk

¾ teaspoon dried leaf thyme, crumbled

½ teaspoon salt

¼ teaspoon ground allspice

¼ teaspoon freshly ground black pepper

⅛ teaspoon freshly grated nutmeg

Broth:

2 quarts rich beef broth (preferably homemade)

SWABIAN BROTH
WITH SPINACH-AND-
MEAT-STUFFED
"RAVIOLI"

Makes 6 to 8 servings

For the dough: Whirl the egg, oil, and water for 2 to 3 seconds in a food processor to combine. Add half the flour and pulse 3 to 4 times to mix. Add the remaining flour and the salt, and again pulse 3 to 4 times to combine. Don't overmix or the dough will be rubbery. Divide the dough in half, wrap each half snugly in plastic wrap, and let stand at room temperature for 1 hour.

For the filling: Sauté the bacon in a small skillet over low heat for 4 to 5 minutes; drain on paper toweling. Pour off the drippings in the skillet, add the butter and, when it melts, the onion. Stir-fry over low heat for 3 to 4 minutes, until translucent; remove from the heat and cool 5 minutes.

Pulse the onion in the food processor with the bacon and all remaining filling ingredients until uniformly fine, scraping down the workbowl as needed. The mixture will be quite thick and pastelike.

To shape the Maultaschen: The easiest way is to use a ravioli maker (available at specialty kitchen shops and not at all expensive). Divide each dough half in half again; roll one portion at a time on a lightly floured pastry cloth with a lightly floured stockinette-covered rolling pin until as thin as tissue paper and slightly larger than the dimensions of the ravioli maker. Fold the dough over the rolling pin and ease on top of the ravioli maker; unfold the dough and fit it into the depressions. Spoon 1 teaspoon of the filling into each depression. Roll a second piece of dough as before and ease on top of the ravioli maker; unfold. Remove the stockinette from the rolling pin and roll hard over the ravioli maker so that you cut and seal the Maultaschen in one operation. Flip the ravioli maker upside down to remove them and arrange in one layer on a large tray; cover snugly with plastic wrap to prevent drying. Roll, fill, and cut the remaining Maultaschen the same way. Add to the tray and re-cover. (These may be made as much as a day ahead and kept refrigerated until

101

continued on next page

about 1 hour before serving. Just make certain that the Maultaschen are tightly sealed with plastic wrap so they don't dry out or absorb refrigerator odors.)

To cook the Maultaschen: Let the tightly covered Maultaschen stand at room temperature for 45 minutes. Pour the broth into a large shallow kettle, set over moderate heat, and bring to a simmer, uncovered. Adjust the heat so the surface of the broth just trembles, add 6 to 8 Maultaschen (or as many as possible without crowding), and cook, uncovered, 8 minutes; turn them all over, cover, and cook 8 minutes longer. With a slotted spoon, remove to a heated platter, cover with a bowl turned upside down, and keep warm. Cook the remaining Maultaschen the same way.

To serve the Maultaschen: Place 4 to 5 Maultaschen in each of 6 to 8 large soup plates, ladle in enough broth to cover, and serve as a main course. The perfect accompaniment: green beans or asparagus vinaigrette.

Note: The Maultaschen can also be served without the broth. A favorite way is to toss them with melted butter or margarine (preferably in which a tablespoon or two of minced onion or shallots have been sautéed).

GOULASH SOUP
Gulaschsuppe

This simple but hearty soup – a thin stew, really – is a cold-weather favorite throughout Germany. Home cooks make it often and chefs at nearly every Ratskeller *and village* Gasthof *keep a big pot of it bubbling on the back of the stove. Recipes vary, of course. But all contain boneless cubes of a richly flavored, muscular cut*

2 pounds boneless beef chuck, cut into ½-inch cubes

3 tablespoons unsalted butter, margarine, or bacon drippings

4 medium-size yellow onions, peeled and coarsely chopped

1 large garlic clove, peeled and minced

2 tablespoons Hungarian sweet rose paprika

1 teaspoon dried leaf thyme, crumbled

4 cups cold water

2 cups rich beef broth (preferably homemade)

GOULASH SOUP

of beef, potatoes, plenty of onions, and a blush of sweet paprika (a staple of the pre–World War I Austro-Hungarian Empire, which Bavaria once bordered).

4 medium-size Maine or Eastern potatoes, peeled and cut into ½-inch cubes

1 pound green beans, tipped and snapped into 1-inch lengths (optional)

3 tablespoons tomato paste

½ teaspoon salt

½ teaspoon freshly ground black pepper

Makes 6 to 8 servings

Brown the beef in two batches in 2 tablespoons of the butter in a large heavy kettle over high heat. As the beef browns, transfer with a slotted spoon to a large heatproof bowl.

Add the remaining tablespoon of butter to the kettle, then the onions and garlic, and stir-fry about 5 minutes, until translucent. Return the beef to the kettle, add the paprika and thyme, and mellow over moderate heat for 1 to 2 minutes, stirring often. Add the water and broth, bring to a boil, adjust the heat so the mixture simmers easily, cover, and cook 45 minutes.

Add the potatoes and optional beans. Re-cover and simmer slowly 45 minutes longer, or until the beef, potatoes, and beans are all tender. Smooth in the tomato paste, salt, and pepper. Taste and adjust the salt as needed. Ladle into heated soup plates and serve as the main course of a casual lunch or supper.

103

BAVARIAN SAUSAGE HOT POT

Bayerischer Würsteltopf

Germans like to layer meats and vegetables in a pot and leave them to cook. Not all their hot pots are all-day affairs, however. This one, a hearty main dish, is ready to serve in half an hour. Most of its liquid cooks away, so this is actually a mélange of broth-poached vegetables and sausage.

1 pound cabbage, cored and sliced ½ inch thick

2 medium-size carrots, peeled and sliced ¼ inch thick

6 ounces green beans, tipped and snapped into 1-inch lengths

1 pound Maine or Eastern potatoes, peeled and cut into ½-inch cubes

2 cups shelled fresh green peas or frozen green peas (do not thaw)

3 cups rich beef broth (preferably homemade)

½ teaspoon salt

⅛ teaspoon freshly ground black pepper

⅛ teaspoon freshly grated nutmeg

1 teaspoon caraway seeds

1 teaspoon dried leaf marjoram, crumbled

¾ pound knockwurst or kielbasa, sliced ¼ inch thick

2 tablespoons coarsely chopped flat-leaf parsley

Makes 6 Servings

Place the cabbage, carrots, beans, potatoes, the fresh peas, if using, the broth, salt, pepper, and nutmeg in a large heavy kettle. Set over moderate heat and bring to a boil. Adjust the heat so the broth bubbles gently, cover, and cook without stirring for 20 minutes. Add the caraway seeds, marjoram, knockwurst, and frozen peas, if using, and toss lightly to mix. Re-cover and simmer 10 minutes. Add the parsley, toss lightly, and serve in soup plates with crusty chunks of bread.

ROSA'S LIVER SPAETZLE SOUP
Rosas Leberspätzle-Suppe

Hedy's mother's delicate rendition of a hearty Bavarian soup.

10 ounces calf's liver, thinly sliced

1 medium-size yellow onion, peeled and cut into eighths

8 tablespoons (1 stick) unsalted butter or margarine, cut into tablespoons and softened to room temperature

2 tablespoons minced flat-leaf parsley

1 teaspoon finely grated lemon zest

½ teaspoon minced fresh marjoram, or ¼ teaspoon dried leaf marjoram, crumbled

½ teaspoon salt

¼ teaspoon freshly grated nutmeg

⅛ teaspoon freshly ground black pepper

5 (⅜-inch-thick) slices firm white bread, reduced to very fine crumbs

4 extra-large eggs

2 quarts rich beef broth (preferably homemade)

¼ cup finely snipped fresh chives

Makes 8 servings

Pulse the liver 8 to 10 times in a food processor until thick, smooth, and pastelike. Add the onion, butter, parsley, lemon zest, marjoram, salt, nutmeg, and pepper and process for about 40 seconds, until absolutely smooth, scraping down the workbowl as needed. Add the bread crumbs and eggs and pulse several times until smooth. Refrigerate the mixture (no need to remove it from the processor workbowl).

Heat the beef broth, uncovered, in a large heavy saucepan over moderate heat just until it simmers; do not boil. Spoon some of the liver mixture into a spaetzle maker (a gadget available in specialty kitchen shops that resembles a potato

105

continued on next page

ROSA'S LIVER
SPAETZLE SOUP (cont.)

ricer) or spoon into a colander. Gently press the liver mixture through the holes into the broth. Repeat with the
remaining mixture. Simmer, uncovered, just until all the
spaetzle rise to the surface – this will take about 5 minutes.
Don't boil the broth at any time or these delicate spaetzle
will disintegrate.

Ladle the soup into bowls, garnish each portion with a
sprinkling of chives, and serve.

TRIPE SOUP WITH MORELS
Kuttelsuppe mit Morcheln

*This surprisingly deli-
cate soup is the creation
of Peter Wehlauer,
formerly chef-owner of
Burg Windeck near
Baden-Baden, one of the
Black Forest's most
delightful inns. Located
in a small medieval
castle atop a high hill,
Burg Windeck overlooks
miles of vineyards that
twill the Rhine slopes
and plain.*

1 ounce dried morels (available in specialty food shops)

1 pound fresh honeycomb tripe (or frozen, thawed), washed
   well and cut into fine julienne

1 small yellow onion, peeled and stuck with 4 cloves

2 cups rich chicken broth (preferably homemade)

2 cups rich beef broth (preferably homemade)

2 tablespoons unsalted butter or margarine

¼ cup fine carrot julienne

¼ cup fine celery julienne

¼ cup fine leek julienne

¾ cup Riesling wine

½ cup half-and-half

½ cup heavy cream

Pinch of freshly grated nutmeg

½ teaspoon salt

⅛ teaspoon white pepper

Makes 8 servings

Soak the morels in 1½ cups cold water for 2 to 3 hours,
until soft; drain, reserving the liquid. Pour the soaking

TRIPE SOUP WITH MORELS

liquid through a cheesecloth-lined sieve (to remove the grit) and reserve. Cut the morels into fine julienne, then soak about 1 hour in enough cold water to cover, drain, discard this second soaking water, and rinse the morels well again. Set aside.

Blanch the tripe for 2 to 3 minutes in a large kettle of lightly salted boiling water, drain, and rinse well. Transfer the tripe to a large heavy saucepan and add the onion and chicken and beef broths. Cover and simmer for 3 hours, or until the tripe is tender. Drain the tripe and reserve; strain and reserve the cooking broth.

Melt the butter in a large sauté pan over moderate heat. Add the carrot and sauté 4 minutes; add the celery and sauté 3 minutes; then add the leek and sauté 1 minute. Add the tripe and toss lightly, then mix in the reserved broth, morel liquid and morels, the Riesling, half-and-half, and heavy cream. Simmer, uncovered – *do not boil* – for 10 minutes. Season to taste with nutmeg, salt, and white pepper and serve as a first course or as an entrée accompanied by a crisp green salad and crusty chunks of bread.

107

PHEASANT AND LENTIL SOUP

Fasanen-und Linsensuppe

Don't be put off by this soup's lengthy ingredients list or by the fact that it's the specialty of one of Germany's most gifted chefs, Claus Köchling of the Atlantic Hotel Kempinski in Hamburg. Though long-winded, the soup isn't difficult to prepare. Besides, it's hearty enough to serve as a main dish, the recipe makes gobs, and it freezes beautifully.

1 frozen pheasant (about 2¼ pounds), thawed

1 large whole bay leaf

2 medium-size yellow onions, peeled, 1 stuck with 2 whole cloves and the second coarsely chopped

2 medium-size carrots, peeled, 1 cut into 1-inch chunks and the second into ¼-inch dice

1 medium-size leek, trimmed, washed well, and cut into 1-inch chunks

1½ teaspoons salt

½ teaspoon freshly ground black pepper

continued on next page

PHEASANT AND
LENTIL SOUP (cont.)

3½ to 4 quarts cold water

1 tablespoon lard, unsalted butter, or margarine

¼ pound smoked slab bacon, cut into ¼-inch dice
(about 1 cup bacon cubes)

1 medium-size celery rib, cut into ¼-inch dice

2 tablespoons tomato paste

1 cup dry red wine (preferably German)

1½ cups lentils

½ cup medium-dry sherry

2 to 3 tablespoons balsamic vinegar

1 teaspoon Dijon mustard

¼ teaspoon freshly grated nutmeg

¼ cup moderately finely snipped fresh chives

Makes 8 servings

Place the pheasant in a large heavy kettle, add the bay leaf, clove-stuck onion, chunked carrot, leek, 1 teaspoon of the salt, ¼ teaspoon of the pepper, and enough water just to cover the pheasant. Set, uncovered, over moderate heat and bring to a boil. Adjust the heat so the water bubbles gently, then simmer, uncovered, about 1½ hours, until the pheasant is very tender. Lift the pheasant from the cooking liquid and cool until easy to handle. Meanwhile, continue simmering the pheasant stock, uncovered, until reduced to 2 ½ quarts. Strain the stock, discarding the solids, and reserve.

Wipe the kettle dry, add the lard and bacon, and sauté over moderate heat, stirring often, until all drippings cook out of the bacon and only crisp brown bits remain – about 5 minutes. With a slotted spoon, lift the bacon bits to paper toweling and reserve. Add the chopped onion, diced carrot, and celery to the kettle and sauté over moderate heat, stirring often, for 8 to 10 minutes, until golden brown. Mix in the

PHEASANT AND LENTIL SOUP

tomato paste, wine, and reserved pheasant stock. Bring to a boil, add the lentils, and return to the boil. Adjust the heat so the mixture bubbles gently, then simmer, uncovered, for 45 minutes, until the lentils are tender.

Meanwhile, skin the pheasant, discarding the skin. Take the meat from the bones, cut into 1½ x ½ x ½-inch strips, and reserve. As soon as the lentils are tender, stir in the sherry, vinegar, mustard, nutmeg, and the remaining salt and pepper. Return the pheasant meat to the kettle and bring just to serving temperature. Remove the bay leaf, taste for salt and pepper, and adjust as needed.

Ladle the soup into soup plates and scatter a little of the chives and reserved bacon on top of each portion.

BLACK FOREST TROUT SOUP

Schwarzwälder Forellensuppe

Wherever we travel in Germany, we're constantly on the lookout for unusual recipes. This smooth trout soup begins with a rich stock brewed of trout (in Germany it would come from one of the Black Forest's fast-flowing streams), carrot, celery, leek, and onion, then is finished off with egg yolks and cream.

1 fresh trout (about 14 ounces), cleaned but head and tail left on

6 cups cold water

1 whole bay leaf

1 whole clove

1 medium-size carrot, peeled and thickly sliced

1 medium-size celery rib, thickly sliced

6 large flat-leaf parsley sprigs

1 large yellow onion, peeled and thinly sliced

1 large leek, trimmed, washed well, and thinly sliced

1½ cups half-and-half

2 extra-large egg yolks, lightly beaten

¾ teaspoon salt

¼ teaspoon freshly ground black pepper

continued on next page

109

BLACK FOREST TROUT SOUP (cont.)

¼ pound skinned smoked fillet of trout, cut into bite-size pieces

Garnishes:

½ cup heavy cream, stiffly whipped

4 small dill sprigs

Makes 4 servings

Cut the fresh trout into 2-inch chunks. Place in a large heavy saucepan, add the water, bay leaf, clove, carrot, celery, parsley, onion, and leek and bring to a simmer. Adjust the heat so the mixture bubbles gently and simmer, uncovered, for 20 minutes. Fish out the pieces of trout, wrap in a clean dish towel, and squeeze hard directly over the saucepan to extract as much liquid as possible; discard the solids. Now boil the soup, uncovered, over high heat for 15 to 18 minutes, until reduced to 4 cups. Put through a large fine sieve set over a large heatproof bowl, pressing the solids to extract as much liquid as possible (you should have 3 cups strained stock). Again, discard the solids.

Return the stock to the saucepan, add 1 cup of the half-and-half, and bring to a simmer over moderate heat. In a small bowl, whisk the remaining half-and-half with the egg yolks until well blended. Whisk a little of the hot soup into the yolk mixture, then stir back into the saucepan. Cook, stirring constantly, over moderately low heat, for 2 to 3 minutes, until slightly thickened, then season with salt and pepper. *Do not allow the mixture to boil or it may curdle.*

Add the smoked trout to the soup and warm 1 to 2 minutes longer. Ladle into soup bowls, then float a dollop of whipped cream on top of each portion and sprig with dill.

LÜBECK SHRIMP SOUP

Lübecker Krabbensuppe

This recipe comes from Helga Brenner, a German now working in New York. Helga says she tasted this soup not long ago in a quaint restaurant in the old Hanseatic port of Lübeck and liked it so much she asked for the recipe. The restaurant obliged. Its name, should you be in Lübeck or neighboring Hamburg and care to dine there, is Weinstuben unter dem Heiligen Geist Hospital, which means "the Wine Tavern below the Holy Ghost Hospice." The shrimp used in the original recipe are the Baltic variety and so tiny you get about 200 of them to the pound. They're available here only in jars or tins and are too salty for this delicate soup. For that reason, we've substituted the smallest American shrimp we could find – with excellent results.

2 tablespoons unsalted butter or margarine

1 pound very small shrimp, shelled and deveined (reserve shells)

1 large yellow onion, peeled and thinly sliced

1 small celery rib, thinly sliced

1 small carrot, peeled and thinly sliced

1 medium-size garlic clove, peeled and minced

2 tablespoons all-purpose flour

3½ cups rich fish stock, or 2 cups bottled clam juice mixed with 1½ cups cold water

½ cup Riesling or other dry white wine

3 juniper berries

½ teaspoon dried leaf thyme, crumbled

1 tablespoon finely snipped fresh dill, or 1 teaspoon dillweed

½ teaspoon salt

¼ teaspoon freshly ground black pepper

1 cup half-and-half

2 tablespoons finely ground blanched almonds

1 to 2 teaspoons freshly squeezed lemon juice

Makes 6 cups

Melt the butter in a heavy medium-size saucepan over moderate heat, add ¼ pound of the shrimp, the reserved shells, onion, celery, carrot, and garlic and sauté 3 minutes, stirring occasionally. Blend in the flour and cook and stir 2 minutes. Add the stock, wine, juniper berries, thyme, dill, salt, and pepper and bring to a boil. Adjust the heat so the liquid

continued on next page

111

LÜBECK SHRIMP SOUP
(cont.)

bubbles gently, then cover and simmer 25 minutes. Put the soup through a fine sieve set over a second medium-size saucepan, pressing the solids to extract as much liquid as possible; discard the solids.

Add the remaining shrimp to the saucepan along with the half-and-half and almonds and bring to a simmer over moderate heat, stirring often. Adjust the heat so the soup bubbles gently and simmer, uncovered, for 5 minutes, just until the shrimp are pink, opaque, and firm. Stir in 1 teaspoon of the lemon juice, taste, and add more, if needed. Also taste the soup for salt and pepper and adjust as needed. Ladle into soup bowls and serve.

HAMBURG MUSSELS SOUP
Hamburger Muschelsuppe

Founded in the ninth century, Hamburg grew rich and powerful during the Middle Ages as a member of the Hanseatic League. It remains Germany's great maritime city, and today its port sprawls for 100 square kilometers down the right bank of the Elbe toward the North Sea. Hamburg's modern docks and shipyards now throng with sea-tainers, supertankers, and freighters. Still, much to the relief of the Hamburgers, who prefer seafood to meat, fishing hasn't been abandoned.

6 pounds mussels in the shell (about 3½ dozen large mussels), well scrubbed and bearded

1 quart cold water

2 tablespoons unsalted butter or margarine

1 medium-size leek, trimmed, washed well, and coarsely chopped

1 medium-size celery rib, coarsely chopped (include some green tops)

1 small carrot, peeled and coarsely chopped

8 medium-size flat-leaf parsley sprigs

2 large whole bay leaves

5 juniper berries

2 whole cloves

½ teaspoon salt

½ cup Riesling or other dry white wine

2 extra-large egg yolks

¼ cup crème fraîche or heavy cream

112

HAMBURG MUSSELS
SOUP

2 to 3 teaspoons lemon juice (or to taste)

Makes 6 servings

Place the mussels and water in a large heavy kettle. Set,
uncovered, over high heat and bring to a boil. Adjust the
heat so the water bubbles continuously but not too furiously,
cover the kettle, and cook just until the mussels open –
about 5 minutes; discard any that do not open. With a slotted
spoon, transfer the mussels to a large bowl and reserve.
Strain the cooking liquid through a fine sieve lined with
a double thickness of cheesecloth wrung out in cool water.
Shuck the mussels, discarding the shells and reserving
the meat.

Melt the butter in a large heavy saucepan over moderate
heat, add the leek, celery, and carrot, and sauté 5 minutes,
stirring occasionally, until translucent. Add the reserved
mussel broth, the parsley, bay leaves, juniper berries,
cloves, and salt and bring to a boil. Adjust the heat so the
mixture bubbles gently, then simmer, uncovered, for 20 minutes. Strain the broth into a large bowl, discarding the solids,
and return the broth to the pan. Add the wine and reserved
mussels and bring just to a simmer over moderate heat, stirring now and then.

Meanwhile, whisk together the egg yolks and crème fraîche.
Blend a little of the hot mussel broth into the egg mixture,
then stir back into the pan and cook, stirring constantly, over
low heat for 2 to 3 minutes longer. Stir in lemon juice to
taste, ladle into soup plates, and serve at once.

EEL SOUP FROM HAMBURG

Hamburger Aalsuppe

What's odd about Hamburg's Aalsuppe *is that the original contained no eel. In the local dialect it was* Aolsuppe *(all soup), an odds-and-ends chowder brewed from whatever was at hand. That usually meant a ham bone and fruit and vegetable scraps. To Hamburg visitors,* Aolsuppe *sounded like* Aalsuppe, *and after listening for years to complaints that his eel soup contained no eel, one enterprising Hamburg restaurateur slipped some eel into his* Aolsuppe *and jacked up the price. This all took place several hundred years ago and explains how such an unlikely medley of eel, fruits, and vegetables has become a Hamburg classic. There is, by the way, no authentic recipe. Everyone makes* Aalsuppe *differently. Most Hamburg cooks agree, however, that it should begin with a rich ham broth – water in which you've simmered a ham long and slow. That's what gives* Aalsuppe *its slightly smoky flavor. So, the next time you boil or simmer a ham – even*

Eel:

2 pounds eel, skinned and rinsed well, or 1¼ pounds mackerel fillets

1 medium-size yellow onion, peeled and thinly sliced

4 cups ham broth (see headnote) or water

1 tablespoon white wine vinegar

2 large whole bay leaves

6 large flat-leaf parsley sprigs

½ teaspoon dried leaf marjoram, crumbled

½ teaspoon dried leaf thyme, crumbled

¼ teaspoon (approximately) salt

Vegetables:

2 tablespoons unsalted butter or margarine

1 cup moderately finely diced peeled celery root

1 medium-size leek, trimmed, washed well, and finely diced

1 medium-size kohlrabi, peeled and moderately finely diced (optional)

1 medium-size carrot, peeled and moderately finely diced

¼ teaspoon salt

2 cups ham broth (see headnote) or rich beef broth (preferably homemade)

1 cup shelled green peas, either fresh or frozen, thawed

3 medium-size asparagus stalks, trimmed of tough stem ends and cut into 1-inch lengths, or ½ (10-ounce) package frozen cut asparagus (do not thaw)

Fruit:

2 ounces pitted prunes

EEL SOUP FROM HAMBURG

ham hocks – save the cooking water and freeze it to use when you're in the mood for Aalsuppe.

2 ounces dried apricots

1 cup hot water

1 cup dry red wine (preferably German)

2 tablespoons sugar

1 cinnamon stick

1 medium-size ripe Bosc pear, peeled, cored, and cut into ½-inch dice

1 medium-size McIntosh apple, peeled, cored, and cut into ½-inch dice

Dumplings:

1 cup water

2 tablespoons unsalted butter or margarine

½ teaspoon salt

1 cup sifted all-purpose flour

1 extra-large egg, lightly beaten

4 quarts water

Makes 6 servings

For the eel: Cut the eel crosswise into 1-inch chunks and place in a large heavy saucepan. Add the onion, ham broth, vinegar, bay leaves, parsley, marjoram, thyme, and salt. Cover and simmer slowly over moderately low heat for 15 minutes, just until the eel flakes. Dump the saucepan mixture into a large fine sieve set over a large heatproof bowl. Transfer the eel to a large plate, then discard the solids left behind in the sieve; reserve the cooking liquid.

For the vegetables: Wipe the saucepan in which you cooked the eel, add the butter, and melt over moderately low heat. Add the celery root, leek, optional kohlrabi, and carrot and sauté 5 minutes, stirring occasionally. Add the salt and ham broth and simmer, uncovered, for 10 minutes. Add the peas

continued on next page

115

EEL SOUP FROM
HAMBURG (cont.)

and asparagus and simmer, uncovered, for 5 minutes. Add the eel cooking liquid and the eel, remove from the heat, and keep warm.

For the fruit: Soak the prunes and apricots in the hot water in a medium-size bowl for 15 minutes. Drain the fruit, reserving the soaking liquid. Coarsely chop the fruit and place in a medium-size heavy saucepan. Add the soaking liquid, wine, sugar, cinnamon stick, pear, and apple and bring to a boil over moderate heat. Adjust the heat so the mixture bubbles gently, cover, and simmer 5 to 8 minutes, just until the fruit is tender. Discard the cinnamon stick, then add the fruit mixture to the eel mixture and keep warm.

For the dumplings: Bring the water, butter, and salt to a boil in a medium-size heavy saucepan over moderate heat, stirring constantly. Reduce the heat to low, blend in the flour, and stir briskly until the mixture rolls into a ball and holds together. Off heat, beat in the egg and continue beating until smooth. With dampened hands, shape into balls about 1 inch in diameter. Bring the water to a boil in a medium-size heavy saucepan over moderate heat, adjust the heat so the water barely simmers, then drop in the dumplings. Cover and simmer 5 to 8 minutes, stirring at halftime. With a slotted spoon, lift the dumplings to a plate lined with paper toweling to drain, then add to the eel mixture.

To finish the soup: Simmer the eel mixture, covered, for 5 minutes. Taste for salt and sugar and adjust as needed (the mixture should be only slightly sweet), then ladle into soup plates and serve.

BLACK FOREST SNAIL SOUP

Badische Schneckensuppe

This is our adaptation of the exquisite snail soup served at Hotel-Restaurant Ritter, the Willi Brunner family's cozily beamed and paneled turn-of-the-century Black Forest inn in the town of Durbach. The restaurant's new German cooking has won it a Michelin star.

4 tablespoons (½ stick) unsalted butter or margarine

2 tablespoons finely minced shallots

1 medium-size garlic clove, minced

½ pound mushrooms, wiped clean and minced

1 cup Riesling wine

1 cup rich beef broth (preferably homemade)

1 cup rich chicken broth (preferably homemade)

1 cup crème fraîche, or ½ cup each light cream and half-and-half

¼ teaspoon pulverized aniseeds

1 (7½-ounce) can escargots, drained (reserve liquid) and minced

1 tablespoon minced chives

1 tablespoon minced parsley

1 tablespoon flour

2 extra-large egg yolks, lightly beaten

2 teaspoons Pernod

Makes 6 servings

117

Melt 3 tablespoons of the butter in a large heavy saucepan over low heat. Add the shallots and sauté 5 minutes; add the garlic and sauté 1 minute longer (do not brown or the garlic will be bitter). Add the mushrooms and stir-fry 15 minutes over lowest heat. Mix in the wine, beef and chicken broths, and crème fraîche and simmer, uncovered, for 10 minutes. *Do not allow the mixture to boil or it may curdle.*

Add the aniseeds, escargots and their liquid, the chives, and parsley. Knead the remaining 1 tablespoon of butter with

continued on next page

BLACK FOREST
SNAIL SOUP (cont.)

the flour to form a *beurre manié*. Pinch off bits of it and whisk into the simmering soup, one at a time, so that the mixture thickens slowly and evenly. Beat 2 tablespoons of the hot soup into the egg yolks, then add 3 additional table-spoons, one at a time, whisking vigorously. Stir back into the soup. Mix in the Pernod and let the soup mellow a minute or two over low heat. Again, do not let it boil. Ladle into soup bowls and serve as a first course.

VEGETABLE SOUP WITH SAUERKRAUT AND SMOKED TURKEY BREAST
Gemüsesuppe mit Sauerkraut und geräucherter Truthahnbrust

A quick and easy soup that's indicative of the way busy young Germans cook today. The soup bursts with flavor, yet is ready to serve in about 45 minutes. Add a salad and crusty chunks of whole-grain bread and you've a nourishing lunch or supper. Smoked turkey breast is available at the deli counters of most good supermarkets, also at specialty food shops.

3 tablespoons unsalted butter or margarine

1 large yellow onion, peeled and coarsely chopped

1 large leek, trimmed, washed well, and thinly sliced

2 medium-size carrots, peeled, halved lengthwise, then each half thinly sliced

1 medium-size celery rib, thinly sliced

1 large whole bay leaf (preferably fresh)

¼ teaspoon freshly ground black pepper

1 large baking potato, peeled and coarsely shredded

1 cup fresh sauerkraut, drained well

3 cups rich beef broth (preferably homemade)

2½ cups rich chicken broth (preferably homemade)

⅓ cup Riesling or other dry white wine

1 extra-large egg yolk

½ cup crème fraîche or sour cream, at room temperature

¼ pound thinly sliced smoked turkey or chicken breast, cut into matchstick strips

2 tablespoons minced flat-leaf parsley

Makes 6 to 8 servings

VEGETABLE SOUP
WITH SAUERKRAUT
AND SMOKED TURKEY
BREAST

Melt the butter in a large heavy saucepan over moderate heat. Add the onion, leek, carrots, celery, bay leaf, and pepper and sauté, stirring often, about 2 minutes, until the onion, leek, and celery are limp and golden. Add the potato, sauerkraut, beef and chicken broths, and Riesling and bring to a simmer over high heat. Adjust the heat so the mixture bubbles gently, cover, and simmer 30 minutes.

Blend the egg yolk with the crème fraîche in a small heat-proof bowl until creamy. Whisk in about 1 cup of the hot soup liquid, then stir back into the pan, cook and stir for 2 minutes. *Do not allow the soup to boil or the crème fraîche may curdle.* Add the turkey and cook and stir for 2 minutes longer. Sprinkle in the parsley and simmer 1 minute more. Remove the bay leaf, ladle into soup plates, and serve.

ASPARAGUS-RICE SOUP

Spargel-Reis Suppe

Modern German cooks, every bit as frugal as their mothers and grandmothers, waste nothing. For example, they intensify the flavor of this lovely, light, low-calorie soup by boiling the woody asparagus stalks, even the parings of asparagus skin, into an infusion in which the asparagus itself cooks.

1 pound tender young asparagus (preferably white)

3¼ cups cold water

⅓ cup long-grain white rice

1 tablespoon unsalted butter or margarine

2 tablespoons minced fresh chervil, or 1 tablespoon each minced fresh tarragon and flat-leaf parsley

2½ cups rich chicken broth (preferably homemade)

½ teaspoon salt

⅛ teaspoon freshly ground black pepper

Pinch of freshly grated nutmeg

2 teaspoons freshly squeezed lemon juice

Makes 4 servings

Wash the asparagus well, snap off the tough stem ends, and place in a heavy medium-size saucepan. Cut the asparagus

119

continued on next page

ASPARAGUS-RICE
SOUP (cont.)

tips off, drop into a small bowl, and set aside. Using a swivel-bladed vegetable peeler, peel the tender asparagus stalks over the saucepan, letting the parings fall in. Cut the stalks into 1-inch lengths and add to the bowl with the tips. Add 2½ cups of the water to the pan, set uncovered over moderate heat, and bring to a boil. Adjust the heat so the water bubbles gently, then simmer, uncovered, for 15 minutes.

Meanwhile, bring the remaining ¾ cup water to a boil in an uncovered small saucepan over moderate heat. Add the rice, return to the boil, adjust the heat so the water simmers slowly, and cook, uncovered, for 12 to 15 minutes, until the rice is *al dente* and all water has been absorbed. Rinse the rice under cool running water, drain well, and reserve. Strain the asparagus cooking liquid, discarding all solids, and set aside. Quickly rinse out the pan.

Melt the butter in the pan over moderate heat, add the chervil, and mellow 2 minutes to release the flavor. Add the chicken broth, reserved asparagus liquid, and asparagus stalks and tips and bring to a boil. Cook, uncovered, for 3 minutes. Add the rice, salt, pepper, and nutmeg and bring just to a simmer. Stir in the lemon juice, taste for salt and pepper, and adjust as needed. Ladle into soup plates and serve at once.

CLEAR ASPARAGUS SOUP WITH TARRAGON-SCENTED VEAL DUMPLINGS

Klare Spargelsuppe mit Kalbfleischklösschen

Here's another fine asparagus soup, this one plumped up with little veal dumplings. The food processor can grind the veal and blend the dumpling mixture in less than two minutes. If you have no processor and are determined to make this soup, you'll have to put the veal through the finest blade of a meat grinder – twice.

For Cooking the Dumplings:

1½ gallons water mixed with 1 tablespoon salt

Soup:

2 pounds asparagus (preferably white)

3 large tarragon sprigs

3 large flat-leaf parsley sprigs

2 quarts rich chicken broth (preferably homemade)

½ teaspoon salt

⅛ teaspoon freshly ground black pepper

⅓ cup Riesling or other dry white wine

Dumplings:

½ pound boned lean veal shoulder, cut into ½-inch cubes

1 extra-large egg

¼ cup finely chopped yellow onion

¾ teaspoon salt

¼ teaspoon freshly grated nutmeg

⅛ teaspoon freshly ground black pepper

Makes 6 servings

For cooking the dumplings: Bring the salted water to a boil in a large pasta kettle over moderately low heat.

For the soup: Snap the tough ends off the asparagus and place in a large heavy saucepan. Peel the asparagus stalks and add the peelings to the saucepan. Strip the leaves from the tarragon and parsley sprigs. Chop the leaves fine and reserve for the dumplings, but toss the tarragon and parsley stems into the saucepan. Add the broth, salt, and pepper,

121

continued on next page

CLEAR ASPARAGUS
SOUP WITH
TARRAGON-SCENTED
VEAL DUMPLINGS
(cont.)

set over moderate heat, and bring to a boil. Adjust the heat so the broth bubbles gently, cover, and boil 15 minutes.

For the dumplings: Place all ingredients, including the reserved chopped tarragon and parsley, in a food processor fitted with the metal chopping blade and process 30 seconds. Scrape down the sides of the workbowl and process 30 seconds longer. Once again scrape down the sides of the workbowl and process 30 seconds more, until thick and pastelike.

With wet hands, shape the dumpling mixture into 1-inch balls. Adjust the heat under the pasta kettle so the salted water bubbles gently, add all the dumplings, cover, and simmer 2 minutes. With a skimmer or slotted spoon, lift the dumplings to a large wet plate and reserve.

To finish the soup: Cut the asparagus stalks on the diagonal into 1-inch chunks and set aside. Line a large fine sieve with several thicknesses of cheesecloth and set over a large heatproof bowl. Pour in the broth and asparagus stems and trimmings and let as much liquid drip through as possible; discard all solids. Return the broth to the saucepan, set over moderate heat, and bring to a boil. Add the asparagus, cover, and cook 4 minutes. Add the dumplings and Riesling, re-cover, reduce the heat to moderately low, and simmer 2 minutes. Taste for salt and pepper and add a little more of each, if needed. Ladle into soup plates, making sure that everyone gets plenty of asparagus and dumplings.

BEAN SOUP

Bohnensuppe

Two kinds of beans go into this soup, which is popular in the Hamburg area – dried white beans and fresh green beans. But that's only the beginning. This hearty cold-weather soup is loaded with smoky bacon, onions, carrots, leeks, and potatoes. It is thickened, just before serving, with a rich brown roux that mellows over low heat for a full hour, developing color and flavor along the way. You must keep the heat low under the roux and stir from time to time so it browns evenly. In the end, it should be the color of pale caramel.

The beans should soak overnight in cold water, so plan accordingly. Or you can use the quick method: Bring the beans and 1 quart cold water to a boil in a large heavy kettle, cover, and boil 5 minutes, then turn off the heat and let the beans cool to room temperature in the covered kettle. You are now ready to proceed with the recipe.

1 pound dried Great Northern or pea beans, washed and sorted

2½ quarts cold water

½ pound lean double-smoked bacon, cut into ¼-inch cubes (about 2 cups bacon cubes)

½ pound green beans, tipped and cut into 1-inch lengths

½ medium-size celery root, peeled and cut into ¼-inch cubes, or 2 large celery ribs, thinly sliced (include some of the tops)

2 large carrots, peeled and cut into ¼-inch cubes

1 large leek, trimmed, washed well, and thinly sliced

1 large yellow onion, peeled and coarsely chopped

1 large parsley root, trimmed, peeled, and cut into ¼-inch cubes, or ½ cup coarsely chopped flat-leaf parsley

¾ pound new potatoes, peeled and cut into ½-inch cubes

1 tablespoon dried leaf marjoram, crumbled

1 teaspoon dried leaf thyme, crumbled

2 large whole bay leaves

3 tablespoons unsalted butter or margarine

4 tablespoons all-purpose flour

1 tablespoon salt

½ teaspoon freshly ground black pepper (optional)

⅓ cup coarsely chopped flat-leaf parsley (use the full amount even if you substitute parsley for parsley root, above)

Makes 10 to 12 servings

Soak the dried beans overnight in 1 quart of the water in a large heavy kettle. Next day, add the remaining 1½ quarts

continued on next page

BEAN SOUP (cont.)

water and the bacon, set over moderately high heat, and bring to a boil. Adjust the heat so the mixture bubbles very gently, cover, and cook 1 hour.

Add the green beans, celery root, carrots, leek, onion, parsley root, potatoes, marjoram, thyme, and bay leaves, re-cover, and simmer 1 hour.

Meanwhile, melt the butter in a heavy 8-inch skillet over low heat, blend in the flour, and let the roux brown very slowly, stirring occasionally – this will take about 1 hour if you keep the heat low enough. Blend a little of the hot soup liquid into the browned roux, stir into the kettle, add the salt and pepper, and cook, uncovered, stirring often, for 10 minutes. Mix in the parsley, remove the bay leaves, taste for salt and pepper, and adjust as needed. Ladle into soup plates and accompany with crusty chunks of Wheat (White) Bread (page 295).

CUCUMBER SOUP

Gurkensuppe

In the Lüneburg Heath southeast of Hamburg, there's a delightful manor-house hotel called Der Fürstenhof. One of the specialties of its restaurant, Endtenfang, is this tart cucumber soup aromatic with fresh dill. Endtenfang serves the soup hot, strewn with crisp butter-browned croutons, but it's equally delicious cold and needs nothing more to garnish than a frilly sprig of dill. The best cucumbers to use are the small, compact Kirbies, which have fewer seeds and

Soup:

1 pound unwaxed cucumbers, peeled, halved lengthwise, seeded, and thinly sliced (reserve skins)

5 cups water

1 teaspoon salt

1½ teaspoons dried leaf marjoram, crumbled

¾ teaspoon dried leaf thyme, crumbled

2 tablespoons unsalted butter or margarine

1 small yellow onion, peeled and coarsely chopped

1 medium-size garlic clove, peeled and minced

¼ teaspoon freshly grated nutmeg

4 tablespoons all-purpose flour

½ cup finely snipped fresh dill

CUCUMBER SOUP

mellower flavor than the everyday garden variety.

2 cups dry white wine (not too tart)

1 cup heavy cream

¼ teaspoon freshly ground white pepper

Optional Garnishes:

1 cup butter-browned croutons, or 6 fresh dill sprigs

Makes 6 servings

For the soup: Place the cucumber skins in a large heavy saucepan. Add the water, salt, marjoram, and thyme. Set over moderate heat, uncovered, and bring to a boil. Adjust the heat so the mixture simmers slowly, cover, and cook 45 minutes.

Melt the butter in a heavy 10-inch skillet over moderate heat. Add the cucumbers and onion and sauté about 5 minutes, stirring often, until golden. Add the garlic and nutmeg, reduce the heat to its lowest point, cover, and steam 20 minutes. Sprinkle the flour evenly over the cucumber mixture, mix in, then allow to mellow over low heat for 1 to 2 minutes.

Place a large fine sieve over a large heatproof bowl. Pour in the cucumber skin mixture, pressing out as much liquid as possible, and discard the skins. Blend about 1 cup of the hot liquid into the skillet mixture, then transfer to the pan in which you cooked the cucumber skins. Add the remaining liquid and cook, stirring constantly, over moderate heat for 3 to 5 minutes, until slightly thickened. Mix in ¼ cup of the dill, the wine, cream, and pepper. Bring to a boil, then adjust the heat so the soup bubbles very gently and cook, uncovered, for 30 minutes. Strain, reserving both the solids and the liquid.

Transfer the solids and 1 cup of the liquid to a food processor fitted with the metal chopping blade and cool 10 minutes. Pulse 8 to 10 times, add another cup of the liquid, and purée 60 seconds, until smooth. Combine the purée and remaining liquid.

continued on next page

125

CUCUMBER SOUP
(cont.)

To serve the soup hot: Return the soup to the pan and bring just to serving temperature over moderately low heat. Taste for salt and pepper and adjust, as needed. Stir in the remaining ¼ cup snipped dill, ladle into soup plates, and, if you like, scatter a few croutons on top of each portion.

To serve the soup cold: Mix the remaining ¼ cup snipped dill into the soup, cover, and chill several hours. Taste for salt and pepper and adjust, as needed. Ladle into soup plates, then garnish, if you like, with dill sprigs and serve.

FENNEL SOUP WITH BACON
Fenchelsuppe mit Speck

This delicate soup successfully teams the very German flavors of browned bacon and onions with the subtle licorice one of fennel.

1½ pounds fennel (about 1 large bulb)

2 ounces double-smoked slab bacon (not too lean), cut into ¼-inch cubes (about ½ cup bacon cubes)

1 tablespoon unsalted butter or margarine

2 large yellow onions, peeled and coarsely chopped

1 large all-purpose potato, peeled and coarsely chopped

1 teaspoon fennel seeds

¼ teaspoon aniseeds

1 large whole bay leaf

¼ teaspoon freshly ground nutmeg

4 cups rich chicken broth (preferably homemade)

1 teaspoon salt

¼ teaspoon freshly ground black pepper

½ cup heavy cream

Makes 6 servings

126

FENNEL SOUP WITH
BACON

Remove the young, feathery fennel tops, chop them moderately fine, then measure and reserve ½ cup of them; they'll be added at the last minute. Discard all withered or woody fennel stalks, also any discolored core. Coarsely chop the remaining fennel and set aside.

Sauté the bacon in a medium-size heavy kettle over moderately low heat, stirring often, until all drippings cook out and only crisp brown bits remain – about 10 minutes. With a slotted spoon, lift the bacon bits to paper toweling and reserve. Add the butter, onions, chopped fennel, potato, fennel seeds, aniseeds, bay leaf, and nutmeg and turn in the drippings 2 to 3 minutes, until nicely glazed. Reduce the heat to low, cover, and steam 15 minutes. Add the broth, bring to a boil over moderate heat, then adjust the heat so the mixture bubbles gently. Cover and simmer 1½ hours, stirring occasionally, until the vegetables are very soft; remove and discard the bay leaf. Cool the soup mixture for 15 minutes, then purée in batches in a food processor fitted with the metal chopping blade for 15 to 20 seconds.

Return the soup to the kettle, add the salt, pepper, and cream and bring slowly to serving temperature. Stir in the chopped fennel tops and reserved bacon crumbles (reserve a little of each, if you like, to sprinkle over each portion), then ladle into soup plates and serve.

127

KALE SOUP

Grünkohlsuppe

Sylt, the major island of the North Frisians off the west coast of Schleswig-Holstein, is a popular North Sea resort in summer. But in winter, "soup weather" prevails, with one raw blustery day after another. Few Frisian soups are better than this one, which contains plenty of pork, lamb, and onions as well as kale. The principal flavoring is mustard – a richly flavored spicy brown one is what's needed or a Dijon. Like most soups, Grünkohlsuppe is even better the second day.

½ pound double-smoked bacon, snipped crosswise into ¼-inch strips (about 2 cups bacon strips)

1 pound well-trimmed boneless pork rump, cut into 1-inch cubes

1 pound well-trimmed boneless lamb shoulder, cut into 1-inch cubes

1½ cups rich beef broth (preferably homemade)

2 quarts water

1 large whole bay leaf

3 tablespoons lard, unsalted butter, or margarine

3 large yellow onions, peeled and coarsely chopped

2 pounds kale, stemmed, washed well, then the leaves sliced crosswise ½ inch thick

¼ cup prepared spicy brown mustard or Dijon

2 tablespoons sugar

2 teaspoons salt

½ teaspoon freshly ground black pepper

Makes 8 servings

Brown the bacon in a medium-size Dutch oven over moderate heat for about 5 minutes, until all the drippings have cooked out and only crisp brown bits remain. Using a slotted spoon, lift the bacon bits to paper toweling to drain.

Brown the pork in the drippings in two batches over high heat for 3 to 5 minutes. With a slotted spoon, transfer the pork to a large heatproof bowl. Brown the lamb in the drippings the same way and add to the bowl. Pour all drippings into a large heavy kettle and reserve. Add the broth to the Dutch oven and boil 1 to 2 minutes over high heat, scraping

KALE SOUP

up all browned bits on the bottom of the Dutch oven. Add the water, bay leaf, lamb, pork, and all accumulated meat juices and bring to a boil. Adjust the heat so the liquid bubbles very gently, set the lid on askew, and simmer 1 hour.

Meanwhile, add the lard to the large heavy kettle, set over moderate heat, and as soon as it melts, add the onions and sauté 8 to 10 minutes, stirring often, until nicely browned. Add the kale and stir-fry 1 to 2 minutes to wilt. Turn the heat to the lowest point, cover, and steam the kale and onions for 10 minutes. Turn the heat off and leave the kettle covered.

When the meats have cooked 1 hour, lift them to a large heatproof bowl with a slotted spoon and cool until easy to handle. Add all the meat stock and the bay leaf to the kale mixture and bring to a boil over moderate heat. Adjust the heat so the stock bubbles gently, cover, and simmer 45 minutes.

Meanwhile, cut each piece of pork and lamb crosswise into thirds and reserve. When the kale mixture has cooked 45 minutes, smooth in mustard, then add the sugar, salt, and pepper and stir well. Discard the bay leaf, add the lamb and pork, and bring just to serving temperature.

Ladle into soup plates and scatter a little of the reserved bacon over each portion.

FRESH PARSLEY SOUP

Petersilien-Suppe

Long a staple in
Germany, parsley root
is at last becoming
available in American
supermarkets. It looks
like a small parsnip,
tastes a bit like parsnip,
too, and is essential to
this delicate soup, along
with gobs of chopped
flat-leaf parsley.
Although Germans serve
this soup hot, it is equally
delicious cold. For extra
flavor, reserve the flat-
leaf parsley stems and
simmer them along with
the parsley roots.

4 tablespoons (½ stick) unsalted butter or margarine

5 medium-size shallots, peeled and minced

5 medium-size celery ribs, trimmed and coarsely chopped

1 pound medium-size parsley roots, stemmed, peeled,
   and coarsely chopped

2 large leeks, trimmed, washed well, and coarsely chopped

¼ teaspoon freshly grated nutmeg

5 cups rich chicken broth (preferably homemade)

1 cup heavy cream

½ cup crème fraîche

1 teaspoon salt

¼ teaspoon freshly ground black pepper

1 tablespoon freshly squeezed lemon juice

5 cups loosely packed flat-leaf parsley leaves, moderately
   finely chopped

Makes 6 to 8 servings

Melt the butter in a large heavy kettle over moderate heat.
Add the shallots, celery, parsley roots, leeks, and nutmeg
and sauté 2 to 3 minutes, stirring constantly, until lightly
glazed. Turn the heat to its lowest point, cover, and steam
20 minutes.

Add the broth and, if you like, the flat-leaf parsley stems.
Bring to a boil over high heat, then adjust the heat so the
mixture bubbles gently. Cover and simmer 45 minutes.
Cool the kettle mixture, still covered, for 30 minutes. Set
a large fine sieve over a large heatproof bowl and pour in
the kettle mixture.

Purée the strained-out solids (include a few of the parsley
stems, if you like) along with 2 cups of the soup liquid in

FRESH PARSLEY SOUP

a food processor fitted with the metal chopping blade for 1 minute. Scrape down the sides of the workbowl and purée 1 minute longer. Return all soup liquid and the purée to the kettle. Set over moderate heat and heat, uncovered, for 3 to 4 minutes, just until the mixture simmers. Smooth in the cream and crème fraîche, the salt, pepper, and lemon juice and stir for 2 to 3 minutes. Taste for salt and pepper and adjust as needed. Finally, stir in the parsley and heat 1 minute longer – just until the parsley turns a vivid emerald. Ladle into soup plates and serve at once. Or, if you prefer, chill well and serve cold.

Variation

Fresh Chervil Soup (Kerbelsuppe): Prepare as directed, but substitute 1 pound (about 1 medium-size bulb) trimmed and coarsely chopped fennel for the parsley roots and 3 cups loosely packed fresh chervil (or 2½ cups flat-leaf parsley and ½ cup tarragon leaves) for the parsley.

CREAM OF POTATO SOUP
Kartoffelcremesuppe

This smooth-as-silk soup owes its creaminess to puréed vegetables, not to cream or egg yolks – or even milk.

2 tablespoons unsalted butter or margarine

2 large yellow onions, peeled and thinly sliced

1 small leek, trimmed, washed well, and thinly sliced

1 small celery rib, thinly sliced

2 thick slices double-smoked bacon, halved crosswise

1 teaspoon dried leaf marjoram, crumbled

1 teaspoon dried leaf thyme, crumbled

¼ teaspoon freshly grated nutmeg

1 pound Maine or Eastern potatoes, peeled and thinly sliced

1 quart rich chicken broth (preferably homemade)

1 teaspoon salt

¼ teaspoon freshly ground black pepper

continued on next page

CREAM OF POTATO SOUP (cont.)

2 tablespoons freshly snipped chives for garnish

Makes 4 to 6 servings

Melt the butter in a large heavy saucepan over moderate heat. Add the onions, leek, celery, bacon, marjoram, thyme, and nutmeg and stir-fry about 2 minutes, until nicely glazed. Reduce the heat to low, cover, and steam 15 minutes, until the onions are very limp; remove and discard the bacon. Raise the heat to moderate, add the potatoes and broth, bring to a simmer, uncovered, then adjust the heat so the broth bubbles gently. Cover and simmer 40 minutes, until the potatoes are mushy. Remove the pan from the heat and cool the soup, still covered, for 15 minutes.

Purée the soup mixture in two batches by blending in a food processor or an electric blender at high speed for 1 minute. Return the soup to the pan, mix in the salt and pepper, then taste and adjust the seasonings as needed. Heat the soup, uncovered, to serving temperature, ladle into bowls, and sprinkle each portion with snipped chives.

POTATO SOUP WITH WHITE TRUFFLE À LA TANTRIS

Kartoffelsuppe mit weisser Trüffel à la Tantris

This is our version of a stellar soup prepared by Chef Heinz Winkler, who until recently held forth at Tantris Restaurant in Munich, which Michelin blessed with three stars (Michelin subtracted a star when Winkler left to open his own inn, Residenz, in Aschau). The truffle is not only shaved into the soup, but also scattered over each portion. Truffle is an extravagance, to be sure, but you need only ½ ounce. If you can't afford fresh truffle, use the canned. This soup is glorious served cold – something to bear in mind come summer.

4 tablespoons (½ stick) unsalted butter or margarine

3 medium-size Maine or Eastern potatoes, peeled and diced

1 medium-size yellow onion, peeled and coarsely chopped

2 medium-size leeks, trimmed, washed well, and thinly sliced

1½ teaspoons minced fresh marjoram, or ½ teaspoon dried leaf marjoram, crumbled

1½ teaspoons minced fresh chervil, or ½ teaspoon dried leaf chervil, crumbled

⅛ teaspoon freshly grated nutmeg

2 cups rich beef broth (preferably homemade)

1½ cups rich chicken broth (preferably homemade)

½ ounce fresh white truffle, scrubbed well, or ½ ounce canned white truffle, with its liquid

1 tablespoon top-quality olive oil

1 cup heavy cream

½ teaspoon salt

⅛ teaspoon white pepper

Makes 4 servings

Melt the butter in a large heavy saucepan over moderately low heat. Add the potatoes, onion, and leeks and stir-fry 8 to 10 minutes, until limp and golden. Add the marjoram, chervil, and nutmeg and mellow 1 to 2 minutes. Add the beef and chicken broths. Bring to a simmer, uncovered, adjust the heat so the mixture bubbles gently, then simmer, uncovered, for 1½ hours, until the vegetables are soft.

Pour the soup into a large fine sieve set over a large heat-proof bowl. Transfer the solids and 1½ cups of the liquid to

133

continued on next page

POTATO SOUP WITH
WHITE TRUFFLE À LA
TANTRIS (cont.)

a food processor fitted with the metal chopping blade. Purée about 30 seconds, until smooth, scraping down the workbowl midway.

Return the puréed solids and the soup liquid to the pan. Using a swivel-bladed vegetable peeler, shave half the truffle into thinnest slices and add to the soup, along with the olive oil, cream, salt, and pepper. (If using canned truffle, add all truffle liquid to the soup along with half the truffle.) Set, uncovered, over low heat and mellow the soup for 30 minutes, stirring occasionally. Taste for salt and pepper and adjust as needed.

Ladle the soup into soup plates, then shave the remaining truffle into thinnest slices on top each of portion, dividing the total amount evenly. Serve at once.

MÜNSTERLAND TOMATO SOUP WITH BACON
Münsterland Tomatensuppe mit Speck

If fresh, homegrown tomatoes are available, by all means use them as the foundation of this robust soup. If not, you're better off substituting a favorite brand of canned crushed tomatoes than relying on the pithy, tasteless tomatoes stacked up in supermarket bins.

2 ounces double-smoked slab bacon (not too lean), cut into ⅛-inch cubes (about ½ cup bacon cubes)

2 large yellow onions, peeled and coarsely chopped

¼ cup finely chopped shallots

1 large whole bay leaf

1 teaspoon dried leaf marjoram, crumbled

½ teaspoon dried leaf thyme, crumbled

3½ cups coarsely chopped, peeled, cored, and seeded very ripe tomatoes (5 to 6 medium-size tomatoes), or 3½ cups canned crushed tomatoes

2 cups rich beef or chicken broth (preferably homemade)

1 tablespoon sugar

1 teaspoon salt

¼ teaspoon freshly ground black pepper

MÜNSTERLAND
TOMATO SOUP WITH
BACON

½ cup heavy cream

1 tablespoon unsalted butter or margarine

2 tablespoons finely snipped fresh chives or minced flat-leaf
parsley

Makes 6 servings

Sauté the bacon over moderate heat, stirring often, in a
medium-size heavy kettle until all drippings cook out and
only crisp brown bits remain – about 5 minutes. With a slotted spoon, lift the bacon bits to paper toweling and reserve.
Add the onions, shallots, bay leaf, marjoram, and thyme and
sauté 5 minutes, stirring often, until the onions are glassy.
Reduce the heat to its lowest point, cover, and steam 20
minutes.

Add the tomatoes, raise the heat to moderately low, and simmer, uncovered, 20 minutes, stirring often. Mix in the broth
and sugar. Bring to a boil, adjust the heat so the soup bubbles gently, then simmer, uncovered, 30 minutes, stirring
now and then; remove and discard the bay leaf. Cool the
soup 15 minutes, then purée in batches in a food processor
fitted with the metal chopping blade for 15 to 20 seconds.
(For an absolutely smooth, more elegant soup, force the
purée through a fine sieve.)

Return the soup to the kettle, add the salt, pepper, and
cream and bring slowly to serving temperature, stirring now
and then. Add the butter and, as soon as it melts, stir the
soup well and ladle into soup plates. Sprinkle the chives and
reserved bacon bits over each portion and serve.

135

ZUCCHINI SOUP

Zucchinisuppe

This unusual wine-based soup is the invention of Christa Jüngling of Winery Paulinshof in the town of Kesten on the Moselle River. It took a lot of refining, she admits, before she got the flavor and consistency just right. Frau Jüngling serves her zucchini soup warm – not hot – but we like it well chilled, too.

2 tablespoons unsalted butter or margarine

1 large yellow onion, peeled and moderately finely chopped

1 large garlic clove, peeled and minced

1 pound medium-size zucchini, peeled, halved, seeded, then cubed or coarsely chopped

¼ teaspoon freshly ground black pepper

1¾ cups dry Mosel or other white wine

1 cup rich beef broth (preferably homemade)

½ teaspoon salt

⅔ cup heavy cream, at room temperature

2 tablespoons coarsely chopped flat-leaf parsley

½ cup butter-browned croutons (optional garnish)

Makes 4 servings

Melt the butter in a large heavy saucepan over moderate heat and allow it to brown lightly. Add the onion and garlic, reduce the heat to moderately low, and sauté, stirring often, for 5 minutes, until golden. Add the zucchini and pepper, reduce the heat to low, and sauté 15 minutes, stirring often, until limp and lightly browned. Add the wine and broth and bring to a boil over moderate heat. Adjust the heat so the mixture bubbles gently, cover, and simmer 40 minutes. Mix in the salt, cool 20 minutes, then purée 1 minute in a food processor fitted with the metal chopping blade. Add the cream and pulse quickly to combine. Taste the soup for salt and pepper and adjust as needed. Ladle at once into soup bowls – do not reheat – sprinkle each portion with parsley, and, if you like, with croutons. Or, if you prefer, chill the soup well and serve cold.

BEEF, VEAL, LAMB, PORK, HAM, AND OTHER MAIN DISHES

Rind, Kalb, Lamm, Schwein, Schinken, und andere Hauptgerichte

ROULADES OF BEEF

Rindsrouladen

This old family recipe of Hedy's, lightened for today's health-conscious cooks, should be made with an evenly grained lean cut of beef. German cooks simply ask the butcher for "Rouladen" and he knows that they need thin scallops of top round. Each one should measure about 6 inches long, 3 inches wide, and ⅜ inch thick. The scallops should then be pounded – gently but thoroughly – until they're only ⅛ inch thick and about ¾ inch larger all around than they were when first cut. Pound the meat carefully so that there are no ragged edges, thin spots, or holes through which the filling can ooze. It's also important that the dill pickles and bacon you use in the filling aren't so salty or strong that they overpower the flavor of the beef. Serve the Roulades with boiled new potatoes or Egg Spaetzle (page 230). You can prepare the roulades a full day or two in advance, then

Roulades:

3 pounds top round, sliced and pounded thin as described in the headnote (you should have 18 to 20 beef scallops in all)

¼ teaspoon freshly ground black pepper

6 tablespoons Dijon mustard

Filling:

4 medium-size yellow onions, peeled and finely chopped

½ pound mildly smoked lean slab bacon, finely diced (about 2 cups)

1 cup minced parsley

3 medium-size dill pickles (not too sour), minced

For Cooking the Roulades:

2 tablespoons unsalted butter or margarine

2 tablespoons peanut oil

1 large carrot, peeled and coarsely chopped

1 large yellow onion, peeled and thinly sliced

1 large celery rib, peeled and thinly sliced

½ cup minced parsley

3½ cups rich beef broth (preferably homemade)

Gravy:

The roulades cooking mixture (liquid and solids)

¼ cup tomato paste

¼ cup half-and-half

continued on next page

137

ROULADES OF BEEF
(cont.)

*bring slowly to serving
temperature in a covered
skillet over low heat.*

138

¼ cup evaporated skim milk

Salt and freshly ground black pepper to taste

Makes 8 servings

For the roulades: Spread the beef scallops on a wax-paper-
covered counter. Trim off and discard any ragged edges, then
sprinkle both sides of each with the pepper. Thinly spread
the top side of each scallop with the mustard, using about
1 level teaspoon for each. Set aside.

For the filling: Stir-fry the onions and bacon in a large heavy
skillet over moderate heat for 8 to 10 minutes, just until the
onions are nicely glazed. Mix in the parsley, remove the
skillet from the heat, and cool to room temperature. Stir in
the pickles.

Place a mounded tablespoon of filling at one end of a
scallop, then spread evenly over the meat, leaving ⅜ inch
margins to the right and left and a full inch at the far end.
Roll the scallop up tightly toward the unspread end and
secure the seam with toothpicks. Pinch each end of the roll
together so that the filling does not ooze or fall out as the
roulades cook. Fill, roll, and seal the remaining roulades the
same way.

To cook the roulades: Warm the butter and oil in a heavy
12- to 14-inch skillet over moderately high heat for 1 to 2
minutes, until sizzling. Add the roulades and brown well on
all sides – this will take 5 to 10 minutes, but keep turning
the roulades so they brown evenly and don't burn. Reduce
the heat to moderate, add the carrot, onion, celery, and parsley and sauté about 5 minutes with the roulades. Add the
broth, bring to a simmer, then adjust the heat so the liquid
just trembles. Cover the skillet and simmer the roulades for
1¼ to 1½ hours, or until a fork pierces them easily. Using
a slotted spoon, lift the roulades to a shallow pan, cover with
foil, and keep warm while you prepare the gravy.

For the gravy: Strain the roulades cooking liquid, saving
both the solids and the liquid. Return the liquid to the skil-

ROULADES OF BEEF

let, set over high heat, and boil hard, uncovered, to reduce by about one third. Meanwhile, purée the solids by blending 15 to 20 seconds in an electric blender at high speed or in a food processor fitted with the metal chopping blade. Smooth the purée into the skillet and lower the heat so the mixture simmers gently. Smooth in the tomato paste, half-and-half, and evaporated skim milk, then season as needed with salt and pepper.

Return the roulades to the skillet, cover, and warm slowly in the gravy for 5 to 10 minutes, basting often. *Do not let the gravy boil or it may curdle.* Serve at once.

MEAT-STUFFED ROULADES OF RED CABBAGE
Gefüllte Rotkrautrouladen

These red-cabbage roulades, plumped with meat and vegetables, are merely a new twist on an old theme. And because they simmer in a vinegar-spiked broth, they retain their bright ruby color. The extra cabbage cooks along with the roulades, making this a nutritious one-dish meal.

4 tablespoons (½ stick) unsalted butter or margarine

1 large yellow onion, peeled and finely chopped

⅓ cup long-grain white rice

1⅔ cups rich beef broth (preferably homemade)

1 medium-size red cabbage (about 2 pounds)

¼ cup finely chopped celery root or celery

¼ cup finely chopped leek

¼ cup finely chopped carrot

¼ cup finely chopped flat-leaf parsley

1 pound meat loaf mix (or a half-and-half mix of ground beef chuck and ground pork shoulder)

2 extra-large eggs

¼ teaspoon freshly grated nutmeg

1½ teaspoons salt

½ teaspoon freshly ground black pepper

2 tablespoons cider vinegar

139

continued on next page

MEAT-STUFFED
ROULADES OF RED
CABBAGE (cont.)

½ cup crème fraîche

2 tablespoons dry red wine

Makes 6 servings

Melt 1 tablespoon of the butter in a small heavy saucepan over moderate heat. Add half the onion and sauté 3 to 5 minutes, stirring often, until limp and golden. Add the rice and ⅔ cup of the broth and simmer, uncovered, for 10 to 12 minutes, until the rice is just tender and all liquids absorbed; cool and reserve.

Meanwhile, remove 12 leaves from the cabbage and cook 5 to 8 minutes in lightly salted boiling water until soft; drain well and set aside. Quarter the remaining cabbage, core, and slice each quarter thin; set aside. Melt 1 tablespoon of the butter in a medium-size heavy saucepan over moderately low heat. Add the celery root, leek, carrot, and parsley, cover and cook 5 minutes, stirring occasionally. Transfer to a large bowl, add the meat loaf mix, rice mixture, eggs, nutmeg, and half the salt and pepper and mix well.

Trim the coarse central vein from each cabbage leaf so it is flush with the leaf. Lay 2 leaves flat on a dampened clean dish towel on a flat surface. Spoon a sixth of the meat mixture onto the leaves, roll up, jelly-roll style, using the cloth to compact the roulades. Stuff and roll the remaining cabbage leaves the same way, compacting each with the towel.

Melt the remaining 2 tablespoons butter in a 6-quart flameproof casserole over moderate heat. Arrange the roulades in the butter, seam sides down, and cook 1 minute. Turn gently and cook 1 minute longer. Transfer the roulades to a platter. Add the sliced cabbage and the remaining onion, broth, salt, and pepper to the casserole, and cook 3 minutes, stirring often. Mix in the vinegar, return the roulades to the casserole, again arranging seam sides down. Bring the casserole liquid to a simmer, adjust the heat so it bubbles gently, then cover the casserole and cook the roulades 30 to 35 minutes, until their juices run clear when pierced with a fork.

140

MEAT-STUFFED
ROULADES OF RED
CABBAGE

Transfer the roulades to a platter, cover loosely with foil, and keep warm. Mix the crème fraîche into the casserole mixture, bring to a boil, then stir in the wine. Simmer, uncovered, for 5 minutes, until slightly thickened.

To serve, slice the roulades ½ inch thick and arrange around the edge of a large platter. Pile the cabbage mixture in the center. Pass the sauce separately.

BOILED BEEF WITH HORSERADISH SAUCE

Gekochtes Ochsenfleisch mit Meerrettichsauce

The traditional accompaniments are peeled, boiled potatoes and steamed wedges of cabbage.

Beef:

2 quarts cold water

¼ cup matchstick strips of celery root

1 medium-size carrot, peeled and thinly sliced

2 medium-size leeks, washed, trimmed, and thinly sliced

½ medium-size bunch flat-leaf parsley

2 teaspoons salt

12 peppercorns

4 whole allspice

1 medium-size whole bay leaf

1 (3-pound) boneless beef rump roast, sirloin tip, or bottom round

Horseradish Sauce:

4 tablespoons (½ stick) unsalted butter or margarine

¼ cup unsifted all-purpose flour

½ cup heavy cream

¼ cup prepared horseradish, well drained

1 tablespoon freshly squeezed lemon juice

1½ teaspoons sugar

141

continued on next page

BOILED BEEF WITH
HORSERADISH SAUCE
(cont.)

⅛ teaspoon freshly ground black pepper

Makes 6 servings

For the beef: Place the water in a medium-size Dutch oven, add the celery root, carrot, leeks, parsley, salt, peppercorns, allspice, and bay leaf. Set, uncovered, over moderate heat and bring to a simmer. Ease the beef into the Dutch oven and return the water to a simmer, skimming it occasionally to remove any scum. Adjust the heat so the water barely simmers, cover, and cook the beef about 2 hours, or until fork-tender. Transfer the beef to a large heated platter, tent with foil, and keep warm. Strain the cooking water and reserve.

For the sauce: Melt the butter in a medium-size heavy saucepan over low heat. Blend in the flour and cook and stir for 2 minutes. Mix in 2 cups of the reserved beef cooking water. Increase the heat to moderate and simmer 3 to 5 minutes, stirring constantly, until thickened and smooth. Mix in the cream, horseradish, lemon juice, sugar, and pepper. Reduce the heat to low and cook, uncovered, 5 minutes longer, stirring often, until no raw starch taste remains.

To serve: Slice the beef across the grain about ¼ inch thick and arrange on a large heated platter, overlapping the slices slightly. Spoon some of the reserved cooking water over the beef. Ladle the sauce into a gravy boat and pass separately.

RHINELAND-STYLE SAUERBRATEN WITH RAISIN GRAVY

Rheinischer Sauerbraten mit Rosinensauce

Although he hails from Bremerhaven in the north of Germany, Karl Uwe Woggon collects recipes wherever he travels in his post as a government official. His favorite sauerbraten is this one from the Rhineland. The beef must marinate for four full days in a cooked marinade before it is set to simmer. Karl sometimes accompanies his sauerbraten with Potato Dumplings (page 221), sometimes with Egg Spaetzle (page 230), sometimes, even, with mashed potatoes, which he learned to appreciate while working in New York.

Marinade:

4 cups dry red wine (preferably German)

1 cup water

2 ½ tablespoons freshly squeezed lemon juice

1 small yellow onion, peeled and finely chopped

10 peppercorns

2 medium-size whole bay leaves

4 whole cloves

Sauerbraten:

1 (3-pound) boneless top round roast with a thin outer layer of fat

2 tablespoons minced parsley

1 teaspoon salt

½ teaspoon freshly ground black pepper

3 tablespoons all-purpose flour

3 tablespoons unsalted butter or margarine

2 medium-size carrots, peeled and thinly sliced

2 large yellow onions, peeled and coarsely chopped

1 tablespoon tomato paste

1 tablespoon sugar

2 tablespoons sweet sherry

½ cup medium-dry red wine (preferably German)

1 cup seedless raisins

1 to 2 tablespoons red currant jelly or orange marmalade (if needed to mellow the tartness of the gravy)

Makes 4 to 6 servings

continued on next page

143

For the marinade: Bring all ingredients to a fairly rapid boil in an uncovered medium-size heavy saucepan over moderate heat and cook 5 minutes.

For the sauerbraten: Place the beef in a large, heatproof, nonmetallic bowl. Pour in the hot marinade and cool to room temperature. Add the parsley, turn the beef in the marinade, cover, and marinate in the refrigerator for 4 days, turning the beef in the marinade every 8 hours.

On the 5th day, remove the beef from the marinade and pat it dry. Strain the marinade, reserving both liquid and solids. Rub the beef with half the salt and pepper, then dredge with the flour.

Melt 2 tablespoons of the butter in a medium-size heavy kettle over moderate heat, add the beef, and brown well on all sides; this will take 8 to 10 minutes. Transfer the beef to a plate, pour off and discard all casserole drippings, then add the remaining 1 tablespoon butter to the casserole and melt over moderate heat. Add the carrots, onions, and reserved marinade solids and sauté, stirring often, for 5 minutes. Return the beef to the casserole, add 2 cups of the reserved marinade and the tomato paste and bring to a boil over high heat. Adjust the heat so the marinade bubbles gently, cover the kettle with a round of foil, set the lid in place, then simmer the sauerbraten 3½ to 4 hours, turning occasionally, until tender. Carefully replace the foil and kettle lid each time you turn the meat.

As soon as the sauerbraten is tender, remove it to a large plate and cover loosely with foil to keep warm. Skim as much fat as possible from the marinade, then strain it, discarding the solids. Return the marinade to the casserole, add the remaining reserved marinade along with the sugar, sherry, red wine, and raisins and boil, uncovered, over high heat for 5 to 7 minutes, until reduced by half and of good gravy consistency. Taste, and if the gravy is too sour, smooth in 1 to 2 tablespoons of the jelly. Season the gravy with the remaining salt and pepper.

To serve: Slice the sauerbraten across the grain about ¼ inch thick, arrange on a large heated platter, overlapping the slices slightly, and smother with the gravy. Pass any extra gravy separately.

OXTAIL RAGOUT

Ochsenschwanz Ragout

Another of the splendid meat recipes Karl Woggon has picked up on his travels about Germany. It's a cold-weather favorite and, because it has plenty of rich brown gravy, should be accompanied by boiled or mashed potatoes, Egg Spaetzle (page 230), or boiled and buttered egg noodles.

4½ pounds oxtail, cut into 2-inch lengths

10 cups water

2 teaspoons salt

2 medium-size yellow onions, peeled and coarsely chopped

2 medium-size carrots, peeled and coarsely chopped

2 medium-size celery ribs, coarsely chopped (include some leafy tops)

¼ cup coarsely chopped flat-leaf parsley

6 peppercorns

3 whole cloves

3 medium-size whole bay leaves

4 tablespoons (½ stick) unsalted butter or margarine

4 tablespoons all-purpose flour

3 tablespoons tomato paste

1½ cups dry red wine (preferably German)

½ cup sour cream, at room temperature

Makes 4 to 6 servings

Place the oxtail in a large heavy kettle and add the water, salt, onions, carrots, celery, parsley, peppercorns, cloves, and bay leaves. Bring to a boil over moderate heat, skim off any scum that has accumulated, then adjust the heat so the water bubbles gently. Cover and simmer 4 hours, until the meat is fork-tender.

Remove the meat from the kettle and cool until easy to handle. Strain the cooking liquid, discarding the solids, then skim as much fat from the liquid as possible. Remove the meat from the bones and coarsely chop it.

continued on next page

145

OXTAIL RAGOUT (cont.)

Melt the butter in the kettle over moderate heat, blend in the flour, and cook and stir 2 minutes. Add the strained cooking liquid, bring to a boil, then cook, uncovered, for 10 minutes, stirring and skimming often. Smooth in the tomato paste and wine and simmer, uncovered, for 10 minutes, again stirring often.

Return the meat to the kettle, blend in the sour cream, taste for salt and pepper, and adjust as needed. Bring the mixture just to a simmer, stirring often, then serve.

BEEF POT WITH BEER
Rindfleischtopf mit Bier

Like most stews, this one will be better if made one day and served the next. The recipe comes from Hedy's sister-in-law, Hannelore Würz, who grew up in Erfurt in what had been East Germany. What makes this particular stew unusual is that thick slices of toast are spread with mustard, then plopped down on top of it. As the stew cooks, they puff up like dumplings (you must take care whenever you stir the stew not to shatter them). The bread you use for the "dumplings" should be from a very firm, chewy loaf that measures at least four inches across and three high. Hannelore serves the stew with mashed or boiled potatoes, sometimes with rice. Because of the saltiness

3 tablespoons corn oil

3 tablespoons unsalted butter or margarine

4 pounds boned lean beef chuck, cut into 1-inch cubes

2 large yellow onions, peeled and coarsely chopped

1 teaspoon dried leaf thyme, crumbled

¼ cup coarsely chopped flat-leaf parsley

3 tablespoons freshly snipped or frozen chives

2 large whole bay leaves

¼ teaspoon freshly ground black pepper

8 (¾-inch-thick) slices French or Italian bread, toasted

4 teaspoons Dijon mustard

3 cups beer (use a German lager)

Salt, if needed

Makes 8 servings

Heat 2 tablespoons of the oil and 1 tablespoon of the butter in a large heavy kettle over moderately high heat for 1 minute. Add one fourth of the beef and brown well on all sides. This will take 3 to 5 minutes. Using a slotted spoon,

146

BEEF POT WITH BEER

of the mustard, you may not need to salt the stew. Taste first.

transfer the browned beef to a large heatproof bowl and reserve. Brown the remaining beef the same way in three batches, adding additional oil and butter as needed and transferring each browned batch to the bowl. Add any remaining butter or oil to the kettle, add the onions, reduce the heat to moderate, and stir-fry 2½ to 3 minutes, until lightly browned. Add the thyme, parsley, chives, bay leaves, and pepper and mellow over moderate heat about 1 minute.

Spread one side of each slice of toast with ½ teaspoon of mustard and set aside for the moment. Add the browned beef and beer to the kettle, bring to a boil, then adjust the heat so the mixture barely bubbles. Arrange the slices of toast, spread sides down, over the surface of the stew. Cover the kettle and simmer slowly about 2 hours, until the beef is tender. Check the kettle from time to time to see that the stew is not bubbling too furiously or threatening to scorch. If it is, stir very carefully so as not to break up the slices of toast, then turn the heat lower still or, if necessary, use a Flame Tamer. Taste the stew for salt and add as needed. Remove and discard the bay leaves. To serve, place a slice of toast in each of 8 large soup plates and ladle the stew on top.

147

HESSIAN BEEF STEW
Hessisches Paprikafleisch

Helga Brenner, who comes from the town of Offenbach near Frankfurt, shared this favorite family recipe with us. It's typical of the hearty winter stews that bubble on the backs of stoves throughout the Hesse region of Germany. Helga likes to add ripe tomatoes toward the end of cooking, but in winter really good tomatoes are difficult to find, so she substitutes tomato paste.

6 tablespoons corn oil

3 pounds boned, lean beef chuck, cut into 1-inch cubes

6 large yellow onions, peeled and coarsely chopped

3 large garlic cloves, peeled and minced

2 tablespoons caraway seeds

1 tablespoon dried leaf marjoram, crumbled

3 tablespoons all-purpose flour

2 teaspoons salt

½ teaspoon freshly ground black pepper

1 quart hot water

continued on next page

HESSIAN BEEF
STEF (cont.)

What gives this stew its distinctly German flavor are caraway seeds. Serve with crusty chunks of Wheat (white) Bread (page 295), boiled potatoes, or rice plus a tartly dressed crisp green salad.

148

1 (6 ounce) can tomato paste

4 large sweet green peppers, cored, seeded, and cut into 1-inch squares

Makes 8 to 10 servings

Heat 4 tablespoons of the oil in a large heavy kettle over high heat for 2 minutes. Add one third of the beef and brown 3 to 4 minutes. With a slotted spoon, transfer the browned meat to a large heatproof bowl. Brown the remaining beef the same way in two batches and add to the bowl.

Add the remaining 2 tablespoons oil to the kettle, reduce the heat to moderately low, and stir in the onions, garlic, caraway seeds, and marjoram. Sauté, stirring often, for 10 minutes, until limp and golden.

Return the beef to the kettle along with all juices that have accumulated in the bowl, then sprinkle with the flour, salt, and pepper. Toss well. Add the water, raise the heat to high, and bring to a boil. Adjust the heat so the water bubbles very gently, cover, and simmer 1 hour.

Blend in the tomato paste, re-cover, and cook 1 hour longer. Add the green peppers, pushing them down into the stew, re-cover, and simmer 30 minutes. Uncover the stew and cook 30 minutes longer just to thicken the liquid a bit, then serve.

VEAL TENDERLOINS IN RIESLING SAUCE WITH MUSHROOMS AND PEARL ONIONS

Kalbslende in Rieslingsauce mit Champignons und Perlzwiebeln

A marvelous family recipe from Beatrix Carolyn Schmitt of Hermannshof, the winery of Hermann Franz Schmitt in Nierstein on the Rhine. It couldn't be easier to prepare and is perfect for a small, elegant dinner, but you should have all ingredients measured and at the ready before you begin. If the veal is to remain succulent, tender, and tinged with pink, it must be coddled: simmered very slowly in the sauce after the initial browning and turned often so it cooks evenly. You need nothing more to accompany than boiled rice (for sopping up every last drop of sauce), a crisp green salad, and a nicely chilled Riesling. Frau Schmitt makes her sauce with veal stock, but because few Americans have veal stock on hand, we've substituted—with excellent results—a half-and-half mix of beef and chicken broth.

2 center-cut veal tenderloins, each measuring about 6 inches long and 2½ to 3 inches in diameter (1¾ pounds in all)

¾ teaspoon salt

¼ teaspoon freshly ground black pepper

3 tablespoons unsalted butter or margarine

¼ pound small mushrooms, trimmed and wiped clean

¾ cup canned pearl or baby onions, drained and rinsed

1 cup heavy cream

½ cup rich beef broth (preferably homemade)

½ cup rich chicken broth (preferably homemade)

1 tablespoon tarragon or Dijon mustard

2 tablespoons freshly squeezed lemon juice

1 cup Riesling or other dry white wine

2 tablespoons all-purpose flour blended with 3 tablespoons cold water (flour paste)

2 tablespoons coarsely chopped fresh tarragon, or 1½ teaspoons dried leaf tarragon, crumbled

3 tablespoons Cognac

Makes 4 to 6 servings

Sprinkle the veal evenly with half the salt and pepper and set aside. Melt 2 tablespoons of the butter in a heavy 12-inch skillet over high heat. Let it foam up and subside, then add the veal and brown evenly on all sides; this will take about 5 minutes. Transfer the veal to a heated large plate, cover with foil, and keep warm.

Reduce the heat under the skillet to moderate, add the remaining 1 tablespoon butter and, when it melts, stir in

149

continued on next page

VEAL TENDERLOINS
IN RIESLING SAUCE
WITH MUSHROOMS
AND PEARL ONIONS
(cont.)

the mushrooms and onions and sauté 1 minute, stirring often. Add the cream, beef and chicken broths, and mustard and boil, uncovered, stirring often, about 10 minutes, until reduced by half. Blend in the lemon juice, wine, and flour paste and cook, stirring constantly, for 2 to 3 minutes, until the mixture bubbles up and thickens slightly.

Return the veal to the skillet together with any accumulated juices. Adjust the heat so the sauce bubbles *very* gently and cook, uncovered, for 30 to 35 minutes, turning the veal every 5 minutes, until an instant-register thermometer inserted in the center of a tenderloin registers 140° to 145° F (the veal will be pink but not rare).

Transfer the veal to a cutting board and let rest 5 minutes. Meanwhile, raise the heat under the sauce to moderate, add the tarragon, Cognac, and remaining salt and pepper and boil, uncovered, for 5 minutes, until slightly thickened. Taste for salt and pepper and adjust as needed. Slice the tenderloins ½ inch thick and arrange in rows on a heated platter, overlapping the slices. Spoon some of the sauce over the veal and pass the rest in a gravy boat.

BREADED VEAL CUTLETS
Wiener Schnitzel

Wiener means Viennese, but this recipe is a mainstay throughout Germany, too. Every "typically German" restaurant serves it. The hallmark of perfectly cooked Wiener Schnitzel: a crumb coating that's crisp and brown yet doesn't stick to the meat (you should be able to slide a table knife between the two). The trick is to bread the scallops just before you cook them, no earlier, because the coating will then cling to the meat. The temperature of the fat used for browning is critical, too – it should be hot enough to brown the scallops in about three minutes, but not so hot that it blackens the breading or so low that the Wiener Schnitzel is greasy. For best results, use a mixture of clarified butter and peanut or other vegetable oil.

1 pound veal scallops, pounded very thin as for scaloppine

½ teaspoon salt

⅛ teaspoon freshly ground black pepper

⅓ cup unsifted all-purpose flour

3 extra-large eggs, lightly beaten

1 cup fine dry white bread crumbs

3 tablespoons clarified butter

3 tablespoons peanut or other vegetable oil

1 large lemon, thinly sliced

Makes 4 servings

Preheat the oven to 275° F. Halve any scallops that are large, sprinkle both sides of each piece with the salt and pepper, and let stand at room temperature for 10 to 15 minutes.

Place the flour on a piece of wax paper, the eggs in a pie plate, and the crumbs in a second pie plate. Line the three up on a counter near the stove so that you don't waste time breading and browning the veal scallops.

Heat the clarified butter and oil in a heavy 12-inch skillet over moderately high heat about 2 minutes, or until a cube of bread sizzles in it. Brown half the breaded scallops quickly – about 3 minutes to a side. Remove to a shallow pan lined with paper toweling and set, uncovered, in the oven. Brown the remaining scallops the same way. Serve at once with the lemon slices.

151

VEAL SCALLOPS IN CREAM SAUCE
Rahmschnitzel

This German classic remains as popular as ever and appears on the menus of fine restaurants across the country. Rahmschnitzel is similar to the émincé de veau *of Switzerland, but in Germany the veal is cut into larger pieces. There's another difference, too. The Swiss like* rösti *(a shredded potato pancake) with their creamed veal and the Germans prefer Egg Spaetzle (see page 230).*

1½ pounds veal scallops, pounded very thin as for scaloppine, then cut into strips about 3 inches long and 1½ inches wide

1 teaspoon salt

¼ teaspoon freshly ground black pepper

⅓ cup unsifted all-purpose flour

¼ cup clarified butter

1 cup rich beef broth (preferably homemade)

½ cup heavy cream blended with ½ cup half-and-half

Makes 4 servings

Sprinkle the veal with salt and pepper and toss well. Scatter the flour evenly on top and toss well again to dredge.

Heat the clarified butter in a heavy 12-inch skillet over moderately high heat for about 2 minutes, or until a cube of bread sizzles in it. Shake the excess flour off the veal, add the veal to the skillet, and sauté, tossing and turning with a spatula, for 2 to 3 minutes, until no longer pink. Remove to a shallow pan lined with paper toweling, cover loosely with foil, and keep warm. Pour all drippings from the skillet, add the broth, and boil rapidly, scraping up the browned bits, until reduced by half. Add the cream mixture and boil, uncovered, stirring often, until reduced by half. Turn the heat to low, return the veal to the skillet, and warm, uncovered, for 2 to 3 minutes, stirring occasionally. Serve at once.

Variation

Paprika Schnitzel (Paprikaschnitzel): Prepare the Rahmschnitzel as directed, but mix 2 tablespoons Hungarian sweet rose paprika with the dredging flour and smooth 2 tablespoons crème fraîche or sour cream into the veal mixture just before serving.

SCHNITZEL POT
Schnitzeltopf

Few recipes are more geared to entertaining than this one from Angelika Miebs of the Hesse region of Germany. Schnitzeltopf can be prepared well ahead, baked while guests sip cocktails, then be brought to the table – or buffet – in its own baking dish.
Don't be shocked by the amount of butter and oil in the recipe. It's needed because bits of breading drop off the veal and begin to char before all cutlets have been browned. The only solution is to begin anew with fresh butter and oil. As for the amount of heavy cream, you can substitute a 50-50 mix of heavy cream and half-and-half, if you like. Also note that the recipe feeds an army.

1½ pounds veal scallops, pounded very thin as for scaloppine, then cut into 6 x 3-inch pieces

1 tablespoon Hungarian sweet rose paprika mixed with 2 teaspoons salt and 1 teaspoon freshly ground black pepper

3 extra-large eggs, lightly beaten

2 cups fine dry white bread crumbs

8 tablespoons (1 stick) unsalted butter or margarine

6 tablespoons corn oil

1 pound medium-size mushrooms, trimmed, wiped clean, and thinly sliced

½ pound sliced boiled ham, cut into 2 x ¼-inch strips

1 very large Spanish onion (1 pound), peeled, quartered, then each quarter thinly sliced

3 cups heavy cream, or 1½ cups each heavy cream and half-and-half

1½ teaspoons dried leaf marjoram, crumbled

¾ teaspoon dried leaf thyme, crumbled

¼ teaspoon freshly grated nutmeg

¼ teaspoon freshly ground black pepper

Makes 8 to 10 servings

Rub each side of each piece of veal lightly with the paprika mixture; dip into the eggs, then into the crumbs, until nicely coated. Place on a rack on a wax-paper-covered counter and let air-dry for 10 minutes.

Heat 2 tablespoons each of the butter and oil in a heavy 12-inch skillet over moderately high heat for 1 minute. Add 3 to 4 pieces of the veal and brown about 2 minutes on each side. Remove to several thicknesses of paper toweling to drain.

continued on next page

153

SCHNITZEL POT (cont.)

Add another 1 tablespoon each butter and oil to the skillet, heat 1 minute, then brown another 3 to 4 pieces of veal on each side as before and drain on paper toweling. Pour all drippings from the skillet, wipe it clean, then add another 2 tablespoons each of the butter and oil and heat 1 minute over moderately high heat. Add another 3 to 4 pieces of the veal, brown as before, and drain on paper toweling. Add 1 more tablespoon of the butter and the final tablespoon of oil to the skillet, heat 1 minute, then brown the remaining veal the same way and drain on paper toweling.

Preheat the oven to 400° F. Once again, drain all drippings from the skillet, wipe it clean, add the remaining 2 table-spoons butter, and melt over moderate heat. Add the mush-rooms and sauté 5 minutes, stirring often, until all juices cook out and evaporate. Transfer the mushrooms to a large heatproof mixing bowl, add the ham, onion, cream, marjo-ram, thyme, nutmeg, and pepper, and toss well to mix.

Arrange the pieces of veal, slightly overlapping, in the bottom of an ungreased large shallow baking dish (approximately 14 x 11 x 2½ inches). Pour in the mushroom mixture, smoothing it well to the corners, then cover with foil and bake for 1 hour. Serve at once.

VEAL SHANKS NORTHERN GERMAN STYLE

Gebratene Kalbskeule Norddeutsche Art

You might call this German ossobuco. Like the Italian original, it's made with thickly sliced veal shanks. But thanks to two pivotal ingredients – smoky bacon and sour cream – the flavor is entirely German. Serve with new potatoes, boiled in their skins, and buttered garden-fresh green peas.

¼ pound thickly sliced double-smoked bacon

3 pounds veal shanks, cut about 2 inches thick

½ teaspoon salt

¼ teaspoon freshly ground black pepper

1 large yellow onion, peeled and moderately finely chopped

1 small carrot, peeled and moderately finely chopped

1 teaspoon dried leaf thyme, crumbled

1 teaspoon dried leaf marjoram, crumbled

VEAL SHANKS
NORTHERN GERMAN
STYLE

1 cup hot water

1 cup sour cream, at room temperature

1 tablespoon all-purpose flour

Makes 4 servings

Preheat the oven to 350° F.

Sauté the bacon in a large heavy Dutch oven over moderate heat, turning once or twice, until translucent – about 3 minutes. Drain the bacon on paper toweling and reserve.

Add the veal shanks to the Dutch oven and brown 2 to 3 minutes on each side. Transfer to a large plate, season with the salt and pepper, and reserve. Add the onion, carrot, thyme, and marjoram to the Dutch oven and sauté 3 minutes, stirring occasionally, until the onion is translucent. Cut the bacon crosswise into 1-inch pieces and return to the kettle along with the veal shanks. Add ⅓ cup of the hot water, cover the kettle, transfer to the oven, and braise 1½ hours, until the veal shanks are fork-tender.

Lift the shanks to a heated platter, cover loosely with foil, and keep warm. Skim the fat from the pan drippings and add the remaining ⅔ cup hot water. In a small bowl, whisk the sour cream with the flour until smooth, add to the Dutch oven, set over moderately low heat, and cook 3 to 5 minutes, stirring constantly, until thickened and smooth. *Don't allow the sauce to boil or it may curdle.* Strain the sauce over the veal shanks and serve.

155

CALF'S LIVER IN HORSERADISH-MUSTARD CREAM SAUCE

Kalbsleber in Meerrettichsenf-Rahmsauce

There's a stellar family-run inn in the wine town of Durbach where we pause for lunch or dinner whenever we're in the neighborhood. This recipe is our adaptation

3 tablespoons unsalted butter or margarine

1½ pounds calf's liver, sliced ¼ inch thick

½ teaspoon salt

¼ teaspoon freshly ground black pepper

continued on next page

CALF'S LIVER IN HORSERADISH-MUSTARD CREAM SAUCE (cont.)

of a memorable liver dish we once enjoyed there. The original Ritter recipe called for a small amount of whipped cream to be folded into the sauce just before serving. Easy enough for chefs because they keep whipped cream at the ready. Not so practical, however, for home cooks who have no way to whip just a few tablespoons. It's important that the liver be sliced no more than ¼ inch thick because you must bounce it in and out of a hot skillet. The liver should be served rare or medium-rare, never well done because it will toughen, dry, and intensify in flavor. This is one of those recipes that must move like clockwork, so have all ingredients measured and ready. Also have at hand a cooking fork, wooden spoon, and a large plate to receive the slices of liver the instant they brown. You'll need nothing more to accompany this dish than a tartly dressed salad of crisp greens.

156

1 large yellow onion, peeled and moderately coarsely chopped

1 cup heavy cream

4 teaspoons prepared horseradish

1 tablespoon Dijon mustard

Makes 6 servings

Heat the butter in a heavy 12-inch skillet over high heat for 1 to 1½ minutes, until it melts, foams up, then subsides. Add half the liver and brown 1 to 1½ minutes on a side, depending on whether you prefer liver rare or medium-rare. Lift the browned slices to a plate and sprinkle each lightly with salt and pepper. Add the remaining liver to the skillet and brown as before. Transfer to the plate and season with salt and pepper. Cover the liver and keep warm.

Stir-fry the onion in the skillet over moderately high heat about 1 minute, scraping up all caramelized juices on the bottom of the skillet. Add the cream, horseradish, and mustard, raise the heat to high, and boil 3 to 4 minutes, stirring often, until slightly reduced.

Arrange the liver on a heated platter, pour any juices that may have accumulated on the plate into the skillet, mix in, then pour artfully over the liver and serve at once.

CALF'S LIVER BERLIN STYLE

Kalbsleber Berliner Art

A perfectly wonderful recipe from Hedy's personal file of favorites.

6 tablespoons unsalted butter or margarine

2 large Spanish onions, peeled and halved, then each half sliced ¼ inch thick

2 large Golden Delicious or Rome Beauty apples, peeled, cored, and cut into wedges ½ inch thick

1½ pounds calf's liver, sliced ¼ inch thick

3 tablespoons all-purpose flour

½ teaspoon salt

¼ teaspoon freshly ground black pepper

2 tablespoons minced parsley

Makes 6 servings

Melt 2 tablespoons of the butter in a heavy 12-inch skillet over moderate heat. Add the onions and sauté 5 to 7 minutes, stirring often, until limp and golden; transfer to a large bowl and reserve. Melt 2 more tablespoons of the butter in the skillet, add the apples, and sauté about 5 minutes, stirring often, until golden; transfer to a separate bowl and reserve.

Dredge the liver in the flour, shaking off any excess. Melt the remaining butter in the skillet over high heat and, as soon as it foams up and subsides, add half the liver and brown 1 to 1½ minutes on a side, depending on whether you like liver rare or medium-rare. Lift the browned slices to a heated platter and sprinkle each lightly with salt and pepper. Tent with foil to keep warm. Add the remaining liver to the skillet and brown as before. Transfer to the platter and season with salt and pepper. Pile the onions and apples on top of the liver, sprinkle with the parsley, and serve.

LAMB POT
Lammtopf

Except in the flat agricultural north, where sheep graze the salt marshes much as they do in Normandy, lamb was never fashionable in Germany. "It was always equated with mutton," explained a German friend. In fact, it was only recently when Turks began coming to Germany to work the menial jobs that lamb began to show up in butcher shops and curious German cooks began to try it. One such cook is Chef Joachim Möhringer at Hotel Römerbad, in the Black Forest spa of Badenweiler. His Lammtopf is a mix of the classic and contemporary with the vegetables being steamed on top of the lamb. It contains two relatively-new-to-Germany vegetables – a huge white Japanese radish and a sweet red American pepper – and is accompanied by Saffron Rice.

4 tablespoons (½ stick) unsalted butter or margarine

4 pounds boned lean lamb shoulder, cut into 1-inch cubes

8 large shallots, peeled and finely chopped

2 large garlic cloves, peeled and minced

1 large sweet red pepper, cored, seeded, and cut into ¼-inch dice

3 cups rich beef broth (preferably homemade)

1 teaspoon salt

½ teaspoon freshly ground black pepper

1 pound green beans, tipped and snapped into 1-inch lengths

4 medium-size scallions (about ¼ pound), trimmed and sliced ½ inch thick (include some green tops)

1 large white Japanese radish (1 pound), peeled and cut into ½-inch cubes, or 1 medium-size bunch (½ pound) red radishes, trimmed and cubed

½ cup coarsely chopped fresh mint

3 tablespoons all-purpose flour blended with 5 tablespoons cold water (flour paste)

1½ times the recipe for Saffron Rice (page 236)

Makes 6 to 8 servings

Melt 3 tablespoons of the butter in a large heavy kettle over moderately high heat. Add one third of the lamb and brown well on all sides – this will take about 5 minutes. Lift the browned lamb to a large bowl and reserve. Brown the remaining lamb the same way in two batches and add to the bowl.

Add the remaining 1 tablespoon butter to the kettle and, when it melts, add the shallots, garlic, and red pepper and

LAMB POT

sauté 2 minutes, stirring often. Reduce the heat to its lowest point, cover the kettle, and steam the shallot mixture 10 minutes. Add the broth, salt, and black pepper and stir well.

Return the lamb and any accumulated lamb juices to the kettle and bring to a boil over moderate heat. Adjust the heat so the broth bubbles gently, then cover and simmer 1 hour and 10 minutes. Uncover the kettle and simmer 20 minutes longer, until the lamb is almost tender and the juices have reduced somewhat.

Lay the beans on top of the lamb – don't stir – cover, and simmer 30 minutes. Lay the scallions, radish, and mint on top of the beans, cover, and simmer 10 minutes. Blend in the flour paste and cook 5 minutes, stirring often, until the stew is slightly thickened and no longer tastes of raw starch. Taste for salt and pepper and adjust as needed.

To serve, wreathe the Saffron Rice around the edge of a large deep platter and mound the stew in the center.

159

POACHED LOIN OF PORK ON A BED OF POTATOES, SAUERKRAUT, AND ONIONS
Gräwes

An old family recipe from Dr. Willkomm'sche Weingutsverwaltung, one of the important estates that grows grapes for Weinkellerei Peter Mertes at Bernkastel-Kues. Hedy explains that the recipe's one-word German title, which requires a 12-word English translation, is probably the local dialect. She adds that Bernkastel-Kues is a half-timbered, turreted town on the Moselle (its market square is one of the most photographed spots in

Pork:

2 pounds boneless pork loin, trimmed of excess fat

3 cups rich chicken broth (preferably homemade)

Potatoes, Sauerkraut, and Onions:

¼ pound double-smoked slab bacon, cut into ¼-inch dice (about 1 cup diced bacon)

2 medium-size yellow onions, peeled and coarsely chopped

1 pound Maine or Eastern potatoes, peeled and cut into 1-inch cubes

1 pound fresh sauerkraut, drained

½ cup Mosel or other dry white wine

1 teaspoon sugar

continued on next page

POACHED LOIN
OF PORK ON A
BED OF POTATOES,
SAUERKRAUT, AND
ONIONS (cont.)

Germany).
If the pork is to be moist
and tender, you must
keep the stock in which
it cooks at a gentle sim-
mer. Because of the
saltiness of the sauer-
kraut and bacon, you're
not likely to need any
additional salt.

¼ teaspoon freshly ground black pepper

Makes 6 servings

For the pork: Place the pork fat side up in a heavy saucepan just large enough to hold it comfortably with no more than a 1-inch clearance at either end of the loin. Add the broth and, if it doesn't cover the pork by about ½ inch, add a little additional broth. Set, uncovered, over moderate heat and bring to a simmer. Adjust the heat so the broth barely trembles. Cover and poach the pork 1½ to 2 hours, until an instant-register meat thermometer, inserted in the center of the loin, reaches 160° F. (Unlike many Americans, Germans do not like their pork pink. When cooked this way, 160-degree pork is supremely moist and tender.)

For the potatoes, sauerkraut, and onions: Sauté the bacon in a heavy 10-inch skillet over moderately low heat for 10 minutes, stirring often, until all the drippings cook out and only crisp brown bits remain. Using a slotted spoon, lift the bacon bits to paper toweling to drain. Add the onions to the skillet drippings and sauté 8 to 10 minutes, stirring often, until nicely browned; remove from the heat and reserve.

About 40 minutes before the pork is done, start the potatoes. Boil them in just enough water to cover in a covered, medium-size heavy saucepan over moderate heat for about 15 minutes, until tender. Drain well, return the potatoes to the heat, and shake briefly to drive off excess moisture. Mash the potatoes well – right in the pan; cover and set at the back of the stove to keep warm.

Place the sauerkraut in a second medium-size saucepan and add the wine. Bring to a boil, uncovered, over moderate heat. Adjust the heat so the mixture bubbles gently and cook 12 to 15 minutes, stirring occasionally, until almost all liquid has evaporated. Stir in the sugar and pepper, then mix the sauerkraut into the mashed potatoes along with the reserved onions and bacon bits.

POACHED LOIN OF PORK ON A BED OF POTATOES, SAUERKRAUT, AND ONIONS

To serve: Bed the sauerkraut mixture on a small heated platter, cover loosely with foil, and keep warm. Lift the pork loin to a cutting board, slice ¼ to ½ inch thick, and arrange on top of the sauerkraut mixture.

Note: Save the pork cooking liquid to use in making vegetable soup another day.

MEDALLIONS OF PORK WITH MUSHROOMS IN COGNAC-CREAM SAUCE
Schweinemedaillons in Weinbrand-Sauce

If this recipe is to have the proper Black Forest flavor, you should use Steinpilze (the meaty yellow boletus mushrooms that thrive in this part of Germany). If you can't find them, substitute white cultivated mushrooms and, to intensify the flavor, add a tablespoon of dried minced Black Forest mushrooms (which can be found in fancy food shops) or dried Polish mushrooms (now stocked by many supermarkets). Serve with Egg Spaetzle (page 230).

1 to 1¼ pounds fresh pork tenderloin, sliced ½ inch thick

5 tablespoons unsalted butter or margarine

¼ cup Cognac

¼ cup Riesling wine

½ cup rich beef broth (preferably homemade)

1 pound small Portobello (boletus) mushrooms, wiped clean and thinly sliced, or 1 pound medium-size white cultivated mushrooms, wiped clean and thinly sliced, plus 1 tablespoon dried minced Black Forest mushrooms or finely chopped dried Polish mushrooms

¼ cup minced shallots

2 cups half-and-half

Salt and freshly ground black pepper to taste

Makes 4 to 6 servings

Preheat the oven to 150° to 200° F.

Brown the pork in 2 tablespoons of the butter in a large heavy skillet over moderately high heat; remove to a shallow baking dish, cover with foil, and keep warm.

Add the Cognac and wine to the skillet and heat 1 to 2 minutes, scraping up any browned bits. Add the broth and boil, uncovered, until reduced by two thirds. Pour the Cognac mixture over the pork, re-cover, and set in the oven.

continued on next page

161

MEDALLIONS OF PORK WITH MUSHROOMS IN COGNAC-CREAM SAUCE (cont.)

Add the remaining 3 tablespoons butter to the skillet, add the mushrooms and shallots, and sauté 8 to 10 minutes, until the mushrooms are limp and their juices have evaporated. Stir the pork medallions (and all liquid) back into the skillet, add the half-and-half, and simmer, uncovered – but do not boil – over moderately low heat for 10 to 15 minutes, until the cream reduces by half and is the consistency of thin white sauce. Season to taste with salt and pepper and serve at once.

VINTNER'S PÂTÉ À LA SCHÄTZEL
Winzerpastete à la Schätzel

This main-dish pâté is actually a pork and mushroom pie with fruity wine flavor. It's the specialty of Annemarie Schätzel, whose family owns the Kapellenhof Weingut in Selzen, about an hour's drive southwest of Frankfurt.

162

Pâté:

1 pound boneless pork neck or shoulder, cut into 1-inch cubes

1 small yellow onion, peeled and moderately finely chopped

2 tablespoons minced flat-leaf parsley

1 tablespoon finely snipped fresh chives

1 tablespoon minced fresh herbs of Provence (equal parts thyme, rosemary, and bay leaf), or 1 teaspoon combined dried leaf thyme, rosemary, and bay leaf, crumbled

2 teaspoons minced fresh chervil, or 1 teaspoon dried leaf chervil, crumbled

2 teaspoons minced fresh tarragon, or 1 teaspoon dried leaf tarragon, crumbled

1½ teaspoons salt

1 teaspoon freshly ground black pepper

2 teaspoons Worcestershire sauce

1 cup dry Franconian wine or Riesling

3 tablespoons unsalted butter or margarine

1 pound medium-size mushrooms, wiped clean and thinly sliced

VINTNER'S PÂTÉ À LA
SCHÄTZEL

1 tablespoon cornstarch

⅔ cup heavy cream

Pastry:

2¾ cups sifted all-purpose flour

1 teaspoon salt

½ pound (2 sticks) minus 2 tablespoons cold unsalted butter
or margarine, cut into bits

1 extra-large egg

8 tablespoons ice water

1 extra-large egg yolk beaten with 2 teaspoons cold water
(egg glaze)

Makes 6 servings

For the pâté: Place the pork, onion, parsley, chives, all the
herbs, 1 teaspoon of the salt, ½ teaspoon of the pepper, the
Worcestershire sauce, and wine in a large ceramic bowl and
toss well. Cover and marinate 12 hours in the refrigerator.
Drain well, discarding the liquid.

Melt the butter in a heavy 12-inch skillet over moderately
high heat, add the mushrooms and remaining salt and pepper, and sauté 5 minutes, stirring occasionally. Add the pork
mixture and sauté, stirring occasionally, for 5 minutes, or
until the pork is no longer pink. Raise the heat to high and
simmer, uncovered, until almost all liquid has evaporated.

Combine the cornstarch and cream in a small bowl, add to
the skillet, and cook, stirring constantly, until the mixture
bubbles up, thickens, and clears – about 3 minutes. Remove
from the heat and reserve.

For the pastry: Combine the flour and salt in a large mixing
bowl. With a pastry blender, cut in the butter until the mixture resembles coarse meal. Whisk the egg into the ice
water. Forking the flour mixture briskly, drizzle in the egg

163

continued on next page

VINTNER'S PÂTÉ À LA
SCHÄTZEL (cont.)

mixture. As soon as mixture holds together, shape into a ball, wrap in plastic wrap, and chill 30 minutes.

Preheat the oven to 375° F.

With a lightly floured stockinette-covered rolling pin, roll two thirds of the dough on a lightly floured pastry cloth into a 14-inch circle. Fit into a 10-inch round shallow casserole that is at least 1½ inches deep. Add the filling, smoothing it into an even layer. Roll the remaining dough into an 11-inch circle and ease on top of the filling. Trim the pastry overhang (top and bottom crusts) so it is about 1 inch larger all around than the casserole, then roll top and bottom overhangs together onto the rim and crimp, making a high fluted edge. With a sharp knife, cut several decorative steam vents in the top crust, then brush the crust with the egg glaze, taking care not to clog the vents.

Bake the pâté, uncovered, for 1 to 1½ hours, until bubbly and golden brown. Serve the pâté hot with a salad of seasonal greens.

164

VINTNER'S FONDUE
Winzer Fondue

Another good recipe from Annemarie Schätzel of Selzen. It's a variation of fondue bourguignonne, in which Frau Schätzel substitutes pork for beef and mulled white wine for boiling oil. She recommends accompanying Winzer Fondue *with a Riesling Kabinett semidry (she would serve a Hahnheimer Knopf). And she wishes you "Guten Appetit!"*

1 recipe Red Currant Sauce (page 392)

1 recipe Apple-Cheese Sauce (page 391)

6 cups Riesling (not too dry)

10 bruised coriander seeds tied in cheesecloth with
    1 broken cinnamon stick and 5 bruised whole allspice

2 pounds pork or veal tenderloin, cut into ¾-inch cubes

Makes 6 servings

Prepare the sauces as directed and chill until ready to serve.

Bring the Riesling to a simmer in a large nonmetallic saucepan, transfer to a fondue pot, add the spice bag, and adjust the flame so the wine stays at a simmer.

VINTNER'S FONDUE

Arrange the pork decoratively on a large platter, put out 6 fondue forks, 6 serving plates, and 6 dinner forks. Also arrange the two sauces so everyone can reach them easily.

First, tell your guests you'll demonstrate how to cook the pork: Spear a cube of pork, thrust it into the simmering wine, and cook 2 to 3 minutes, until no longer pink in the center. Transfer the pork to your plate, dunk it in one or the other of the sauces, then eat. Let your guests follow suit, each taking turns cooking his or her meat. No more than two persons should cook their pork at the same time or the temperature of the wine will drop too low to cook the meat properly.

Note: Caution your guests to transfer their pork to their plates before eating. If they eat it directly from their fondue forks, they may burn their mouths.

RAT TAILS
Rattenschwänze

There's a reason for this recipe's less than appetizing name. It's the specialty of Hamelin, the Pied Piper town, located north of Frankfurt near Hanover. The restaurant that made the recipe famous is a historic one called Rattenfängerhaus ("The Rat Catcher's House"). Don't be put off by the polyglot list of ingredients – these Rat Tails are delicious, especially when ladled, the restaurant way, over boiled rice.
The pork will be far easier to cut into "rat tails" if you partially freeze it – an hour in the freezer should do it.

8 tablespoons (1 stick) unsalted butter or margarine

1 pound boneless pork loin, trimmed of excess fat and cut into 3½ x ⅛ x ⅛-inch strips

¼ cup Calvados or applejack

1 teaspoon salt

¼ teaspoon freshly ground black pepper

3 tablespoons all-purpose flour

1 cup rich beef broth (preferably homemade)

1 large yellow onion, peeled and coarsely chopped

½ pound medium-size mushrooms, wiped clean and thinly sliced

¼ cup Riesling or other dry white wine

¼ cup dry red wine (preferably German)

2 medium-size vine-ripe tomatoes, peeled, cored, seeded, and coarsely chopped, or 1 cup canned crushed tomatoes

continued on next page

RAT TAILS (cont.)

3 tablespoons coarsely chopped pimiento-stuffed olives

¼ cup thinly slivered pimientos

1 tablespoon Dijon mustard

1 teaspoon Worcestershire sauce

¼ teaspoon hot red pepper sauce

¼ cup ruby port

½ cup heavy cream

4 ears pickled baby corn, cut lengthwise into fine slivers

Makes 6 servings

Heat 3 tablespoons of the butter in a heavy 12-inch skillet over high heat for 1½ to 2 minutes, until it melts, foams up, then subsides. Add half the pork and stir-fry 3 minutes, until no longer pink. With a slotted spoon, lift to a large heatproof bowl and reserve. Brown the remaining pork the same way. Return the first batch of pork to the skillet, pour in the Calvados, heat for about 1 minute, then blaze with a match – easy does it! As soon as the flames subside, transfer the skillet mixture to the bowl, sprinkle with ½ teaspoon of the salt and the pepper and set aside. Keep the skillet handy.

In a small heavy saucepan, melt 2 tablespoons of the remaining butter over moderate heat. Blend in the flour to make a smooth paste. Add the broth and remaining ½ teaspoon salt; cook 3 to 5 minutes, stirring constantly, until thickened and smooth. Set the sauce off heat and reserve.

Add the final 3 tablespoons butter to the skillet and set over moderate heat. When it melts, add the onion and sauté about 5 minutes, stirring often, until limp and golden. Add the mushrooms, reduce the heat to low, and sauté 5 minutes, stirring often, until the mushrooms have released their juices and these evaporate. Add the Riesling and red wine, raise the heat to moderately high, and boil, uncovered, for 3 to 4 minutes, until the skillet liquid is reduced by two thirds. Add the tomatoes, olives, and pimientos and bring to a sim-

RAT TAILS

mer over moderate heat. Mix in the reserved sauce, mustard, Worcestershire, red pepper sauce, port, and cream. Bring to a boil over moderate heat. Adjust the heat so the mixture bubbles gently and simmer, uncovered, for 25 to 30 minutes, stirring often, until the skillet liquid is reduced by about half and is the consistency of gravy. Mix in the corn, reserved pork, and all pork liquid and simmer, uncovered, for 3 to 5 minutes, just until serving temperature. Ladle over fluffy boiled rice and serve at once.

HAM SCALOPPINE FROM POMERANIA
Pommerscher Klopfschinken

This unusual recipe was given to us by Edith Müllenbrock, an octogenarian who grew up in the village of Stolp, Pommern, near Danzig, in what is now a part of Poland. Today Frau Müllenbrock lives in Stuttgart, but counts this Pomeranian recipe among her favorites. Although you begin with scallops of Westphalian or Black Forest ham and pound them thin, these resemble grilled ham sandwiches more than they do scaloppine. The ham slices are dipped in a thick batter and quickly browned on both sides, creating the illusion, at least, of a sandwich. Frau Müllenbrock's "grilled ham

Ham:

4 (⅛-inch-thick) slices Black Forest or Westphalian ham (about ¾ pound), halved crosswise

1½ cups milk

½ cup unsifted all-purpose flour (for dredging)

Batter:

1 cup sifted unbleached, all-purpose flour

½ cup milk (use that in which you marinated the ham, above)

1 extra-large egg

1½ teaspoons sugar

½ teaspoon salt

For Frying the Ham:

4 tablespoons clarified butter

Makes 4 servings

For the ham: Using a cutlet bat or the side of a meat cleaver, pound the ham between sheets of plastic wrap to thin the slices slightly. Transfer to a 9 x 9 x 2-inch baking dish, pour in the milk, cover with plastic wrap, and marinate 2 hours in

167

continued on next page

HAM SCALOPPINE
FROM POMERANIA
(cont.)

*sandwiches," by the
way, put ours to shame.
We used the nutty Black
Forest ham when testing
this recipe because it's
widely available across
the United States. If this
scaloppine is to cook
properly, it's imperative
that you have the ham
sliced ⅛ inch thick – no
thicker, no thinner. Also
that you choose a ham
that's 7 to 8 inches
across and 3½ to 4 inches
high so the scallops
won't be skimpy.*

168

the refrigerator. Pour off the milk, reserving ½ cup of it for the batter. Pat the ham slices dry on each side and set aside for the moment. Place the dredging flour in a 9-inch pie tin and set aside.

For the batter: Place the flour in a small mixing bowl and make a well in the center. Whisk together the milk, egg, sugar, and salt in a 2-cup measure until smooth, pour into the well in the flour, then beat just until combined and reasonably smooth. The batter will be quite stiff – no matter if there are a few small lumps; overbeating the batter will toughen it. Transfer the batter to a second 9-inch pie tin so it's easier to dip the ham slices.

To fry the ham: Heat the clarified butter in a heavy 12-inch skillet over moderately high heat about 2 minutes, or until a cube of bread sizzles in it. Quickly dredge half the scallops in the flour, shaking off the excess, then dip into the batter so that each side is nicely coated. Brown the scallops in the clarified butter for 1½ to 2 minutes on each side, then lift to paper toweling to drain. Dredge, batter-dip, and brown the remaining scallops the same way. Serve as the main course of a family lunch or supper and accompany with a tartly dressed salad of crisp greens.

GARLIC HAM
Knoblauch-Schinken

*Angelika Miebs, who
comes from a town near
Frankfurt in the Hesse
region, graciously
shared this family recipe
with us. She cautions
not to use a fork when
turning or lifting the
ham because juices will
seep out of the pricks
and the ham won't be as
succulent as it should.*

5½ pounds smoked ham

1½ quarts milk

5 large garlic cloves, peeled and minced

1½ teaspoons salt

¾ teaspoon freshly ground black pepper

¾ pound unwaxed zucchini, cut into 2 x ¼ x ¼-inch strips

¾ pound unwaxed kirby cucumbers, halved, seeded, and cut into 2 x ¼ x ¼-inch strips

GARLIC HAM

*Angelika also says you
can halve the vegetable
cooking time if you like
your vegetables crisp.
The ham must marinate
overnight, so plan
accordingly.*

1 large Bermuda onion (1 pound), peeled, quartered, then each quarter sliced ¼ inch thick

1 cup crème fraîche

Makes 8 servings

Place the ham in a deep bowl just large enough to accommodate it. Combine the milk, garlic, and ½ teaspoon each of the salt and pepper and pour over the ham. Cover and marinate up to 24 hours in the refrigerator, turning the ham occasionally in the marinade.

When ready to cook the ham, preheat the oven to 350° F.

Pour off and reserve all marinade. Transfer the ham to an ungreased 13 x 9 x 2-inch baking pan, then pour the marinade into the pan to a depth of ¼ inch, letting it trickle down over the surface of the ham. Bake the ham, uncovered 1½ hours, basting every 20 minutes with ½ cup more of the marinade.

169

Remove the ham from the oven and from the pan. Add the zucchini, cucumbers, onion, and crème fraîche to the pan and sprinkle with the remaining 1 teaspoon salt and ¼ teaspoon pepper; toss well. Center the ham on top of the vegetables, cover all snugly with foil, and bake 20 minutes. Remove the foil, raise the heat to 425° F., and bake 20 minutes longer. Let the ham rest at room temperature for 15 to 20 minutes before carving to allow the juices to settle and the meat to firm up. Slice the ham thin and top each portion with some of the vegetables and pan liquid.

ALLGÄU EMMENTALER CAKE WITH HAM

Allgäuer Emmentalerkuchen mit Schinken

Erika Wedell, a Frank-furter who was born in what had been East Germany, shared this unusual recipe with us. It comes from the Allgäu region of Bavaria and is perfect for a casual lunch or supper. Erika adds seedless green grapes to the filling, but we've made them optional because we prefer the cake without them. Like quiche, this main dish is best served slightly warm or at room temper-ature – not oven-hot or refrigerator-cold.

Pastry:

1 recipe Murbteig Pastry (page 398)

Filling:

2 tablespoons unsalted butter or margarine

1 large yellow onion, peeled and moderately coarsely chopped

1 medium-size sweet green pepper, cored, seeded, and moderately coarsely chopped

½ pound mushrooms, trimmed, wiped clean, and moderately coarsely chopped

½ pound boiled ham, moderately finely chopped

½ pound well-aged Emmentaler cheese, moderately finely chopped

¼ pound small seedless green grapes, stemmed and halved lengthwise (optional)

2 tablespoons minced parsley

5 extra-large eggs

½ cup heavy cream

1 teaspoon salt

¼ teaspoon freshly ground black pepper

Makes 8 to 10 servings

For the pastry: Prepare the pastry according to the recipe, then roll and fit into an ungreased 10-inch springform pan as directed. Set aside. Preheat the oven to 350° F.

For the filling: Heat the butter in a heavy 12-inch skillet over moderately high heat for 1 minute and add the onion, green pepper, and mushrooms. Reduce the heat to moderate

ALLGÄU EMMENTALER
CAKE WITH HAM

and sauté 8 to 10 minutes, stirring often, until all juices have been released, these have evaporated, and the mixture is touched with brown. Remove from the heat and cool 10 minutes.

Place the ham and cheese, the grapes, if you like, and the parsley in a large mixing bowl. In a separate bowl, whisk the eggs with the cream, salt, and black pepper until smooth. Add the mushroom mixture to the ham mixture and toss well with your hands. Pour in the egg mixture and, using a large rubber spatula, mix thoroughly.

Pour the filling into the pastry shell and bake, uncovered, for 1 hour, until set and a toothpick inserted midway between the rim and the center comes out clean. Cool the cake in the upright pan on a wire rack for 45 minutes before serving. (If you should make the cake ahead and refrigerate it, let stand at room temperature for 30 to 40 minutes before serving.) Accompany with a crisp green salad.

RHEINPFALZ POACHED MEATBALLS
"Pälzer Fleschknepp"

"Pälzer Fleschknepp," explains Petra Schuster of the Eduard Schuster Winery in Kallstadt/Rheinpfalz, "is local dialect for Pfälzer Fleischklösse.*" English translation: "Meatballs from the Rheinpfalz." The recipe is a family favorite, delicious, yet easy to make. Frau Schuster serves these delicate meatballs with horseradish sauce and mashed potatoes or sauerkraut that has been simmered in white wine. If these meatballs are to be nice and light, you must never let the poaching broth boil.*

Meatballs:

½ pound lean beef chuck

½ pound ground veal shoulder

½ pound ground pork shoulder

1¾ cups soft, moderately fine kaiser roll crumbs (you'll need a 2-ounce roll or an equal amount of French or Italian bread), soaked in ⅓ cup water 5 minutes (do not squeeze dry)

1 extra-large egg

2 tablespoons minced flat-leaf parsley

½ teaspoon dried leaf marjoram or thyme, crumbled

¼ teaspoon ground caraway or cloves

¼ teaspoon freshly grated nutmeg

1 teaspoon salt

¼ teaspoon freshly ground black pepper

For poaching the meatballs:

7 cups rich beef broth (preferably homemade)

Accompaniment:

1 recipe Warm Horseradish Sauce (page 389)

Makes 6 servings

For the meatballs: Using your hands, mix all ingredients together well in a large bowl. Cover and refrigerate 1 hour.

For poaching the meatballs: Pour the broth into a medium-size heavy kettle (it should be 9 to 10 inches across and 4½ to 5 inches deep), set over moderately low heat, and bring slowly to a simmer. Meanwhile, pinch off bits of the meat mixture and shape into ovals about the size of large eggs.

172

RHEINPFALZ POACHED
MEATBALLS

When the broth steams, ease in half the meatballs, distributing them so they don't touch, and simmer, uncovered, for 10 minutes. Cover and simmer 10 minutes longer, or until the meatballs float. (Keep adjusting the heat as needed to keep the broth at a tremble.) Using a skimmer or slotted spoon, transfer the meatballs to a heated platter, tent with foil, and keep warm while you poach the remaining meatballs the same way.

While the second batch simmers, prepare the Warm Horse-radish Sauce.

To serve: Mound the meatballs on a platter, ladle a little of the horseradish sauce on top, if you like, and pass the rest.

Note: Strain the poaching broth, pour into a sterilized half-gallon preserving jar, screw the lid down tight, and store in the refrigerator. The broth will keep fresh for about a week and can be used for making soups, sauces, and gravies.

LEEK STEW WITH BOCKWURST

Porree-Eintopf mit Bockwurst

You can halve the amount of bockwurst in this recipe or, if you prefer, eliminate it. But if you do, the recipe will serve only 4, or at the very most, 6.

1 tablespoon vegetable oil

3 ounces double-smoked bacon, cut into ¼-inch cubes (about ¾ cup bacon cubes)

2 large carrots, peeled and cut into ½-inch cubes

1 large yellow onion, peeled and diced

¼ pound celery root, peeled and cut into ¼-inch cubes, or 1 large celery rib, diced

1 ½ pounds baking potatoes, peeled and cut into ½-inch cubes

5 cups rich beef broth (preferably homemade)

1 pound bockwurst or knockwurst

2 pounds leeks, trimmed, quartered lengthwise almost, but not quite, through the root end, washed well, then sliced ½-inch thick

continued on next page

LEEK STEW WITH
BOCKWURST (cont.)

½ teaspoon salt

¼ teaspoon freshly ground black pepper

2 tablespoons coarsely chopped flat-leaf parsley

Makes 8 servings

Heat the oil 1 minute in a medium-size heavy kettle over moderately high heat. Add the bacon and sauté 3 to 4 minutes, stirring often, until all the drippings cook out and only crisp brown bits remain. Using a slotted spoon, lift the bacon bits to paper toweling to drain. Pour all drippings from the kettle, measure out 3 tablespoons, and return to the kettle. Add the carrots, onion, and celery root, reduce the heat to moderate, and sauté about 10 minutes, stirring often, until golden brown. Add the potatoes and broth and bring to a boil. Adjust the heat so the mixture bubbles very gently, lay the bockwurst on top, cover, and simmer 40 to 45 minutes, until the carrots and potatoes are tender. Remove the bockwurst, slice ¼ inch thick, and return to the kettle. Stir in the leeks, salt, and pepper. Cover and cook 12 to 15 minutes over lowest heat, just until the leeks are crisp-tender. Taste for salt and pepper and adjust as needed. Sprinkle the parsley and reserved bacon over the stew, ladle into large bowls, and serve with chunks of crusty bread.

GAME, GAME BIRDS, AND POULTRY
Wild, Wildgeflügel, und Geflügel

ROAST SADDLE OF VENISON WITH SPICED VEGETABLE GRAVY
Gebratener Rehrücken mit würziger Gemüsesauce

The Black Forest is a rumpled piece of real estate, part woodland (filled with deer and half a dozen different kinds of mushrooms), part vineyard, part orchard (with apples and plums, but especially cherries, from which the famous kirschwasser comes). There is no shortage of good cooks either at home or in the little inns that proliferate. The ultimate tribute, surely, is the number of French who cross the Rhine to feast on Black Forest venison. It may be roasted – as it is here – or simmered into a rich brown ragout with wild mushrooms and chestnuts (see the recipe on page 178). If you cannot obtain fresh venison for this recipe, buy a frozen saddle and let it thaw before you roast it. You can use this same recipe – with great success – for a saddle of baby lamb of approximately the same weight.

Venison:

1 (5-pound) saddle of venison, trimmed of sinew and larded well (ask the butcher to grind the trimmings for you)

8 large juniper berries, very finely minced

12 large black peppercorns, pulverized

1 tablespoon kosher (coarse) salt

½ pound thinly sliced bacon

Gravy:

1 medium-size yellow onion, peeled and coarsely chopped

1 medium-size carrot, peeled and coarsely chopped

¼ cup minced celery root

3 tablespoons unsalted butter or margarine

¼ pound ground venison trimmings (see above)

¼ teaspoon dried leaf thyme, crumbled

¼ teaspoon dried leaf rosemary, crumbled

⅛ teaspoon ground cloves

⅛ teaspoon freshly ground black pepper

1 cup drained canned tomatoes

1¾ cups beef rich broth (preferably homemade)

½ cup dry red wine (preferably German)

½ cup heavy cream

Salt to taste

Makes 6 servings

ROAST SADDLE OF
VENISON WITH SPICED
VEGETABLE GRAVY
(cont.)

For the venison: Rub the venison all over with a mixture of juniper berries, peppercorns, and salt. Let stand at room temperature for 1 hour.

For the gravy: Stir-fry the onion, carrot, and celery root in 2 tablespoons of the butter in a heavy skillet over moderate heat about 10 minutes, until lightly browned. Transfer to a medium-size heavy saucepan and set aside.

Melt the remaining 1 tablespoon butter in the skillet and brown the venison trimmings 2 to 3 minutes over high heat. Add the thyme, rosemary, cloves, and pepper, reduce the heat to moderate, and allow to mellow 1 to 2 minutes. Transfer to the saucepan. Add the tomatoes, broth, and wine, reduce the heat to low, and simmer, uncovered, for 1½ hours.

To roast the venison: After the gravy has simmered about ½ hour, preheat the oven to 450°F.

Stand the venison on its rib ends in a shallow roasting pan, then drape the bacon slices on top, overlapping slightly, so that the venison is completely covered.

Roast the venison, uncovered, for 40 to 45 minutes (the meat will be rare, but this is as it should be; overcooking will toughen venison). Remove the venison from the oven and let stand 15 to 20 minutes, to allow the juices to settle.

To complete the gravy: After the saucepan mixture has simmered 1½ hours, purée it in two batches in a food processor or electric blender. Return to the pan, add the cream and salt, and simmer slowly, uncovered, for 15 minutes, until slightly thickened. *Do not allow the gravy to boil or it may curdle.*

To serve: Carve the venison into thick slices by cutting down between the ribs. Pass the gravy separately so that guests may help themselves.

CHESTNUT-WRAPPED TENDERLOIN OF VENISON
Rehfilet im Maronenmantel

In the village of Eschen-lohe within plain view of the Bavarian Alps, there's a cozy inn run with grace and style by the Josef Huber family. Each Christmas Eve, Hotel-Restaurant Tonihof lays on a holiday feast and one recent Weihnachtsmenu featured a glorious filet of venison cloaked in chestnut pastry. This is our adaptation of the Tonihof recipe, and very like the original it is, too.

If the venison is to cook in the short time allot-ted, it must be at room temperature before you wrap the chestnut pastry around it. Serve with Egg Spaetzle (page 230) and Braised Red Cabbage with Onions and Apples in Red Wine Sauce (page 250), or, if you prefer, with buttered, steamed broccoli or Brussels sprouts.

1 (1¼- to 1½-pound) tenderloin of venison, measuring 11 to 12 inches long and 2½ to 3 inches in diameter

1 (15½-ounce) can unsweetened whole chestnuts, drained and rinsed

3 to 4 tablespoons all-purpose flour

1½ teaspoons salt

½ teaspoon freshly ground black pepper

Sauce:

2 tablespoons unsalted butter or margarine

½ cup finely minced shallots

2 tablespoons all-purpose flour

1½ cups rich beef broth (preferably homemade)

½ teaspoon dried leaf thyme, crumbled

¼ teaspoon salt

⅛ teaspoon freshly ground black pepper

½ cup coarsely chopped canned unsweetened chestnuts

Makes 4 servings

Preheat the oven to 400°F.

Pat the venison dry and set aside.

Purée the chestnuts in a food processor fitted with the metal chopping blade. Add 3 tablespoons of the flour and pulse 15 to 20 seconds, just until the mixture holds together. If it is too wet, add the additional 1 tablespoon flour, a bit at a time. Add ½ teaspoon of the salt and ¼ teaspoon of the pepper and pulse briefly to combine. Once again, pat the venison dry, then sprinkle with the remaining salt and pepper.

Pat the chestnut mixture all around the venison in a smooth

continued on next page

177

layer about ¼ inch thick. Carefully ease the venison into an oiled shallow roasting pan and roast, uncovered, for 15 to 18 minutes. (The venison will be very rare, but if you cook it further you risk burning the chestnut pastry and toughening the meat.) Remove the venison from the oven and let stand 10 minutes.

For the sauce: Melt the butter in a medium-size heavy saucepan over moderate heat. Add the shallots and sauté, stirring occasionally, for 2 minutes, until translucent. Blend in the flour and cook and stir over moderately low heat for 2 minutes, until golden. Add the broth, thyme, salt, and pepper and cook 10 minutes, stirring often. Strain the sauce into a small heavy saucepan, add the chestnuts, taste for salt and pepper, and adjust as needed. Cover and keep warm.

To Serve: Slice the venison ¾ inch thick, divide the slices among 4 heated dinner plates, puddle some of the sauce around each portion, and serve.

178

RAGOUT OF VENISON WITH CHESTNUTS AND MUSHROOMS
Rehgulasch mit Maronen und Pilzen

German cooks would use fresh wild Black Forest mushrooms for this recipe – Pfifferlinge *(chanterelles),* Steinpilze *(yellow boletus),* Speise-morcheln *(morels), or* Waldegerlinge *(brown field mushrooms) – or more likely a combination of them. We've substituted the more widely available white cultivated mushrooms, then added dried chanterelles and a dried mixture of Black Forest mushrooms for extra flavor. The dried mushrooms are available*

3 pounds boned venison shoulder, cut into 1-inch cubes

5 tablespoons unsalted butter or margarine

5 tablespoons vegetable oil

1 tablespoon minced shallots or scallions

3 medium-size yellow onions, peeled and coarsely chopped

1 pound medium-size mushrooms, wiped clean and thinly sliced

½ teaspoon dried leaf thyme, crumbled

¼ teaspoon dried leaf rosemary, crumbled

¼ teaspoon freshly grated nutmeg

¼ pound slab bacon, cut into ½-inch cubes (about 1 cup bacon cubes), blanched 15 minutes in boiling water to cover, then drained well

RAGOUT OF VENISON WITH CHESTNUTS AND MUSHROOMS

in most specialty food stores (even in some supermarkets), and produce a nicely flavored ragout. This stew freezes splendidly, so if there are any leftovers, pop them into the freezer.
You can substitute lean beef chuck, if you like, for the venison, or pork or lamb shoulder. The frozen chestnuts called for can be found in most specialty food shops. Serve with boiled new potatoes, egg noodles, or Egg Spaetzle (page 230) and a salad of crisp greens or, if you prefer, steamed broccoli, green beans, or asparagus.

1¾ cups rich beef broth (preferably homemade)

2 cups dry red wine (preferably German)

1 (¼-ounce) package dried minced chanterelle mushrooms

1 (¼-ounce) package dried minced Black Forest mushrooms

½ pound frozen, shelled, and peeled Italian chestnuts

1 cup whole cranberry sauce

1 cup heavy cream

Salt and freshly ground black pepper to taste

Makes 8 to 10 servings

Brown one fourth of the venison cubes in 1 tablespoon each of the butter and oil in a large heavy kettle over high heat; transfer to a large bowl. Brown the remaining venison in three batches, adding more butter and oil as needed; transfer to the bowl.

Stir-fry the shallots and onions in 1 tablespoon more of the butter and oil over moderately high heat for 8 to 10 minutes, until lightly browned; add to the bowl with the venison. Stir-fry the mushrooms in 1 to 2 tablespoons more of the butter and oil about 10 minutes, until lightly browned.

Return the venison, shallots, and onions to the kettle; add the thyme, rosemary, and nutmeg and mellow 3 to 4 minutes over low heat. Add the bacon, broth, wine, and dried mushrooms (both kinds), cover, and simmer slowly 2 to 3 hours. Add the chestnuts and cranberry sauce, re-cover, and simmer 1 to 2 hours longer, or until the venison is fork-tender. The cooking time will vary considerably depending upon the age of the animal and how well exercised it was (the older, more active animal will be tougher than the young one). Stir in the cream, salt, and pepper and simmer, uncovered, about ½ hour, or until the flavors are well blended.

179

JUGGED RABBIT OR HARE
Hasenragout

The rethinking of old German recipes begins these days with the "white brigade," young chefs who have traveled the world, then returned home to take up the tasting spoons. Walter Carle, executive chef of the Hotel Gravenbruch Kempinski Frankfurt, is just such an innovator. His culinary dues include hitches in both the United Arab Emirates and the United States. He also served as chef de partie with the Holland-America Line. Before baking his Jugged Rabbit, Carle seals the pot with a rope of sourdough (by all means try it, if you should have enough sourdough on hand to coil around the rim of the casserole before clapping on the lid).

180

3 tablespoons unsalted butter or margarine

1 (2½-pound) rabbit, cleaned, dressed, disjointed, and patted dry on paper toweling

¾ teaspoon salt

½ teaspoon freshly ground black pepper

2 large yellow onions, peeled, halved, then each half thinly sliced

2 medium-size carrots, peeled and thinly sliced

½ medium-size celery root, peeled and thinly sliced, or 1 medium-size celery rib, thinly sliced

1 large leek, trimmed, washed well, halved lengthwise, then each half thinly sliced

2 medium-size vine-ripe tomatoes, peeled, cored, seeded, and coarsely chopped, or 1 cup canned crushed tomatoes

2 tablespoons tomato paste

4 cups (approximately) dry red wine (preferably German)

1⅔ cups coarsely crumbled dark pumpernickel bread

2 tablespoons red currant jelly

2 whole cloves

6 juniper berries

2 medium-size whole bay leaves

Makes 4 servings

Preheat the oven to 375° F.

Melt the butter in a large Dutch oven over moderately high heat. Quickly season the pieces of rabbit with salt and pepper, using ¼ teaspoon of each. Brown the rabbit on all sides in the melted butter; this will take about 6 minutes. As the

JUGGED RABBIT
OR HARE

rabbit pieces brown, lift to a large heatproof bowl and reserve. Add the onions, carrots, celery root, leek, tomatoes, and tomato paste to the Dutch oven. Reduce the heat to moderate and cook 2 minutes, stirring often. Return the rabbit to the Dutch oven together with any juices that have accumulated in the bottom of the bowl. Pour in enough wine to cover the rabbit, add the pumpernickel, and bring to a boil over moderate heat. Mix in the jelly, then add the cloves, juniper berries, bay leaves, and remaining salt and pepper.

Cover the Dutch oven with foil, set the lid in place, and transfer to the oven. Bake 1½ hours, until the rabbit is fork-tender. Taste the gravy for salt and pepper and adjust as needed. Remove the bay leaves and serve at once with peeled, boiled potatoes.

HARE BRAISED IN RED WINE
Hasenpfeffer

Karl Uwe Woggon, a German railroad official who once worked in the United States, makes this recipe with both rabbit and hare – rabbit if he's in the United States, hare if he's in Germany, where it's readily available. We've used farm-raised rabbit with equally delicious results. Serve with Potato Dumplings II (page 222), Egg Spaetzle (page 230), or peeled, boiled potatoes.

3 cups dry red wine (preferably German)

½ cup red wine vinegar

1 large Spanish onion, peeled and coarsely chopped

¾ teaspoon salt

¾ teaspoon freshly ground black pepper

8 juniper berries

6 large whole bay leaves

4 whole cloves

1 (2½-pound) rabbit, cleaned, dressed, quartered, and patted dry on paper toweling

½ cup unsifted all-purpose flour

2 tablespoons unsalted butter or margarine

1 tablespoon vegetable oil

Makes 4 servings

continued on next page

HARE BRAISED IN
RED WINE (cont.)

Place the wine, vinegar, onion, ½ teaspoon each of the salt and pepper, the juniper berries, bay leaves, and cloves in a large nonmetallic bowl. Add the rabbit, turn well in the marinade, cover, and marinate in the refrigerator for 36 to 48 hours, turning occasionally.

Remove the rabbit from the marinade and reserve the marinade. Pat the rabbit dry on paper toweling and dredge in the flour, shaking off the excess. Sprinkle with the remaining salt and pepper.

Heat the butter and oil in a heavy medium-size Dutch oven over moderate heat for 1 minute. Add the rabbit and brown well on all sides – 5 to 7 minutes. Add the marinade, bring to a boil, and adjust the heat so the mixture bubbles gently. Cover and simmer 1½ hours, until the rabbit is tender.

Transfer the rabbit to a heated deep platter, cover loosely with foil, and keep warm. Strain the cooking liquid into a medium-size heavy saucepan and boil, uncovered, over moderately high heat until reduced by half, about 10 minutes. Pour the sauce over the rabbit and serve.

FRISIAN-STYLE DUCKS WITH SAVOY CABBAGE

Friesische Ente in Wirsing

The Frisians, a string of North Sea islands off the west coast of Schleswig-Holstein (Germany's northernmost state), are a nesting ground for a variety of marine ducks. And these are the birds that local cooks would be most likely to use in this hearty one-dish dinner. Farm-raised ducks work equally well, although they lack the flavor of wild ducks. You'd be wise to sweet-talk your butcher into

2 (4- to 5-pound) oven-ready ducks

1 teaspoon salt

½ teaspoon freshly ground black pepper

1 tablespoon unsalted butter or margarine

2 cups Riesling or other dry white wine

Stock:

The bones and trimmings from the ducks

1 large yellow onion, peeled and quartered

1 large celery rib, thinly sliced (include leaves)

1 small carrot, peeled and thinly sliced

FRISIAN-STYLE DUCKS WITH SAVOY CABBAGE

boning the ducks for you. Ask him to save the bones and chop them into large chunks. You'll need them for stock.

8 large flat-leaf parsley sprigs

2 small fresh thyme sprigs, or 1 teaspoon dried leaf thyme, crumbled

4 whole cloves

2 large whole bay leaves

Cabbage and Sautéed Vegetables:

2 small heads (about 4 pounds) young savoy cabbage

2 tablespoons unsalted butter or margarine

2 large yellow onions, peeled and coarsely chopped

1 cup finely diced, peeled celery root (about 1 small root)

1 small leek, trimmed, washed well, halved lengthwise, then each half thinly sliced

1 small carrot, peeled and finely diced

Makes 6 servings

183

For the ducks: Remove the legs from the ducks, separate into thighs and drumsticks, and bone each piece. It's easy: With a sharp boning or paring knife, cut the length of the drumstick or thigh, right to the bone, then peel away the flesh. That's all there is to it. Also remove the breasts from the ducks and halve each crosswise. Chop the carcasses and leg and thigh bones into largish pieces and save, along with all trimmings, for the stock. Rinse the pieces of duck well, pat dry, cover, and refrigerate while you prepare the stock.

For the stock: Place the duck bones and trimmings, onion, celery, carrot, parsley, thyme, cloves, and bay leaves in a large heavy kettle and add just enough cold water to cover. Bring to a boil over high heat, adjust the heat so the water bubbles very gently, then simmer slowly, uncovered, skimming off the froth as it gathers, for 3 hours. Strain the stock through a large fine sieve into a large heavy saucepan, discarding the solids. Skim the stock of all fat, then boil,

continued on next page

FRISIAN-STYLE DUCKS
WITH SAVOY
CABBAGE (cont.)

uncovered, over moderately high heat until reduced to 2 cups – this will take 8 to 10 minutes.

For the cabbage and sautéed vegetables: Halve each cabbage, core, then separate into leaves. Blanch the cabbage in two batches in a large kettle of lightly salted boiling water for 3 to 5 minutes, just until limp. Drain the cabbage well and pat dry on paper toweling. Melt the butter in a large heavy kettle over moderately low heat. Add the onions, celery root, leek, and carrot and turn in the butter just enough to coat. Cover and cook 5 minutes, stirring once or twice. Transfer the vegetables to a bowl.

To finish the ducks: Sprinkle the pieces of duck with ¼ teaspoon of the salt and ⅛ teaspoon of the pepper. Melt the 1 tablespoon butter in the kettle over moderately high heat and, as soon as it foams up and subsides, add the duck and brown 2 minutes on each side, until golden.

Transfer the duck to a large plate and pour the drippings from the kettle. Arrange one third of the cabbage in the bottom of the kettle, top with half the sautéed vegetables, and sprinkle with half the remaining salt and pepper. Add another third of the cabbage and the remaining sautéed vegetables; sprinkle with the remaining salt and pepper. Top with the last of the cabbage and arrange the pieces of duck on top.

Pour in the reduced duck stock and the wine and bring to a boil over moderately high heat. Adjust the heat so the liquid bubbles gently, cover, and simmer 1 to 1¼ hours, until the duck and cabbage are tender. Serve at once – directly from the kettle if it is pretty enough to take to the table. Otherwise, bed the cabbage and sautéed vegetables on a large deep platter and arrange the duck pieces artfully on top.

ROAST DUCK WITH APPLE AND HAM STUFFING

Gebratene Ente mit Apfel-Schinken-Füllung

Stuffing duck with ham may seem like overkill, but do try this northern German recipe before passing judgment. Accompany with boiled new potatoes or Egg Spaetzle (page 230).

1 (4½-pound) oven-ready duck

3 tablespoons unsalted butter or margarine

3 medium-size McIntosh or Granny Smith apples, peeled, cored, and sliced ¼ inch thick

½ pound boiled ham, very finely diced

¼ cup fine dry bread crumbs

¾ teaspoon salt

½ teaspoon freshly ground black pepper

3 tablespoons all-purpose flour

2 cups rich beef broth (preferably homemade)

¼ cup crème fraîche or heavy cream

½ teaspoon Worcestershire sauce

Makes 4 servings

Preheat the oven to 450° F.

Pat the duck dry, then prick all over with the point of a small, sharp knife.

Melt the butter in a heavy 9-inch nonstick skillet over moderate heat, add the apples and ham, and sauté 5 minutes, stirring occasionally, until the apples are golden. Transfer to a large bowl, mix in the bread crumbs, and ¼ teaspoon each of the salt and pepper, then cool to room temperature.

Spoon the stuffing loosely into the body cavity of the duck, then sew the vent shut. Sprinkle the outside of the duck with the remaining salt and pepper. Arrange the duck breast side up on a rack in a large shallow roasting pan and roast, uncovered, for 30 minutes, until golden brown. Reduce the oven temperature to 350° F. and roast 1 hour longer, or until the duck juices run clear when you pierce the leg with a fork.

185

continued on next page

ROAST DUCK WITH APPLE AND HAM STUFFING (cont.)

Transfer the duck to a heated platter, cover loosely with foil, and let stand while you prepare the gravy.

Heat 2 tablespoons of the duck drippings in a small heavy saucepan over moderately low heat for 1 minute. Blend in the flour and cook 3 minutes, whisking constantly, until pale golden. Add the broth and cook, again whisking constantly, for 3 to 5 minutes, until thickened and smooth. Raise the heat to moderately high and boil, uncovered, about 5 minutes longer, stirring occasionally, until the gravy thickens a bit. Smooth in the crème fraîche and Worcestershire, then taste for salt and pepper and adjust as needed. Strain the gravy into a gravy boat and serve with the duck.

BRAISED DUCK WITH TURNIPS

Geschmorte Ente mit Weissen Rübchen

First the duck roasts at high heat until nicely browned, then it simmers – whole – in a rich wine broth in the company of turnips and onions.

1 (4- to 4½-pound) oven-ready duck

½ teaspoon salt

¼ teaspoon freshly ground black pepper

5 tablespoons unsalted butter or margarine

2 tablespoons all-purpose flour

1 cup dry red wine (preferably a German red such as Spätburgunder, Portugieser, or Trollinger)

2 cups rich beef broth (preferably homemade)

2 tablespoons tomato sauce

1 tablespoon sweet Hungarian rose paprika

10 ounces small white onions, no more than 1 inch in diameter, peeled

2 pounds medium-size turnips, peeled and cut into eighths

1 teaspoon sugar

¼ cup sour cream, at room temperature

Makes 4 servings

**BRAISED DUCK
WITH TURNIPS**

Preheat the oven to 450° F.

Pat the duck dry, then prick all over with the point of a small, sharp knife. Sprinkle the duck with half the salt and pepper, arrange breast side up on a rack in a large shallow roasting pan, and roast uncovered, 45 minutes, until richly brown, basting occasionally with the pan juices.

Melt 2 tablespoons of the butter in a large heavy flameproof casserole (preferably one pretty enough to carry to the table) over moderately low heat. Blend in the flour and cook and stir 2 minutes, until pale golden. Blend in the wine, broth, tomato paste, and paprika and cook 3 minutes, stirring constantly, until thickened and smooth. Add the duck to the casserole, spoon some of the sauce over it, and adjust the heat so the sauce bubbles gently. Cover and simmer 30 minutes, basting the duck occasionally with the sauce.

Meanwhile, melt the remaining 3 tablespoons butter in a heavy 12-inch skillet over moderate heat. Add the onions and sauté 5 minutes, stirring often, until golden brown. Add the turnips, remaining salt and pepper, and the sugar and sauté 5 minutes, stirring occasionally, until lightly caramelized.

Add the onions and turnips to the casserole with the duck, cover, and simmer 10 to 15 minutes, until the duck is tender. Smooth in the sour cream, warm 1 to 2 minutes, then carry the casserole to the table and serve. The duck will be tender enough to carve right in the casserole.

187

ROAST GOOSE WITH GINGER, CORIANDER, AND APPLES

Gebratene Gans mit Ingwer, Koriander, und Äpfeln

Germans rarely stuff goose with anything but fruit and herbs or spices. This modern recipe calls for apples, chopped fresh ginger, and coriander seeds. The best accompaniments are classic: red cabbage and potato dumplings.

1 (8- to 10-pound) oven-ready goose

12 small McIntosh apples (about 2¼ pounds)

6 cinnamon sticks

½ cup seedless raisins

2 tablespoons coarsely chopped fresh ginger

6 whole cloves

2 teaspoons juniper berries

½ teaspoon coriander seeds

6 tablespoons apple schnapps or Calvados

1 cup Riesling or other dry white wine

2 cups cold water

2 tablespoons sugar

1½ teaspoons salt

1 teaspoon dried leaf marjoram, crumbled

¾ teaspoon freshly ground black pepper

1 cup hot water

Gravy:

2 cups rich chicken broth (preferably homemade)

3 tablespoons roast goose drippings

1 small yellow onion, peeled and minced

3 tablespoons all-purpose flour

½ teaspoon salt

⅛ teaspoon freshly ground black pepper

Makes 6 servings

ROAST GOOSE WITH GINGER, CORIANDER, AND APPLES

Preheat the oven to 325° F. Remove the neck and giblets from the goose and save to use in a stock. Remove as much fat from the body cavities of the goose as possible and also trim the tail of excess fat. Either discard the fat or save to render (see note). Pat the goose dry and set aside.

Peel and core 6 of the apples but leave them whole. Put a cinnamon stick in the hole of each apple, then drop several raisins into the holes, using ¼ cup of them in all. Sprinkle the ginger, cloves, juniper berries, and coriander seeds over the bottom of a medium-size heavy saucepan. Arrange the apples on top, then add the schnapps, wine, cold water, sugar, and ¼ teaspoon of the salt. Set over moderate heat and bring to a boil. Adjust the heat so the liquid bubbles gently, cover, and simmer 6 to 8 minutes, just until the apples are tender.

Cool the apples in the liquid, then drain them, reserving the liquid, spices, and juniper berries. Transfer the apples to a bowl, pour the cooking liquid over them, and set aside. Sprinkle the reserved spices and juniper berries over the bottom of a large shallow roasting pan fitted with a rack and set aside.

Peel, core, and dice the remaining 6 apples, letting them fall into a medium-size bowl. Add the remaining ¼ cup raisins, ½ teaspoon of the remaining salt, the marjoram, and ¼ teaspoon of the pepper and toss well to mix. Stuff the neck cavity of the goose loosely with a little of the mixture and enclose by skewering the neck skin flat against the back of the bird. Stuff the body cavity loosely with the remaining apple mixture, then skewer shut with poultry pins and tightly lace with twine. Fold the wings flat against the back of the bird.

Prick the goose well with a skewer and sprinkle with the remaining ¾ teaspoon salt and ½ teaspoon pepper. Arrange the goose breast side down on the rack in the roasting pan, pour the hot water over the goose, and roast, uncovered, 1½ hours, basting with the reserved apple cooking liquid from time to time.

continued on next page

189

ROAST GOOSE WITH
GINGER, CORIANDER,
AND APPLES (cont.)

Turn the goose breast side up. Pour 1 cup of the apple cooking liquid over it and continue roasting, uncovered, 1 to 1½ hours, again basting with the pan juices, until an instant-register meat thermometer, inserted in the fleshy part of a thigh, registers 175° F. Transfer the goose to a heated platter, cover loosely with foil, and let stand while you prepare the gravy. Spoon off and reserve 3 tablespoons of the fatty pan drippings to use in making the gravy, then discard all remaining pan juices.

For the gravy: Add 1 cup of the broth to the roasting pan and deglaze by heating over moderate heat for 3 minutes, scraping up all browned bits; reserve the deglazing liquid.

Heat the goose drippings in a medium-size saucepan over moderate heat for 1 minute. Add the onion and sauté 5 minutes, stirring occasionally. Blend in the flour and cook and stir 2 minutes, until pale golden. Add the deglazing liquid and the remaining 1 cup broth and simmer, uncovered, for 10 minutes, stirring often. Season with the salt and pepper, cover with a round of wax paper, and keep warm.

Quickly remove the skewers and trussing strings from the goose and surround with the poached stuffed apples. Pour the gravy into a gravy boat and pass separately.

Note: If you can't bear to discard the goose fat, render it, then use in place of butter or oil when browning meat, poultry, or potatoes. Here's how: Pull all fat from the body cavities of the goose and cut into ¾-inch squares. Place in a medium-size heavy skillet, add enough cold water to cover, and bring to a boil over moderate heat. Adjust the heat so the water bubbles gently, cover, and simmer 20 to 25 minutes. Remove the skillet lid and continue simmering over lowest heat until all water evaporates and only the goose fat remains. Strain the fat through a fine sieve, pour into a small crock or ramekin, cover with foil or plastic wrap, and store in the refrigerator.

· CHRISTMAS GOOSE

Weihnachtsgans

The centerpiece of the traditional German Christmas dinner is goose, plump of breast and crisp of skin. The stuffing, usually a mixture of herbs, fruits, and vegetables, is for flavor only and discarded before the goose is served. This particularly festive roast goose comes from the cozy little Post-Hotel Partenkirchen in the Bavarian Alps. It is presented in the inn's beamed-ceiling dining rooms on a platter wreathed with Baked Wine-Glazed Apples Stuffed with Marzipan, Cranberries, and Raisins.

1 (10- to 12-pound) oven-ready goose

1 teaspoon salt

½ teaspoon freshly ground black pepper

4 large thyme sprigs

4 large flat-leaf parsley sprigs

3 medium-size tart apples, quartered but not peeled or cored

2 medium-size yellow onions, peeled and quartered

2 celery ribs, cut into 2-inch chunks

5 cups cold water

6 tablespoons all-purpose flour

1 cup (approximately) rich beef broth (preferably homemade)

1 recipe Baked Wine-Glazed Apples Stuffed with Marzipan, Cranberries, and Raisins (page 395)

Makes 8 servings

Preheat the oven to 500° F.

Remove the neck and giblets from the goose and set aside. Remove as much fat from the body cavities of the goose as possible, also trim the tail of excess fat, then either discard or save to render (see note, page 190). Pat the goose dry, then rub inside and out with the salt and pepper. Place the thyme, parsley, apples, onions, and celery in the body cavity, skewer shut with poultry pins, and tightly lace with twine. Fold the wings flat against the back of the bird and skewer the neck skin to the back.

Place the goose breast side down in a lightly oiled large shallow roasting pan. Prick the skin well all over with a fork, then roast the goose, uncovered, for 30 minutes. Reduce the

191

continued on next page

CHRISTMAS GOOSE
(cont.)

oven temperature to 400° F and roast, uncovered, 30 minutes longer. Pour off all pan drippings and reserve. Protecting your hands with several thicknesses of paper toweling, very carefully turn the goose breast side up and roast, uncovered, for 1 hour.

Bring the neck, giblets, and 3 cups of the water to a simmer in an uncovered medium-size saucepan over moderately low heat. Simmer, uncovered, for 10 minutes. Remove the liver, place in a small bowl, cover, and refrigerate until ready to use. Reduce the heat to low and continue simmering the neck and remaining giblets, uncovered, about 1½ hours, until all are tender. Drain, reserving 1½ cups of the giblet stock. Discard the neck and add the heart and gizzard to the bowl with the liver; keep refrigerated. Also skim as much fat from the giblet stock as possible.

Again pour all drippings from the roasting pan and reserve. Prick the goose well again with a fork, pour the remaining 2 cups water into the roasting pan, and continue roasting the goose, uncovered, for 1 to 1½ hours, or until a leg moves easily in its hip socket and the juices run clear when a thigh is pierced. Once again, pour off all pan drippings and reserve. Remove the goose from the oven, tent loosely with foil, and let stand for 30 minutes, to allow the meat to firm up and the juices to settle.

To prepare the gravy, chop the giblets very fine and set aside. Skim 6 tablespoons of the fat from the pan drippings and heat for 1 minute in a heavy 10-inch skillet over low heat. Blend in the flour and cook and stir for 3 minutes. Degrease the remaining drippings and add to the giblet broth; measure and add enough beef broth to total 3 cups. Add to the skillet, raise the heat to moderately high, and cook, whisking constantly, until thickened and smooth. Mix in the giblets, taste for salt and pepper, and season as needed. Reduce the heat under the gravy to its lowest point and allow the gravy to mellow, uncovered, while you attend to the goose.

CHRISTMAS GOOSE

Remove the poultry pins and strings from the goose and discard the stuffing. Set the goose on a large heated platter and garnish with the wine-glazed apples. Pour the gravy into a heated sauceboat and pass separately.

ROAST PHEASANT WITH RED CURRANT GRAVY

Gebratener Fasan mit Johannisbeersauce

Germans prefer pork to poultry, but will never refuse roast pheasant if it's good and succulent. This Bavarian recipe explains why.

2 (1½-pound) oven-ready pheasants, quartered

2 tablespoons freshly squeezed lemon, lime, or orange juice

¾ teaspoon salt

¼ teaspoon freshly ground black pepper

2 ounces double-smoked slab bacon, cut into ¼-inch cubes (about ½ cup)

3 small leeks, trimmed, washed well, and thinly sliced

2 medium-size carrots, peeled and coarsely chopped

½ cup coarsely chopped celery root, or 1 large celery rib, coarsely chopped

⅓ cup coarsely chopped parsley root, or 1 medium-size parsnip, peeled and coarsely chopped

1 medium-size tart apple, peeled, cored, and coarsely chopped

1 large whole bay leaf

½ teaspoon dried leaf thyme, crumbled

½ teaspoon dried leaf marjoram, crumbled

6 peppercorns

4 whole allspice berries

2 cups rich beef broth (preferably homemade)

½ cup dry red wine (preferably German)

1 tablespoon all-purpose flour

2 teaspoons Dijon mustard

continued on next page

193

ROAST PHEASANT
WITH RED CURRANT
GRAVY (cont.)

2 tablespoons red currant jelly or jellied cranberry sauce

1 cup crème fraîche or heavy cream

Makes 4 to 6 servings

Preheat the oven to 450°F. Rub the pheasant quarters all over with the lemon juice, salt, and pepper and set aside.

Sauté the bacon in a heavy 12-inch skillet over moderately low heat, stirring often, for 5 minutes, until all the drippings cook out and only crisp brown bits remain. Add the leeks, carrots, celery and parsley root, the apple, bay leaf, thyme, marjoram, peppercorns, and allspice. Raise the heat to moderate and sauté 10 to 12 minutes, stirring often, until all vegetables are tender. Add the broth and wine and simmer, uncovered, for 10 minutes.

Transfer the skillet mixture to a lightly greased 13 x 9 x 2-inch baking pan. Quickly dust the skin side of each piece of pheasant with flour, then arrange floured side up on the bed of vegetables. Bake, uncovered, about 25 minutes, until the pheasant is golden brown and its juices run clear (to test, pierce a piece of pheasant with a sharp-tined fork). Transfer the pheasant to a heated platter, tent with foil, and keep warm while you prepare the gravy.

Strain the pan juices into a heavy 10-inch skillet, pressing the vegetables to extract as much liquid as possible. Boil, uncovered, over moderate heat until only a thick glaze remains on the skillet bottom; this will take 12 to 15 minutes. Quickly blend in the mustard and jelly, then the crème fraîche. Boil, uncovered, about 5 minutes, stirring often, until the consistency of a thin gravy. Drizzle some of the gravy over the pheasant and pass the rest.

194

CORNISH HENS WITH SAUERKRAUT

Hühnchen auf Sauerkraut

The chickens of choice in Germany, particularly the Black Forest, are infants no bigger than the poussins *of France. They aren't widely available here, so we've substituted Cornish hens. The recipe produces plenty of meaty pan drippings to ladle over mashed potatoes – the traditional accompaniment.*

2 tablespoons unsalted butter or margarine

2 medium-size yellow onions, peeled and coarsely chopped

1 pound fresh sauerkraut, drained and rinsed if extra salty

5 juniper berries

¼ cup heavy cream

¾ cup Riesling or other dry white German wine (not too tart)

2 tablespoons bacon drippings

2 Rock Cornish hens (about 1¼ pounds each), halved
(freeze the giblets to use another time)

½ teaspoon salt

½ teaspoon freshly ground black pepper

8 small fresh thyme sprigs

1 cup rich beef broth (preferably homemade)

4 thin slices Black Forest ham or boiled ham

Makes 4 servings

Melt the butter in a heavy 12-inch skillet over moderate heat. Add the onions and sauté about 5 minutes until limp and touched with brown, stirring often. Mix in the sauerkraut, juniper berries, cream, and wine. Bring to a simmer, then turn the heat down very low, cover, and simmer 1 hour, stirring often and adding a little water if the mixture threatens to cook dry.

Preheat the oven to 350°F.

Heat the bacon drippings in a second heavy 12-inch skillet over moderately high heat for 1 minute. Place the hens skin side down in the drippings and brown 4 minutes, then turn and brown the flip sides 1 to 2 minutes. Sprinkle the undersides of the hens with ¼ teaspoon of the salt and ⅛ teaspoon

195

continued on next page

CORNISH HENS WITH
SAUERKRAUT (cont.)

of the pepper. Arrange the hens skin side up in an ungreased 13 x 9 x 2-inch baking pan, placing them so they don't touch one another or the sides of the pan. Sprinkle with the remaining salt and another ⅛ teaspoon pepper. Tuck 2 thyme sprigs underneath each hen, pour the skillet drippings evenly over all, and roast, uncovered, for 30 minutes, basting with ½ cup of the broth at halftime. Drape a slice of ham over each hen, baste with the remaining broth, and roast, uncovered, for 10 minutes longer. Turn the ham, baste the ham and birds well with the pan drippings, and roast 10 minutes longer. Baste once again with pan drippings.

Bed the sauerkraut on a heated large, deep platter and arrange the hens on top, discarding the thyme sprigs. Once again turn the ham slices so they cup nicely around the hens. Spoon 2 tablespoons pan drippings over each hen and serve. Pour the remaining drippings into a small sauceboat and pass separately.

FISH AND SHELLFISH
Fisch und Schalentiere

FILLETS OF SALMON AND TURBOT WITH MELON BALLS
Lachs- und Steinbutt-Filets mit Melonenbällchen

Pairing fish with melon balls was the inspiration of Bernhard Schuster, not yet 35, the innovative chef at Düsseldorf's Hotel Breidenbacher Hof. To finish the plate, Schuster adds a scoop of rice reddened with beet juice and a garnish of blanched snow peas. It's a combination that exemplifies his culinary creed: Fresh products at the right time, of the appropriate size and composition, nutritionally prepared and presented in an attractive manner. "This," Schuster says, "is what I call my honest cuisine."

4 tablespoons (½ stick) unsalted butter or margarine

4 skinned salmon fillets (2½ ounces each)

4 skinned turbot fillets (2½ ounces each)

½ teaspoon salt

½ cup small (½- to 1-inch) honeydew melon balls

½ cup small (½- to 1-inch) cantaloupe or Crenshaw melon balls

½ cup small (½- to 1-inch) watermelon balls

1 teaspoon minced fresh tarragon, or ½ teaspoon dried leaf tarragon, crumbled

1 recipe Red Rice (page 237)

Makes 4 servings

Melt 3 tablespoons of the butter in a heavy 12-inch skillet over moderately high heat. As soon as it foams and subsides, add the salmon and turbot, reduce the heat to moderately low, and sauté 2 minutes on each side. Sprinkle the fish with salt, transfer to a heated platter, cover with foil, and keep warm.

Add the remaining butter to the skillet and, when it melts, add all the melon balls and sauté about 2 minutes, stirring gently, until heated through. Sprinkle the melon balls with the tarragon. Arrange the fish on a heated platter, spoon the melon balls on top, and accompany with Red Rice.

TERRINE OF SOLE AND SALMON WITH LOBSTER AND SORREL SAUCE

Terrine von Seezunge und Wildlachs mit Hummer und Sauerampfersauce

In the Rhine River town of Assmannshausen west of Wiesbaden, there's a popular restaurant called Krone. Its chef, Herbert Pucher, created this terrine for Georg Breuer, a Rheingau producer of fine dry and medium-dry Rieslings. Breuer published the terrine recipe in a booklet designed to show how well its wines pair with today's lighter German cooking. We include it here with Breuer's permission.

Terrine:

4 large fillets of sole (about 1 pound)

½ teaspoon salt

¼ teaspoon freshly ground black pepper

10 ounces salmon fillets, cut into 2-inch squares

1 extra-large egg

½ cup heavy cream

¼ pound cooked lobster meat, cut into small cubes

3 tablespoons finely snipped fresh dill

1 tablespoon kirschwasser

¼ cup heavy cream, stiffly whipped

Sorrel Sauce:

1 cup sour cream

1½ cups loosely packed sorrel leaves

½ cup finely snipped fresh dill

1 tablespoon freshly squeezed lemon juice

2 teaspoons Dijon mustard

½ teaspoon salt

¼ teaspoon freshly ground black pepper

Makes 6 to 8 servings

For the terrine: Butter a 9 x 5 x 3-inch loaf pan, line the bottom with wax paper, and butter the paper. Flatten the fillets of sole by patting lightly with your hand, then sprinkle with half the salt and pepper. Line the bottom and sides of the pan with the sole, cutting and piecing the fillets as needed.

Purée the salmon with the egg and remaining salt and pepper by pulsing 30 seconds in a food processor fitted with

TERRINE OF SOLE
AND SALMON WITH
LOBSTER AND SORREL
SAUCE

the metal chopping blade. Scrape down the sides of the workbowl, and, with the motor running, pour the heavy cream down the feed tube. Purée 30 seconds longer, scraping the bowl at halftime. Transfer the salmon mixture to a bowl, cover with plastic wrap, and refrigerate 30 minutes.

Preheat the oven to 350° F.

Add the lobster, dill, and kirschwasser to the chilled terrine mixture and stir well to combine. Fold in the whipped cream and pour the mixture into the prepared pan. Rap gently on the counter to expel any air bubbles, cover with a double thickness of buttered aluminum foil, buttered side down, and transfer to a shallow baking pan. Pour enough hot water into the pan to come halfway up the sides of the loaf pan and bake 35 to 45 minutes, until a skewer inserted in the center of the terrine comes out clean.

For the sorrel sauce: Blend all ingredients for 20 seconds in a food processor fitted with the metal chopping blade. Transfer to a serving bowl, cover, and chill until ready to serve.

To serve: Cool the terrine in the upright pan on a wire rack for 10 minutes. Loosen carefully around the edge and invert on a small heated platter. Peel off the wax paper. Slice the terrine about ¾ inch thick and pass the sauce separately.

HAMBURG PAN-FISH

Hamburger Pfannenfisch

The farther north you travel in Germany, the nearer you approach the North Sea and Baltic, the more popular fish becomes. At the Atlantic Hotel Kempinski in Hamburg, Chef Claus Köchling capitalizes upon the local catch, but few of his recipes are more popular than this homey pan roast of turbot, onion, and potatoes accompanied by a zippy sauce.

Fish:

1¾ pounds small new potatoes (about 2 inches in diameter)

1 large yellow onion, peeled and thinly sliced

1 teaspoon salt

¼ teaspoon freshly ground black pepper

3 tablespoons unsalted butter or margarine

1 pound skinned turbot or flounder fillets

1 tablespoon finely snipped fresh chives

Sauce:

2 tablespoons unsalted butter or margarine

3 tablespoons finely chopped shallots

2 tablespoons all-purpose flour

1½ cups milk

½ cup half-and-half

3 tablespoons Dijon mustard blended with 2 tablespoons Riesling or other dry white wine

2 teaspoons freshly squeezed lemon juice

¼ teaspoon salt

¼ teaspoon freshly ground black pepper

Makes 4 to 6 servings

For the fish: Preheat the oven to 400° F. Lightly butter a 13 x 9 x 2-inch baking pan and set aside.

Cook the potatoes in boiling water to cover in a large heavy saucepan over high heat for 10 to 15 minutes, until firm-tender. Drain the potatoes, cool until easy to handle, peel, slice ¼ inch thick, and arrange over the bottom of the

HAMBURG PAN-FISH

prepared baking pan. Top with the onion slices and sprinkle with half the salt and pepper. Dot with the butter and roast, uncovered, stirring once or twice, about 1 hour, until the potatoes and onions are golden brown.

For the sauce: Melt the butter in a medium-size saucepan over moderate heat, add the shallots, and sauté 3 minutes, stirring occasionally, until translucent. Blend in the flour and cook and stir 2 minutes. Whisk in the milk and half-and-half, reduce the heat to moderately low, and cook about 5 minutes, stirring constantly, until thickened and smooth. Whisk in the mustard mixture, lemon juice, salt, and pepper. Taste for lemon juice and add a bit more, if needed. Cover the sauce with a buttered round of wax paper and keep warm.

To finish the fish: Cut the turbot into ¾-inch cubes. Add to the browned potatoes and onion, toss lightly, return to the oven, and roast, uncovered, for 5 to 8 minutes, until the fish just flakes at the touch of a fork. Sprinkle with the remaining salt and pepper, toss lightly, then mound on a large heated platter. Sprinkle with the chives and serve. Pass the sauce separately.

PLAICE WITH BACON IN THE STYLE OF FINKENWERDER
Finkenwerder Scholle mit Speck

Finkenwerder is a small fish-loving town near Hamburg in northern Germany. And plaice is a lean, white, sweet-meated fish – a European first cousin to flounder, which we've substituted here. In Finkenwerder, this recipe would be served with boiled potatoes and cucumber salad (we suggest Cucumber Salad with Mustard Dressing, page 288).
Because there's plenty of salty bacon in this recipe, you won't need any salt.

4 (5- to 6-ounce) flounder or sole fillets

⅓ cup freshly squeezed lemon juice

3 tablespoons all-purpose flour

¼ pound double-smoked slab bacon, cut into ¼-inch cubes (about 1 cup)

1 medium-size lemon, quartered

4 small parsley sprigs

Makes 4 servings

Rinse the flounder fillets, pat dry on paper toweling, then lay flat in a shallow baking dish large enough to hold them in a single layer. Sprinkle the lemon juice evenly over the fish, turn, and sprinkle the flip sides. Place the flour in a 9-inch pie tin and set aside.

Sauté the bacon in a heavy 12-inch skillet over moderate heat, stirring often, until most of the drippings cook out and the bacon is translucent and lightly browned – about 3 minutes. Push the bacon to the edge of the skillet, quickly dredge the fish fillets on both sides in the flour mixture, add to the skillet, and brown 2 minutes. Carefully turn the fish and brown the flip sides 3 minutes. Using a slotted spatula, lift the fish to paper toweling to drain, then transfer to a heated platter. With a skimmer or slotted spoon, lift the bacon cubes from the skillet, letting the excess drippings drain off, and sprinkle on top of the fish. Discard the bacon drippings. Garnish the fish with lemon and parsley and serve.

PLAICE BAKED IN FOIL WITH TOMATOES AND ONIONS

Schollen in Alufolie mit Tomaten und Zwiebeln

Frau Margot von Glasenapp of Pinneberg, near Hamburg, sent us this marvelous modern recipe. Like the one that precedes, it can be made with flounder or sole if plaice isn't available. They all belong to a huge family of flatfish. In the Hamburg fish market, old-timers like to tell this fish story. The flounder, it seems, always considered itself superior to the herring. One day, when it couldn't stand the smelly little fish any longer, it haughtily asked a fellow flatfish, "Is the herring also a fish?" And as punishment for its arrogance, the flounder's face was twisted so that both eyes landed on the same side and its mouth was screwed into a crooked grin. And this, Hamburg fishermen will tell you, is why the flounder remains lopsided to this day.

4 (5- to 6-ounce) flounder or sole fillets, each halved lengthwise so that you have 8 pieces of fish

4 teaspoons freshly squeezed lemon juice

1 teaspoon salt

½ teaspoon freshly ground black pepper

2 medium-size, firm-ripe tomatoes, sliced ⅜ inch thick but not peeled or cored

⅔ cup finely chopped flat-leaf parsley

2 tablespoons unsalted butter or margarine, cut into bits

6 medium-size yellow onions, peeled and coarsely chopped

¼ cup rich beef broth (preferably homemade)

Makes 4 servings

Preheat the oven to 400° F.

Pat the fish dry and sprinkle each side with the lemon juice, salt, and pepper. Arrange 4 pieces of fish on a work surface, top each with tomato slices, dividing the total amount evenly, then sprinkle with ¼ cup of the parsley. Dot with the butter, then lay the remaining 4 pieces of fish on top of the tomato, forming 4 fish stacks.

Cut heavy-duty aluminum foil into 4 (9 x 12-inch) rectangles and butter the dull side of each. Working with one piece of foil at a time, arrange about ½ cup of the chopped onions lengthwise down the center in a little mound, then sprinkle the onions with 1½ teaspoons of the broth. Carefully center a fish stack on top of the onions. Top each fish stack with ½ cup more of the chopped onions and sprinkle with 1½ teaspoons more of the broth. Wrap the foil around the fish, twisting the ends to seal.

Arrange the packets of fish on an ungreased baking sheet

continued on next page

203

**PLAICE BAKED IN FOIL
WITH TOMATOES AND
ONIONS** (cont.)

and bake 20 minutes, until the fish flakes easily. Puncture each foil packet before removing from the oven, then very carefully slit lengthwise with a sharp knife, partially open the foil, cupping the edge of it around the fish stack so the juices remain inside. Place a heated plate upside down over the opening in each fish packet, then invert quickly so the fish, vegetables, and juices tumble out onto the plate. Remove the foil, sprinkle the fish stacks with the remaining parsley, and serve. Accompany with boiled new potatoes.

HADDOCK IN MUSTARD SAUCE
Angelschellfisch in Senfsauce

A superb fish recipe from the north of Germany given to us by Monika Dorman of the Hamburg North American Representation Office in New York.

4 pounds haddock, cleaned and filleted (trimmings, heads, tails, and bones reserved)

1 large yellow onion, peeled and stuck with 2 cloves

2 large whole bay leaves

12 peppercorns

1 large leek, trimmed, washed, and thickly sliced

⅔ cup diced celery root, or 1 medium-size celery rib, thickly sliced

8 flat-leaf parsley sprigs

4 cups cold water

1 cup milk

¼ teaspoon salt

¼ teaspoon freshly ground black pepper

½ cup heavy cream

3 tablespoons Dijon mustard

¼ teaspoon sugar

2 tablespoons sour cream

4 tablespoons (½ stick) unsalted butter, cut into bits, at room temperature

HADDOCK IN
MUSTARD SAUCE

2 tablespoons minced flat-leaf parsley

Makes 4 to 6 servings

Place the haddock trimmings, heads, tails, and bones in a large heavy saucepan, along with the onion, bay leaves, peppercorns, leek, celery root, parsley sprigs, and water. Set, uncovered, over moderately high heat and bring to a boil. Adjust the heat so the mixture bubbles gently, then simmer, uncovered, for 20 minutes, skimming off the froth occasionally. Strain the stock through a large cheesecloth-lined sieve set over a large heatproof bowl; discard all solids.

Combine the strained stock and the milk in a skillet large enough to hold the haddock fillets in a single layer. Set, uncovered, over moderate heat and bring to a simmer. Add the haddock, salt, and pepper and simmer, uncovered, for 5 to 7 minutes, until the fish just flakes at the touch of a fork. With a spatula, carefully remove the haddock to a heated platter, cover loosely with foil, and keep warm.

Boil the poaching liquid, uncovered, over moderately high heat about 10 minutes, until reduced to 1 cup. Smooth in the heavy cream and boil, uncovered, for 2 to 3 minutes, until slightly reduced. Blend in the mustard, sugar, and sour cream and bring the sauce back to a simmer. Whisk in the butter, bit by bit. Pour any fish juices that have accumulated on the platter into the skillet, heat briefly, then strain the sauce over the fish. Sprinkle with the minced parsley and serve.

PIKE WITH RAISIN SAUCE

Hecht mit Rosinensauce

There's something almost Moorish about this combination of fish, fruit, and nuts, yet the recipe is wholly German. A Hamburg specialty, at that.

1 whole pike (about 2 pounds), cleaned, dressed, and cut into 2-inch chunks but not boned or skinned

2 cups white wine vinegar

1 cup cold water

½ teaspoon salt

2 tablespoons unsalted butter or margarine

1 tablespoon all-purpose flour

⅔ cup Riesling or other dry white wine

⅔ cup fish stock (preferably homemade), or ⅓ cup each bottled clam juice and cold water

2 tablespoons dried currants

¼ cup seedless raisins

3 tablespoons finely ground blanched almonds

½ teaspoon sugar

1 extra-large egg yolk

¼ cup heavy cream

⅛ teaspoon freshly grated nutmeg

1 to 2 teaspoons freshly squeezed lemon juice (or to taste)

Makes 4 servings

Preheat the oven to 150° to 200° F.

Place the pike in a medium-size heavy saucepan, add the vinegar, water, and ¼ teaspoon of the salt. Bring the fish to a simmer over moderately low heat, then cover and poach 4 to 5 minutes, just until it flakes easily. Transfer the fish to a heated platter, cover loosely with foil, and set in the warm oven. Discard the cooking liquid.

Melt the butter in the same saucepan over moderately low

PIKE WITH RAISIN
SAUCE

heat, blend in the flour, and cook and stir 2 minutes, just until pale golden. Mix in the wine and stock and cook 3 to 5 minutes, stirring constantly, until thickened and smooth. Add the currants, raisins, almonds, sugar, and remaining salt and simmer, uncovered, for 5 minutes, stirring occasionally.

Meanwhile, whisk the egg yolk with the cream in a small bowl. Blend a little of the hot sauce into the yolk mixture, then stir back into the pan and cook and stir 2 minutes. Mix in the nutmeg, season to taste with lemon juice, then bring just to serving temperature, stirring often. Ladle a little of the hot sauce over the pike and pass the rest. Serve at once.

FILLETS OF PIKE-PERCH BADEN STYLE
Zanderfilets nach Badischer Art

The American fish that most resembles Zander *(the pike-perch of Germany) is the walleye, and like its Old-World cousin, it is best when taken from crystalline rivers or deep cold lakes. In Germany* Zander *may not have the cachet of trout or salmon, but it is popular. This quick and easy way to prepare it comes courtesy of Harald Schmitt, the up-and-coming young chef at the Orangerie in Wiesbaden's Hotel Nassauer Hof.*

1¼ pounds skinned fillets of pike-perch, walleye, ocean perch, or other lean white fish such as flounder

4 teaspoons freshly squeezed lemon juice

½ teaspoon salt

¼ teaspoon freshly ground black pepper

4 tablespoons (½ stick) unsalted butter or margarine

3 medium-size mushrooms, wiped clean and finely diced

2 large shallots, peeled and minced

½ cup Riesling or other dry white wine

⅙ cup heavy cream

½ cup crème fraîche

½ small garlic clove, peeled and crushed

1 tablespoon finely snipped fresh chives

1 tablespoon minced fresh chervil, or 1½ teaspoons each minced fresh tarragon and flat-leaf parsley

Makes 4 servings

continued on next page

207

FILLETS OF PIKE-PERCH
BADEN STYLE (cont.)

Preheat the oven to 400° F.

Cut the fish into 4 equal portions. Sprinkle both sides of each portion using 3 teaspoons of the lemon juice and half the salt and pepper.

Melt 2 tablespoons of the butter in a 12-inch gratin pan over moderate heat. Add the mushrooms and shallots and sauté 5 minutes, stirring often, until the mushrooms have released their juices and these have evaporated. Mix in the Riesling and heavy cream and arrange the fish on top in a single layer. Quickly bring the pan liquid to a simmer. Transfer the pan to the oven and bake the fish, uncovered, 10 minutes, until it just flakes at the touch of a fork.

Arrange the fish on a heated platter, cover loosely with foil, and keep warm. Return the pan to moderate heat and boil the pan liquid, uncovered, over moderately high heat about 2 minutes, until lightly thickened. Carefully add the remaining 2 tablespoons butter, bit by bit, stirring all the while. Blend in the crème fraîche, garlic, and remaining 1 teaspoon lemon juice, salt, and pepper. Heat and stir 1 minute longer, but do not allow to boil or the crème fraîche may curdle. Ladle the sauce over the fish. Quickly mix the chives and chervil and sprinkle evenly over all. Serve at once.

FISH DUMPLINGS IN GREEN SAUCE
Fisch Klösschen in würziger Kräutersauce

This is the way Berliners like their fish dumplings. Two things make them unique: The dumplings are baked, not poached, and the green sauce contains sage. This recipe comes to us courtesy of Berlin's Bristol Hotel Kempinski.

Fish Dumplings:

¾ pound pike fillets

5 ounces perch or other lean white fish fillets (preferably freshwater fish)

2 extra-large eggs

¼ cup soft white bread crumbs

½ teaspoon salt

¼ teaspoon white pepper

FISH DUMPLINGS IN
GREEN SAUCE

⅛ teaspoon freshly grated nutmeg

1 cup heavy cream

Green Sauce:

3 tablespoons unsalted butter or margarine

2 large shallots, peeled and minced

2 tablespoons soft white bread crumbs

1 cup rich fish stock or rich chicken broth
   (preferably homemade)

2 tablespoons finely chopped spinach

2 tablespoons finely chopped sorrel

2 tablespoons minced flat-leaf parsley

2 tablespoons finely snipped fresh dill

2 tablespoons finely snipped fresh garlic chives or chives

1 teaspoon finely minced fresh sage, or ¼ teaspoon rubbed
   sage

1 cup sour cream, at room temperature

¼ teaspoon salt

⅛ teaspoon freshly ground black pepper

Makes 6 servings

For the dumplings: Process the pike and perch for 30 seconds in a food processor fitted with the metal chopping blade, or until smooth and thick. Place the workbowl in the refrigerator for 30 minutes. Return the workbowl to the processor, add the eggs, bread crumbs, salt, pepper, and nutmeg and pulse 10 seconds to combine. With the motor running, drizzle the cream down the feed tube, then process 20 seconds until fine and smooth. Transfer the mixture to a bowl, cover with plastic wrap, and chill 30 minutes.

Preheat the oven to 150° to 200° F. Butter a 13 x 9 x 2-inch baking dish.

continued on next page

FISH DUMPLINGS IN
GREEN SAUCE (cont.)

Wet one hand and with the other take up a rounded table-spoon of the chilled fish mixture and shape it into an egg shape on your wet hand. Set in the prepared baking dish. Repeat until all dumplings are shaped, arranging in the baking dish so they neither touch one another nor the walls of the dish (there will be 18 to 20 dumplings in all). Cover the dumplings with foil and bake 30 to 40 minutes, until firm.

For the green sauce: Melt the butter in a medium-size heavy saucepan over moderate heat. Add the shallots, sauté for 3 minutes, until golden. Add the bread crumbs and stock and simmer 10 minutes, stirring occasionally. Add the spinach, sorrel, parsley, dill, garlic chives, and sage and simmer 5 minutes, stirring occasionally. Smooth in the sour cream, salt, and pepper and simmer 5 minutes longer, stirring occasionally, until lightly thickened. *Do not allow the sauce to boil or it may curdle.*

To serve: Transfer the dumplings to a heated deep platter and smother with the sauce.

210

COLD TROUT IN SEKT DRESSING
Forelle (kalt) in Sektsauce

Sekt (the German "champagne") imparts zing to the dressing of this lovely light dish, which can be served as an appetizer, salad, or main dish. There will be enough for six appetizers or salads and four entrées.

Trout:

2 (1-pound) trout, cleaned, dressed, and boned (have your fishmonger do this messy job for you)

2 quarts cold water

1 small yellow onion, peeled and stuck with 4 cloves

1 tablespoon red wine vinegar

1 teaspoon salt

Sekt Dressing:

¼ cup heavy cream, whipped

2 tablespoons sour cream

1 tablespoon mayonnaise (preferably homemade)

1 tablespoon ketchup

COLD TROUT IN SEKT
DRESSING

2 tablespoons freshly squeezed lemon juice

3 tablespoons freshly squeezed orange juice

2 teaspoons prepared horseradish

⅓ cup finely snipped fresh dill

⅓ cup Sekt (dry German champagne)

3 tablespoons Cognac or brandy

¼ teaspoon Hungarian sweet rose paprika

¼ teaspoon salt

Pinch of white pepper

Garnishes:

1 medium-size head Boston lettuce, or 1 large head radicchio,
  trimmed, washed, and patted dry on paper toweling

5 small dill fronds

8 to 12 small ripe cherry tomatoes (optional)

Makes 4 to 6 servings

For the trout: Place the trout side by side on a poaching rack
– either the rack of a fish poacher or one that will accommodate the fish and fit into a large shallow kettle. Bring the
water, onion, vinegar, and salt to a simmer over moderate
heat in the poacher or kettle. Lower the rack of fish into the
liquid and, as soon as it returns to a gentle simmer, adjust
the burner heat to keep it merely trembling. Poach the trout,
uncovered, for 7 to 8 minutes, just until it flakes at the touch
of a fork. Lift the trout from the kettle, plunge into ice water,
and leave for 3 to 4 minutes to quick-chill. Then remove
from the water, drain well, and set aside.

For the dressing: Whisk all ingredients together briskly to
combine. Taste for salt and add more, if needed.

To serve: Cut the trout into chunks about 1 inch thick and
arrange on a small platter on which you have already

continued on next page

COLD TROUT IN SEKT
DRESSING (cont.)

arranged perfect leaves of lettuce. Spoon the dressing evenly over the trout and sprig with dill. If you'd like to add a little extra color, add a few clusters of cherry tomatoes. Serve with a crisp, dry Sekt and buttered toast points.

COD WITH SAUERKRAUT AND TARRAGON SAUCE
Kabeljaufilet mit Sauerkraut und Estragonsauce

By borrowing the breading and browning technique from Wiener Schnitzel and by teaming two of Germany's mainstays – cod and sauerkraut – Chef Heinz Wehmann of Landhaus Scherrer in Hamburg has come up with something altogether unique. What follows is our adaptation of the restaurant recipe. Use only top-quality eggs from a reliable source for this recipe; the mayonnaise-like sauce may not reach the temperature (or stay at that temperature long enough) to kill salmonella bacteria, an ongoing problem in the American poultry industry.

Cod:

5 tablespoons unsalted butter or margarine

4 slices bacon, snipped crosswise into 1/4-inch strips

1 medium-size yellow onion, peeled and coarsely chopped

1 pound fresh sauerkraut, drained well

½ cup Sekt (dry German champagne) or Riesling

¼ teaspoon freshly ground black pepper

1½ pounds skinned, ¾-inch-thick cod or halibut fillets, cut into 4 pieces of equal size

¼ teaspoon salt

2 tablespoons freshly squeezed lemon juice

½ cup unsifted all-purpose flour

2 extra-large eggs, lightly beaten

1 cup fine dry white bread crumbs

2 tablespoons corn or vegetable oil

Tarragon Sauce:

2 tablespoons tarragon vinegar

2 extra-large egg yolks, well beaten

⅔ cup melted unsalted butter or margarine

¼ teaspoon salt

1 tablespoon minced fresh tarragon, or 1 teaspoon dried leaf tarragon, crumbled

Makes 4 servings

COD WITH
SAUERKRAUT
AND TARRAGON
SAUCE

For the cod: Melt 2 tablespoons of the butter in a heavy 12-inch skillet over moderate heat. Add the bacon and sauté 2 minutes, stirring often. Add the onion and sauté 2 minutes, until limp. Add the sauerkraut, reduce the heat to moderately low, and sauté 5 minutes, turning often until nicely glazed. Add the Sekt, reduce the heat to low, and simmer, uncovered, for 10 minutes. Season with the pepper, cover, remove from the heat, and set at the back of the stove to keep warm. Sprinkle both sides of each cod fillet with the salt and lemon juice, then dredge in the flour, shaking off any excess. Dip the dredged fillets into the beaten eggs, then into the bread crumbs, again shaking off the excess. Heat the remaining 3 tablespoons butter and the oil in a large heavy skillet over moderately high heat for 1½ minutes. Add the cod, reduce the heat to moderately low, and brown 4 to 5 minutes on each side; drain on paper toweling and keep warm.

For the tarragon sauce: Boil the vinegar, uncovered, in a ½ cup metal measure over moderate heat until reduced to ½ tablespoon; this will take about 2 minutes. Whisk the hot vinegar into the egg yolks, then add the melted butter drop by drop, whisking vigorously until the mixture begins to thicken. Continue adding the butter in a thin stream, whisking all the while. Mix in the salt and tarragon. Set the bowl of sauce in a large pan of simmering water – off the heat – and keep warm, whisking occasionally, while you arrange the platter.

To serve: Arrange the sauerkraut mixture on a heated platter, top with the cod, then a generous ladling of hot sauce. Pass any remaining sauce separately. Accompany with boiled potatoes.

213

GREEN EEL

Grüner Aal

No seafood is more beloved in Hamburg than eel, and no method of preparing it is more popular than this one. If fresh eel isn't available, substitute a firm oily fish such as mackerel. If eel is available, ask your fishmonger to skin it for you (it's not as neat as peeling a potato).

2 pounds eel, skinned and rinsed well, or 1¼ pounds mackerel fillets

2 tablespoons freshly squeezed lemon juice

1 cup Riesling or other dry white wine

2 cups water

1 large yellow onion, peeled and thinly sliced

6 juniper berries

6 peppercorns

8 large flat-leaf parsley sprigs

½ teaspoon salt

2 (2-inch) strips lemon zest

Green Sauce:

Cooking liquid from cooking the eel

3 tablespoons unsalted butter or margarine

3 tablespoons all-purpose flour

½ cup heavy cream

1 extra-large egg yolk

¼ cup minced fresh green herbs, such as dill, chervil, flat-leaf parsley, sorrel, watercress, or better yet, a mixture of several of them

Makes 4 servings

Preheat the oven to 150° to 200° F. Cut the eel crosswise into 1-inch chunks and sprinkle with the lemon juice. Place in a medium-size heavy saucepan, add the wine, water, onion, juniper berries, peppercorns, parsley, salt, and lemon zest. Cover and simmer slowly over moderately low heat for 15 minutes, until the eel flakes easily. Dump the saucepan

GREEN EEL

mixture into a large fine sieve set over a large heatproof bowl. Transfer the eel to a large heatproof plate, cover loosely with foil, and set in the warm oven. Discard the solids left behind in the sieve but reserve the cooking liquid.

For the green sauce: Pour the reserved cooking liquid into a medium-size heavy saucepan and boil, uncovered, over moderately high heat for about 5 minutes, until reduced to 1¼ cups. Melt the butter in a second medium-size saucepan over moderately low heat, blend in the flour, and cook and stir 2 minutes, until golden. Add the reduced cooking liquid and ¼ cup of the cream and cook 3 to 5 minutes, stirring constantly, until thickened and smooth. In a small bowl, whisk the remaining ¼ cup cream with the egg yolk. Blend in ½ cup of the hot sauce, then stir back into the saucepan. Cook and stir over moderately low heat for 3 minutes – just until steaming. Mix in the green herbs, pour the sauce over the eel, and serve at once.

POTATOES, DUMPLINGS, SPAETZLE, RICE, AND OTHER SIDE DISHES
Kartoffeln, Klösse (Knödel), Spätzle, Reis, und andere Beilagen

POTATOES WITH ROSEMARY
Rosmarinkartoffeln

Astonishing as it may seem, Margot von Glasenapp of Pinneberg, near Hamburg, who sent us this easy recipe, says she would prepare this amount for one person. "Don't worry if this sounds like a bit much for one person," she wrote. "I would even suggest that you use a few more potatoes because they will shrink somewhat as they cook, also because you will eat more than you think." Frau von Glasenapp uses the newest potatoes she can find, preferably tiny ones no bigger than Brussels sprouts that can be cooked whole, in their skins. If you must use larger new potatoes, peel and cut them into cubes about "the size of one thumb joint." Frau von Glasenapp recommends serving these potatoes with a hearty piece of meat – a nice slice of roast beef, for example, or a good, thick schnitzel – and tall glasses of beer.

1 tablespoon corn oil

2 ounces double-smoked slab bacon, cut into small dice (about ½ cup dice)

1 pound tiny new potatoes, scrubbed (they should be no bigger than Brussels sprouts)

½ teaspoon dried leaf rosemary, finely crumbled

¼ teaspoon freshly ground black pepper

3 medium-size yellow onions, peeled and coarsely chopped

2 large garlic cloves, peeled and finely minced

½ teaspoon salt

Makes 4 servings

Preheat the oven to 400° F.

Heat the oil for 1 minute over moderate heat in a heavy 12-inch skillet with a heatproof handle. Add the bacon, reduce the heat to moderately low, and sauté about 5 minutes, stirring often, until translucent. Add the potatoes, rosemary, and pepper and toss well to mix. Cover snugly with aluminum foil, transfer to the oven, and bake 30 minutes. Remove from the oven, discard the foil cover, and add the onions, garlic, and salt. Stir well, return to the oven, and bake, uncovered, for 15 minutes, stirring every 5 minutes, until the onions are golden brown. Serve at once.

GLAZED POTATOES
Glasierte Kartoffeln

Here's another of Margot von Glasenapp's easy but unusual potato recipes. She says it's important that you use very new, very small potatoes — never bigger than golf balls — so they can be glazed and served whole. Frau von Glasenapp likes to serve these potatoes with pork, but they're also integral to one of her particular favorites, Kale with Chestnuts and Glazed Potatoes (page 264). Frau von Glasenapp neither salts nor peppers these potatoes and we like them her way.

2 pounds small new potatoes, scrubbed

4 tablespoons (½ stick) unsalted butter or margarine

2 tablespoons sugar

Makes 4 to 6 servings

Cook the potatoes in lightly salted boiling water in a covered, large heavy saucepan over moderate heat for 20 to 25 minutes, just until firm-tender. Drain well, cool until easy to handle, then peel.

Melt the butter in a heavy 12-inch skillet over moderate heat. As soon as it bubbles up and subsides, add the potatoes and shake over moderate heat about 1 minute, until the butter coats them well. Sprinkle the sugar evenly over the potatoes, reduce the heat to moderately low, and cook the potatoes, uncovered, for 10 to 12 minutes, shaking the skillet often, until nicely glazed and honey-gold. Serve at once.

217

STUFFED POTATOES FROM THE MOSELLE
Moselländische gefüllte Kartoffeln

A strictly regional dish that's eaten only in the Mosel region of Germany. It comes from Christa Jüngling of the Paulinshof Winery, headquartered in the Moselle River town of Kesten. Although it may seem a bit tricky to make, it isn't. All you need is a bit of patience – plus the right potatoes. Choose Maine or Eastern potatoes that won't disintegrate during long, slow baking in a bath of Mosel wine. Also uniformly shaped ones that are as big and round as navel oranges (each potato should weigh about ½ pound).

Potatoes:

8 large Maine or Eastern potatoes of equal size, peeled (about 4 pounds)

Stuffing:

1 tablespoon unsalted butter or margarine

1 large yellow onion, peeled and moderately finely chopped

¼ cup minced flat-leaf parsley

1 pound ground round, ground again with 6 ounces smoked bacon (ask the butcher to do this)

2 ounces liverwurst

¾ teaspoon salt

¼ teaspoon freshly ground black pepper

1 extra-large egg, lightly beaten

For Cooking the Stuffed Potatoes:

3 tablespoons unsalted butter or margarine

1½ cups Mosel or other dry white wine

Makes 6 to 8 servings

For the potatoes: Using a melon baller, and starting from the top of each potato, very carefully scoop out the center, leaving walls and bottoms about ¼ inch thick. Submerge the potato shells in cold water until ready to stuff. Save the scooped-out centers for mashed potatoes another day.

For the stuffing: Melt the butter in a heavy 10-inch skillet over moderate heat and sauté the onion and parsley for 1 minute. Turn the heat to its lowest point, cover the skillet, and steam the mixture 5 minutes; cool 10 minutes. Using your hands, combine the beef mixture, liverwurst, salt, and pepper. Add the cooled onion mixture and work in with your hands also.

STUFFED POTATOES
FROM THE MOSELLE

Lightly brush the insides and rims of the potato shells with the beaten egg, then combine the remaining egg with the meat mixture. Pack into the potato shells, rounding the mixture up a bit on top and pressing it firmly onto the rims of the potato shells so it won't separate from them during baking.

To cook the potatoes: Preheat the oven to 300° F. Melt the butter in a heavy 12-inch skillet over moderately high heat, then let it foam up and subside. Carefully place the potatoes in the skillet, stuffing side down, and brown 2 minutes. Using a small spatula, gently turn each potato, stuffing side up, and brown 2 minutes longer.

Arrange the potatoes in a lightly greased shallow roasting pan just large enough to accommodate them without touching one another or the pan sides. Pour the wine evenly over the potatoes and cover snugly with foil. Bake about 1½ hours, until the potatoes are tender.

To serve: Arrange the potatoes on a deep platter and spoon some of the pan liquid on top. Pour a bit of the remaining liquid into a gravy boat and pass separately, if you like.

219

PURÉE OF POTATOES AND APPLES

Kartoffel-Apfelpüree

This inspired combination comes from Alfons Schuhbeck, chef-owner of Kurhaus Stüberl, a delightful Bavarian inn at Waging am See between Munich and the Austrian border. Serve with ham, roast pork, or poultry, even with roast venison.

1 pound baking potatoes, well scrubbed

2 tablespoons unsalted butter or margarine

1 pound Granny Smith or other apples (not too sweet), peeled, cored, and thinly sliced

1 tablespoon freshly squeezed lemon juice

1 teaspoon sugar

¼ teaspoon freshly grated nutmeg

1 teaspoon salt

¼ teaspoon freshly ground black pepper

⅓ cup hot milk

¼ cup heavy cream, sour cream, or crème fraîche

Makes 4 servings

Cook the potatoes in their skins in a covered, large heavy saucepan of lightly salted boiling water over moderate heat for about 1 hour, until a fork easily pierces them.

Melt the butter in a heavy 12-inch skillet over moderate heat. Add the apples, lemon juice, sugar, and nutmeg and toss well to mix. Sauté 5 minutes, stirring often, until the apples are golden. Reduce the heat to its lowest point, cover, and cook 10 minutes. Transfer the skillet mixture to a food processor fitted with the metal chopping blade, add the salt and pepper, and process 30 seconds, scraping down the sides of the workbowl at halftime. Transfer to a large heat-proof bowl and set aside.

As soon as the potatoes are tender, peel, chunk, and add to the apple mixture. Pour in the milk and cream and, using a potato masher, mash until smooth and fluffy. Serve at once.

Note: Do not attempt to mash the potatoes in the food processor; they will turn to paste.

POTATO DUMPLINGS I
Kartoffelklösse

In the Rhineland and north of Germany, these dumplings are the classic accompaniment to sauerbraten. They can be mixed and shaped ahead – but don't hold them in the refrigerator for more than four hours or the dumplings will absorb moisture and be difficult to handle. When cooking the dumplings, boil them for exactly 3 minutes after *the cooking water returns to a boil, otherwise they may disintegrate.*

5 medium-size baking potatoes, scrubbed and boiled until tender

3 slices lean bacon, snipped crosswise into ¼-inch strips

1½ teaspoons salt

3 extra-large eggs

1 cup plus 2 tablespoons sifted all-purpose flour

½ cup farina

2 slices stale firm-textured white bread, cut into ¼-inch cubes

¼ teaspoon freshly grated nutmeg

Pinch of ground cinnamon

2 tablespoons minced parsley

Makes 8 servings

Drain the potatoes very dry, cool until easy to handle, then peel and rice or mash. Spread the potatoes on a clean, dry dish towel and allow to stand, uncovered, for 20 minutes (to keep the dumplings from going soggy, the towel must absorb as much potato moisture as possible).

Meanwhile, brown the bacon in a small heavy skillet over moderate heat about 5 minutes, until crisp; drain off all drippings, then crumble the bacon as fine as possible. Spread on a piece of paper toweling and set aside.

Empty the potatoes into a large bowl and make a well in the center. Add the salt and the eggs, breaking them one by one into the well. Sift the flour on top, then add the reserved bacon and all remaining ingredients and knead with your hands until uniformly mixed. Shape into balls just slightly larger than golf balls and arrange in a single layer on a wax-paper-lined tray or baking sheet. Refrigerate, uncovered,

continued on next page

221

POTATO DUMPLINGS I
(cont.)

until ready to cook (but for no longer than 4 hours).

Preheat the oven to 150° to 200° F.

Cook the dumplings in two batches in a large covered kettle of lightly salted *very gently* boiling water for 3 minutes exactly (start timing after the dumplings have been added and the water returns to the boil). Using a slotted spoon, lift the cooked dumplings from the water and arrange in a single layer on a large heatproof plate. Place a large colander upside down over the dumplings, then set in the oven to keep warm while you cook the remaining dumplings. Serve hot.

POTATO DUMPLINGS II
Gekochte Kartoffelknödel

Unlike the previous recipe, these dumplings from the south of Germany are made with two kinds of potatoes: cooked Maine or Eastern (all-purpose) potatoes, which are waxy enough to bind the dumpling mixture, and raw grated russets or baking potatoes, which provide texture. It's imperative that the grated potatoes be wrung as dry as possible, otherwise the dumplings may fall apart as they cook. Make certain, too, that the baking potatoes you choose are dry, firm, and mealy, not soft or watery. With their butter-browned bread-crumb topping, these dumplings are dressy enough to accompany a

Dumplings:

2 pounds Maine or Eastern potatoes, boiled in their skins until tender

1 pound baking potatoes, peeled and moderately finely grated

1 gallon cold water mixed with 1 tablespoon cider vinegar (acidulated water)

2 extra-large eggs

2 teaspoons salt

¼ teaspoon white pepper

¼ teaspoon freshly grated nutmeg

8 slices stale, firm-textured white bread, soaked in 1 cup milk and squeezed very dry

3 slices stale, firm-textured white bread, cut into ½-inch cubes

6 tablespoons unsalted butter or margarine

POTATO DUMPLINGS II

Christmas goose. They're also the perfect sop for its gravy.

Crumb Topping:

½ cup fine, soft white bread crumbs, lightly browned in 2 teaspoons unsalted butter or margarine

Makes 8 servings

Drain the boiled potatoes, cool until easy to handle, then peel, quarter, and spread out between two clean dry dish towels; let stand at least 15 minutes.

Meanwhile, soak the grated potatoes in the acidulated water for 15 minutes. Working with half the potatoes at a time, bundle in clean dish towels and wring bone dry. This is tedious work, but keep at it, wringing the potatoes again and again until every drop of moisture is forced out. Spread the grated potatoes between clean dry dish towels and set aside for the moment.

Place the boiled potatoes in a large bowl and mash well. Add the eggs, salt, pepper, nutmeg, and squeezed-out bread and beat hard until fluffy. Stir in the grated potatoes. (If the mixture seems too soft to shape, mix in 1 to 2 slices or more white bread, buzzed to fine, soft crumbs in a food processor.) Cover the dumpling mixture and refrigerate. Brown half the bread cubes in 3 tablespoons of the butter in a heavy 10-inch skillet over moderately low heat, stirring or shaking the skillet often so the cubes brown evenly; drain on paper toweling. Brown the remaining bread cubes in the remaining butter the same way and drain.

To shape the dumplings: Take up 3 to 4 browned croutons in one hand and drop about 1 cup of the dumpling mixture on top. Shape into a ball about the size of a baseball, enclosing the croutons. Repeat until all the croutons and potato mixture are used. Arrange the dumplings in a single layer on a wax-paper-covered tray or baking sheet, cover loosely with wax paper, and chill several hours, until quite firm. Or, if you prefer, freeze the dumplings.

223

continued on next page

POTATO DUMPLINGS II
(cont.)

To cook the dumplings: Bring a large kettle of lightly salted water to a simmer. Drop in the dumplings, spacing them evenly so they don't touch one another or the sides of the kettle. Adjust the heat so the water barely trembles, cover, and cook 30 minutes. No peeking or the dumplings won't be light. Drain the dumplings well, then lightly sprinkle each with a little of the crumb topping. Serve at once with plenty of gravy.

POTATO PANCAKES I

Kartoffelpuffer I

These potato pancakes couldn't be easier. And if you don't fry them all at the outset, you can refrigerate the balance of the potato mixture and cook it the next day. Shredded raw potatoes will darken on standing, but once they're browned no one will be the wiser. Serve these potato pancakes with sauerbraten, pot roast, or roast pork, along with applesauce or cranberry sauce and sour cream.

1¾ pounds baking potatoes, peeled and coarsely shredded

1 medium-size yellow onion, peeled and moderately coarsely chopped

5 tablespoons all-purpose flour

1 teaspoon salt

½ cup clarified butter or corn or other vegetable oil

Makes 6 to 8 servings

Place the potatoes, onion, flour, and salt in a large mixing bowl. Using your hands, mix well until the mixture holds together nicely.

Heat the clarified butter in a heavy 12-inch skillet over moderate heat for 1½ to 2 minutes (just until a shred of potato will sputter vigorously when dropped into the skillet). Scoop up the potato mixture by level ¼ cup measures and drop into the skillet. With an oiled pancake turner, flatten into cakes about ¼ inch thick. Don't try to cook more than 4 pancakes at a time. Brown them 2½ to 3 minutes on each side, until crisp and brown. Lift the browned pancakes to a baking sheet lined with several thicknesses of paper toweling and top with more paper toweling. Cook the remaining potato pancakes the same way and serve hot.

POTATO PANCAKES II

Kartoffelpuffer II

These potato pancakes contain egg and are a little richer than Potato Pancakes I. They're also more oniony. Any leftover batter can be refrigerated and cooked the next day.

1¼ pounds baking potatoes, peeled and coarsely shredded

1 medium-size yellow onion, peeled and moderately coarsely chopped

3 tablespoons all-purpose flour

1½ teaspoons freshly squeezed lemon juice

1 extra-large egg

¾ teaspoon salt

⅛ teaspoon freshly ground black pepper

⅓ cup clarified butter or corn or other vegetable oil

Makes 4 to 6 servings

Bundle about one fourth of the potatoes in a clean dish towel and, working over the sink, squeeze out as much liquid as possible; transfer to a large bowl. Repeat until all the potatoes have been squeezed dry. Add the onion and flour and toss well to mix. Add the lemon juice, egg, salt, and pepper and mix well.

Heat the clarified butter in a 12-inch heavy skillet over moderately high heat for 1½ to 2 minutes. Scoop up the potato mixture by level ¼ cup measures, add to the skillet, and flatten with an oiled spatula to a thickness of ¼ inch. Cook 4 pancakes at a time for 2½ to 3 minutes on each side. Lift the browned pancakes to a baking sheet lined with several thicknesses of paper toweling and top with more paper toweling. Cook the remaining pancakes the same way. Serve hot with sour cream or applesauce as an accompaniment to roasts or pot roasts.

225

BREAD DUMPLINGS
Semmelknödel

These fluffy dumplings are served throughout southern Germany as an accompaniment to roasts and stews – any meat, in fact, with gravy. The most traditional combination, however, is roast pork, Semmelknödel, and sauerkraut. These dumplings are also delicious smothered in a sauce of wild mushrooms (see Forest Mushroom Sauce, page 387) and are then hearty enough to serve as the main course of an informal lunch or supper. If the dumplings are to be light, the dough must be just the right consistency – like moist mashed potatoes. You must use hard rolls several days old and slice them very thin (the food processor's 4-millimeter slicing disk does the job to perfection). Some Germans make Semmelknödel just so they'll have leftovers to slice and brown. You'll find several of their favorite ways to recycle Semmelknödel at the end of this recipe.

Dumplings:

4 quarts ⅛-inch-thick slices stale hard rolls or French or Italian bread

1 cup (approximately) coarse hard roll crumbs (left from slicing the rolls)

2 cups lukewarm milk

2 extra-large eggs

4 teaspoons unsalted butter or margarine

1 medium-size yellow onion, peeled and moderately coarsely chopped

½ cup moderately coarsely chopped flat-leaf parsley

1½ teaspoons salt

For Cooking the Dumplings:

3 gallons boiling water mixed with 2 tablespoons salt

Makes 4 to 6 servings

Place the sliced rolls and crumbs in a large mixing bowl and drizzle the milk evenly over all. Toss well and let stand, uncovered, at room temperature for 30 minutes, tossing once after 15 minutes. If, after 30 minutes, there is any unabsorbed milk in the bowl, pour it off. Add the eggs to the roll mixture and knead in with your hands.

Melt the butter in a heavy 10-inch skillet over moderate heat, add the onion, reduce the heat to low, and sauté 5 to 6 minutes, stirring now and then, just until translucent. Add the parsley and sauté 2 minutes longer, stirring often. Add the onion mixture and salt to the roll mixture and knead in with your hands until smooth and pastelike. Scoop up a bit of the dumpling mixture with wet hands and shape into a ball 2 inches in diameter. Using a perforated ladle, slotted

BREAD DUMPLINGS

spoon, or skimmer, ease this test dumpling into the boiling salted water, let the water return to a boil, then adjust the heat so that it stays at a slow boil. Cover the kettle and boil the dumpling for 15 minutes.

Lift the test dumpling from the kettle with the perforated ladle to a platter lined with several thicknesses of paper toweling. If the dumpling has fallen apart in the cooking water, work a few more crumbs into the remaining dumpling mixture and try a second test dumpling. If the dumpling has not fallen apart, gently pull it apart with two forks – never cut Semmelknödel with a knife because you'll compact them. The dumpling should be cooked all the way through and have a feathery texture. If it is doughy inside, you will know to cook the remaining dumplings 3 to 5 minutes longer. Taste the dumpling and, if not salty enough, add a bit more salt to the remaining dumpling mixture.

Shape the remaining dumpling mixture into 2-inch balls. Ease them into the boiling salted water, let the water return to the boil, then adjust the heat so the water boils gently but steadily. Cover the kettle and cook the dumplings for 15 minutes, or until cooked through. Lift from the kettle with the perforated ladle, roll quickly on several thicknesses of paper toweling, and serve with a roast or stew, topping with plenty of the gravy. Or, to serve as a main course, smother with Forest Mushroom Sauce (page 387).

What to Do with Leftover Bread Dumplings

These are just some of the ways Germans like to recycle *Semmelknödel*. You can be as inventive as you like

Bread Dumplings with Onions (Geröstete Semmelknödel mit Zwiebeln): Place any leftover dumplings on a plate, cover loosely with plastic wrap, and refrigerate overnight. Next day, slice the dumplings ½ inch thick and set aside. In a heavy 10-inch skillet, melt 3 to 4 tablespoons unsalted butter or margarine over moderate heat, add 1 to 2 thinly sliced large yellow onions (quantities will depend on how many dumplings you have), then sauté, stirring often, over moder-

227

continued on next page

BREAD DUMPLINGS
(cont.)

ate heat, about 10 minutes, until richly browned. When the onions are almost done, melt 2 to 3 tablespoons unsalted butter or margarine in a heavy 12-inch skillet over moderate heat (again the quantity will depend on the number of dumplings), then brown the sliced dumplings about 2 minutes on each side. Serve topped with the browned onions.

Bread Dumplings with Bacon (Geröstete Semmelknödel mit Geräuchertem Speck): Chill and slice the dumplings as directed above; set aside. Depending on the amount of leftover dumplings, snip ¼ to ½ pound sliced bacon crosswise into ¼-inch strips and brown in a heavy 12-inch skillet over moderate heat about 5 minutes. Using a slotted spoon, lift the browned bacon bits to paper toweling to drain. Pour off all but 2 to 3 tablespoons bacon drippings from the skillet, add the sliced dumplings, and brown about 2 minutes on each side. Serve topped with the crisp bacon bits.

Bread Dumplings with Bacon and Eggs (Geröstete Semmelknödel mit Speck und Eiern): Chill and slice the dumplings as directed above, set aside. Also brown and drain the bacon as directed. Lightly beat 4 eggs with ½ teaspoon salt and ¼ teaspoon freshly ground black pepper and mix in, if you like, ¼ cup moderately coarsely chopped flat-leaf parsley; set aside. Pour off all but 2 to 3 tablespoons bacon drippings from the skillet, add the sliced dumplings, and brown about 2 minutes on each side. Lift to a heated platter and reserve. Add an additional 2 tablespoons bacon drippings to the skillet, pour in the eggs, and scramble over moderate heat until softly set. Spoon the scrambled eggs over the dumplings and scatter with the bacon.

SPAETZLE
Spätzle

Spaetzle, the pasta of Germany, are little squiggles or teardrops of dough thought to have originated in Swabia in the southwestern part of the country. Today, however, they're popular throughout Germany. They are usually served in place of potatoes – most often with venison, Roulades of Beef (page 137), or gravy-rich ragouts. If there is to be no gravy, the spaetzle are simply tossed with a little melted butter.

Sometimes spaetzle are layered in a casserole with cheese, butter, and onions (see Spaetzle with Cheese, page 231). And sometimes they're sauced (Green Spaetzle, page 233) and browned in the oven. In both instances, the recipes are rich enough to serve as a main course. But the traditional role of spaetzle is as a potato substitute.

There are several ways to shape spaetzle. You can push the batter through a spaetzle maker, which resembles a potato ricer and can be bought at specialty kitchen shops. You can push it through the holes of a fine colander, or you can do as German chefs do and scrape it off a wooden paddle in slender strands. Stiffer doughs can be dropped from a teaspoon into bubbling broth or water, or simply rolled into little logs with your fingers.

EGG SPAETZLE

Eierspätzle

If the flour in your area contains a high proportion of hard wheat, as it does in much of the West and Midwest, you may need to reduce the amount of flour in this recipe by about ¼ cup to achieve a workable spaetzle batter.

1 cup plus 2 tablespoons sifted all-purpose flour

⅛ teaspoon freshly grated nutmeg

½ teaspoon salt

1 extra-large egg

6 tablespoons milk

3 tablespoons unsalted butter or margarine, melted

Makes 4 servings

Combine the flour, nutmeg, and salt in a small bowl and make a well in the center.

Whisk the egg with the milk in a measuring cup, pour into the well in the dry ingredients, and beat hard with a wooden spoon until the batter is bubbly and elastic (or mix the batter in a food processor, then give it 3 to 4 one-minute pulses until smooth and elastic).

Push the batter through a spaetzle maker into a large kettle of rapidly boiling salted water. Cook the spaetzle, uncovered, for 8 minutes, stirring occasionally. With a slotted spoon, lift the spaetzle to a large bowl of ice water and let stand until ready to serve – but no longer than an hour or two.

Drain the spaetzle well in a colander, then warm 4 to 5 minutes in the melted butter in a large sauté pan over moderately low heat, stirring now and then. Serve at once.

SPAETZLE WITH CHEESE
Käse-Spätzle

You might call this the German macaroni and cheese. It isn't a difficult recipe, but it does require a bit of dexterity and careful choreography. German cooks have plenty of practice, so preparing a big casserole of Käse-Spätzle is as easy for them as making macaroni and cheese is for us. The first requisite is a well-aged Emmentaler cheese that won't go rubbery when it melts. The second is to get the consistency of the spaetzle batter precisely right. It should be quite thick and elastic (like a very soft yeast dough) so the spaetzle won't disintegrate in the cooking water or turn to mush. But the batter must also be thin enough to push through the holes of a colander or spaetzle maker. It's also important to have everything else at the ready before you begin cooking the spaetzle: a well buttered 3-quart casserole, the finely grated Emmentaler, a skillet of butter-browned onions. The spaetzle should be cooked in four batches, each layered into the casserole as soon as it's drained, then

For Cooking the Spaetzle:

1½ gallons water mixed with 3 tablespoons salt

Topping:

3 tablespoons unsalted butter or margarine

3 large yellow onions, peeled and thinly sliced

Spaetzle:

5 cups sifted unbleached all-purpose flour

1 teaspoon salt

5 extra-large eggs

1 cup plus 2 tablespoons cold water

1 pound well-aged Emmentaler or Gruyère cheese, finely grated

Makes 6 to 8 servings

For cooking the spaetzle: Bring the salted water to a boil in a large pasta kettle over moderate heat. Preheat the oven to 325° F.

For the topping: Melt the butter in a heavy 12-inch skillet over moderate heat. Add the onions and stir-fry 8 to 10 minutes, until richly browned. Turn the heat to its lowest point and keep the onions warm while you prepare the spaetzle.

For the spaetzle: Sift the flour and salt into a large mixing bowl and make a well in the center. Break 1 egg into the well and, using your hands, work a bit of the flour into the egg. Add the remaining 4 eggs, one by one, each time working in the flour. Add the water and beat hard with a wooden spoon until the spaetzle batter is smooth and elastic; it will be quite thick. Lift up a gob of dough on the spoon; if it is the proper consistency, it will drop from the spoon in long doughy strands, not in a single large blob. If the dough is too

231

continued on next page

SPAETZLE WITH
CHEESE (cont.)

_sprinkled with cheese
and set in a moderately
low oven while you cook
the next batch of spaet-
zle. You'll need nothing
more to accompany this
dish than a crisp green
salad to round out a
light lunch or supper._

stiff, work in an additional tablespoon or two of cold water.

To cook the spaetzle: Place a large heatproof bowl on the stove beside the kettle and set a large fine sieve in the bowl. Place the grated cheese nearby, also the skillet of onions, and a well buttered 3-quart casserole that is at least 2½ inches deep. Adjust the heat under the kettle so the water boils rapidly. Lay the spaetzle maker across the rim of the kettle (the bottom of the spaetzle maker should be several inches above the boiling water). (If you push the spaetzle batter through a colander, you must hold the colander with one hand several inches above the water so that you can fish out the cooked spaetzle with the other. Not the easiest trick, but manageable nonetheless.) Spoon one fourth of the spaetzle batter into the spaetzle maker or colander and push it through the holes into the bubbling water in little dribbles.

Once the first batch of spaetzle is in the kettle, cover and return the water to a boil. As soon as the water boils vigorously, uncover the kettle and stir gently so the spaetzle are in perpetual motion. Once they pop up and float, cook 1 minute longer – from start to finish, each batch of spaetzle should cook no more than 3 minutes. Using a skimmer or slotted spoon, remove the cooked spaetzle at once to the sieve in the bowl and shake well to drain.

Arrange the spaetzle in the bottom of the casserole and sprinkle with one fourth of the grated cheese. Set, uncovered, in the oven. Cook and drain a second batch of spaetzle exactly as you did the first, layer into the casserole, and top with another one fourth of the cheese; return to the oven. Repeat twice more so you have four layers of spaetzle and cheese.

After the final layer of spaetzle and cheese is added, return the casserole to the oven for about 2 minutes – just long enough to melt the top layer of cheese. Remove the _Käse-Spätzle_ from the oven, quickly scatter the browned onions over the melted cheese, and serve at once.

GREEN SPAETZLE
Grüne Spätzle

These little green noodles, creamed and gratinéed, are hearty enough to serve as the main course of a light lunch or supper. All that's needed to round out the meal are a tartly dressed green salad and a fruit dessert.

Green Spaetzle:

2⅔ cups sifted all-purpose flour

1 teaspoon salt

½ teaspoon freshly grated nutmeg

¼ teaspoon freshly ground black pepper

2 extra-large eggs, lightly beaten

½ cup milk

1 tablespoon vegetable oil

4 teaspoons cooked sieved spinach (use baby food, if you like)

Cheese Sauce:

2 ounces double-smoked bacon, cut into fine julienne strips (about ½ cup bacon strips)

1 small yellow onion, peeled and finely chopped

1 cup beef broth

1 cup light cream

½ cup heavy cream

¼ teaspoon freshly ground black pepper

3 tablespoons freshly grated Parmesan cheese

Topping:

3 tablespoons freshly grated Parmesan cheese

Makes 4 to 6 servings

For the spaetzle: Combine the flour, salt, nutmeg, and pepper in a food processor by pulsing 2 to 3 times. Quickly whisk together the eggs, milk, oil, and spinach. Add to the processor and pulse 4 to 5 times to make a stiff, sticky dough.

233

continued on next page

GREEN SPAETZLE
(cont.)

Scrape onto a floured piece of wax paper, cover with an upside-down bowl, and let rest 15 minutes.

Preheat the oven to 400° F.

With well-floured hands, pinch off pea-size bits of dough, roll quickly into little logs, and drop into a large kettle of *very gently* boiling salted water. Work as fast as possible, reflouring hands as needed, and poach the spaetzle in 5 to 6 batches. They'll take about 2 minutes to cook — when they float, they're done, so lift out with a skimmer and plunge into a large bowl of cold water. Continue until all spaetzle are cooked. Let stand in cold water while you prepare the sauce.

For the sauce: Lightly brown the bacon in a 12-inch heavy skillet over moderate heat for 4 to 5 minutes; add the onion and sauté 4 to 5 minutes, until translucent. Add the broth and boil, uncovered, for 4 to 5 minutes, until only a glaze remains on the bottom of the skillet. Add the two creams and boil, uncovered, for 2 to 3 minutes, to thicken slightly. Meanwhile, drain the spaetzle well, add to the skillet, reduce heat to low, and simmer, uncovered, for 3 to 4 minutes, stirring often. Stir in the pepper and Parmesan.

Transfer all to a buttered 2½-quart gratin pan, top with the Parmesan, and bake, uncovered, about 15 minutes, until bubbling and touched with brown. Serve at once as the main course of a light lunch or supper.

234

· RICE CAKES

Reisplätzchen

Young German cooks, like their American counterparts, are traveling the world and trying new foods, although when it comes to preparing them, they often revert to traditional German cooking techniques. These rice cakes, for example, have the

½ cup wild rice, washed

2¾ cups boiling water

½ cup long-grain white rice

½ cup moderately coarsely shredded carrot (about 1 medium-size carrot)

⅓ cup finely chopped shelled, unblanched, salted pistachio nuts

RICE CAKES

crunch, even a bit of the nutty flavor, of classic German potato pan-cakes. Like them, too, they are crisply browned in sweet butter. But these pancakes are made with wholly American wild rice plus long-grain rice, whole wheat flour, and finely chopped pista-chios. The recipe comes from Angelika Miebs of the Hesse region (the area Frankfurt is in), who worked in New York for a spell, first at the German National Tourist Office, then at the German Consulate. "These rice cakes taste good with almost any kind of meat with or without gravy," says Angelika. They are equally good as a light main course accompa-nied by a tossed salad of greens. Angelika sometimes even tops her rice cakes with fried eggs à la veal Holstein.

½ cup unsifted whole wheat flour

2 extra-large eggs

1 teaspoon salt

¼ teaspoon freshly ground black pepper

4 tablespoons (½ stick) unsalted butter or margarine

Makes 8 (4-inch) cakes, 6 to 8 servings

Cook the wild rice in 1½ cups of the boiling water in a cov-ered, small heavy saucepan over moderately low heat for 45 to 50 minutes, until tender and all water is absorbed. At the same time, cook the long-grain rice in the remaining boiling water in a second covered, small heavy saucepan over low heat for 20 minutes, until tender and all water is absorbed.

Place the two rices in a large mixing bowl and cool to room temperature. Add all remaining ingredients except the but-ter and stir well to mix.

Melt 2 tablespoons of the butter in a heavy 12-inch skillet over moderate heat and, as soon as it foams, scoop a little of the rice mixture into a ½-cup measure (be generous). With your fingers, pat the mixture into the measure. Invert in the hot butter in the skillet. With a small pancake turner, flatten firmly into a cake about 4 inches across and ½ inch thick. Shape three more rice cakes the same way and brown all four about 2 minutes on each side, until crisp and richly browned. Transfer at once to a baking sheet lined with several thicknesses of paper toweling. Quickly melt the remaining butter in the skillet, then shape and brown the remaining rice cakes the same way. Serve at once.

235

SAFFRON RICE

Safran-Reis

Here's another rice recipe that shows how global the thinking of German cooks is today. It's the specialty of Chef Joachim Möhringer of Hotel Römerbad, in the Black Forest spa of Badenweiler, who serves it with his vegetable-laden Lamb Pot (page 158).

¼ teaspoon crumbled saffron threads

¼ cup hot water

4 cups cold water

1½ teaspoons salt

¼ teaspoon freshly ground black pepper

1 tablespoon unsalted butter or margarine

2 cups long-grain white rice

Makes 4 to 6 servings

Stir the saffron into the hot water and set aside. Bring the cold water, salt, pepper, and butter to a boil in a large heavy saucepan over high heat. Add the rice and the saffron mixture, return to the boil, then adjust the heat so the water bubbles gently. Cook, uncovered, for 20 minutes, until the rice is *al dente* and almost all water has been absorbed. Cover the rice, reduce the heat to its lowest point, and steam 5 minutes. Fluff the rice with a fork and serve as an accompaniment to stews, pot roasts, or other meat dishes that have plenty of gravy.

RED RICE

Roter Reis

Unlike the classic red rice, this one from Bernhard Schuster of Düsseldorf's Hotel Breidenbacher Hof gets its color from beet juice, not tomatoes. In truth, the rice is more rose than red. Schuster serves Red Rice with fish, but we think it's equally good with ham, pork, or chicken.

1½ cups rich chicken broth (preferably homemade)

1½ cups fresh or canned beet juice or bottled borscht

1 teaspoon salt

1½ cups long-grain white rice

Makes 4 servings

Bring the broth, beet juice, and salt to a boil in an uncovered medium-size heavy saucepan over moderate heat. Add the rice, adjust the heat so the liquid bubbles gently, then cover and cook 18 to 20 minutes, until the rice is tender. Fluff with a fork and serve.

237

VEGETABLES
Gemüse

THE CLASSIC WAY TO SERVE ASPARAGUS
Das klassische Spargel-Rezept

The asparagus beloved by all Germans is white – smooth, buttery stalks the color of ivory (only recently has green asparagus begun appearing in high-end markets). During Germany's brief asparagus season (early May to the end of June), every restaurant has a special Spargel-Karte, *or Asparagus Menu. It always includes everyone's favorite:* al dente *asparagus (cooked with a little sugar, butter, and salt) served with an assortment of sauces – clarified butter, hollandaise, and béarnaise. Sometimes restaurants get fancy and offer asparagus Greek style, Provençal style, even Chinese style. For most Germans, however, white asparagus is too good to gussy up. They like platters piled high with it, the requisite sauces, and, of course, the traditional accompaniments: tiny new potatoes parsleyed in butter, boiled or air-cured ham sliced fairly thick, or perhaps a small veal steak.*

2½ pounds asparagus (white, if at all possible)

6 cups boiling water mixed with 1 tablespoon sugar and 1½ teaspoons salt

1 tablespoon unsalted butter or margarine

Makes 4 servings

Snap the tough woody ends off each asparagus stalk and discard. Using a swivel-bladed vegetable peeler, peel the stalks upward from the bottom. Make sure you remove all tough, fibrous skin at the base of the stalks so they'll cook as fast as the tender tips.

Lay the asparagus flat in a single layer in a heavy 12-inch skillet with the tips all pointing the same direction. Pour in the sugared and salted boiling water, drop in the butter, cover tight, and boil 6 minutes over moderate heat, until crisp-tender. Drain the asparagus well, return to the heat, and shake the skillet briefly to drive off excess moisture. Pile the asparagus on a huge heated platter and serve at once with the sauce of your choice (see headnote).

ASPARAGUS STEW

Spargelgemüse

White asparagus is what Germans would use in preparing this easy but elegant recipe. But Helga Brenner, who comes from Offenbach near Frankfurt and whose recipe this is, says it's equally delicious made with green asparagus.

1 pound asparagus

1½ cups boiling water mixed with ½ teaspoon salt

¼ teaspoon freshly grated nutmeg

⅛ teaspoon freshly ground black pepper

2 tablespoons all-purpose flour blended with 3 tablespoons cold water (flour paste)

1 extra-large egg yolk, lightly beaten

1 tablespoon unsalted butter or margarine (optional)

Makes 2 to 4 servings

Cut 1 inch from the bottom of each asparagus stalk. With a swivel-bladed vegetable peeler, peel the stalks upward from the bottom. Make sure you remove all tough, fibrous skin at the base of the stalks so they'll cook as fast as the tender tips. Cut the asparagus on the diagonal into 2-inch chunks.

Cook in the boiling salted water with the nutmeg and pepper in a covered, medium-size heavy saucepan over moderate heat for 6 minutes, until crisp-tender. Drain the asparagus, reserving the cooking water. Mix a little of the cooking water into the flour paste, then return to the pan along with all remaining cooking water. Set over low heat and cook 2 to 3 minutes, stirring constantly, until thickened and smooth. Blend a little of the hot sauce into the egg yolk, stir back into the pan, and cook 2 minutes, stirring constantly. Return the asparagus to the pan, stir in the butter, if you like, and bring just to serving temperature – 2 to 3 minutes. Serve at once with mashed potatoes.

239

ASPARAGUS WITH MUSHROOMS
Spargel mit Pilzen

For this recipe, German cooks choose small, tender morels – some even gather the mushrooms themselves. If you're unable to buy fresh morels, substitute medium-size white cultivated mushrooms. They lack the earthy flavor of morels, but are also delicious teamed with asparagus. Serve as an accompaniment to red meat, pork or poultry, fish or shellfish. And the more simply prepared they are, the better.

2 pounds fresh asparagus (preferably white)

½ pound small morels or medium-size white cultivated mushrooms

3 tablespoons unsalted butter or margarine

½ teaspoon dried leaf marjoram, crumbled

¼ teaspoon dried leaf thyme, crumbled

¼ teaspoon freshly grated nutmeg

3 tablespoons all-purpose flour

1½ cups rich chicken broth (preferably homemade)

½ teaspoon salt

¼ teaspoon freshly ground black pepper

1 extra-large egg yolk, lightly beaten

Makes 4 to 6 servings

Snap the tough woody ends off each asparagus stalk and discard. With a swivel-bladed vegetable peeler, peel the stalks upward from the bottom. Make sure you remove all tough, fibrous skin at the base of the stalks so they'll cook as fast as the tender tips. Cut the asparagus on the diagonal into 1-inch chunks. Parboil the asparagus in lightly salted boiling water in a covered, medium-size heavy saucepan over moderate heat for 4 minutes. Drain well, then quick-chill in ice water and set aside.

If using morels, wash very carefully, pat dry on paper toweling, then halve lengthwise. If using white mushrooms, discard the stems, wipe the caps clean with a damp cloth, then slice about ⅛ inch thick. Melt the butter in a heavy 10-inch skillet over moderate heat, add the mushrooms, and sauté 3 minutes, stirring often. Add the marjoram, thyme, and nutmeg and cook and stir 1 minute. Sprinkle the flour evenly over the mushrooms, then mix in. Reduce the heat to low,

ASPARAGUS WITH MUSHROOMS

pour in ¾ cup of the broth, and stir quickly to combine with the flour. Add the remaining broth, the salt, and pepper and cook 5 minutes, stirring constantly, until thickened. Raise the heat to moderately low and boil the mushroom mixture, uncovered, for 10 minutes, stirring now and then.

Meanwhile, drain the asparagus thoroughly and pat dry on paper toweling. When the mushroom mixture has reduced for 10 minutes, whisk a little of the skillet liquid into the egg yolk, stir back into the skillet, and cook for 1 minute over moderately low heat, stirring constantly. Add the asparagus and heat, uncovered, for 2 to 3 minutes longer, stirring often, just until of serving temperature. Serve at once.

GREEN BEANS, PEARS, AND BACON
Bohnen, Birnen, und Speck

In this day of vegetables so crisp they skip off the plate as they're cut, 45 minutes may seem overly long to cook green beans. Not if the pot is heavy enough and the flame low enough. They will, in fact, be crisp-tender. The pears soften and, when tossed with the beans and kettle liquid, emerge as a sort of sweet-sour sauce. This unlikely pairing of ingredients is a particular favorite in Hamburg, indeed the recipe is popular throughout the northerly Schleswig-Holstein region of Germany. Integral to this dish is Bohnenkraut, *or bean herb, which is nothing more than summer savory. If it's unavailable, substitute a half-and-half mixture of thyme and marjoram, which, though not the same, is equally delicious.* Bohnen, Birnen, und Speck *is filling enough to serve as the main course of a light lunch or supper. To round out the meal, add a husky whole grain bread and a dessert of mixed citrus sections.*

½ cup water

1 teaspoon salt

1 pound green beans, tipped and snapped into 1½- to 2-inch lengths

1 pound small firm-ripe pears, peeled, halved, cored, then sliced crosswise ¼ inch thick

6 ounces lean double-smoked bacon, cut into ¾-inch cubes (about 1½ cups bacon cubes)

½ teaspoon dried leaf summer savory, crumbled, or ¼ teaspoon each dried leaf thyme and marjoram, crumbled

¼ teaspoon freshly ground black pepper

2 tablespoons minced flat-leaf parsley

Makes 4 to 6 servings

Bring the water and salt to a boil in a large heavy saucepan over high heat, then reduce the heat to very low. Add the beans, layer the pears on top, then the bacon. Sprinkle evenly with the savory and pepper, cover tight, and simmer very slowly for 45 minutes. Sprinkle in the parsley, toss well, ladle into soup plates, and serve.

242

ROSA WÜRZ'S GREEN BEANS
Grüne Bohnen von Rosa Würz

The title hardly does justice to the recipe because, prepared Hedy's mother's way, tenderest young green beans simmer with onion, herbs, and tomatoes, then are tossed, just before serving, with minced parsley and crisp bacon crumbles. These beans are equally delicious with pork, ham, beef, veal, lamb, or chicken.

¼ pound sliced double-smoked bacon, snipped crosswise into ¼-inch strips (about 1 cup bacon strips)

1 large yellow onion, peeled and moderately coarsely chopped

1 medium-size bay leaf, crumbled

1 teaspoon dried leaf marjoram, crumbled

¼ teaspoon dried leaf thyme, crumbled

1¾ pounds vine-ripe tomatoes, peeled, cored, seeded, and coarsely chopped

½ cup rich beef broth (preferably homemade)

1 to 2 teaspoons sugar, depending on the tartness of the tomatoes

½ teaspoon salt

¼ teaspoon freshly ground black pepper

1¼ pounds tender young green beans, tipped and snapped in half

3 tablespoons moderately coarsely chopped flat-leaf parsley

Makes 6 servings

Sauté the bacon in a heavy 12-inch skillet over moderate heat for 3 to 4 minutes, stirring often, until all the drippings cook out and only crisp brown bits remain. With a slotted spoon, lift the bacon bits to paper toweling to drain.

Pour all drippings from the skillet; measure out 2 tablespoons and return those to the skillet. Add the onion and sauté 8 to 10 minutes, stirring often over moderately low heat, until golden brown. Mix in the bay leaf, marjoram, and thyme and allow to mellow over low heat for 1 minute. Mix in the tomatoes, broth, 1 teaspoon of the sugar, the salt, and pepper. Cover and simmer 10 minutes over moderately low

continued on next page

243

ROSA WÜRZ'S GREEN
BEANS (cont.)

heat. Stir well, raise the heat to moderately high, and boil, uncovered, for 5 minutes, stirring often. Lay the beans on top – do not stir – then adjust the heat so the tomato mixture bubbles gently, cover, and simmer 15 to 20 minutes, until the beans are crisp-tender. Taste for sugar, salt, and pepper and adjust, as needed. Sprinkle with the parsley and reserved bacon, toss lightly, and serve.

QUARK TART WITH BRUSSELS SPROUTS
Quarkkuchen mit Rosenkohl

Brussels sprouts aren't yet as popular in Germany as other members of the cabbage family, but they are gaining ground. Some cooks batter-dip them and fry in deep fat, some toss them into a Topf *(hot pot) with chunks of wurst or ham, and others slice them into this quiche-like tart, which we think splendid. Serve as the main course of a light lunch or supper, as an appetizer, or as a side dish with roast pork, baked ham, or simply prepared chicken or turkey. Quark (page 51) is available in specialty German groceries and many greenmarkets now carry it. If you can't find it, substitute ricotta and "sour" it with a bit of sour cream. Also, if you use a frozen pie shell, make sure it's the deep-dish variety, otherwise you'll have too much filling.*

1 pint (10 ounces) fresh Brussels sprouts, trimmed of stems and coarse outer leaves, or 1 (10-ounce) package frozen Brussels sprouts (do not thaw)

¼ pound double-smoked slab bacon, cut into ¼-inch cubes (about 1 cup bacon cubes)

3 medium-size leeks, trimmed, washed well, and thinly sliced

⅔ cup quark, or ½ cup ricotta blended with 2 tablespoons sour cream

¾ cup heavy cream

2 tablespoons freshly grated Parmesan cheese

½ teaspoon freshly grated nutmeg

½ teaspoon salt

¼ teaspoon freshly ground black pepper

2 extra-large eggs

1 cup coarsely shredded Emmentaler cheese

1 (9-inch) unbaked pie shell with a high fluted edge

Makes 6 to 8 servings

Preheat the oven to 400° F.

Boil the Brussels sprouts, covered, in a large heavy saucepan of lightly salted boiling water for about 20 min-

244

QUARK TART WITH
BRUSSELS SPROUTS

utes, until crisp-tender. If using frozen sprouts, cook by package directions. Drain the sprouts well, return to the pan, and shake briskly over the heat for 1 to 2 minutes, to drive off excess moisture. Set the sprouts aside.

Sauté the bacon in a heavy 12-inch skillet over moderately low heat for 15 minutes, stirring often, until all the drippings cook out and only crisp brown bits remain; transfer the browned bits to paper toweling to drain. Add the leeks to the drippings and sauté about 5 minutes, stirring often, until limp and lightly browned. Slice the sprouts crosswise ¼ inch thick, add to the skillet, toss lightly to mix, then transfer all to a large mixing bowl.

Whisk the quark, cream, Parmesan, nutmeg, salt, pepper, and eggs until creamy. Or, even easier, process the quark, cream, Parmesan, nutmeg, salt, and pepper in a food processor fitted with the metal chopping blade for about 20 seconds, until smooth. Pulse in the eggs, one by one. Pour the quark mixture into the bowl, add the Emmentaler and reserved bacon, and toss well to mix.

Set the pie shell on a heavy-duty baking sheet and pour in the quark mixture. Bake, uncovered, for 10 minutes. Reduce the oven temperature to 325° F. and bake 30 to 35 minutes longer, until lightly browned and set like custard. Remove the tart from the oven and cool 45 minutes before cutting. To serve, cut into slim wedges.

245

BRAISED CABBAGE
Geschmortes Weisskraut

Helga Brenner, who hails from the town of Offenbach near Frankfurt, has adopted an Eastern way to cook cabbage because her husband is from Bangladesh. The ingredients, however, are purely German and the results superb. Serve with baked ham or roast pork.

2 tablespoons corn oil

1 large yellow onion, peeled and coarsely chopped

1 large green cabbage (about 3 pounds), trimmed, cored, and moderately finely chopped (see note)

1 tablespoon caraway seeds

2 large ripe tomatoes, peeled, cored, seeded, and coarsely chopped, or 1 cup canned crushed tomatoes

1½ teaspoons salt

¼ teaspoon freshly ground black pepper

Makes 6 to 8 servings

Heat the oil in a heavy 12-inch skillet over moderate heat for 1 minute. Add the onion and sauté 5 minutes, stirring often, until limp and golden. Add the cabbage and caraway seeds and toss carefully over moderate heat for 2 minutes. Reduce the heat to low, cover the skillet, and cook the cabbage 35 to 40 minutes, until crisp-tender; stir from time to time to move the browned cabbage on the bottom of the skillet up to the top. Mix in the tomatoes, salt, and pepper, cover, and cook over low heat 5 minutes longer. Serve at once.

Note: The easiest way to chop cabbage is in a food processor fitted with the metal chopping blade. Once you've trimmed and cored the cabbage, cut into 1½-inch chunks, then chop in two batches, giving each about 22 quick pulses in the processor. That's all there is to it.

SWEET-SOUR SAVOY CABBAGE

Wirsinggemüse süss-sauer

Superb with roast pork or baked ham. If you can't find savoy cabbage, substitute green cabbage, even the red. Both are delicious cooked this way.

2 tablespoons unsalted butter or margarine

2 tablespoons corn oil

2 large yellow onions, peeled and coarsely chopped

½ cup rich beef broth (preferably homemade)

1 large savoy cabbage (about 2½ pounds), trimmed, cut into eighths, then each eighth sliced crosswise ½ inch thick

¾ pound carrots, peeled and coarsely shredded

1½ tablespoons sugar

1 teaspoon salt

¼ teaspoon freshly ground black pepper

¾ cup cider vinegar

Makes 6 to 8 servings

247

Heat the butter and oil in a heavy 12-inch skillet over moderate heat for 1 minute. Add the onions and sauté 10 minutes, stirring often, until lightly browned. Add the broth and pile the cabbage into the skillet. Reduce the heat to low, cover snugly, and steam 20 minutes. Pile the carrots on top of the cabbage, re-cover, and steam 20 minutes longer. Sprinkle with the sugar, salt, and pepper, then pour in the vinegar and toss gently but well. Raise the heat to moderate and boil, uncovered, stirring occasionally, for 3 to 5 minutes, just until the skillet juices reduce a bit. Taste for salt and adjust, as needed. Serve at once.

SAVOY CABBAGE AND ONION CAKE WITH BACON
Wirsing-Zwiebelkuchen mit Speck

You might call this the German pizza. The yeast-raised crust is similar, and the filling is scattered on and baked the same way. But the filling itself is altogether German – onions, savoy cabbage, caraway seeds, and bacon. Accompany this cabbage and onion cake with a tartly dressed crisp green salad and a fruit dessert and you have all you need for a light lunch or supper.

248

Crust:

3¾ cups sifted unbleached all-purpose flour

1 package active dry yeast

½ teaspoon salt

⅓ cup corn oil

1 cup warm water (105° to 115° F)

Filling:

6 ounces sliced double-smoked bacon, snipped crosswise into ¼-inch strips (about 1½ cups bacon strips)

3 tablespoons unsalted butter or margarine

1 large leek, trimmed, washed, and thinly sliced

2 large yellow onions, peeled and coarsely chopped

¼ teaspoon freshly grated nutmeg

¼ teaspoon ground caraway seeds (see note)

1 large savoy cabbage (about 3 pounds), trimmed, cut into eighths, cored, and each eighth sliced crosswise ¼ inch thick

1 tablespoon whole caraway seeds

2 teaspoons salt

¼ teaspoon freshly ground black pepper

1¼ cups crème fraîche, or 1 cup heavy cream blended with ¼ cup sour cream

½ cup rich beef broth (preferably homemade)

5 extra-large eggs

¼ cup coarsely chopped flat-leaf parsley

Makes 8 to 10 servings

SAVOY CABBAGE
AND ONION CAKE
WITH BACON

For the crust: Put the flour, yeast, and salt in a food processor fitted with the metal chopping blade and pulse 8 to 10 times to combine. Add the oil and water and pulse 8 to 10 times. Scrape down the sides of the workbowl and process 20 to 30 seconds nonstop, until the dough forms a ball and rides up on the central spindle. (If you don't have a food processor, combine the flour, yeast, and salt in a large bowl, mix in the oil and water, then knead briskly 2 to 3 minutes on a lightly floured pastry cloth.) Scoop the dough into a well-buttered, warm, large bowl, then, with well-buttered hands, pat the surface of the dough so it is nicely buttered, too. Cover with a clean dry cloth and set to rise in a warm dry spot, away from drafts, until doubled in bulk. This will take about 2 hours.

For the filling: Sauté the bacon in a heavy 12-inch skillet over moderate heat for 3 to 5 minutes, stirring often, until lightly browned. Using a slotted spoon, lift the browned bacon bits to paper toweling to drain. Add the butter to the skillet and, when it melts, add the leek and onions and sauté 10 minutes, stirring often, until nicely browned. Mix in the nutmeg and ground caraway and mellow 1 minute over moderate heat. Pile the cabbage into the skillet and sprinkle the caraway seeds, salt, and pepper evenly over all. Cover snugly, reduce the heat to low, and steam 20 minutes. Toss the skillet mixture well, re-cover, and steam 10 minutes longer, just until the cabbage is crisp-tender. Remove from the heat and set aside to cool, still covered.

When the dough has risen for almost 2 hours, preheat the oven to 400° F. Lightly butter a 15½ x 10½ x 1 inch jelly roll pan and set aside.

Spread a pastry cloth on the counter and sprinkle with flour. Punch down the dough, place on the floured cloth, and knead briskly 12 to 14 times. Shape the dough into a brick, then, with a floured, stockinette-covered rolling pin, roll into a rectangle about 1 inch larger all around than the jelly roll pan. Lop half the dough over the rolling pin, then ease into the pan, patting the dough firmly across the bottom, into the

continued on next page

249

SAVOY CABBAGE
AND ONION CAKE
WITH BACON (cont.)

corners, and up the sides. With a sharp knife, trim the dough overhang so it is ½ inch larger all around than the pan. Patch any skimpy spots with the trimmings, then roll the overhang under so it rests on the rim of the pan and crimp to make a high fluted edge. Set aside while you finish the filling.

Whisk the crème fraîche with the broth and eggs just until creamy, pour into the cooled skillet mixture, add the parsley, and toss carefully to mix. Ladle the filling into the crust, distributing it as evenly as possible. Sprinkle with the reserved bacon and bake uncovered, 35 to 40 minutes, until the crust is nicely browned and the filling is set like custard. Remove from the oven and cool 40 to 45 minutes. To serve, cut into large squares.

Note: If you can't find ground caraway seeds, buy them whole and grind to powder in a little electric coffee grinder or pulverize with a mortar and pestle.

BRAISED RED CABBAGE WITH ONIONS AND APPLES IN RED WINE SAUCE
Rotkraut mit Zwiebeln und Äpfeln in Rotweinsauce

This recipe is Hedy's own and it is the perfect accompaniment to her Roulades of Beef (page 137), also to venison, pork, and ham.

1 large red cabbage (about 2 pounds)

2 tablespoons unsalted butter or margarine

1 tablespoon sugar

1 large yellow onion, peeled and finely chopped

2 large tart green apples, peeled, cored, and coarsely chopped

¼ cup red wine vinegar

1 cup rich beef broth (preferably homemade)

½ teaspoon salt

2 large whole bay leaves

2 tablespoons all-purpose flour

1 cup dry red wine (preferably German)

2 tablespoons red currant jelly

BRAISED RED CABBAGE
WITH ONIONS AND
APPLES IN RED WINE
SAUCE

Makes 6 to 8 servings

Trim the coarse outer leaves from the cabbage and discard;
quarter the cabbage, slice off the hard white core at the
point of each quarter and discard, then slice each quarter
very thin. Set the cabbage aside.

Melt the butter in a very large heavy skillet over moderately
high heat, sprinkle in the sugar, and heat 2 to 3 minutes –
just until dissolved. Add the onion and apples and stir-fry
about 5 minutes, until limp and golden. Add the cabbage
and stir-fry about 5 minutes, until nicely glazed. Pour in the
red wine vinegar and ½ cup of the beef broth. When the mixture simmers, adjust the heat so that the liquid bubbles very
gently. Sprinkle in the salt and add the bay leaves, pushing
them down into the cabbage. Cover the skillet and simmer
20 to 25 minutes, until the cabbage is crisp-tender.

Sprinkle the flour over the cabbage and toss well to mix.
Add the wine and the remaining ½ cup beef broth. Heat, stirring gently, for 3 to 5 minutes, until the liquids are thickened and no raw starch taste remains. Remove and discard
the bay leaves, add the jelly, and toss lightly to mix. Warm,
uncovered, for another 5 minutes and serve.

251

SAUERKRAUT AND APPLES COOKED IN WHITE WINE

Sauerkraut und Äpfel in Weisswein

Most Germans like their sauerkraut good and tender, which means that it must cook long and slow. "I remember my mother cooking it for hours," Hedy says. "And when we complained about it smelling up the house, she began using a pressure cooker." This particular recipe is one of Hedy's favorites, albeit a somewhat lighter version than the one her mother used to make. "If you like your sauerkraut crisper," Hedy adds, "simply reduce the cooking time by about an hour." Of course, it all depends upon how crisp the kraut is at the outset. Some brands are much softer than others. If the sauerkraut seems unusually salty, rinse it well before using. This recipe is not likely to need any additional salt, but taste before serving and adjust as needed.

2 pounds fresh sauerkraut, drained well

3 medium-size Golden Delicious or other sweet apples, peeled, cored, and quartered, then each quarter thinly sliced

6 juniper berries

3 large whole bay leaves

2½ cups Riesling or other white German wine (not too dry)

2½ cups water

1 tablespoon Hungarian sweet rose paprika

¼ teaspoon freshly ground black pepper

½ cup heavy cream

Salt, if needed, to taste

1 tablespoon superfine sugar, if needed to temper the tartness of the sauerkraut

Makes 6 servings

Place the sauerkraut, apples, juniper berries, bay leaves, wine, and water in a medium-size, heavy, nonmetallic kettle, and bring to a boil over moderate heat. Adjust the heat so the mixture bubbles gently, cover, and simmer 1½ to 1¾ hours, stirring occasionally, until the sauerkraut is tender. Uncover and raise the heat to moderate. Boil, uncovered, stirring often, for 15 minutes, to reduce the liquid somewhat; remove and discard the juniper berries and bay leaves. Redden the surface of the sauerkraut with the paprika, add the pepper and cream, and toss well to mix. Taste, and if not salty enough to suit you, adjust as needed. If too tart, mix in the sugar. Serve hot as an accompaniment to pork, bockwurst, or knackwurst.

RED SAUERKRAUT
Rotes Sauerkraut

This is not sauerkraut made with red cabbage. It's plain sauerkraut reddened with shredded beets, and it's a delicious accompaniment to roast venison, pork, turkey, chicken, or game birds. The recipe makes a lot, but you'll be happy to have leftovers. Red Sauerkraut is even better the second time around.

1 pound beets, trimmed of all but 1 inch of the tops and scrubbed

6 ounces double-smoked slab bacon, snipped crosswise into ¼-inch strips (about 1½ cups bacon strips)

2 medium-size red onions, peeled and coarsely chopped

2 pounds fresh sauerkraut, drained

2 whole bay leaves

½ cup dry red wine (preferably German)

½ cup sweet Madeira wine (Malmsey or Bual)

⅛ teaspoon freshly ground black pepper

Makes 6 to 8 servings

Parboil the beets in an uncovered saucepan in enough boiling water to cover for 20 minutes. Meanwhile, brown the bacon in a heavy 12-inch skillet over moderate heat about 5 minutes, until all the drippings have cooked out and only crisp brown bits remain. Using a slotted spoon, lift the bacon bits to paper toweling to drain. Pour off the drippings, reserving 3 tablespoons, and return these to the skillet. Add the onions to the skillet and stir-fry over moderately low heat for 8 to 10 minutes, until richly browned (the browning is important for flavor).

Drain the parboiled beets, cool by plunging into cold water, then peel and shred coarsely. Add the beets to the skillet and toss with the onions over moderate heat for 1 to 2 minutes, until nicely glazed. Add the sauerkraut and stir for 2 to 3 minutes to glaze well. Add the bay leaves, red wine, and Madeira, reduce the heat so the mixture bubbles gently, cover snugly, and simmer 20 minutes, until the beets are tender. Remove and discard the bay leaves, raise the heat under the skillet to high, and boil hard for a minute or two until most of the skillet juices have evaporated. Mix in the pepper and serve.

253

RHINELAND SAUERKRAUT CASSEROLE

Rheinischer Sauerkrautauflauf

Serve as an accompaniment to pork or as the main course of a casual supper.

1 pound fresh sauerkraut, with its liquid

1 large Golden Delicious or other sweet apple, peeled, cored, cut into eighths, then each eighth thinly sliced

1 medium-size yellow onion, peeled and coarsely chopped

½ cup rich beef broth (preferably homemade)

2 teaspoons sugar

½ teaspoon freshly ground black pepper

2¼ pounds baking potatoes (about 3 large), scrubbed well

½ pound double-smoked slab bacon, cut into ¼-inch cubes (about 2 cups bacon cubes)

1¼ cups hot milk

¾ teaspoon salt

¼ teaspoon freshly grated nutmeg

1 tablespoon unsalted butter or margarine, cut into bits

2 tablespoons freshly grated Parmesan cheese

Makes 6 to 8 servings

Place the sauerkraut, apple, onion, broth, sugar, and ¼ teaspoon of the pepper in a large, heavy, nonmetallic saucepan and bring to a boil over moderate heat. Adjust the heat so the mixture bubbles gently, cover, and simmer 1 hour, stirring occasionally.

At the same time, cook the potatoes in lightly salted boiling water to cover in a covered large, heavy saucepan over moderate heat for 1 hour, until tender.

Meanwhile, sauté the bacon in a heavy 10-inch skillet over moderately low heat for 15 minutes, stirring often, until all the drippings cook out and only crisp brown bits remain; transfer the browned bits to paper toweling to drain and

254

RHINELAND SAUERKRAUT CASSEROLE

reserve; save the drippings to use another day.

About 15 minutes before the potatoes and sauerkraut are done, preheat the oven to 375° F. Butter a 3-inch-deep 2½-quart casserole and set aside.

Drain the potatoes, peel, and place in a large heatproof bowl. Cut back and forth through the potatoes with a sharp knife so they'll be easier to mash. Add the milk, salt, nutmeg, and remaining pepper and mash well with a potato masher.

Spread one third of the mashed potatoes in the prepared casserole and sprinkle with one fourth of the bacon. Arrange half the sauerkraut in an even layer on top and scatter with another fourth of the bacon. Add another third of the potatoes, another fourth of the bacon, then the remaining sauerkraut and bacon. Finally, top with the remaining mashed potatoes, keeping the surface rough. Dot with the butter and sprinkle with the Parmesan. Bake, uncovered, 40 to 45 minutes, until browned and bubbly. Serve at once.

255

PURÉE OF CARROTS

Karottenpüree

This is our version of a carrot purée we enjoyed at Alfons Schuhbeck's Kurhaus Stüberl, a marvelous Bavarian restaurant at Waging am See, about an hour southeast of Munich. We've duplicated the purée's meaty flavor by using a rich brown beef glaze to season, together with a little rosemary and butter. You'll find that this purée partners perfectly with roast beef, veal, venison, pork, or poultry.

1 pound medium-size carrots, peeled and cut into 1-inch chunks

1 medium-size leek, trimmed, washed well, and thinly sliced

1 small fresh rosemary or lemon thyme sprig, or ¼ teaspoon dried leaf rosemary or thyme, crumbled

2 cups boiling water

½ cup rich beef broth (preferably homemade)

2 teaspoons unsalted butter or margarine

⅛ teaspoon freshly grated nutmeg

½ teaspoon salt

⅛ teaspoon freshly ground black pepper

Makes 4 servings

continued on next page

PURÉE OF CARROTS
(cont.)

Boil the carrots, leek, and rosemary in the water in a covered, medium-size, heavy saucepan over moderate heat for 25 to 30 minutes, until very tender. At the same time, simmer the beef broth, uncovered, in a very small heavy saucepan or butter warmer over very low heat until reduced to about 1 tablespoon of rich brown glaze. This may take slightly less time than the carrots, so watch carefully and remove from the heat the instant the broth is sufficiently reduced.

When the carrots are done, drain well, then return to the heat and shake the pan 1 to 2 minutes to drive off all moisture. This step is crucial. If the carrots aren't dry, the purée will be too thin. It should be about the consistency of whipped potatoes.

Remove and discard the rosemary stem. Place the carrot mixture in a food processor fitted with the metal chopping blade. Add the beef glaze, butter, nutmeg, salt, and pepper and purée 10 seconds. Scrape down the sides of the workbowl and purée 10 to 15 seconds longer, until silky smooth. Serve at once.

SHREDDED CARROTS WITH LIME AND ROSEMARY

Geriebene Karotten mit Limonensaft und Rosmarin

A perfect example of how modern German cooks are lightening up. Carrots prepared this way are delicious with all meats, but particularly so with pork, ham, and poultry. If this recipe is to be properly flavorful, you must use the freshest carrots you can find, not those that have languished in storage for weeks. You must also use freshly squeezed lime juice and, if at all possible, fresh rosemary.

2 tablespoons unsalted butter or margarine

1 pound carrots, peeled and coarsely shredded

¼ cup rich beef or chicken broth (preferably homemade)

4 small fresh rosemary sprigs, or ¼ teaspoon dried leaf rosemary, crumbled

1 tablespoon freshly squeezed lime or lemon juice

¼ teaspoon salt

¼ teaspoon freshly ground black pepper

Makes 4 servings

SHREDDED CARROTS WITH LIME AND ROSEMARY

Melt the butter in a heavy 12-inch skillet over moderate heat. Add the carrots, broth, and rosemary and toss well to mix. If you use fresh rosemary, make sure the sprigs are well distributed and tucked down underneath the carrots. Reduce the heat to low, cover tightly, and simmer 15 minutes, stirring once at halftime. Remove the rosemary sprigs, if used, add the lime juice, salt, and pepper and toss well. Serve at once.

CAULIFLOWER CUSTARD WITH SPINACH SAUCE

Blumenkohlpudding mit Spinatsauce

All members of the cabbage family are popular throughout Germany, with the exception, possibly, of broccoli. This delicate cauliflower custard – our variation of a cauliflower cake created by Chef Heinz Wehmann of Landhaus Scherrer in Hamburg – makes a lovely light entrée, but can also be served as an accompaniment to meat. It's especially good with smoked tongue or ham.

Cauliflower Custard:

2½ cups tiny cauliflower florets no more than ½ inch across

¼ large lemon

4 extra-large eggs

1 cup milk

¾ teaspoon salt

¼ teaspoon white pepper

¼ teaspoon freshly grated nutmeg

Spinach Sauce:

2½ tablespoons unsalted butter or margarine

2 medium-size shallots, peeled and minced

1 cup loosely packed tender young spinach leaves, stemmed, washed, patted dry on paper toweling, and coarsely chopped

1 cup loosely packed parsley sprigs, stemmed

1 cup rich chicken broth (preferably homemade)

2 tablespoons all-purpose flour

½ cup heavy cream

¼ cup dry white wine (Riesling or Mosel)

½ teaspoon salt

257

continued on next page

CAULIFLOWER
CUSTARD WITH
SPINACH SAUCE
(cont.)

⅛ teaspoon freshly grated nutmeg

⅛ teaspoon freshly ground black pepper

Makes 4 to 6 servings

For the cauliflower custard: Boil the cauliflower, uncovered, with the lemon quarter in a large heavy saucepan of salted boiling water for 8 to 10 minutes until crisp-tender; drain well and spread on a clean dish towel to dry.

Whisk the eggs, milk, salt, pepper, and nutmeg in a large bowl and stir in the cauliflower. Pour into a well-buttered 1½-quart gugelhupf mold (preferably ceramic) or Bundt pan, cover with foil, and punch a few holes in the foil to allow steam to escape. Stand the mold on a rack in a large deep kettle, then pour in enough hot water to come two thirds of the way up the sides of the mold. Bring the water in the kettle to a simmer, adjust the heat so that it bubbles very gently, then cover the kettle and let the mold simmer 35 minutes.

For the spinach sauce: Melt 1½ tablespoons of the butter in a small heavy saucepan and sauté the shallots over moderate heat for 2 to 3 minutes, until golden brown. Add the spinach and parsley and stir-fry 1 to 2 minutes, until wilted. Transfer to a food processor or electric blender, add ½ cup of the chicken broth, and process about 30 seconds, until smooth; set aside. Melt the remaining 1 tablespoon butter in the same small saucepan over moderate heat and blend in the flour. Reduce the heat to low and mellow about 1 minute. Combine the remaining chicken broth with the cream and wine, add to the saucepan, whisking constantly, then cook and whisk 3 to 5 minutes, until thickened and smooth. Reduce the heat to low and let the sauce bubble, uncovered, for 15 minutes, to reduce slightly. Stir the spinach-parsley purée into the sauce along with the salt, nutmeg, and pepper; taste for seasoning and adjust as needed. Keep the sauce warm until ready to serve.

To serve: Carefully lift the mold from the hot water bath and let stand upright on a wire rack for 5 minutes. Uncover,

CAULIFLOWER CUSTARD
WITH SPINACH SAUCE
then, using a small thin-bladed spatula, carefully loosen the custard around the edge and central tube and gently invert on a heated serving plate. Ladle a little of the spinach sauce on top and pass the rest.

CAULIFLOWER WITH HAM
Blumenkohl mit Schinken

This recipe comes from Edith Müllenbrock, an octogenarian who grew up in the village of Stolp, Pomerania, near Danzig, in what is now Poland. Today she lives in Stuttgart and still loves to cook. This dish, a particular favorite, is hearty enough to serve as the main course of a light lunch or supper.

Cauliflower Mixture:

1 large cauliflower (about 3 pounds), trimmed

½ pound Westphalian or Black Forest ham, cut into very fine dice or coarsely chopped

2 extra-large egg yolks, lightly beaten

½ cup sour cream

½ cup heavy cream

¼ teaspoon freshly grated nutmeg

½ teaspoon salt

¼ teaspoon pepper

Topping:

½ cup fine dry bread crumbs (do not use seasoned crumbs)

¼ cup freshly grated Parmesan cheese

2 tablespoons unsalted butter or margarine, cut into bits

Makes 4 to 6 servings

Preheat the oven to 375° F. Butter a 5-cup gratin dish and set aside.

For the cauliflower mixture: Place the head of cauliflower in a steamer and steam 15 to 20 minutes, until crisp-tender. Lift the cauliflower from the steamer. When it is cool enough to handle, break into florets about 1½ inches across. Also cut the heavy stems into 1-inch cubes. Arrange the cauliflower in a single layer in the prepared gratin dish. Sprinkle the ham evenly on top.

continued on next page

259

CAULIFLOWER WITH
HAM (cont.)

Quickly whisk together the egg yolks, sour cream, heavy cream, nutmeg, salt, and pepper and pour evenly over the ham and cauliflower.

For the topping: Toss the crumbs and Parmesan well to combine, then scatter evenly over the cauliflower mixture. Dot well with the butter.

Bake, uncovered, 25 to 30 minutes, until bubbling and touched with brown. Serve at once.

BRAISED CELERY ROOT WITH BACON
Selleriegemüse mit Speck

In Germany, Sellerie means celery root, or knob celery. Indeed, stalk celery, so popular throughout the United States, isn't often used by home cooks. Stronger than stalk celery, celery root is nuttier, too, and far more versatile. This recipe and the one that follows prove the point. Celery root prepared this way is particularly compatible with pork and poultry.

1¾ pounds celery root (about 3 medium-large), washed well and trimmed

6 ounces double-smoked slab bacon, cut into ¼-inch cubes (about 1½ cups bacon cubes)

4 tablespoons all-purpose flour

2 cups rich beef broth (preferably homemade)

1 teaspoon lemon juice

¼ teaspoon salt

¼ teaspoon freshly ground black pepper

1 extra-large egg yolk, lightly beaten

3 tablespoons minced flat-leaf parsley

Makes 6 servings

Peel the celery root, slice thin, then quarter each slice and set aside.

Sauté the bacon in a heavy 12-inch skillet over moderately low heat for 15 minutes, stirring often, until all the drippings cook out and only crisp brown bits remain; transfer the browned bits to paper toweling to drain. Add the celery root to the drippings and sauté about 5 minutes, stirring often, until lightly browned. Sprinkle the flour evenly over the celery root, then toss well to mix. Add ¾ cup of the broth and

BRAISED CELERY ROOT
WITH BACON

cook and stir quickly just until blended with the flour. Mix in the remaining broth, the lemon juice, salt, and pepper and bring to a boil. Adjust the heat so the mixture bubbles gently, cover, and simmer 12 to 15 minutes, until the celery root is crisp-tender.

Whisk a little of the hot skillet liquid into the egg yolk, stir back into the skillet, and cook, stirring constantly, for 2 to 3 minutes. Reduce the heat to low and cook, uncovered, for 5 minutes longer, stirring now and then, just to thicken the sauce a bit. *Do not allow the sauce to boil or it may curdle.* Stir in the parsley and reserved bacon bits and serve.

CELERY ROOT SCHNITZEL
Sellerie-Schnitzel

You might call this "vegetarian Wiener Schnitzel." It is hearty enough to serve as a main course, yet it can also be served as an accompaniment to meat or poultry – provided they're not overly rich.

1½ pounds celery root (about 2 large), washed well and trimmed

¾ cup unsifted all-purpose flour

1 extra-large egg, lightly beaten with 1 tablespoon freshly squeezed lemon juice, ¾ teaspoon salt, and ¼ teaspoon freshly ground black pepper

1 cup fine dry bread crumbs

½ cup clarified butter

1 large lemon, quartered

4 small curly parsley or watercress sprigs

Makes 4 servings

Peel the celery root, slice ¼ inch thick, and parboil 10 minutes in a covered large saucepan of lightly salted boiling water. Drain well, then pat dry between several thicknesses of paper toweling.

Place the flour, egg mixture, and crumbs in separate 8- or 9-inch pie tins and line them up on a counter in that order. Dredge the celery root slices in flour, shaking off any excess,

261

continued on next page

CELERY ROOT
SCHNITZEL (cont.)

then dip into the egg mixture, then coat evenly with crumbs.

Heat half the clarified butter in a heavy 12-inch skillet over moderately high heat for 2 minutes, or until a cube of bread will sizzle. Add half the breaded celery root slices – the biggest ones first – and sauté 2 to 2½ minutes on each side, until crisp and golden brown. Lift to paper toweling to drain. Discard the blackened bits in the skillet, wipe out the skillet, then add the remaining clarified butter. Heat 2 minutes over moderately high heat, then brown the remaining breaded celery root slices as before and drain on paper toweling. Arrange on a small heated platter, garnish with the lemon quarters and parsley sprigs, and serve.

Variation

Kohlrabi Schnitzel (Kohlrabi-Schnitzel): Prepare as directed, substituting large kohlrabi for celery root and beef broth, milk, or water for the lemon juice in the egg mixture.

PURÉE OF CELERY ROOT AND POTATOES
Püree von Sellerie und Kartoffeln

Normally, you cannot whip potatoes in a food processor – they'll turn to glue. But there is just enough celery root in this recipe to make it possible. If you have no food processor, you'll have to force the mixture through a coarse sieve and that's pesky work. You must also reheat the purée. Superb with pork and poultry.

1½ pounds celery root (about 2 large), peeled and cut into 1-inch chunks

1 pound baking potatoes, peeled and cut into 1-inch chunks

2 cups boiling water mixed with 1 tablespoon freshly squeezed lemon juice (acidulated water)

2 tablespoons unsalted butter or margarine

1 tablespoon heavy cream

1 teaspoon salt

¼ teaspoon freshly ground black pepper

⅛ teaspoon freshly grated nutmeg

Makes 4 to 6 servings

Boil the celery root and potatoes in the acidulated water in a covered, large heavy saucepan over moderate heat for 20 to

PURÉE OF CELERY
ROOT AND POTATOES

25 minutes, until soft. Drain well, return to the heat, and stir 4 to 5 minutes to drive off all moisture. This is crucial. If the mixture isn't dry, the purée will be too thin.

Add all remaining ingredients and mash well with a potato masher. Transfer to a food processor fitted with the metal chopping blade and purée 20 seconds. Scrape down the workbowl and purée 20 to 30 seconds longer, until absolutely smooth. Taste for salt and pepper and adjust as needed, then serve.

KALE WITH BACON
Grünkohl mit Speck

In Germany, where the Christmas season begins the first Sunday of Advent and lasts a month or more, the colorful accompaniments to the big brown goose served on Christmas Day are always green kale and red cabbage.

2 pounds fresh kale, trimmed of coarse stems and veins

4 thick slices lean double-smoked bacon, snipped crosswise into ¼-inch strips

1 large yellow onion, peeled and coarsely chopped

2½ cups rich beef broth (preferably homemade)

2 tablespoons potato starch

½ teaspoon salt

¼ teaspoon freshly ground black pepper

Makes 8 servings

Wash the kale in several changes of cool water, then parboil, uncovered, in a large saucepan of salted boiling water for 5 minutes. Drain thoroughly and squeeze as dry as possible. Slice the kale thin and set aside.

Cook the bacon in a 12-inch heavy skillet over moderate heat for 4 to 5 minutes, until crisp and brown; remove with a slotted spoon to paper toweling to drain. Add the onion to the skillet and sauté about 10 minutes, stirring occasionally, until lightly browned. Add the kale and cook, uncovered, for 10 minutes, stirring occasionally, until slightly wilted. Return the bacon to the skillet. Add 2 cups of the beef broth

continued on next page

263

KALE WITH BACON
(cont.)

and bring to a simmer. Adjust the heat so that the broth bubbles very gently, cover, and simmer about 1 hour, until the kale is tender and almost all liquid has cooked away.

Blend the potato starch with the remaining ½ cup broth in a measuring cup. Add to the skillet along with the salt and pepper and cook over moderate heat for about 3 minutes, stirring constantly, until thickened and smooth. Reduce the heat to low and cook, uncovered, for 5 minutes to blend the flavors. Taste and adjust the salt and pepper as needed. Serve hot.

KALE WITH CHESTNUTS AND GLAZED POTATOES

Grünkohl mit Kastanien und glasierten Kartoffeln

What a wonderful combination this is! The recipe comes to us from Margot von Glasenapp of Pinneberg, near Hamburg, who likes to serve it with pork chops or ham and tall glasses of beer.

¼ pound dried, peeled Italian chestnuts (see note)

½ the recipe for Glazed Potatoes (page 217)

2 pounds kale, trimmed of coarse stems and veins, then washed well

2 tablespoons lard or bacon drippings

¼ teaspoon freshly grated nutmeg

1 cup rich beef broth (preferably homemade)

½ teaspoon salt

¼ teaspoon freshly ground black pepper

1 tablespoon all-purpose flour

Makes 4 servings

Bring the chestnuts to a boil in a large saucepan of water, adjust the heat so the water bubbles gently, cover, and boil 5 minutes. Turn the heat off and let the chestnuts stand 1 hour. Turn the heat on under the chestnuts again and simmer them, covered, for 30 minutes, until firm-tender.

Meanwhile, prepare the potatoes as directed and keep warm over low heat. Also spin the kale dry in a salad spinner or

264

KALE WITH CHESTNUTS
AND GLAZED POTATOES

pat dry on paper toweling, then stack the leaves in batches and cut crosswise into 1-inch strips.

Melt the lard in a medium-size Dutch oven over moderate heat, add the kale and nutmeg, and turn in the hot lard 2½ to 3 minutes, until the kale is slightly wilted and intensely green. Add the broth, bring to a boil, then adjust the heat so it bubbles gently. Cover the kale and cook 10 minutes. Sprinkle in the salt, pepper, and flour and cook and stir about 2 minutes, just until the liquid thickens a bit.

Drain the chestnuts well and cut into quarters. Add to the kale, tossing lightly to mix. Re-cover and cook 5 minutes. To serve, mound the kale and chestnuts in the middle of a deep platter and cluster the potatoes around the edge. Serve at once.

Note: Frau von Glasenapp uses fresh chestnuts, but we find the dried, peeled Italian chestnuts (now available in many specialty food shops) equally good and more convenient because they eliminate the pesky job of peeling and blanching. Dried chestnuts do need about 1½ hours of preparation before they can be added to the kale, however, so plan accordingly.

SHREDDED KOHLRABI IN ONION-PARSLEY SAUCE

Geriebene Kohlrabi in Zwiebel-Petersiliensauce

Choose young kohlrabi and trim away all woody portions. Two pounds may seem like too much for four to six servings, but once you've peeled the kohlrabi, the edible portion will be about 1 pound. Serve with roast pork, game, game birds, or chicken.

1¾ cups rich chicken broth (preferably homemade)

2 pounds trimmed small kohlrabi, peeled and coarsely shredded

2 tablespoons unsalted butter or margarine

1 medium-size yellow onion, peeled and moderately finely chopped

¼ teaspoon freshly grated nutmeg

3 tablespoons all-purpose flour

⅓ cup heavy cream or half-and-half

½ teaspoon salt

⅛ teaspoon freshly ground black pepper

⅓ cup coarsely chopped flat-leaf parsley

Makes 4 to 6 servings

Bring the broth to a boil in a large heavy saucepan over moderate heat. Add the kohlrabi, cover, and boil 5 minutes. Place the kohlrabi in a large fine sieve set over a large heatproof bowl and drain as dry as possible; reserve broth.

Melt the butter in the same pan over moderate heat, add the onion and nutmeg, and stir-fry 3 minutes, until the onion is golden. Turn the heat to its lowest point, cover the onion, and steam 10 minutes, stirring often. During this period, the onion will brown nicely, which is important for flavor.

Blend the flour into the onion mixture, then slowly mix in the reserved broth and cream. Raise the heat to moderately low and cook 3 to 5 minutes, stirring constantly, until the mixture thickens and no raw starch remains. Return the kohlrabi to the pan, add the salt, pepper, and parsley, and toss well to mix. Serve at once.

STUFFED KOHLRABI
Gefüllte Kohlrabi

Marvelous with roast pork or fowl, also with baked ham.

4 medium-size kohlrabi (about 1½ pounds), trimmed and peeled

Stuffing:

¼ cup cold water

1 small hard French roll (1 ounce), crumbled

1 tablespoon unsalted butter or margarine

2 tablespoons finely minced yellow onion

½ cup finely chopped, peeled, seeded tomato (about 1 medium-size)

½ cup chopped scooped-out kohlrabi centers (reserved from the kohlrabi, above)

2 tablespoons finely minced smoked ham

2 tablespoons finely minced flat-leaf parsley

¼ teaspoon salt

⅛ teaspoon freshly ground black pepper

⅛ teaspoon freshly grated nutmeg

1 extra-large egg, lightly beaten

Cooking the Stuffed Kohlrabi:

2 tablespoons unsalted butter or margarine

1 cup rich chicken broth (preferably homemade)

½ cup heavy cream

2 teaspoons tomato paste

Makes 4 servings

Cook the kohlrabi in a large heavy saucepan of lightly salted boiling water for 15 to 18 minutes, until crisp-tender. Drain the kohlrabi well, slice 1 inch off the top of each, and

continued on next page

267

STUFFED KOHLRABI
(cont.)

reserve. With a melon baller, scoop out the centers of each kohlrabi, leaving shells ⅜ inch thick. Level the bottoms of the kohlrabi, if necessary, to make them stand straight without wobbling. Finely chop and reserve enough of the scooped-out centers to total ½ cup.

For the stuffing: Place the water in a small bowl, crumble in the roll, soak 15 minutes, then squeeze as dry as possible and set aside. Melt the butter in a heavy 10-inch skillet over moderate heat and sauté the onion 3 minutes, stirring occasionally, until pale golden. Add the tomato and reserved chopped kolhrabi centers and sauté, stirring now and then, for 3 minutes. Add the ham, parsley, and squeezed-out roll and cook 2 minutes longer, stirring occasionally. Remove from the heat and mix in the salt, pepper, nutmeg, and egg. Spoon the mixture into the scooped-out kohlrabi and set the caps firmly into place.

For cooking the stuffed kohlrabi: Melt the butter in a medium-size heavy saucepan over moderate heat, stand the kohlrabi upright in the butter, and brown the bottoms 2 minutes. Combine the broth, cream, and tomato paste, add to the saucepan, and bring to a boil. Adjust the heat so the mixture bubbles gently, cover tightly, and simmer 40 to 45 minutes, until a fork will pierce the kohlrabi easily. Transfer the kohlrabi to a serving dish and keep warm. Boil the cooking liquid, uncovered, over moderately high heat for 2 to 3 minutes, until lightly thickened. Pour over the kohlrabi and serve at once.

LEEK TART

Lauchkuchen

Although the Germans call this a cake, it is really a quichelike tart baked in a multilayered phyllo crust. This particular recipe comes from Burg Windeck, a medieval mountaintop castle-inn near Baden-Baden.

Pastry:

8 sheets fresh or frozen and thawed phyllo pastry (available at supermarkets)

8 tablespoons (1 stick) unsalted butter or margarine, melted

Filling:

2 tablespoons unsalted butter or margarine

3 large leeks, trimmed, washed, and thinly sliced

½ pound Emmentaler cheese, coarsely grated

3 extra-large eggs, lightly beaten

1¼ cups milk

1¼ cups half-and-half

1 tablespoon kirschwasser

½ teaspoon salt

⅛ teaspoon freshly grated nutmeg

⅛ teaspoon white pepper

Makes 6 to 8 servings

For the pastry: Butter the bottom and sides of a 9 x 9 x 2-inch baking dish. Brush the first sheet of phyllo with melted butter, fold in half horizontally, and gently but firmly press into the baking dish, allowing an equal amount of overhang on opposite sides. Brush the pastry overhang well with butter to prevent drying. Brush a second sheet of phyllo with butter, fold in half horizontally, and place in the dish at right angles to the first layer. Brush the overhang with butter as before. Repeat with the 6 remaining sheets of phyllo, placing each at right angles to the previous one and brushing the overhang well with butter. When the last sheet is in place, roll the overhang under just to cover the rim of the dish. Set aside.

continued on next page

269

LEEK TART (cont.)

Preheat the oven to 300° F.

For the filling: Melt the butter in a small heavy skillet over moderately high heat and sauté the leeks until golden, about 5 minutes. Sprinkle the leeks and cheese over the pastry. Whisk the eggs, milk, half-and-half, kirschwasser, salt, nutmeg, and pepper in a large bowl, blending well. Pour into the pastry-lined pan, then bake, uncovered, for 50 to 60 minutes, until set. To test, insert a toothpick midway between the center and the rim; if it comes out clean, the tart is done. Cool the tart in the pan for 30 minutes, cut into large squares, and serve. Cut into 1- to 1 ½-inch squares, the tart is good cocktail party food.

ONION CAKE FROM THE RHEINPFALZ
Rheinpfälzer Zwiebelkuchen

This onion cake recipe is our adaptation of one sent us by Alice Fitz of Weingut Fitz-Ritter in Bad Dürkheim, Rheinpfalz. She says that Zwiebelkuchen *is especially popular during the harvest season, also that it's customary to wash it down with a glass of Federweisser (a new wine that hasn't finished fermenting). Of course Federweisser is available only at German wineries at harvest time. So Frau Fitz suggests accompanying her* Rheinpfälzer Zwiebelkuchen *with a full-bodied dry or medium-dry Rheinpfalz Riesling.*

6 ounces double-smoked slab bacon, cut into ¼-inch cubes (about 1½ cups bacon cubes)

2 medium-size Spanish onions (1¾ pounds), peeled, halved lengthwise, then each half thinly sliced (about 6 cups sliced onions)

2½ teaspoons caraway seeds

½ teaspoon freshly grated nutmeg

12 ounces frozen puff pastry, thawed

1¾ cups heavy cream, or 1 cup heavy cream and ¾ cup milk

3 extra-large eggs, lightly beaten

½ teaspoon salt

¼ teaspoon freshly ground black pepper

Makes 8 appetizer servings, 6 main-course servings

Preheat the oven to 350° F.

Sauté the bacon in a heavy 12-inch skillet over low heat for about 5 minutes, until all the drippings cook out and only

ONION CAKE FROM
THE RHEINPFALZ

crisp browned bits remain. Using a slotted spoon, lift the bacon bits to paper toweling to drain and reserve. Pour off all but 1 tablespoon drippings from the skillet (save for another use, if you wish).

Add the onions to the skillet, sprinkle with the caraway seeds and nutmeg, and sauté 5 minutes over moderate heat, stirring often. Reduce the heat to its lowest point, cover the skillet, and steam the onions for 15 minutes. Remove from the heat and set aside.

With a floured stockinette-covered rolling pin, roll the puff pastry on a well-floured surface into a 14-inch circle. Set a 12-inch tart tin on a baking sheet. Lop the pastry over the rolling pin, then ease into the tin, pressing it in to form a neat pastry shell. Trim the pastry overhang so it is ½ inch larger all around than the tart tin, then roll under so it rests on top of the tin and crimp, making a high fluted edge.

Pile the onion mixture into the pastry shell, spreading to the edges as smoothly as possible, then scatter the reserved bacon evenly on top. Bake the onion cake, uncovered, for 20 minutes. Meanwhile, whisk the cream, eggs, salt, and pepper until well blended and set aside.

Remove the partially baked onion cake from the oven and raise the heat to 400° F.

Slowly pour the cream mixture over the onion and bacon, distributing it as evenly as you can. Return the onion cake to the oven and bake, uncovered, 20 to 25 minutes, until the filling is set like custard and lightly browned. Remove the onion cake from the oven and cool 30 minutes.

To serve, cut into slim wedges (for appetizer portions) or medium-size wedges (for a main course). If you serve the onion cake as a main course, you will need nothing more to accompany it than a salad of crisp greens.

271

THE BAMBERG ONION
Die Bamberger Zwiebel

The half-timbered town of Bamberg is known as "The Rome of Franconia" because, like the Italian capital, it is built on seven hills. This particular recipe, given to us by Franconia native Werner Pompl, is nicknamed "The Onion Squasher" after the men whose job it was to tramp through the fields crushing young onion sprouts so the onions underground would grow big and flavorful. Despite its name, The Bamberg Onion – nothing more than big yellow onions stuffed with a ground pork mixture – is a main course. Serve with mashed potatoes, boiled potatoes, rye bread, or even sauerkraut. And, of course, a glass of beer.

Onions:

8 large yellow onions (about 4 pounds)

5 cups rich beef broth (preferably homemade and only lightly salted because the broth will be reduced for a sauce)

Stuffing:

½ kaiser roll or other hard roll (you'll need 1½ ounces in all)

⅓ cup water

½ pound lean ground pork

1½ cups moderately finely chopped yellow onion (from the insides of the onions above)

1 medium-size garlic clove, peeled and minced

1 extra-large egg

2 tablespoons coarsely chopped flat-leaf parsley

1 teaspoon dried leaf marjoram, crumbled

½ teaspoon finely grated lemon zest

½ teaspoon salt

¼ teaspoon freshly ground black pepper

¼ teaspoon freshly grated nutmeg

¼ teaspoon ground or pulverized caraway seeds

Sauce:

Casserole juices (from cooking the onions)

½ cup dark beer

1 tablespoon unsalted butter or margarine

Makes 8 servings

For the onions: Peel the onions very carefully, leaving the tops and root ends intact; set aside.

272

THE BAMBERG ONION

Bring the broth to a boil over moderate heat in a large heavy saucepan. Add the onions, cover, and parboil 5 minutes. Lift the onions from the broth and cool until easy to handle. Reserve the broth. Slice 1 inch off the top of each onion and save for another use. Using a small sharp paring knife, make crisscross cuts deep into the center of each onion, taking care not to nick the outer two layers. With a melon baller, very carefully scoop out the centers of each onion, leaving walls two-ply thick. Chop the onion centers moderately fine, measure out and reserve 1½ cups for the filling, and save the balance to use another day for soups, stews, burgers, or meat loaf. Let the hollowed-out onions drain upside down on several thicknesses of paper toweling while you prepare the stuffing.

Preheat the oven to 400° F.

For the stuffing: Crumble the roll into the water in a small bowl and let stand 10 minutes. Squeeze the pieces of roll lightly to extract some of the water, then place in a food processor fitted with the metal chopping blade. Add remaining stuffing ingredients and pulse 8 to 10 times to combine. (If you don't have a food processor, simply knead the mixture with your hands until well mixed.) Spoon the stuffing into the scooped-out onions, mounding it up a bit on top. Stand the onions in an ungreased round casserole just large enough to accommodate them without their touching one another. Prop the onions, as needed, with crumples of foil so that they stand straight without wobbling. Pour the reserved broth into the casserole to a depth of 1 inch. (You won't need all the broth, so save the balance to use for soups or stews another day.) Cover the onions and bake 1 hour, just until they are tender and the stuffing is cooked through. Using a slotted spoon, lift the onions to a heated round platter, cover loosely, and keep warm.

For the sauce: Pour the casserole juices into a small heavy saucepan, add the beer, and boil, uncovered, for 5 minutes over high heat, until the liquid is reduced by about half.

273

continued on next page

THE BAMBERG ONION (cont.)

Add the butter and whisk until it melts. Carefully pour the broth mixture around the onions on the platter, covering the well completely. When serving, make sure that each person gets some of the sauce.

GRATIN OF PORCINI
Gratin von Steinpilzen

This elegant dish of wild forest mushrooms can be served as a first course or as an accompaniment to meat. It is our interpretation of a fabulous chanterelle gratin developed by Chef Günter Scherrer of Victorien Restaurant in Düsseldorf. Chanterelles (Pfifferlinge) are not easily come by in many parts of the United States. Fortunately, almost any fresh mushrooms will do, but we prefer the meaty boletus or porcini (Steinpilze) or the earthy morels (Morcheln). We've even had great success using the big steak-rich Portobello mushrooms, now appearing in American supermarkets. If none of these is available, substitute white cultivated mushrooms.

1 pound porcini or other mushrooms, wiped clean with a damp cloth (see note)

2 tablespoons unsalted butter or margarine

¼ pound Westphalian ham or prosciutto, trimmed of excess fat and cut into small dice

4 large shallots, peeled and minced

1¼ cups heavy cream

⅓ cup minced flat-leaf parsley

2 tablespoons minced fresh chervil, or 1 teaspoon dried leaf chervil, crumbled

⅛ teaspoon freshly ground black pepper

2 extra-large egg yolks, lightly beaten

Makes 4 servings

Preheat the oven to 375° F. Butter a 6-cup gratin dish and set aside.

Stem the porcini, cut off and discard the woody ends, then coarsely chop the remaining stems and set aside. Slice the caps about ¼ inch thick and set aside. If using morels, chanterelles, or white cultivated mushrooms, leave whole, halve, or quarter, depending on their size.

Melt the butter in a heavy 10-inch skillet over moderate heat and sauté the ham for 2 minutes. Add the shallots and sauté 3 to 4 minutes, until golden. Add the mushroom stems and caps and sauté about 5 minutes, just until they release their

274

GRATIN OF PORCINI

juices and these evaporate. Add ¾ cup of the cream and let it come to a boil. Using a slotted spoon, lift the mushrooms to a bowl and keep warm.

Boil the cream, uncovered, for 3 to 4 minutes, until the consistency of a thin white sauce. Mix in the parsley, chervil, and pepper, then return the mushrooms to the skillet along with any liquid that has accumulated in the bottom of the bowl.

Whip the remaining ½ cup heavy cream to soft peaks, blend in the egg yolks, then stir into the mushroom mixture. Spoon into the prepared gratin dish and bake, uncovered, for 25 to 30 minutes, until bubbly and touched with brown. Serve at once.

Note: If you use morels, you'll have to wash them carefully to remove all the grit lurking in their honeycombed caps. Drain well and pat dry on paper toweling before using.

MOREL- OR CHANTERELLE-STUFFED PANCAKES
Pfannkuchen gefüllt mit Morcheln oder Pfifferlingen

If morels or chanterelles are unavailable, use white cultivated mushrooms. They work beautifully but don't have as much flavor. This recipe is hearty enough to serve as the main course of a light lunch or supper.

Pancakes:

1 recipe Basic German Pancakes (page 325)

Mushroom Filling:

2 tablespoons unsalted butter or margarine

1 large yellow onion, peeled and coarsely chopped

1 pound morels or chanterelles, carefully washed, patted dry on paper toweling, then thinly sliced

½ teaspoon dried leaf marjoram, crumbled

¼ teaspoon dried leaf thyme, crumbled

¼ pound sliced boiled ham, cut into fine julienne (1 cup)

Sauce:

2 tablespoons unsalted butter or margarine

continued on next page

MOREL- OR
CHANTERELLE-STUFFED
PANCAKES (cont.)

4 tablespoons all-purpose flour

¼ teaspoon freshly grated nutmeg

1¼ cups milk, at room temperature

1 cup heavy cream, at room temperature

¾ teaspoon salt

⅛ teaspoon white pepper

3 tablespoons freshly grated Parmesan cheese

Topping:

3 tablespoons freshly grated Parmesan cheese

Makes 6 servings

For the pancakes: Prepare and cook the pancakes as directed, stack between sheets of wax paper, and let stand at room temperature for several hours.

For the mushroom filling: Melt the butter in a heavy 12-inch skillet over moderate heat. Add the onion and sauté 2 minutes, stirring often, until limp. Add the morels, marjoram, and thyme and cook and stir 1 minute; reduce the heat to low, cover, and steam 15 minutes. Uncover the skillet, raise the heat to high, and cook 3 to 4 minutes, stirring often, until all juices evaporate. Mix in the ham and remove from the heat.

For the sauce: Melt the butter in a small heavy saucepan over moderate heat, blend in the flour and nutmeg, and cook and stir 1 minute. Add the milk and cream and cook 3 minutes, stirring constantly, until thickened and smooth. Mix in the salt and pepper, reduce heat to its lowest point, and let the sauce mellow, uncovered, for 5 minutes, stirring often. Blend in the Parmesan and remove from the heat. Mix ½ cup of the sauce into the mushroom mixture, set over moderate heat, and cook 2 to 3 minutes, stirring constantly, until thick. Remove from the heat.

MOREL- OR
CHANTERELLE-STUFFED
PANCAKES

To assemble the pancakes: Preheat the oven to 375° F. Lightly butter a 13 x 9 x 2-inch baking pan and set aside.

Place a pancake, prettiest side down, on a wax-paper-covered surface and ladle ½ cup of the mushroom mixture on the lower third of the pancake. Using a spoon, elongate the mixture into a chunky log shape, leaving ½-inch margins at either end. Fold the bottom of the pancake up over the mushroom mixture, then roll jelly-roll style as snugly as possible without forcing the filling out.

Arrange the filled pancake seam side down in the prepared baking pan. Fill and roll the remaining pancakes the same way and arrange seam side down in the pan in a single layer.

Pour the remaining sauce evenly over the pancakes – it won't cover them completely – then scatter the Parmesan cheese on top. Bake, uncovered, for 35 to 40 minutes, until bubbly and touched with brown. Serve at once.

PURÉE OF PARSLEY ROOTS
Petersilienwurzeln-Püree

Good German home cooks slip parsley roots into soups and stews, but Chef Harald Schmitt of the Orangerie at Wiesbaden's Hotel Nassauer Hof whips them into an aromatic purée that can be served in place of mashed potatoes. P.S. Be sure to try the celery root variation that follows.

6 medium-size parsley roots with tops (about 1¾ pounds)

1½ cups half-and-half, or 1 cup milk and ½ cup half-and-half

2 tablespoons unsalted butter or margarine

¾ teaspoon salt

¼ teaspoon freshly ground black pepper

¼ teaspoon freshly grated nutmeg

Makes 4 to 6 servings

Remove the green tops from the parsley roots and chop enough of them to equal ½ cup; set aside. Peel the parsley roots, cut into 1-inch cubes, and place in a medium-size heavy saucepan. Add the half-and-half and gently push the parsley roots underneath the cream (they will float at first).

continued on next page

PURÉE OF PARSLEY
ROOTS (cont.)

Set, uncovered, over moderate heat and bring to a boil.
Adjust the heat so the mixture bubbles gently, then cover
and simmer 30 minutes, until the parsley roots are soft. Add
the reserved tops and cool 10 minutes.

Transfer to a food processor fitted with the metal chopping
blade and purée 20 seconds, until smooth. Return to the
saucepan, add the butter, salt, pepper, and nutmeg, and
bring just to serving temperature over moderate heat,
stirring often.

Variation

Celery Root Purée (Sellerie-Püree): Prepare as directed for
Purée of Parsley Roots but substitute 1¾ pounds peeled and
cubed celery root for the parsley roots. Also season, if you
like, with a pinch each of crumbled dried leaf thyme and
marjoram or rosemary.

SPINACH CASSEROLE WITH CHEESE SOUFFLÉ TOPPING
Spinatauflauf mit Käsehaube

*Hearty enough to
serve as a main course
(especially if you
include the optional
hard-cooked eggs), this
recipe comes from Fée
Steifensand, whose
husband Wilhelm's
family owns the P.J.
Valckenberg Winery in
the Rhine River town of
Worms. It's a popular
family recipe, Frau
Steifensand says. Showy,
too, and easy to make.*

Spinach Mixture:

1 pound fresh spinach, trimmed and well washed, or 1
   (10-ounce) package frozen chopped spinach, cooked by
   package directions and drained

2 extra-large hard-cooked eggs, peeled and moderately
   coarsely chopped (optional)

Soufflé Topping:

3 tablespoons unsalted butter or margarine

5 tablespoons all-purpose flour

1⅓ cups milk

½ cup coarsely shredded Emmentaler cheese (about 2
   ounces)

¼ teaspoon salt

¼ teaspoon freshly ground black pepper

SPINACH CASSEROLE
WITH CHEESE SOUFFLÉ
TOPPING

⅛ teaspoon sugar

¼ teaspoon freshly grated nutmeg

2 extra-large eggs, separated

Makes 4 servings

For the spinach mixture: Place the spinach in a large heavy saucepan, cover, and steam 3 to 5 minutes over moderate heat, until somewhat wilted but still intensely green. Drain well, coarsely chop, then arrange in a buttered 6-cup casserole that is at least 2¾ inches deep. Scatter the hard-cooked eggs on top, if you like, and set aside.

Preheat the oven to 375° F.

For the soufflé topping: Melt the butter in a small heavy saucepan over moderate heat, blend in the flour, then add the milk and cook about 3 minutes, stirring constantly, until thickened and smooth. Add the cheese, salt, pepper, sugar, and nutmeg and cook, stirring constantly, just until the sauce bubbles up and the cheese melts. Remove the sauce from the heat and cool 15 minutes, whisking often to prevent a skin from forming on the surface. Blend in the egg yolks. Beat the egg whites until stiff. Stir a heaping tablespoon of them into the sauce to lighten it, then fold in the balance gently but thoroughly.

Pour the soufflé mixture into the casserole on top of the spinach and bake, uncovered, for 35 to 40 minutes, until puffed and lightly browned. Serve at once before the soufflé topping begins to deflate.

279

GLAZED TURNIPS

Glasierte Weisse Rübchen

Once the turnips are cut, this frugal Bavarian recipe couldn't be easier. Serve with pork or ham.

2 tablespoons bacon drippings

1½ tablespoons sugar (preferably superfine)

1½ pounds large turnips or rutabaga, peeled and cut into strips the size of shoestring potatoes

1 tablespoon all-purpose flour

½ cup rich beef broth (preferably homemade)

½ teaspoon salt

¼ teaspoon freshly ground black pepper

1 large whole bay leaf

1 tablespoon unsalted butter or margarine

Makes 4 to 6 servings

Heat the drippings in a heavy 12-inch skillet over moderate heat for 1 minute. Add the sugar and cook, shaking and tilting the skillet from side to side, about 2 minutes, until the sugar dissolves and begins to caramelize. Add the turnips and toss and turn in the caramel mixture. Bits of it will harden, but these will dissolve as the turnips cook. Sprinkle the flour over the turnips and toss well to mix. Add the broth, salt, and pepper, then tuck in the bay leaf. Adjust the heat so the mixture bubbles gently, cover, and cook 5 minutes, until the turnips are crisp-tender. Remove the bay leaf, add the butter, and toss with the turnips until melted. Serve at once.

SALADS
Salate

SQUAB, GREEN BEAN, AND RED LETTUCE SALAD WITH WARM GRAVY DRESSING
Salat von Tauben, grünen Bohnen, und rotem Kopfsalat mit warmer Sauce

A couple of years ago when we were touring Germany's Black Forest, we ate a memorable warm quail salad at Burg Windeck, a mountaintop restaurant built inside the ruins of a medieval castle near Baden-Baden. Our version of the salad, which substitutes more readily available squab for quail, is otherwise quite like the original. Serve as a first course preceding the entrée of an elegant dinner party. Or serve as the main course of a light luncheon.

Salad:

1 (¾- to 1-pound) oven-ready squab

½ pound young green beans, cut into matchstick strips, parboiled 5 minutes, and drained

2 medium-size leeks, washed, trimmed, cut into matchstick strips, parboiled 2 minutes, and drained

¼ pound celery root, peeled, cut into matchstick strips, parboiled 3 minutes, and drained

1 medium-size head red lettuce, or 2 medium-size heads radicchio, trimmed, washed, and cut into fine shreds

Gravy Dressing:

2 tablespoons finely minced shallots or scallions

⅓ cup squab pan drippings (add olive oil, if necessary, to round out the measure)

2 to 3 tablespoons reduced squab stock (see below)

¼ cup olive oil

1 teaspoon Dijon mustard

1 tablespoon snipped fresh chives

1 tablespoon minced parsley

½ teaspoon dried leaf tarragon, crumbled

⅛ teaspoon dried leaf chervil, crumbled

3 tablespoons tarragon vinegar

½ teaspoon salt

⅛ teaspoon freshly ground black pepper

Makes 4 to 6 servings

continued on next page

281

SQUAB, GREEN BEAN,
AND RED LETTUCE
SALAD WITH WARM
GRAVY DRESSING
(cont.)

For the salad: Preheat the oven to 375° F.

Place the squab in a small shallow roasting pan and roast 35 to 40 minutes, until nicely browned. Remove from the oven and cool until easy to handle. Pour the drippings into a small heavy saucepan and set aside. Remove the squab meat from the carcass and cut into matchstick strips; also cut the crisp skin into thin strips; set both aside. Place the carcass in a small heavy saucepan, add enough cold water to cover, and simmer, uncovered, for 1 hour. Strain the stock (discard the carcass), then boil hard, uncovered, until reduced to 2 to 3 tablespoons (only a thin glaze will coat the bottom of the pan); reserve.

For the gravy dressing: Sauté the shallots 2 to 3 minutes in the reserved squab drippings in a small saucepan over moderate heat, until golden. Remove from the heat, add the reduced squab stock, and all remaining ingredients. Set, uncovered, over lowest heat, and keep hot.

To assemble the salad: Place the reserved squab, squab skin, and all other salad ingredients in a large bowl, pour the hot dressing over all, toss well, and serve at once.

BAVARIAN WURST SALAD
Bayerischer Wurstsalat

You can toss this salad together in no time, but you must let it marinate for several hours. Bavarians make the salad with bockwurst, but we've substituted the more readily available bologna, which looks and tastes very much the same. If you should find a really good bockwurst, by all means use it.

1½ pounds bologna, in one piece

2 medium-size yellow onions, peeled

½ cup corn oil

¼ cup red wine vinegar

1 tablespoon prepared spicy brown mustard

¼ teaspoon salt

⅛ teaspoon freshly ground black pepper

2 tablespoons freshly snipped chives

2 tablespoons coarsely chopped flat-leaf parsley

Makes 6 servings

BAVARIAN WURST
SALAD

Slice the bologna ¼ inch thick, then stack the slices, 3 or 4 at a time, and cut into eighths just as if you were cutting a pie; place in a large bowl.

Slice the onions thin, then stack the slices, 3 or 4 at a time, and quarter; add to the bowl with the bologna. Whisk the oil with the vinegar, mustard, salt, and pepper until creamy, pour over the bologna and onions, and toss well to mix. Cover and let stand at room temperature, tossing occasionally, for 2 hours. (If the kitchen is hot, marinate in the refrigerator.) Taste the salad for salt and pepper and adjust as needed. Add the chives and parsley, toss well again, and serve as a main course.

RAW ASPARAGUS SALAD
Roher Spargelsalat

Germans are so fond of asparagus they are constantly dreaming up new ways to prepare it. This one is unusual – and successful. To keep asparagus from discoloring (especially green asparagus), marinate it with the oil and seasonings, then add the vinegar just before serving.

1¾ pounds tender young asparagus (preferably white), tough
   stem ends removed

1½ tablespoons minced fresh chervil, or 2 teaspoons each
   minced fresh tarragon and flat-leaf parsley

2 to 3 tablespoons corn oil

¼ teaspoon sugar

¼ teaspoon salt

⅛ teaspoon freshly ground black pepper

1 to 2 tablespoons red wine vinegar

Makes 4 servings

Cut the tips off the asparagus and place in a medium-size bowl. Using a swivel-bladed vegetable peeler, peel the asparagus stalks, then slice ¼ inch thick, letting the slices fall into the bowl with the tips. Add the chervil, 2 tablespoons of the oil, the sugar, salt, and pepper and toss lightly. If the asparagus isn't nicely glossed with oil, add the remaining tablespoon and toss again. Cover and marinate at room temperature for 1½ to 2 hours. Add 1 tablespoon of the vinegar, toss lightly, taste, and if the salad isn't tart enough, add the extra tablespoon of vinegar. Toss lightly and serve.

ASPARAGUS, SNOW PEA, AND RADISH SALAD
Spargel, Zuckererbsen, und Radieschen Salat

To give an idea of the lighter dishes modern German cooks are preparing these days, Hedy recently demonstrated this crunchy red, white, and green salad on American television. If it is to have the proper flavor, you must marinate the vegetables with the oil and seasonings for at least an hour. The acidity in the lime juice will ruin the vibrant green of the snow peas, so don't add it until you're ready to serve. This colorful salad is an ideal accompaniment to broiled chicken, salmon, and other firm-fleshed fish like tuna and swordfish.

1¼ pounds asparagus (preferably white), tough stem ends snapped off, then the stalks peeled and cut on the diagonal into 1-inch chunks

½ pound snow peas, stemmed and strings removed

3 medium-size scallions, trimmed and thinly sliced (include some tops)

15 small red radishes, trimmed and thinly sliced

¼ cup freshly snipped dill

3 tablespoons corn oil

1 teaspoon superfine sugar

¾ teaspoon salt

¼ teaspoon freshly ground black pepper

3 to 4 tablespoons freshly squeezed lime juice

Makes 6 servings

Blanch the asparagus in a large kettle of boiling water for 2 minutes. Drain and pat dry on paper toweling. Blanch the snow peas in a large kettle of boiling water for 1 minute. Drain and pat dry on paper toweling. Cut the snow peas crosswise and on the diagonal into 1-inch chunks.

Place the asparagus and snow peas in a large mixing bowl, add the scallions, radishes, and dill, and toss lightly. Quickly whisk the oil with the sugar, salt, and pepper and drizzle evenly over the salad. Toss carefully, then cover and marinate at room temperature for 1 hour, or in the refrigerator for 3 to 4 hours.

When ready to serve, drizzle 3 tablespoons of the lime juice over the salad, toss carefully but thoroughly, taste, and if not tart enough, add the remaining tablespoon lime juice. Toss again. (If the salad is refrigerator-cold, let stand at room temperature for 30 minutes before adding the lime juice.)

COLD MARINATED GREEN BEANS WITH THYME

Bohnensalat mit Thymian

Be sure the beans you use for this modern German recipe are young and tender. Also, do not add the lemon juice, vinegar, and mustard until just before serving, otherwise the beans will turn an unappetizing khaki color.

1 pound green beans, tipped, snapped into 1-inch lengths, boiled until crisp-tender, and drained well

3 medium-size shallots, peeled and minced

1 small garlic clove, peeled and minced

½ teaspoon salt

¼ teaspoon freshly ground black pepper

10 small sprigs fresh thyme, rosemary, marjoram, or oregano (see note)

¼ cup olive or corn oil

2 tablespoons freshly squeezed lemon juice

2 tablespoons balsamic vinegar

1 tablespoon Dijon mustard

1 teaspoon superfine sugar

Makes 4 to 6 servings

Place the beans, shallots, garlic, salt, pepper, thyme sprigs, and oil in a large nonmetallic bowl and toss well to mix. Cover and refrigerate at least 12 hours, or overnight.

Remove from the refrigerator and let stand, still covered, at room temperature for 1 hour. In a small bowl, whisk the lemon juice, vinegar, mustard, and sugar until creamy. Drizzle evenly over the bean mixture and toss well. Remove the thyme sprigs or not, as you like, and serve as a salad.

Note: Fresh thyme is essential for proper flavor; do not substitute the dried, which will give the beans an unpleasant bitter taste.

SHREDDED BEET AND HORSERADISH SALAD

Geriebener Rote Bete-Salat mit Meerrettich

Fresh horseradish is what most Germans use for this salad because it adds plenty of bite. Prepared horseradish (either the red or white) is an acceptable substitute, but it lacks the punch of the freshly grated root. Serve this salad with ham, wursts, or any kind of pork.

2 pounds large beets, trimmed of all but 1 inch of the tops and scrubbed but not peeled (see note)

Dressing:

½ cup cider vinegar

¾ cup water

1 medium-size yellow onion, peeled and finely chopped

2 tablespoon finely grated fresh horseradish, or ¼ cup prepared horseradish

1 tablespoon sugar

1 tablespoon caraway seeds

½ teaspoon salt

2 tablespoons corn oil

Makes 6 servings

Boil the beets in enough water to cover in a covered, large heavy saucepan over moderate heat about 1 hour, or until a fork will pierce them easily.

For the dressing: Place the vinegar, water, onion, horseradish, sugar, caraway seeds, and salt in a small, heavy, nonmetallic saucepan. Set, uncovered, over moderate heat and bring to a boil. Reduce the heat to low and simmer, uncovered, about 20 minutes, until reduced by one third. Turn the heat to its lowest point, set the lid askew, and keep the dressing hot while the beets finish cooking.

Drain the beets well, quick-chill in cold water until easy to handle, then cut off the root ends and tops and peel. Coarsely shred the beets into a large ceramic bowl, pour the dressing evenly over all, and toss well. Cover and marinate at room temperature for 1 hour. Drizzle the oil evenly over the beets and toss well. Taste for salt and adjust, as needed. Toss once again and serve.

286

| SHREDDED BEET AND HORSERADISH SALAD | Note: Mature beets shred more neatly than young and tender ones, so choose those about the size of tennis balls. |

CELERY ROOT AND APPLE SALAD WITH DILL-MUSTARD DRESSING
Sellerie-Apfelsalat mit Dill-Senfsauce

Hedy says this is the salad to serve with chicken – especially cold chicken. Or with leftover turkey.

Salad:

1 large celery root (about 1 pound), peeled and cut into matchstick strips (4 cups)

2 medium-size tart apples, peeled, cored, and cut into matchstick strips (2 cups)

Dressing:

⅓ cup sour cream

⅓ cup mayonnaise (preferably homemade)

1 tablespoon Dijon mustard

1 tablespoon freshly squeezed lemon juice

1 teaspoon sugar

½ teaspoon salt

⅛ teaspoon freshly ground black pepper

1 tablespoon moderately finely snipped fresh dill, or ½ teaspoon dillweed

1 tablespoon minced parsley

Makes 4 to 6 servings

For the salad: Blanch the celery root in a large saucepan of lightly salted boiling water for 3 minutes. With a skimmer or slotted spoon, lift to a large sieve set over a large heatproof bowl and drain 5 minutes. Transfer to a large nonmetallic bowl and add the apples.

For the dressing: Whisk all ingredients together until creamy, drizzle over the salad, and toss lightly. Cover and marinate several hours in the refrigerator. Toss well, taste for sugar, salt, and pepper, adjust as needed, then serve.

287

CUCUMBER SALAD WITH MUSTARD DRESSING

Gurkensalat mit Senfsauce

Hedy's favorite cucumber salad and one she prepares often, it's particularly good with poached salmon, trout, pike, cod, almost any fish. Hedy says that cucumber salad is also often paired with sausages and potato salad. "That's quite traditional."

1 cup half-and-half

½ cup plain low-fat yogurt

2 tablespoons Dijon mustard

¾ teaspoon salt

½ teaspoon freshly ground black pepper

¼ cup moderately finely snipped fresh dill

1¼ pounds Kirby cucumbers, peeled and thinly sliced

Makes 6 to 8 servings

Whisk the half-and-half, yogurt, mustard, salt, pepper, and dill in a large bowl until creamy. Taste for mustard and add a bit more, if needed; there should be a distinct mustard flavor, but take care not to add so much that you overpower the flavor of the cucumbers. Add the cucumbers to the bowl and toss well to mix. Cover with plastic wrap and refrigerate at least 4 hours before serving, or better yet, chill overnight.

WARM COLESLAW WITH BACON AND CARAWAY

Bayrischer Krautsalat

It's imperative that you don't overcook the cabbage – 5 minutes in heavily salted boiling water should be sufficient – and that you drain the cabbage very dry so that it doesn't water down the dressing. This particular slaw is superb with pork chops, roast pork, and a wide variety of wursts.

5 ounces lean smoked slab bacon, cut into ¼-inch cubes (about 1¼ cups bacon cubes)

1 large green cabbage (2 to 2½ pounds), cored and sliced ½ inch thick

4 quarts cold water

5 tablespoons salt (that's right, *tablespoons*)

¼ cup (approximately) bacon drippings

⅓ cup rich beef broth (preferably homemade)

3 tablespoons red wine vinegar

1 tablespoon sugar

WARM COLESLAW WITH BACON AND CARAWAY

2 teaspoons caraway seeds

¼ teaspoon freshly ground black pepper

Makes 8 servings

Sauté the bacon in a medium-size heavy skillet over moderately low heat for 15 to 20 minutes, stirring often, until most of the drippings have cooked out and the bacon is golden and translucent but not brown.

While the bacon cooks, halve or quarter any cabbage slices that are unusually large. Bring the water and salt to a rolling boil in a very large kettle (the type you'd use to cook pasta). Dump in the cabbage and cook, uncovered, for 5 minutes, until barely tender. Drain at once, return the cabbage to the kettle, and shake well over moderate heat for 1 to 2 minutes to drive off all excess moisture. Transfer the cabbage to a large bowl.

Drain the bacon drippings into a measuring cup; you'll need ¼ cup, so if there are insufficient drippings, round out the measure with corn oil. Sprinkle the bacon cubes over the cabbage. Place the drippings in a small saucepan, add the broth, vinegar, sugar, and caraway seeds and bring quickly to the boil. Pour over the cabbage and toss lightly to mix. If the slaw seems skimpily dressed, add another tablespoon or two of bacon drippings (or of corn oil) – every leaf should glisten with dressing. Sprinkle the slaw with the pepper and toss lightly again. Let stand at room temperature for about 15 minutes before serving.

PIQUANT CARROT SALAD

Pikanter Karottensalat

This unusual salad comes from the late Werner Pompl, a great "hobby cook" from Franconia (the region of Nuremberg). It couldn't be easier to make – especially if you have a food processor and fine shredding disk. If you processor-shred the carrots, you can make the dressing in the processor, too. Just re-equip the machine with the metal chopping blade, add all dressing ingredients, and pulse 8 to 10 times. That's all there is to it.

Salad:

1 pound carrots, peeled and finely shredded

Creamy Horseradish Dressing:

3 tablespoons prepared horseradish

2 tablespoons vegetable oil

½ cup half-and-half or heavy cream

2½ tablespoons freshly squeezed lemon juice

2 teaspoons sugar

1 teaspoon salt

¼ teaspoon freshly ground black pepper

Optional Garnish:

4 to 5 small clusters of seedless green and/or red grapes

Makes 4 servings

Place the carrots in a medium-size mixing bowl. Whisk the horseradish with the oil, cream, lemon juice, sugar, salt, and pepper until smooth. Drizzle evenly over the carrots and toss well to mix. Cover and refrigerate until ready to serve (you can make the salad as long as a day or two in advance).

Toss the mixture well again, mound in a salad bowl, and garnish, if you like, with clusters of grapes.

Segads

FENNEL SALAD
Fenchelsalat

Here's an unusual salad from Hedy's file of "new German recipes" that's a little bit tart, a little bit sweet, and wholly refreshing. Like leeks, fresh fennel contains considerable grit and sand, so wash very carefully, separating the stalks, if necessary, then pat dry on paper toweling. Serve this salad with pork, ham, or chicken. Or mound in lettuce or radicchio cups and serve as the main course of a light lunch or supper. Accompany with crusty chunks of Wheat (White) Bread (page 295), Angelika's Rye Bread with Ham (page 303), or Many Grain Bread (page 304).

Salad:

1 cup very coarsely chopped walnuts

¾ pound well-trimmed fennel (white part only; about 4 small bulbs)

2 large navel oranges, peeled, cut into eighths, then each eighth trimmed of all white pith, seeded, and sliced ¼ inch thick

½ pound Emmentaler cheese, cut into matchstick strips

Yogurt Dressing:

1¾ cups plain low-fat yogurt

2 tablespoons olive, corn, or other vegetable oil

3 tablespoons freshly squeezed lemon juice

1 tablespoon sugar

¾ teaspoon salt

¼ teaspoon freshly ground black pepper

Makes 6 to 8 servings

For the salad: Preheat the oven to 350° F. Spread the walnuts in a pie tin and toast in the oven for 12 to 15 minutes, until golden brown. Remove from the oven and set aside.

Quarter each fennel bulb lengthwise and slice each quarter ¼ inch thick; transfer to a large mixing bowl. Add the oranges, cheese, and walnuts and set aside.

For the yogurt dressing: Whisk all ingredients together in a small mixing bowl, pour evenly over the salad, and toss well. Cover with plastic wrap and chill 3 to 4 hours. Toss well again and serve.

HEDY'S HOT BAVARIAN POTATO SALAD
(Hedys Warmer Bayerischer Kartoffelsalat)

Because it contains no eggs or mayonnaise, this potato salad is far less perishable than most and is an ideal choice for picnics. It's equally good at room temperature, but shouldn't be served straight out of the refrigerator. Always let it stand at room temperature for 30 to 45 minutes to take the chill off.

5 pounds baking potatoes, scrubbed but not peeled

1 pound thickly sliced double-smoked bacon, snipped crosswise into ¼-inch strips

2 large yellow onions, peeled and coarsely chopped

1 teaspoon salt

½ teaspoon freshly ground black pepper

⅞ cup bacon drippings (if insufficient drippings cook out of the bacon, add enough corn oil to round out the measure)

1 cup boiling rich beef broth (preferably homemade)

2 tablespoons balsamic vinegar, or for a slightly tarter salad, cider or red wine vinegar

2 tablespoons coarsely chopped flat-leaf parsley

Makes 10 to 12 servings

Cook the potatoes, covered, in a large heavy saucepan of boiling water over moderate heat for about 1 hour, until firm-tender. Meanwhile, sauté the bacon in a heavy 12-inch skillet over moderate heat for 10 minutes, stirring often, until considerable drippings cook out. Reduce the heat to moderately low and continue cooking the bacon for 5 to 10 minutes longer, stirring often, until all the drippings cook out and only crisp brown bits remain. Using a slotted spoon, lift the bacon bits to paper toweling to drain. Pour all drippings from the skillet into a butter warmer or small heavy saucepan and set over lowest heat until ready to use.

Drain the potatoes. Working with about one fourth of the total amount at a time, peel while still hot. Slice ⅛ to ¼ inch thick and layer in a very large heatproof mixing bowl. (Here's an easy way to deal with hot potatoes: Place a potato on several thicknesses of paper toweling and pull the skin off in strips with a paring knife, turning the potato as needed.

With the potato still on the toweling, slice, then lift the toweling and dump the slices into the mixing bowl. This way you scarcely touch the hot potatoes.) Once a fourth of the potatoes are sliced and in the bowl, scatter one fourth each of the chopped onions and bacon bits over the potatoes, then ¼ teaspoon of the salt and ⅛ teaspoon of the pepper. Repeat the layers three times – potatoes, onions, bacon, salt, and pepper – until all are used. Do not toss.

Pour the hot bacon drippings evenly over the salad, then the broth, then sprinkle evenly with the vinegar. Toss well to mix – some of the potatoes will break apart, but this is as it should be. If the mixture seems dry, add a bit more broth. Taste for salt and pepper and adjust as needed. Scatter the parsley over the salad and serve at once.

POTATO SALAD IN LIGHT CHERVIL DRESSING
Kartoffelsalat in Kerbelmarinade

The perennial German favorite considerably lightened by Harald Wohlfahrt, the bright young chef at Schwarzwaldstube in Baiersbronn-Tonbach. For this recipe, which is our interpretation, you must use fresh chervil. The dried merely imparts an unpleasant grassy taste. If fresh chervil is unavailable, a mix of fresh tarragon and parsley approximates – if not duplicates – its delicate anise flavor.

Salad:

2½ pounds new potatoes, scrubbed but not peeled

4 slices double-smoked bacon, snipped crosswise into ¼-inch strips

Light Chervil Dressing:

½ cup coarsely chopped fresh chervil, or ⅓ cup coarsely chopped flat-leaf parsley and 3 tablespoons finely chopped fresh tarragon

4 large shallots, peeled and minced

½ cup plain low-fat yogurt

½ cup mayonnaise (preferably homemade)

¼ cup rich beef broth (preferably homemade)

2 tablespoons bacon drippings

4 teaspoons Dijon mustard

1 tablespoon balsamic or red wine vinegar

293

continued on next page

POTATO SALAD IN
LIGHT CHERVIL
DRESSING (cont.)

1 teaspoon salt

¼ teaspoon freshly ground black pepper

Makes 6 to 8 servings

For the salad: Cook the potatoes, covered, in a large heavy saucepan of boiling water over moderate heat for about 40 minutes, until firm-tender. Meanwhile, sauté the bacon in a heavy 8-inch skillet over moderate heat for 5 minutes, stirring often, until considerable drippings cook out. Reduce the heat to low and continue cooking the bacon for 5 to 10 minutes longer, stirring often, until all the drippings cook out and only crisp brown bits remain. Using a slotted spoon, lift the bacon bits to paper toweling to drain; reserve 2 tablespoons of the drippings for the dressing. When the potatoes are tender, drain well, then cool until easy to handle.

For the dressing: Place all ingredients in a large mixing bowl and whisk briskly to combine. Set aside.

Peel the potatoes and cut into ¾-inch cubes, letting them drop into the dressing in the bowl. Add the bacon bits and toss well to mix. Cover and chill several hours. Toss well again and serve.

BREADS
Brot

WHEAT (WHITE) BREAD
Weizenbrot

To Americans, "white bread" has come to mean lackluster, bland, dull, because millions of us have made squishy mass-produced loaves our daily staple. German white bread couldn't be more different. It's dense and flavorful and it gives the jaws a royal workout. This particular recipe – as well as Angelika's Rye Bread with Ham (page 303) and Many Grain Bread (page 304) – come from a dedicated home baker named Angelika Miebs from the Hesse region (Frankfurt is its major city). In addition to sharing three favorite bread recipes, Angelika offers this tip: "In order to get a nice crunchy crust on the breads, after five minutes of baking, pour a cup of ice water in a pan on the oven floor and close the door immediately." It works. This bread also toasts superbly.

7 cups (approximately) sifted unbleached all-purpose flour

1 (¼-ounce) package active dry yeast

2 teaspoons salt

2 cups warm water (105° to 115° F)

Makes one 11-inch loaf

Mix 5½ cups of the flour, the yeast, salt, and water in a large mixing bowl to make a soft dough, then beat hard until smooth and elastic. This is exhausting, so if you have a heavy-duty food processor or mixer with a dough hook, by all means use it (see note), beating the dough for 1 minute exactly, then letting it rest and cool for 5 minutes. Now beat the dough for 30 seconds by machine and again let rest for 5 minutes. Repeat the beating and resting process four more times. Scoop the dough into a well-buttered, warm, large bowl. With well-buttered hands, pat the surface of the dough so it is nicely buttered, too. Cover with a clean dry cloth and set to rise in a warm dry spot, away from drafts, until doubled in bulk. This will take about 1 hour.

Toward the end of rising, spread a pastry cloth on the counter and sprinkle with ¼ cup of the remaining flour. Punch the dough down, place on the floured cloth, and sift another ¼ cup of the remaining flour on top. Gently but carefully knead in the flour. At first, the dough will be very sticky, but keep adding the remaining flour, ¼ cup at a time, and kneading it in until the dough is smooth and elastic. Once the dough is a good manageable consistency, knead hard for 10 minutes. This extra kneading gives the bread its firm, chewy texture. Shape the dough into an oval loaf 9 to 10 inches long and 4 to 5 inches wide and place on a lightly

continued on next page

WHEAT (WHITE) BREAD
(cont.)

floured baking sheet. Cover with the cloth and let rise in a warm, dry, draft-free spot for 30 minutes.

Meanwhile, preheat the oven to 400° F.

Bake the bread for 1 hour, until nicely tan and hollow-sounding when thumped. Remove the bread from the oven, transfer to a wire rack, and cool to room temperature. To slice, cut crosswise, slightly on the bias, about ½ inch thick, using a sharp serrated knife.

Note: This bread can be made in a heavy-duty food processor or electric mixer with a dough hook, but you must be careful not to overheat the dough by beating or processing it too long; you'll kill the yeast. If you make this bread – or any bread, for that matter – in wet or humid weather, you may need to add more flour to make it a good kneadable consistency.

MUNSTERLAND BUTTERMILK BREAD
Münsterländer Buttermilchbrot

Quark (see page 51) is what gives this bread its unusual dense texture and fine moist crumb. It's a heavy loaf, but it melts in the mouth and toasts superbly. Because the dough is sticky-stiff, it's best to knead it in a heavy-duty food processor or electric mixer with a dough hook. You'll wear yourself out if you try to do the job by hand. When using the processor, take care not to overknead the dough; it will overheat and kill the yeast.

2 (¼-ounce) packages active dry yeast

1 tablespoon sugar

3¾ cups (approximately) sifted unbleached all-purpose flour

1 cup warm buttermilk (105° to 115° F; see note)

½ pound quark or light cream cheese, at room temperature

2 tablespoons lard, unsalted butter, or margarine, melted

1½ teaspoons salt

1½ cups unsifted medium rye flour

Makes one 8-inch round loaf

Combine the yeast, sugar, and ½ cup of the all-purpose flour by pulsing several times in a heavy-duty food processor fitted with the metal chopping blade. Add ¼ cup of the buttermilk and pulse several times more. Let the mixture stand in the covered food processor for 15 minutes, until spongy.

**MUNSTERLAND
BUTTERMILK BREAD**

Add the remaining buttermilk, the quark, lard, and salt and pulse about 5 times, until smooth. Add 1½ cups of the remaining all-purpose flour and all of the rye flour and process for 10 seconds, until smooth. (The mixture is very gluey at this point and the motor may strain. If it does, turn the processor off at once and let rest 2 to 3 minutes.)

Add another 1½ cups all-purpose flour and process for 10 seconds. Scrape down the sides of the workbowl and process 20 to 30 seconds longer, just until the dough rolls into a ball and rides up on the central spindle.

If mixing the dough in a heavy-duty mixer, first combine the yeast, sugar, ½ cup all-purpose flour, and ¼ cup buttermilk by hand in the large mixer bowl. Cover with a cloth and set in a warm spot to rise for 15 minutes. Return the bowl to the mixer, add the remaining buttermilk, the quark, lard, and salt and beat for 1 minute at moderate speed. Add 1½ cups of the remaining all-purpose flour and all of the rye flour and beat at low speed for 1 minute. Add another 1½ cups of the all-purpose flour and beat 1 minute longer at low speed. Remove the mixer beater, attach the dough hook, and knead the dough at moderately low speed for 3 to 5 minutes, until very smooth and elastic.

Shape the dough into a ball and place in a well-buttered, warm large bowl. With well-buttered hands, pat the surface of the dough so it is nicely buttered, too. Cover with a clean dry cloth and set to rise in a warm, dry spot, away from drafts, until doubled in bulk. This will take about 1 hour.

Toward the end of rising, spread a pastry cloth on the counter and sprinkle with the remaining ¼ cup all-purpose flour. Punch the dough down, place on the floured cloth, and knead hard, working in as much flour as needed to make a very stiff dough. Once the dough is a good manageable consistency, knead hard for 5 minutes, until very springy. This extra kneading develops the gluten in the bread and gives it firmer texture.

Shape the dough into a ball, dust all over with flour, and

continued on next page

297

MUNSTERLAND
BUTTERMILK BREAD
(cont.)

place in a lightly buttered 8-inch round layer cake pan. Make a deep X-cut in the top of the ball of dough, cover with the cloth, and let rise in a warm, dry, draft-free spot for 30 minutes.

Meanwhile, preheat the oven to 400° F.

Bake the bread for 35 to 40 minutes, until richly browned and hollow-sounding when thumped. Remove the bread from the oven and from the pan, set on a wire rack, and cool to room temperature. Slice about ½ inch thick, using a sharp serrated knife, and serve.

Note: To keep the buttermilk from curdling as you heat it, pour it into a heatproof measuring cup, stand in a small pan of cold water, set over low heat, and warm slowly, stirring now and then, just until a candy thermometer registers 105° to 115° F.

LIGHT RYE BREAD
Roggenbrot

American rye breads, no matter how dark or light, are likely to contain caraway seeds. Classic German "light ryes" do not, yet they're plenty flavorful. And thanks to the intense heat at which they're baked, they're good and crusty. This bread makes glorious toast.

2 (¼-ounce) packages active dry yeast

1 tablespoon sugar

1 cup warm water (105° to 115° F)

1½ cups unsifted medium rye flour

1 cup warm buttermilk (105° to 115° F; see note)

2 teaspoons salt

1½ cups unsifted whole wheat flour

3 to 3½ cups unsifted unbleached all-purpose flour

Makes one 8-inch round loaf

Dissolve the yeast and sugar in the water in a large warm bowl. Blend in ¾ cup of the rye flour, cover with a clean dry cloth, then set in a warm dry spot, away from drafts, for 20 to 25 minutes, until light and spongy. Stir down the sponge,

LIGHT RYE BREAD

then mix in the buttermilk, salt, remaining ¾ cup of the rye flour, and the whole wheat flour. Finally, mix in enough of the all-purpose flour to make a stiff but manageable dough. Knead hard on a well-floured pastry cloth for about 5 minutes or, if you have a heavy-duty electric mixer with the dough hook attachment, knead at moderately low speed for 5 minutes.

You can also mix and knead the dough in a heavy-duty food processor fitted with the metal chopping blade. Simply transfer the risen sponge to the processor workbowl, add the buttermilk, salt, remaining rye flour, and the whole wheat flour and pulse to combine. Finally, mix in enough of the all-purpose flour, 1 cup at a time and pulsing after each addition to incorporate, to make a stiff but manageable dough. Once all the flour is in, process the dough about 20 seconds, until it rolls into a ball and rides up on the central spindle. It's important that you do not overprocess the dough at this point because it will quickly heat up in the processor and can actually reach temperatures that will kill the yeast.

Shape the dough into a ball and place in a well-buttered, warm large bowl. With well-buttered hands, pat the surface of the dough so it is nicely buttered, too. Cover with a clean dry cloth and set to rise in a warm dry spot, away from drafts, until doubled in bulk. This will take about 1 hour.

Toward the end of rising, spread a pastry cloth on the counter and sprinkle with about ¼ cup unbleached all-purpose flour. Punch the dough down, place on the floured cloth, and knead hard, working in as much flour as needed to make a very stiff dough. Once the dough is a good manageable consistency, knead hard for 5 minutes, until smooth and elastic. This extra kneading gives the bread its firm, chewy texture.

Shape the dough into a ball, dust all over with flour, and place in a lightly buttered 9-inch round cake pan. Make a deep diagonal slash across the top of the ball of dough, cover with the cloth, and let rise in a warm, dry, draft-free spot for 30 minutes.

299

continued on next page

LIGHT RYE BREAD
(cont.)

Meanwhile, preheat the oven to 450° F.

Bake the bread for 40 minutes, until richly browned and hollow-sounding when thumped. Remove the bread from the oven, transfer from the pan to a wire rack, and cool to room temperature. Slice about ½ inch thick, using a sharp serrated knife, and serve.

Note: To keep the buttermilk from curdling as you heat it, pour it into a heatproof measuring cup, stand in a small pan of cold water, set over low heat, and warm slowly, stirring now and then, just until a candy thermometer registers 105° to 115° F.

BLACK BREAD
Schwarzbrot

German black bread isn't black, it's beige or brown. Still, Germans routinely lump nonwhite breads into the Schwarzbrot category. This one is actually a dark rye bread, which owes its toasty color to whole-grain flours (rye and wheat), plus burnt sugar syrup. Molasses is not a common commodity in Germany, so whenever bakers need to darken their breads, they usually rely on caramel, or burnt sugar syrup.

2 teaspoons whole caraway seeds

2 cups warm buttermilk (105° to 115° F; see note above)

½ cup sugar

½ cup boiling water

2 (¼-ounce) packages active dry yeast

½ cup warm water (105° to 115° F)

1 cup unsifted whole wheat flour

¼ cup corn or other vegetable oil

2 teaspoons freshly ground caraway seeds (see notes on page 302)

2 teaspoons salt

2 cups unsifted medium rye flour

4⅔ cups (approximately) sifted bread flour

Glaze:

1 egg white, beaten until frothy with 1 tablespoon cold water

Makes two 10-inch oval loaves

BLACK BREAD

Let the whole caraway seeds soften in the warm buttermilk on the back of the stove while you proceed with the recipe.

Place the sugar in a heavy 10-inch skillet and tilt from side to side so it covers the skillet bottom evenly. Set over moderate heat and let the sugar melt, shaking the skillet often (don't stir or the sugar will clump), then let the sugar caramelize until an even rich brown; this will take about 5 minutes in all. Pour the boiling water slowly into the skillet – it will sputter violently at first, so stand back. Reduce the heat to very low and let the mixture simmer, uncovered, about 10 minutes, stirring occasionally, until all of the hard caramel lumps dissolve. You should have ⅓ cup burnt sugar syrup; if not, round out the measure with a little hot water.

Meanwhile, dissolve the yeast in the warm water, blend in ½ cup of the whole wheat flour, and set in a warm spot for 10 minutes, until light and spongy. Transfer to the large electric mixer bowl (the mixer should be equipped with the "creaming" beater). The food processor won't work for this heavy dough.

Quickly combine the burnt sugar syrup, warm buttermilk and whole caraway seeds, oil, ground caraway seeds, and salt and pour into the mixer bowl. Add the remaining ½ cup whole wheat flour and 1 cup of the rye flour and mix at low speed about 1 minute. Add the remaining rye flour and 4 cups of the bread flour, 1 cup at a time, beating well after each addition, to make a very stiff but manageable dough. Remove the creaming beater from the mixer and insert the dough hook, then knead the dough for 5 minutes at low speed.

Shape the dough into a ball and place in a well-buttered, warm large bowl. With well-buttered hands, pat the surface of the dough so it's nicely buttered, too. Cover with a clean dry cloth and set to rise in a warm dry spot, away from drafts, until doubled in bulk. This will take about 1 hour.

Toward the end of rising, spread a pastry cloth on the counter and sprinkle with ⅓ cup of the remaining bread

301

continued on next page

BLACK BREAD (cont.)

flour. Punch the dough down, place on the floured cloth, and knead hard, working in all the flour. Sprinkle the final ⅓ cup bread flour over the pastry cloth and knead in all of it. This extra kneading gives the bread its firm, chewy texture.

Divide the dough in half and shape each into an oval about 7½ inches long and 4 inches wide. Sift a little flour over a large baking sheet, then arrange the loaves crosswise on the sheet, spacing them 4 to 5 inches apart. Cover with the cloth and let rise in a warm, dry, draft-free spot for 30 minutes.

Meanwhile, preheat the oven to 350° F.

Once the loaves have risen, brush the tops and sides with the beaten egg white, but take care that it doesn't run down onto the baking sheet and "glue" the loaves in place. With a very sharp knife, make three 3-inch-long, diagonal, crosswise slashes in the top of each loaf.

Bake the loaves for 45 to 50 minutes, until richly browned and hollow-sounding when thumped. Remove the bread from the oven, transfer to a wire rack, and cool to room temperature. Slice about ½ inch thick, using a sharp serrated knife, and serve.

Notes: You can use the commercially ground caraway seeds, but only freshly ground seeds will give this bread the proper fragrance and taste. The best way to grind them is in a little electric coffee grinder. You can also pulverize them with a mortar and pestle or by pounding with a kitchen mallet or the bottom of a heavy glass preserving jar – easy does it!

This bread freezes beautifully. Simply double-wrap in plastic wrap, pop into plastic freezer bags, date, label, and store at 0° F.

ANGELIKA'S RYE BREAD WITH HAM

Angelikas Roggenbrot mit Schinken

The best ham to use for this recipe of our Hessian friend Angelika Miebs is Westphalian, an air-cured German ham the color of mahogany that's often available in this country in specialty food shops. If you're unable to find it, substitute a half-and-half mix of deeply smoky baked ham (Vermont or Kentucky, for example) and prosciutto. Be sure to trim the ham of as much fat as possible before weighing.

5 cups (approximately) sifted unbleached all-purpose flour

2⅓ cups unsifted medium rye flour

2 (¼-ounce) packages active dry yeast

2 teaspoons salt

2 cups warm water (105° to 115° F)

½ pound well-trimmed, boneless, baked smoked ham, cut into ¼-inch cubes

Makes one 15-inch loaf

Mix 4¼ cups of the all-purpose flour, the rye flour, yeast, salt, and water in a large mixing bowl to make a soft dough, then beat hard until elastic. It's tough work, so if you have a heavy-duty food processor or mixer with a dough hook, by all means use it, beating the dough for 1 minute exactly.

Spread a pastry cloth on the counter and sprinkle with ¼ cup of the remaining all-purpose flour. Turn the dough onto the pastry cloth and sprinkle with a little more of the flour. Knead lightly to incorporate all flour. Again sprinkle the cloth with a little more of the flour. Flatten the dough into an oval, then sprinkle about a third of the ham over the dough. Fold the dough over to enclose the ham and knead hard to distribute the ham throughout the dough. Repeat twice more, until all the ham is kneaded into the dough, adding more all-purpose flour as needed to keep the dough from sticking to the cloth or your hands. Once all the flour and ham are incorporated, knead the dough hard for 10 minutes, until very smooth and springy.

Shape the dough into a ball, place in a well-buttered, warm large bowl, then turn the dough in the bowl so the buttered side is up. Cover with a clean dry cloth and set to rise in a warm dry spot, away from drafts, until doubled in bulk. This will take about 2 hours.

continued on next page

303

ANGELIKA'S RYE
BREAD WITH HAM
(cont.)

Toward the end of rising, spread a pastry cloth on the counter and sprinkle lightly with flour. Punch the dough down, then knead about 5 minutes on the floured cloth. Shape the dough into an oval loaf about 12 inches long and 4 inches wide and place on a lightly floured baking sheet. Cover with the cloth and let rise in a warm, dry, draft-free spot for 30 minutes.

Preheat the oven 400° F.

Bake the bread for 1 hour, until richly browned and hollow-sounding when thumped. Transfer the bread at once to a wire rack and cool to room temperature. To slice, cut crosswise, slightly on the bias, about ½ inch thick, using a sharp serrated knife.

MANY GRAIN BREAD
Mehrkornbrot

The flax seeds, wheat and rye grains, and buckwheat groats used in this nutritious bread can all be bought in health food stores. Angelika Miebs's original recipe calls for soaking the grains overnight in cold water. But the quick-soak process used for dried beans works equally well and saves time.

⅓ cup buckwheat groats

¼ cup whole hard wheat grains

¼ cup whole rye grains

2 cups cold water

2 tablespoons sesame seeds

2 tablespoons flax seeds (available at health food stores)

1 (2¼-ounce) package salted, toasted, shelled sunflower seeds

7¾ cups (approximately) sifted unbleached all-purpose flour

3½ cups unsifted medium rye flour

2 (¼-ounce) packages active dry yeast

1 tablespoon salt

2½ cups warm water (105° to 115° F)

Makes two 9 x 5 x 3-inch loaves

MANY GRAIN BREAD

Place the buckwheat groats and wheat and rye grains in a small heavy saucepan. Add the cold water, set uncovered over moderate heat, and bring to a boil. Adjust the heat so the water ripples gently and boil the grains, uncovered, for 5 minutes. Turn off the heat, cover the pan, and let stand for 1 hour. As soon as the grains have cooled for 1 hour, turn into a fine sieve and let drain while you proceed with the recipe. Preheat the oven to 325° F.

Spread the sesame and flax seeds in a pie tin, set uncovered in the oven, and toast 10 to 12 minutes, until the sesame seeds are pale tan. Remove from the oven, mix in the sunflower seeds, and set aside. Turn the oven off.

Combine 5½ cups of the all-purpose flour, the rye flour, yeast, and salt by pulsing 4 to 5 times in a heavy-duty food processor, or by beating about 1 minute in a heavy-duty electric mixer fitted with the dough hook. With the processor or mixer running, add the warm water in a slow steady stream, then beat for 1 minute exactly. The dough will be soft and sticky. Sprinkle ¼ cup of the remaining all-purpose flour on a pastry cloth, scrape the dough on top of the flour, then scatter the mixed toasted seeds over the dough and sprinkle with another ¼ cup of the flour. With well-floured hands, gently knead in the flour and seeds, distributing them as evenly as possible. Sprinkle another ¼ cup flour on the cloth underneath the dough and flatten the dough into a large oval. Spread the drained mixed grains over the dough, leaving 2-inch margins all around, then sprinkle another ¼ cup of the flour over the grains. Gather up the edges of the dough and shape into a sort of hobo bundle. Place another ¼ cup flour in the middle of the cloth, flour your hands well, and very gently knead in the grains and the flour. This is a messy, sticky job because the grains are wet and soften the dough. But keep the pastry cloth well floured and persist just long enough to work in the grains fairly well. Scrape the dough into a very large, warm, well-buttered bowl. With clean well-buttered hands, smooth the surface of the dough. Cover with a clean dry cloth and set to rise in a warm dry

continued on next page

MANY GRAIN BREAD
(cont.)

spot, away from drafts, until doubled in bulk. This will take about 1 hour. Butter two 9 x 5 x 3-inch loaf pans and set aside.

Toward the end of rising, spread a pastry cloth on the counter and sprinkle with another ¼ cup of the all-purpose flour. Punch the dough down and divide in half. Place one portion of the dough in the flour on the pastry cloth and sprinkle with another ¼ cup of the flour. Knead hard for 5 minutes, keeping your hands well floured. Shape the dough into a loaf and place in one of the prepared loaf pans. Repeat the kneading and shaping process with the remaining dough, working in the last ½ cup of all-purpose flour, and place in the second loaf pan. Cover the two loaves with cloths and let rise in a warm, dry, draft-free spot for 30 minutes.

Preheat the oven to 400° F.

Bake the loaves, side by side, for 45 to 50 minutes, until richly browned and hollow-sounding when thumped. Transfer the breads at once to a wire rack and cool to room temperature before cutting.

CISSY'S HOUSE BREAD

Cissys Hausbrot

"Cissy" is Cissy Spranger of Munich and she's typical of today's home bakers who love getting their hands in the dough and feeling the yeast spring to life. This recipe is made the modern way – by food processor. But only a sturdy machine can cope with these heavy doughs and you must take care not to overprocess (over-heat) them because you will kill the yeast.

2 (¼-ounce) packages active dry yeast.

4 cups sifted bread flour

2 cups sifted unbleached all-purpose flour

1 cup unsifted medium rye flour

1 tablespoon salt

½ teaspoon freshly ground aniseeds (see notes)

½ teaspoon freshly ground caraway seeds

½ teaspoon freshly ground coriander seeds

½ teaspoon freshly ground fennel seeds

1¼ cups hot water

CISSY'S HOUSE BREAD

1¼ cups hot milk

2 tablespoons flax seeds (available at health food stores)

2 tablespoons sesame seeds

½ cup steel-cut oatmeal

½ cup sunflower seeds (not toasted or salted)

½ cup pine nuts (pignoli)

Makes two 10-inch oval loaves

Combine the yeast, bread flour, 1 cup of the all-purpose flour, and the rye flour, salt, aniseeds, caraway, coriander, and fennel and set aside. Place the water, milk, flax and sesame seeds, and oatmeal in a heavy-duty food processor fitted with the metal chopping blade and process 3 minutes. Let the mixture cool a few minutes (it should register from 105° to 115° F), then add 2 cups of the flour mixture and pulse quickly to combine. Add the sunflower seeds and pine nuts and another 2 cups of the flour mixture and again pulse quickly. Finally, add the remaining flour mixture and process 20 to 25 seconds, until the dough rolls into a ball, rides up on the central spindle, and leaves the sides of the workbowl reasonably clean.

Shape the dough into a ball and place in a well-buttered, warm large bowl. With well-buttered hands, pat the surface of the dough so it's nicely buttered, too. Cover with a clean dry cloth and set to rise in a warm dry spot, away from drafts, until doubled in bulk. This will take about 1 hour.

Toward the end of rising, spread a pastry cloth on the counter and sprinkle with ⅓ cup of the remaining all-purpose flour. Punch the dough down, place on the floured cloth, and knead hard, working in all the flour. Sprinkle another ⅓ cup all-purpose flour over the cloth and knead in all of it. Sprinkle the final ⅓ cup all-purpose flour over the cloth and, again, knead it all in. This additional flour and extra kneading give the bread its firm but springy texture.

continued on next page

307

CISSY'S HOUSE BREAD (cont.)

Divide the dough in half and shape each into an oval about 7½ inches long and 4 inches wide. Arrange the loaves cross-wise on a large baking sheet lined with baking parchment, spacing them 4 to 5 inches apart. Cover with the cloth and let rise in a warm, dry, draft-free spot for 30 minutes.

Preheat the oven to 425° F. Place a large baking pan of water on the oven floor.

When the loaves have risen, bake for 45 minutes, until richly browned and hollow-sounding when thumped. Transfer the loaves at once to a wire rack and cool to room temperature before slicing.

Notes: For truly aromatic bread, grind the anise, caraway, coriander, and fennel seeds, yourself. It's easy. Simply pop ½ teaspoon of each kind of seed into a little electric coffee grinder and pulse until powdery. Or pulverize with mortar and pestle or pound with a kitchen mallet or the bottom of a preserving jar.

This bread freezes beautifully. Simply double-wrap in plastic wrap, pop into plastic freezer bags, date, label, and store at 0° F.

FLATBREAD FROM VINSCHGAU

Vinschgauer

Our Munich friend Gertrud Schaller sent us this unsual recipe. Although popular through-out Bavaria, this bread comes originally from Vinschgau, a county in the South Tyrol (formerly Austria, but now a part of Italy). These loaves resemble pita bread and are marvelous split, then sandwiched back together with slices of good German cheese and/or ham.

5¾ to 6 cups sifted unbleached all-purpose flour

2¾ cups warm water (105° to 115° F)

2 (¼-ounce) packages active dry yeast

2¾ cups unsifted medium rye flour

1 tablespoon salt

2 teaspoons ground fennel

2 teaspoons ground anise

2 teaspoons fennel seeds

2 teaspoons aniseeds

FLATBREAD FROM VINSCHGAU

Makes eight 8-inch round loaves

Beat 4 cups of the all-purpose flour in a large bowl with the water and yeast to form a thick batter. Cover with a clean dry cloth and let stand in a warm dry spot, away from drafts, for 30 minutes, until doubled in bulk. Mix in the rye flour, salt, ground fennel, and anise, then work in enough of the remaining all-purpose flour, 1 cup at a time, to form a stiff but manageable dough. Turn the dough onto a lightly floured pastry cloth and knead 8 minutes, until smooth and elastic.

Shape the dough into a ball; place in a well-buttered, warm large bowl. With well-buttered hands, pat the surface of the dough so it is nicely buttered, too. Cover with a clean dry cloth and set to rise in a warm dry spot, away from drafts, until doubled in bulk, about 1½ hours.

Toward the end of rising, preheat the oven to 425° F. Also place a large baking pan of water on the oven floor. Lightly butter two large baking sheets and set aside.

Punch the dough down. Working on a lightly floured pastry cloth, shape the dough into a rope 3 inches in diameter and 24 inches long. Cut the rope crosswise into 8 pieces of equal size. With a floured, stockinette-covered rolling pin, roll each piece into a 5-inch round about ⅜ inch thick. Space the rounds as far apart as possible on the prepared baking sheets. Brush with lukewarm water, then sprinkle evenly with the fennel and aniseeds.

Bake the loaves for 20 to 25 minutes, until nicely browned and hollow-sounding when tapped. Transfer to wire racks and cool before eating.

ROSA'S CHRISTMAS STOLLEN

Rosas Christstollen

This yeast bread, lavishly strewn with nuts and candied fruits, is the traditional Christmas bread of Germany. Every region has its own version and this one comes from Hedy's mother, who lived in the Bavarian Alps all her life. The dough is so heavy and rich that it may take three to four hours to rise. Stollen is simply wonderful toasted and buttered, but Germans prefer to slice it and eat as is.

¾ cup dried currants

⅓ cup orange juice plus enough light rum to total ½ cup

4 (¼-ounce) packages active dry yeast

½ cup warm water (105° to 115° F)

¾ cup milk

½ pound (2 sticks) unsalted butter or margarine, at room temperature

¾ cup sugar

¼ teaspoon salt

⅔ cup moderately finely diced candied orange peel

⅔ cup moderately finely diced candied citron

⅔ cup moderately finely chopped blanched almonds

7½ to 8 cups sifted all-purpose flour

Topping:

3 tablespoons melted unsalted butter or margarine

¼ cup unsifted confectioners' sugar

Makes two 15-inch loaves

Place the currants in a small bowl, add the orange juice mixture, and let macerate at room temperature for 2 to 3 hours. When ready to proceed, sprinkle the yeast over the warm water and let stand for 15 to 20 minutes. Meanwhile, heat the milk to scalding in an uncovered small saucepan over moderate heat; remove from the heat, add the butter, and when it melts, stir in the sugar and salt. Cool to lukewarm (105° to 115° F). Place the milk mixture in the largest bowl of a heavy-duty mixer or in the workbowl of a heavy-duty food processor fitted with the metal chopping blade. Add the yeast mixture and blend quickly. Set aside for the time being.

ROSA'S CHRISTMAS
STOLLEN

Place the candied orange peel, citron, and almonds in a mixing bowl, add 1 cup of the flour, and toss well to coat; set aside. Add 1 cup of the remaining flour to the yeast mixture and mix quickly. Now blend in 4 additional cups flour, 1 cup at a time. Add the dredged fruits and nuts, all dredging flour, and the currants and orange juice mixture and beat hard to mix. Work in 1½ to 2 additional cups flour to form a stiff but manageable dough. (If the mixer or processor begins to balk at the load, you will have to knead in the remaining flour. Spread ¾ cup of it on a bread board; divide the dough and knead the flour into one half. If the dough still seems sticky, knead in another ¼ cup flour or so. Shape the dough into a ball and set aside. Mix the remaining flour into the remaining dough the same way and shape into a second ball.)

If you have not already divided the dough in half, do so now and shape each half into a ball. Place the balls of dough in two well-buttered large bowls, turn the dough in the bowls so the buttered sides are up, cover with clean dry cloths, and set to rise in a warm dry spot away from drafts. Because of the heaviness of the dough, this first rising will take 3 to 4 hours and the dough will never really double in bulk.

Punch the balls of dough down and knead, one at a time, on a well-floured pastry cloth for 3 to 4 minutes, until satiny and elastic. Now roll the dough, one ball at a time, into a 15 x 8-inch oval. Lay a rolling pin the length of the oval slightly to the right of center and press down hard to crease. Fold the dough over at the crease so that the top portion is slightly smaller all around than the bottom. Moisten the underside edge of the top portion and press into the bottom portion to seal. Ease the stollen onto an ungreased baking sheet, cover with the cloth, and again set to rise in a warm draft-free spot. Roll and shape the remaining dough the same way, place on a second ungreased baking sheet, cover, and set to rise. The second rising will take about 2 hours and, once again, the dough will not fully double in bulk.

Toward the end of the second rising, preheat the oven to 375° F.

continued on next page

ROSA'S CHRISTMAS
STOLLEN (cont.)

Bake the stollen, one loaf at a time, for 40 to 45 minutes, until richly browned and hollow-sounding when thumped. Remove the stollen from the oven and transfer to a wire rack set on a wax-paper-covered counter. Brush at once with the melted butter, then sift the confectioners' sugar lavishly over the stollen until snowy white. Bake the remaining stollen the same way, then brush with butter and dust with confectioners' sugar as before. Cool the stollen to room temperature. To slice, cut crosswise, slightly on the bias, about 1 inch thick, using a sharp serrated knife.

Note: To freeze the stollen, wrap each loaf snugly in plastic wrap, pressing out all air. Overwrap in aluminum foil, again sealing tight. Label and date, then place on the freezing surface of a 0° F freezer. The loaves will keep well for about 3 months at 0° F. Thaw before serving. If you like, unwrap the stollen, rewrap in aluminum foil, and heat in a preheated 300-degree oven for about 20 minutes. Re-dust with confectioners' sugar, if you like, just before serving.

ALMOND STOLLEN
Mandelstollen

Two sweet doughs, one plain, one filled with ground almonds, kneaded into a single loaf. A Christmas favorite across Germany, Mandelstollen *is delicious any time. With a morning cup of coffee, it's a welcome change from the usual doughnuts or Danish.*

Plain Dough:

4 teaspoons active dry yeast

⅓ cup sugar

¾ cup warm milk (105° to 115° F)

4 cups sifted unbleached all-purpose flour

1 extra-large egg

1 vanilla bean, split lengthwise

¼ teaspoon salt

¼ teaspoon almond extract

Almond Dough:

8 tablespoons (1 stick) unsalted butter or margarine, at room temperature

ALMOND STOLLEN

¾ cup sifted unbleached all-purpose flour

1 cup coarsely ground blanched almonds

½ cup finely diced candied lemon peel

Topping:

6 tablespoons melted unsalted butter or margarine

½ cup Vanilla Sugar (page 400)

⅓ to ½ cup confectioners' sugar

Makes one 15-inch loaf

For the plain dough: Dissolve the yeast and 1 tablespoon of the sugar in the milk in a warm medium-size bowl. Set in a warm dry spot, away from drafts, for 5 minutes, until light and spongy. Stir the sponge down, mix in 1 cup of the flour, cover with a clean dry cloth, then set in a warm dry spot, away from drafts, and let rise for 20 to 25 minutes, until doubled in bulk.

In a second bowl, beat the remaining sugar, egg, seeds scraped from the vanilla bean (discard the pod), salt, and almond extract until smooth. Transfer the risen yeast mixture to the large electric mixer bowl or the workbowl of a heavy-duty food processor fitted with the metal chopping blade, add the egg mixture, and beat or pulse quickly to blend. Add enough of the remaining flour, 1 cup at a time, beating or pulsing after each addition, to form a stiff but manageable dough. (You will probably be able to work in only 2⅔ cups flour by machine; you'll use the remaining ⅓ cup flour to knead in the almond dough.)

Shape the dough into a ball and place in a well-buttered, warm, large bowl. With well-buttered hands, pat the surface of the dough so it is nicely buttered, too. Cover with a clean dry cloth and let rise in a warm dry spot, away from drafts, until doubled in bulk. This will take about 45 minutes.

For the almond dough: Place the butter, flour, almonds, and

continued on next page

313

ALMOND STOLLEN
(cont.)

candied lemon peel in a food processor fitted with the metal chopping blade and pulse 20 to 30 seconds, until well combined; set aside.

When the yeast dough has doubled in bulk, punch it down, place on a lightly floured cloth, and knead in the almond dough, sprinkling as you go with the remaining ⅓ cup flour and working all of it in, too. Shape into a ball and transfer to a well-buttered, warm large bowl. With well-buttered hands, pat the surface of the dough so it is nicely buttered, too. Cover with the clean dry cloth and set to rise in a warm dry spot, away from drafts, until almost doubled in bulk. This will take about 1½ hours.

Butter a baking sheet, line with baking parchment and set aside.

To shape the stollen: Punch the dough down and knead on a lightly floured cloth for 2 to 3 minutes, until satiny and elastic. With a lightly floured stockinette-covered rolling pin, roll the dough into a 15 x 8-inch oval. Lay a rolling pin the length of the oval slightly to the right of center and press down hard to crease. Fold the dough over at the crease so that the top portion is slightly smaller all around than the bottom. Moisten the underside edge of the top portion and press into the bottom portion to seal. Ease the stollen onto the prepared baking sheet, cover with the cloth, and let rise in a warm draft-free spot. The second rising will take 1½ to 2 hours and the dough will not fully double in bulk.

Toward the end of this final rising, preheat the oven to 375° F.

Bake the stollen for 40 to 45 minutes, until richly browned and hollow-sounding when thumped. If the stollen is browning too fast, slide a second baking sheet underneath it and cover loosely with foil.

Remove the stollen from the oven and transfer to a wire rack set on a wax-paper-covered counter. Brush at once with the melted butter. Sprinkle a large piece of baking parchment

ALMOND STOLLEN

with the vanilla sugar, place the stollen upside down in the sugar, and roll very carefully to coat. Sprinkle any uncoated portions of stollen with any excess sugar on the paper. Wrap the stollen in foil and let it season for a week. Just before serving, sift the confectioners' sugar lavishly over the stollen until snowy white. To slice, cut crosswise, slightly on the bias, about 1 inch thick, using a sharp serrated knife.

Note: To freeze the stollen, wrap snugly in plastic wrap, pressing out all air. Overwrap in aluminum foil, again sealing tight. Label and date, then place on the freezing surface of a 0° F freezer. This stollen will keep well for about 3 months at 0° F. Thaw before serving. If you like, unwrap the stollen, rewrap in aluminum foil, and heat in a preheated 300-degree oven for about 20 minutes. Dust again with confectioners' sugar, if you like, just before serving.

POPPY SEED STOLLEN
Mohnstollen

You see these black and white pinwheel loaves in Bäckerei *windows all over Bavaria. The black part is a thick poppy seed-almond-raisin paste, the light part, a brioche-rich yeast dough.*

Yeast Dough:

4 teaspoons active dry yeast

½ cup sugar

1 cup warm milk (105° to 115° F)

4 cups (approximately) sifted unbleached all-purpose flour

1 extra-large egg

8 tablespoons (1 stick) unsalted butter or margarine, at room temperature

½ teaspoon salt

Poppy Seed Filling:

⅓ cup seedless raisins

2 tablespoons dark rum

½ cup milk

⅔ cup sugar

continued on next page

POPPY SEED STOLLEN
(cont.)

2½ cups (about ½ pound) finely ground poppy seeds (see notes)

4 tablespoons (½ stick) unsalted butter or margarine, melted

¼ teaspoon ground cinnamon

⅓ cup finely diced candied lemon peel

½ cup finely ground unblanched almonds

¾ teaspoon almond extract

1 extra-large egg

Glaze:

1 cup plus 2 tablespoons sifted confectioners' sugar

1½ tablespoons dark rum

1 tablespoon freshly squeezed lemon juice

Makes one 14-inch loaf

For the yeast dough: Dissolve the yeast and 1 tablespoon of the sugar in ¾ cup of the milk in a warm, medium-size bowl. Set in a warm dry spot, away from drafts, for 5 minutes, until light and spongy. Stir the sponge down, mix in 1 cup of the flour, cover with a clean dry cloth, then set in a warm dry spot, away from drafts, and let rise 20 to 25 minutes, until doubled in bulk.

Transfer to the large electric mixer bowl or the workbowl of a heavy-duty food processor fitted with the metal chopping blade. Add the egg, butter, salt, and remaining sugar and beat or pulse 10 to 15 seconds to blend. Add enough of the remaining flour, 1 cup at a time, beating or pulsing after each addition, to form a stiff but manageable dough.

Shape the dough into a ball and place in a well-buttered, warm large bowl. With well-buttered hands, pat the surface of the dough so it is nicely buttered, too. Cover with a clean dry cloth and let rise in a warm dry spot, away from drafts, until doubled in bulk. This will take about 1½ hours.

POPPY SEED STOLLEN

Line a baking sheet with baking parchment and set aside.

For the poppy seed filling: Place the raisins in a small bowl, add the rum, and allow to plump for 30 minutes. At the same time, bring the milk to a simmer in a medium-size heavy saucepan over moderate heat. Add the sugar and cook 3 to 5 minutes, stirring now and then, until the sugar dissolves. Place the poppy seeds in a large heatproof bowl, add the milk mixture, melted butter, cinnamon, candied lemon peel, almonds, and almond extract and mix well. Finally, mix in the egg and raisins plus any rum left in the bowl.

To shape the stollen: Punch the dough down and knead on a lightly floured cloth for 2 to 3 minutes, until satiny and elastic. With a lightly floured stockinette-covered rolling pin, roll the dough into a 17 x 11-inch rectangle ¼ inch thick. Brush with some of the remaining ¼ cup warm milk, then spread the poppy seed filling evenly on top, leaving a 1-inch border all around. Starting with a short side, roll up, jelly-roll style, just until you reach the center of the dough rectangle. Roll the second half the same way, in toward the center, until it touches the first roll. Brush the two rolls where they meet with a little more of the warm milk and press lightly to seal them together.

Invert the stollen on the prepared baking sheet, cover with a clean dry cloth, and again set to rise in a warm, draft-free spot. The final rising will take about 1 hour and the stollen will not fully double in bulk. To keep the filling from oozing out of the stollen as it bakes, tuck each end underneath and press to seal.

Toward the end of the final rising, preheat the oven to 375° F.

Bake the stollen for 40 to 45 minutes, until richly browned and hollow-sounding when thumped. (If the stollen is browning too fast, slide a second baking sheet underneath it and cover loosely with foil.) Remove the stollen from the oven and transfer to a wire rack set on a wax-paper-covered counter.

continued on next page

317

POPPY SEED STOLLEN
(cont.)

For the glaze: Beat the confectioners' sugar, rum, and lemon juice in a medium-size bowl until creamy, then spoon evenly over the still-hot stollen, letting the excess drip down onto the wax paper.

Cool the stollen to room temperature, wrap in plastic wrap, and let season several days before serving. To slice, cut crosswise, slightly on the bias, about 1 inch thick, using a sharp serrated knife.

Notes: It is imperative that the poppy seeds you use are sweet and fresh – rancid ones will ruin the stollen. If you can't buy freshly ground poppy seeds (many specialty food shops and bakery supply houses sell them), try grinding them yourself in a little electric coffee grinder. For best results, grind about ½ cup poppy seeds at a time, giving each batch 20 to 30 seconds of nonstop grinding.

To freeze the stollen, wrap snugly in plastic wrap, pressing out all air. Overwrap in aluminum foil, again sealing tight. Label and date, then place on the freezing surface of a 0° F freezer. This stollen will keep well for about 3 months at 0° F. Thaw before serving. If you like, unwrap the stollen, rewrap in aluminum foil, and heat in a preheated 300-degree oven for about 20 minutes. Dust with confectioners' sugar, if you like, just before serving.

Breads

DRIED FRUIT BREAD
Früchtebrot

Well before Advent, Bavarian women begin baking fruit breads for the Christmas season. There are three different types, Hedy explains, all of them dark and heavy, all of them crammed with fruit. The first, Kletzenbrot, was originally made only with dried pears (Kletze), *the second, Hutzelbrot, with a combination of dried currants (Hutzel) and other fruits, none of them candied. Finally, there is* Früchtebrot, *loaded with nuts and an assortment of dried and candied fruits. Over time the distinctions between these three fruit breads have blurred to the point that they pretty much resemble one another. Still, there are purists who adhere to the original recipes. The* Früchtebrot *we offer here is a classic. It may look complicated, but it isn't.*

Fruit:

½ pound dried pears

¼ pound dried figs

5 ounces pitted prunes

4 cups cold water

¾ cup coarsely chopped unblanched hazelnuts or walnuts

⅓ cup coarsely chopped unblanched almonds

½ cup finely diced candied orange peel

⅓ cup finely diced candied lemon peel

1 cup seedless raisins

¾ cup dried currants

½ teaspoon ground anise

¼ teaspoon ground cinnamon

¼ teaspoon ground ginger

¼ teaspoon ground cloves

¼ teaspoon salt

¼ cup kirschwasser

Dough:

2 (¼-ounce) packages active dry yeast

3 tablespoons sugar

¾ cup warm milk (105° to 115° F)

4½ to 5 cups sifted unbleached all-purpose flour

½ teaspoon salt

Makes three 9-inch loaves

319

continued on next page

DRIED FRUIT BREAD
(cont.)

For the fruit: Place the pears, figs, prunes, and cold water in a very large bowl and soak for 12 hours at room temperature. Drain the fruits, cut into ¼-inch dice, and return to the bowl. Add the hazelnuts, almonds, candied orange and lemon peel, raisins, currants, all the spices, and the salt. Mix well with your hands. Pour the kirschwasser over all, cover, and let stand at room temperature for 12 hours.

For the dough: Dissolve the yeast and 1 tablespoon of the sugar in the milk in a medium-size warm bowl. Set in a warm dry spot, away from drafts, for 5 minutes, until light and spongy. Stir the sponge down, mix in 1 cup of the flour, cover with a clean dry cloth, then set in a warm dry spot, away from drafts, and let rise 20 to 25 minutes, until doubled in bulk. Add the remaining 2 tablespoons sugar, the salt, and about 2 cups of the remaining flour, 1 cup at a time, kneading the dough until it is stiff but manageable. Cover the bowl with a clean dry cloth and let the dough rest 20 minutes.

Knead the fruit mixture into the dough, a little bit at a time, using the remaining flour to keep it from becoming too sticky. It will take 8 to 10 minutes to knead in all the fruit mixture.

Line a large baking sheet with baking parchment and set aside.

To shape the bread: Divide the dough into three equal parts and shape each into a 7 x 3 x 2-inch oval. Place the loaves on the prepared baking sheet, spacing about 3 inches apart. Cover with a clean dry cloth and let rise in a warm draft-free spot for 30 minutes. These loaves are so heavy they will never double in bulk and the rising is just to lighten them slightly. If you allow them to rise any longer, the loaves will spread and flatten rather than rise.

While the loaves rise, preheat the oven to 425° F.

Bake the loaves on the lower oven rack for 10 minutes. Reduce the oven temperature to 350° F and bake 40 to 45

DRIED FRUIT BREAD

minutes longer, until firm and nicely browned. Remove the Früchtebrot from the oven, transfer to a wire rack, and cool to room temperature.

Wrap each loaf snugly in plastic wrap, overwrap in foil, then allow to season in a cool dry spot for about a week. To serve, slice ½ inch thick, slightly on the bias, with a sharp serrated knife.

Note: Wrapped airtight, these loaves will keep fresh at room temperature for four to five weeks. And in the freezer much longer. Simply date and label the wrapped loaves and store at 0°F.

ROSA'S NUT WREATH
Rosas Nusskranz

Another of Hedy's mother's wonderful Christmas breads. These wreaths can be baked well ahead of the holiday season and frozen.

Dough:

3 (¼-ounce) packages active dry yeast

1½ cups warm milk (105° to 115° F)

½ pound (2 sticks) unsalted butter or margarine, melted and cooled to room temperature

3 extra-large egg yolks

¾ cup sugar

1 teaspoon salt

6 to 7 cups sifted all-purpose flour

Filling:

8 tablespoons (1 stick) unsalted butter or margarine, at room temperature

1 cup sugar

¾ cup finely ground unblanched hazelnuts

1 teaspoon ground cinnamon

1 extra-large egg white

321

continued on next page

ROSA'S NUT WREATH
(cont.)

Glaze:

1¼ cups unsifted confectioners' sugar

2 to 3 tablespoons hot water

½ teaspoon vanilla extract

Makes two 12-inch wreaths

For the dough: Combine the yeast with ½ cup of the milk in a large bowl and let stand 10 minutes, until foamy. Beat in the remaining milk, the butter, egg yolks, sugar, and salt. Mix in the flour, 1 cup at a time, until the mixture forms a stiff but manageable dough. Knead hard on a well-floured pastry cloth for 8 to 10 minutes or, if you have a heavy-duty electric mixer with the dough hook attachment, knead at moderately low speed for 5 to 8 minutes.

You can also mix and knead the dough in a heavy-duty food processor fitted with the metal chopping blade. Simply transfer the risen yeast mixture to the processor workbowl, add the remaining milk, the butter, egg yolks, sugar, and salt and pulse to combine. Finally, mix in enough of the all-purpose flour, 1 cup at a time and pulsing after each addition to incorporate, to make a stiff but manageable dough. Once all the flour is in, process the dough about 20 seconds, until it rolls into a ball and rides up on the central spindle. It's important that you do not overprocess the dough at this point because it will quickly heat up in the processor and can actually reach temperatures that will kill the yeast.

Shape the dough into a ball and place in a well-buttered, warm large bowl. With well-buttered hands, pat the surface of the dough so it is nicely buttered, too. Cover with a clean dry cloth and set to rise in a warm dry spot, away from drafts, until doubled in bulk. This will take 2 to 3 hours.

For the filling: Cream the butter in the small electric mixer bowl at high speed for 3 to 5 minutes, until light, then reduce the mixer speed to medium and gradually add the sugar. Continue creaming until light. Beat in the hazelnuts

ROSA'S NUT WREATH

and cinnamon and set aside. When the dough is properly risen, beat the egg white to stiff peaks and fold into the filling.

To shape the wreaths: Punch the dough down, divide in half, then roll half at a time on a lightly floured pastry cloth into a 17 x 12-inch rectangle about ¼ inch thick. Spread half the filling lengthwise over half the dough rectangle. Fold the unspread half of the dough over the filling to enclose it. Beginning about 1 inch down from the top of the dough, cut the filled rectangle lengthwise into thirds with a sharp knife. Braid the strands of dough and curve into a wreath, pinching the ends to seal. Roll, fill, and shape the remaining wreath the same way.

Line two baking sheets with baking parchment, then ease a wreath into the center of each. Cover with the cloth and let rise in a warm draft-free spot for 1 hour. Toward the end of rising, preheat the oven to 350° F.

Bake the wreaths for about 40 minutes, until golden brown and hollow-sounding when tapped. (If the breads brown too quickly, cover with foil.) Let the breads cool on the baking sheets for 10 minutes, then transfer to wire racks and cool to room temperature.

For the glaze: Whisk all ingredients in a small bowl, adding only enough water to make the glaze a good drizzling consistency. Drizzle over the cooled wreaths as attractively as possible. Let the glaze harden for an hour before cutting the wreaths.

Note: If you do not serve the wreaths immediately, wrap in plastic wrap and store in a cool dry place or in the refrigerator. To freeze the wreaths, do not glaze. Wrap each cooled wreath snugly in plastic wrap, pressing out all air. Overwrap in aluminum foil, again sealing tight. Label, date, and place on the freezing surface of a 0° F freezer. The wreaths will keep well for about 3 months at 0° F. Thaw, then glaze as directed above before serving.

BLACK FOREST HAZELNUT BREAD
Schwarzwälder Haselnussbrot

When we lunched at the Brunner family's splendid Hotel-Restaurant Ritter in the Black Forest town of Durbach some fifteen years ago, we couldn't get enough of this wonderful bread. So we came home and worked out our own version. It tastes very much like the original and is marvelous as is, or spread with unsalted butter or cream cheese.

2 cups sifted all-purpose flour

½ cup unsifted whole wheat flour

⅓ cup firmly packed light brown sugar

1½ teaspoons baking powder

1 teaspoon baking soda

½ teaspoon salt

½ teaspoon freshly grated nutmeg

¼ teaspoon freshly ground black pepper

1¼ cups finely ground, toasted, blanched hazelnuts (see note)

⅓ cup corn oil

1 cup sour milk or buttermilk

1 extra-large egg, lightly beaten

Makes one 9 x 5 x 3-inch loaf

Preheat the oven to 375°F. Butter a 9 x 5 x 3-inch loaf pan and set aside.

Combine the all-purpose and whole wheat flours, the sugar, baking powder, soda, salt, nutmeg, and pepper in a large mixing bowl, pressing out all lumps of sugar with your hands. Add the hazelnuts and toss well to mix. Make a well in the middle of the dry ingredients. In a 1-quart measure, whisk the oil, sour milk, and egg until creamy. Pour all at once into the well in the dry ingredients and stir just enough to mix; the batter should be lumpy. Don't overmix or the bread will be tough.

Spoon the batter into the prepared loaf pan, smoothing the top and spreading well to the corners. Bake uncovered about 45 minutes, or until the bread is richly browned and sounds

BLACK FOREST HAZELNUT BREAD

hollow when thumped. Cool the bread in the upright pan on a wire rack for 15 minutes. Loosen carefully around the edges with a small spatula and turn the bread out on the rack. Turn right side up and cool several hours before slicing. Because of its crumbly and tender texture, this bread will cut more neatly if you wait 24 hours before slicing.

Note: To blanch and toast hazelnuts, spread the nuts in a baking pan and set in a preheated 350-degree oven for 30 to 35 minutes. Cool 10 minutes, bundle in a clean tea towel, and rub briskly to remove the skins. Don't worry about any stubborn bits clinging to the nuts. They will add color to the bread. The easiest way to finely grind hazelnuts is in a food processor fitted with the metal chopping blade. One 15-second churning, a quick scraping down of the sides of the workbowl, then several fast pulses should do the job nicely. But proceed carefully lest you churn the nuts to paste.

BASIC GERMAN PANCAKES
Pfannkuchen Grundrezept

German pancakes resemble French crepes, but they're thicker and softer and can be used as the basis of all manner of sweet and savory recipes. It's essential that you use a well-seasoned, round-bottomed skillet for cooking the pancakes, otherwise they'll stick and break when you try to flip them. Here's a quick way to season a skillet: Spray liberally with nonstick vegetable spray and let stand at room temperature for 30 minutes. With a wad of paper toweling, rub the spray firmly into the skillet bottom and sides.

2 cups sifted unbleached all-purpose flour

¼ teaspoon salt

3 extra-large eggs

1 cup milk

1 cup club soda or sparkling mineral water

3 tablespoons unsalted butter or margarine

Makes 6 (8½-inch) pancakes

Combine the flour and salt in a large mixing bowl and make a well in the center. Break the eggs into the well and add ¼ cup of the milk. Begin mixing the eggs and milk into the flour around the edge of the well by stirring in a rapid circular motion. Then, while stirring briskly, drizzle in the remaining milk and, finally, the club soda. Continue beating hard to make a smooth, slightly elastic batter. This will take

continued on next page

BASIC GERMAN
PANCAKES (cont.)

about 3 minutes by hand, 1 minute by electric mixer (use moderate speed).

To mix the batter in a food processor, place all ingredients except the butter in the workbowl fitted with the metal chopping blade and pulse 4 to 5 times, to combine. Scrape down the sides of the workbowl and process 30 seconds nonstop.

Cover the batter and let stand at room temperature for 30 minutes. The pancake batter will keep for a day in the refrigerator.

To cook the pancakes: Melt 1½ teaspoons of the butter over moderate heat in a heavy, round-bottomed skillet that measures 8 to 9 inches across the bottom and about 10 inches across the top. Add ½ cup of the pancake batter, tilt the skillet so the batter entirely covers the bottom, then cook 2 minutes, until the surface of the pancake is nearly dry. The pancake will bubble and buckle as it cooks, but this is as it should be. If it seems to be browning too fast, reduce the heat to moderately low. In fact, you may need to keep adjusting the heat – between moderate and moderately low – so the pancakes brown properly without burning.

Shake the skillet briskly to loosen the pancake, then, with a broad spatula or pancake turner, turn the pancake and brown the flip side for 1 to 1½ minutes. Ease the pancake onto a large plate and top with a square of wax paper. Continue cooking the pancakes the same way, using 1½ teaspoons of the butter for each. As the pancakes cook, stack them on the plate, using squares of wax paper as dividers. (You can cook the pancakes several hours ahead. In fact, if you plan to stuff and roll them, it's better that you do so because they'll soften and be easier to roll.)

Use these pancakes in any recipe calling for Basic German Pancakes. Or simply drizzle them with melted butter and top with cinnamon sugar, berry jam, or Red Wine Jelly à la Schätzel (page 393) and eat.

326

DESSERTS AND DESSERT SAUCES
Desserts und Dessert Saucen

LEBKUCHEN SOUFFLÉ WITH DARK BEER SABAYON
Lebkuchen-Soufflé mit dunkler Bier-Sabayon

Germany's most famous chef is Austrian Eckhart Witzigmann, owner of the Michelin three-star Aubergine Restaurant in Munich. This ethereal dessert is his way of reinventing a classic German Christmas cookie, and our version is the result of considerable recipe sleuthing.

For the Soufflé Dish:

1 tablespoon unsalted butter or margarine, at room temperature

2 tablespoons sugar

Lebkuchen Soufflé:

¼ cup minced candied orange peel

3 tablespoons minced crystallized ginger

3 tablespoons dark rum

⅔ cup sugar

4 tablespoons all-purpose flour

1 tablespoon finely grated lemon zest

1 teaspoon ground cinnamon

¼ teaspoon freshly grated nutmeg

2 cups half-and-half

4 extra-large egg yolks

⅓ cup finely chopped blanched almonds

6 extra-large egg whites, at room temperature

¼ teaspoon salt

⅛ teaspoon cream of tartar

Dark Beer Sabayon:

3 extra-large egg yolks

1 extra-large egg

¾ cup sugar

327

continued on next page

LEBKUCHEN SOUFFLÉ WITH DARK BEER SABAYON (cont.)

½ cup flat dark German beer

1 tablespoon freshly squeezed lemon juice

½ teaspoon ground cinnamon

Makes 6 to 8 servings

For the soufflé dish: Butter a 2½-quart soufflé dish, add the sugar, tilting the dish from one side to another until the bottom and sides are nicely coated. Tap out any excess sugar and set the dish aside.

For the soufflé: Mix the orange peel and ginger in a small bowl and sprinkle with the rum. Let macerate until ready to use.

Combine the sugar, flour, lemon zest, cinnamon, and nutmeg in a heavy medium-size saucepan. Whisk in the half-and-half and egg yolks. Set over moderate heat and cook and stir for 8 to 10 minutes, until thickened and smooth. Quick-chill in an ice bath, stirring frequently.

Set the oven rack in the middle position and preheat the oven to 400°F.

Fold the rum mixture and almonds into the cooled soufflé mixture. Beat the egg whites, salt, and cream of tartar to soft peaks. Fold about 1 cup of the beaten whites into the cooled soufflé mixture to lighten it, then fold in the balance until no streaks of white remain.

Pour into the prepared soufflé dish and bake for 30 to 35 minutes, until puffed and browned and the soufflé quivers gently when the dish is nudged.

For the sabayon: Ten minutes before the soufflé is done, whisk all sabayon ingredients in the top of a large double boiler set over gently simmering water to combine. Then beat with a portable electric mixer at low speed until the mixture starts to thicken. Increase the speed to moderate and beat until frothy and almost thick enough to form a ribbon when the beaters are withdrawn. Pour into a heated sauceboat.

LEBKUCHEN SOUFFLÉ
WITH DARK BEER
SABAYON

Serve the soufflé the instant it is done and pass the sabayon separately.

BLACK FOREST CHERRY PUDDING
Schwarzwälder Kirschauflauf

Germany's Black Forest isn't black. Or nonstop forest. It's a strip of mountains, vineyards, and fertile plains lying directly east of the Rhine and beginning unofficially at Baden-Baden, the spa of spas where Bismarck and Brahms, Dostoyevski and Dietrich, all came for the cure and the casino. Germany's finest cherries, both sweet and sour, grow up and down the Rhine, and those that aren't distilled into kirschwasser (cherry eau de vie) are stirred into a variety of recipes. We still remember this soufflé-like pudding served to us some years ago by Willi Brunner of Hotel-Restaurant Ritter. This cozy family inn in the little wine town of Durbach is one of the Black Forest's top restaurants. It's a homey place with walls paneled in wood the color of caramel, an old-time porcelain stove, and antique pitchers and platters everywhere.

For the Casserole:

1 tablespoon unsalted butter or margarine, at room temperature

2 tablespoons sugar

Pudding:

½ pound small sour or sweet cherries, stemmed and pitted (see note)

¾ cup sugar

2 tablespoons kirschwasser

4 tablespoons (½ stick) unsalted butter or margarine

6 tablespoons all-purpose flour

1¼ cups milk

3 extra-large eggs, separated

⅛ teaspoon salt

Makes 4 to 6 servings

For the casserole: Butter a 2½- to 3-quart soufflé dish or straight-sided casserole well. Add the sugar, tilting the dish from one side to another until the bottom and sides are nicely coated. Tap out any excess sugar and set the dish aside. Preheat the oven to 350°F.

For the pudding: Macerate the cherries with 2 to 4 tablespoons of the sugar (depending on the tartness of the cherries) and the kirschwasser in a medium-size bowl while you proceed with the recipe, but toss the cherries well from time to time.

329

continued on next page

BLACK FOREST CHERRY
PUDDING (cont.)

Melt the butter in a medium-size heavy saucepan over moderate heat, blend in the flour, then add the milk and remaining sugar and cook 3 to 5 minutes, stirring constantly, until thickened and smooth. Whisk the egg yolks in a large bowl just until liquid, quickly blend in about 1 cup of the hot sauce, then briskly stir in the balance. Pour all liquid in the bowl of cherries into the egg yolk mixture and mix in well. Add the cherries and toss lightly. Beat the egg whites with the salt to soft peaks. Stir about one fourth of the beaten whites into the cherry mixture to lighten it, then gently but thoroughly fold in the balance.

Pour into the prepared soufflé dish and bake, uncovered, 40 to 45 minutes, until puffed and browned and the mixture quivers when you nudge the dish. Rush the pudding to the table and serve.

Note: Brunner made this dessert with sour cherries. If you use sweet cherries, macerate them in 2 tablespoons of sugar instead of 4.

BAVARIAN APPLE STRUDEL

Bayrischer Apfelstrudel

Unlike the wispy, crispy rolled strudels of Hungary, the Bavarian variety is a sort of cobbler – leaves of phyllo pastry layered into a baking pan with apples and rum-soaked raisins, then baked under a coverlet of crème fraîche.

¾ cup golden raisins (sultanas)

⅓ cup light rum

5 pounds Rome Beauty or Granny Smith apples

6 cups cold water mixed with ½ cup freshly squeezed lemon juice (acidulated water)

1½ cups granulated sugar

1 tablespoon finely grated lemon zest

1½ teaspoons ground cinnamon

1 (1-pound) package fresh or frozen and thawed phyllo pastry

½ pound (2 sticks) unsalted butter or margarine, melted

1½ cups crème fraîche

2 cups heavy cream

2 tablespoons rosewater

2 tablespoons confectioners' sugar

Makes 12 servings

Preheat the oven to 475°F. Butter a 13 x 9 x 2-inch baking pan and set aside.

Place the raisins in a small bowl, add the rum, and let macerate while you proceed with the recipe.

Peel and core the apples, cut into eighths, then cut each eighth crosswise into thin slices, letting them drop into a large bowl containing the acidulated water; set aside.

Combine the granulated sugar, lemon zest, and cinnamon in a small bowl and set aside.

Spread the phyllo sheets on a damp cloth. Lightly brush the left half of the top sheet of phyllo with a little of the melted

continued on next page

331

butter and fold in half as if closing a book. Fit into the bottom of the prepared baking pan and brush lightly with more butter. (The phyllo sheets may not fit the pan exactly. If they're too big, tuck any overhang under; if they're too small, simply stagger their placement so that the bottom of the pan is completely covered.) Layer in 5 more sheets of phyllo, buttering, folding, and buttering as before.

Drain the apple slices and pat very dry. Arrange half the apples in the pan on top of the phyllo. Sprinkle with half the sugar mixture and half the raisins and rum, then spread with half the crème fraîche. Top with 4 more phyllo sheets, again brushing each with melted butter before folding and after placing in the pan. Make sure the phyllo covers the apples. Arrange the remaining apples on top of the phyllo, sprinkle with the remaining sugar mixture, rum, and raisins. Spread with the remaining crème fraîche and set aside for the moment.

Bring the cream and rosewater to a simmer in an uncovered, small heavy saucepan over low heat, then pour evenly over the apples. Finally, top with the remaining phyllo sheets (there should be about 8), using the same buttering, folding, and buttering technique. Place the pan of strudel on a baking sheet (to catch any boil-over) and slide onto the middle oven rack.

Bake, uncovered, for 10 minutes. Reduce the oven temperature to 400°F and continue baking, uncovered, until bubbly and richly browned. (If the strudel browns too fast, cover loosely with foil.) Remove from the oven and cool 15 minutes. Sift the confectioners' sugar evenly over the top, cut into large squares, and serve at once.

CRANBERRY-STUFFED APPLES BAKED IN MULLED WINE

Bratäpfel gefüllt mit Preiselbeeren in Glühwein

Here's another of Hedy's favorites. It's lighter than most German desserts. Easier to make, too.

4 large Golden Delicious or Rome Beauty apples (about 2 pounds), peeled and cored to within ¼ inch of the bottom

4 tablespoons (approximately) whole cranberry sauce

1 cup dry red wine (preferably German)

4 whole cloves

1 cinnamon stick, broken into several pieces

2 tablespoons unsalted butter or margarine, cut into bits

4 tablespoons sugar

Optional Topping:

1 cup heavy cream, stiffly whipped with 1 tablespoon sugar and ½ teaspoon vanilla extract

Makes 4 servings

333

Preheat the oven to 350° F. Butter a 3-quart casserole and set aside.

Fill the center of each apple with cranberry sauce, mounding it ever so slightly on top. Stand the apples in the prepared casserole, arranging them so they don't touch the casserole sides or one another.

Pour the red wine evenly over the apples, then drop the cloves, pieces of cinnamon, and butter into the casserole, distributing them evenly. Finally, sprinkle 1 tablespoon sugar over each apple.

Bake the apples, uncovered, for 50 to 60 minutes, until tender, basting with the casserole liquid every 10 minutes. Serve hot or warm, spooning a little of the casserole liquid over each apple and adding, if you like, a dollop of topping.

APPLE PANCAKES

Apfelpfannkuchen

It is imperative that you use a well-seasoned omelet pan or skillet with gently sloping sides for cooking these big pancakes, otherwise they'll stick and be difficult to turn or remove. Old German hands can flip Apfelpfannkuchen without batting an eye, but inexperienced cooks may have trouble. The fastest (but most difficult) method is to brown the pancakes on both sides in the skillet. Slower but practically foolproof is the broiler method (which follows), because the pancakes needn't be flipped at all. Although these pancakes aren't very sweet, they are served as dessert. Germans like them plain, but you may prefer to top them with Vanilla or Lemon Sauce (page 355) or vanilla ice cream.

Pancake Batter:

1¼ cups sifted all-purpose flour

2 tablespoons sugar

1 teaspoon baking powder

¼ teaspoon salt

1¼ cups milk

1 extra-large egg

1 tablespoon melted unsalted butter or margarine

½ teaspoon vanilla extract

Apple Mixture:

3 medium-size Golden Delicious or tart cooking apples (about 1¼ pounds)

2 tablespoons sugar mixed with 1 teaspoon ground cinnamon and ¼ teaspoon freshly grated nutmeg

1 tablespoon freshly squeezed lemon juice

2 tablespoons unsalted butter or margarine

¼ cup water

Topping:

2 tablespoons Vanilla Sugar or Vanilla 10X Sugar (page 400)

Makes 4 (8-inch) pancakes, 4 servings

For the pancake batter: Sift the flour, sugar, baking powder, and salt into a small mixing bowl and make a well in the center. Whisk the milk, egg, melted butter, and vanilla until smooth in a 1-quart measure, pour into the well in the dry ingredients, and whisk until creamy. Cover and let stand while you prepare the apples.

APPLE PANCAKES

For the apple mixture: Quarter each apple, then peel, core, and slice each quarter crosswise ⅛ inch thick, letting the slices fall into a large mixing bowl. Add the sugar mixture and lemon juice and toss well. Melt the butter in a heavy 12-inch skillet over moderate heat, then let it foam up and subside. Add the apple mixture and sauté 2 minutes, stirring often. Pour in the water, reduce the heat to low, cover, and cook 5 minutes. Uncover, raise the heat to moderate, and boil, uncovered, shaking the skillet often, for 1½ to 2 minutes, just until all juices boil away. Scoop the skillet mixture into a 1-quart measure and reserve.

Preheat the oven to 150° to 200° F.

To cook the pancakes: Generously oil the bottom and sides of a well-seasoned 10-inch omelet pan or spray with nonstick vegetable cooking spray and set over moderate heat for 1 minute. Remove the pan from the heat, pour in a scant ⅓ cup of the pancake batter, and tilt the pan first to one side, then to another, until the batter coats the bottom of the pan in a thin, even layer. Set the pan on a hot pad on the counter, then by hand, arrange ½ cup of apple slices on top of the batter in the pan, distributing them as evenly as possible. Pour in another scant ⅓ cup batter, covering the apples as uniformly as possible. Tilt the pan gently to distribute the batter more evenly, if necessary.

Set the skillet over moderate heat and cook the pancake, uncovered, for 1 minute. Reduce the heat to low and cook, uncovered, 2 minutes longer, until the pancake has dried around the edge and holes begin to appear on top. Spray a small, thin-bladed spatula with the cooking spray, carefully loosen the pancake around the edge, then shake the pan over the heat several times until the pancake moves freely. Quickly spray a large, flat round plate with the cooking spray and ease the pancake onto it right side up. Using potholders to protect your fingers, invert the omelet pan on the plate, then invert once again so the pancake is in the pan uncooked side down. Set over moderate heat and cook the

335

continued on next page

APPLE PANCAKES
(cont.)

pancake, uncovered, for 2 minutes. Slide onto a large, round, ovenproof plate, cover with foil, and set in the warm oven. Cook the remaining pancakes the same way, recoating the skillet with cooking spray before each new pancake. As each new pancake finishes cooking, slide on top of the foil-covered pancake, top with more foil, and return to the warm oven. When ready to serve, slide each pancake onto a heated plate and dust with the vanilla sugar.

Broiler Method: Set the broiler rack 6 to 7 inches below the heating element and preheat the broiler. Follow the basic recipe, but be sure that the omelet pan or skillet you use has a flameproof handle. As soon as a pancake has browned 3 minutes in the skillet on top of the stove, transfer to the broiler and broil 3 to 3½ minutes, until nicely tipped with brown. Carefully loosen the pancake around the edge with a spatula, ease right side up onto a large round plate, cover with foil, and keep warm. Cook the three remaining pancakes the same way. Dust with sugar and serve.

CHERRY PANCAKES

Kirschpfannkuchen

If fresh dark sweet cherries are available, by all means use them in this recipe. Frozen cherries work equally well, however, and mean that you can enjoy these pancakes in the dead of winter as well as in the all-too-short cherry season. These pancakes should be served warm, not broiler-hot. They're even good at room temperature – a good thing, too, since you must broil them one by one and can't keep all six sizzling.

2 (12-ounce) packages frozen, pitted, no-sugar-added, dark sweet cherries, thawed and drained very well, or 1½ pounds fresh dark sweet cherries, stemmed and pitted

3 tablespoons kirschwasser

Basic German Pancakes batter (page 325)

3 tablespoons unsalted butter or margarine

6 tablespoons Orange Sugar (page 401)

Topping:

1 cup heavy cream

2 tablespoons superfine sugar

½ teaspoon vanilla extract

1 tablespoon kirschwasser

Makes 6 (8½-inch) pancakes, 6 servings

Halve the cherries, place in a medium-size bowl, add the kirschwasser, and toss well. Cover and macerate at room temperature for 1 hour; drain very well.

Preheat the broiler.

Prepare the pancake batter as directed and let stand at room temperature for 30 minutes. Melt 1½ teaspoons of the butter over moderate heat in a heavy, round-bottomed skillet that measures 8 to 9 inches across the bottom and about 10 inches across the top; it should also have a flameproof handle because you will finish the pancakes in the broiler.

Add ½ cup of the pancake batter to the skillet, tilt so the batter entirely covers the skillet bottom, then quickly distribute a generous ⅓ cup of the cherries evenly over the surface of the pancake. Reduce the heat to moderately low and cook the pancake, uncovered, for about 5 minutes, until the surface is almost dry. Sprinkle 1 tablespoon of the orange sugar

continued on next page

337

CHERRY PANCAKES
(cont.)

evenly over the pancake, transfer the skillet to the broiler, setting 6 inches from the heat, and broil 2½ to 3 minutes, until the pancake is nicely browned. Shake the skillet to dislodge the pancake, then ease, cherry side up, onto a large plate.

Cook the remaining cherry pancakes the same way, and as they come from the broiler, stack one on top of another, using squares of wax paper as dividers.

For the topping: Whip the cream with the sugar and vanilla to stiff peaks, then fold in the kirschwasser.

To serve: Place a warm or room-temperature pancake on each of 6 dessert plates, then drift each with a dollop of the topping.

PLUM CAKE
Zwetschgenkuchen

338

What we would call a tart or open-face pie, Germans often call a cake. This Swabian recipe was passed along to us by Christa Willibald, a German now working in New York. It's a family favorite handed down by her mother, Paula Willibald, who lives in the town of Geienhofen-Horb on Lake Constance. Sometimes Christa and Paula will make their Plum Cakes with the baking powder pastry given here, sometimes they will use the more classic Sweet Murbteig Pastry (page 400), adding 1 to 2 tablespoons kirschwasser

Baking Powder Pastry:

6 tablespoons cold unsalted butter (no substitute), cut into small cubes

¼ cup sugar

2¼ cups sifted all-purpose flour

1 tablespoon baking powder

¼ teaspoon salt

⅓ cup cold milk

1 extra-large egg yolk blended with 1 tablespoon milk (egg glaze)

Filling:

2 pounds Italian black plums, pitted (but not peeled), then quartered, but not cut all the way through so the quarters can be spread like flower petals, or 2 (16-ounce) cans purple plums, drained well, pitted, and halved

¼ cup soft white bread crumbs (optional)

PLUM CAKE

to it for extra flavor. The baking powder pastry contains no egg and only half the quantity of butter, so it's not as flaky as the Murbteig – or as caloric. Take your pick. If you use Sweet Murbteig Pastry, you will have to double the recipe.

⅓ cup sugar mixed with ½ teaspoon ground cinnamon (cinnamon sugar)

Makes an 11-inch tart, 8 to 10 servings

Preheat the oven to 350° F. Generously butter the bottom and sides of an 11-inch, slip-bottom tart tin and set aside.

For the baking powder pastry: Cream the butter in the small electric mixer bowl at high speed for 2 to 3 minutes, until light and fluffy. With the motor still running, add the sugar, 1 tablespoon at a time. Continue beating 2 to 3 minutes longer. By hand, mix in the flour, baking powder, and salt, then the milk, stirring after each addition only enough to combine. Press the pastry smoothly over the bottom and up the sides of the prepared tart tin, brush with the egg glaze, and set aside.

For the filling: If the plums seem very juicy, scatter the bread crumbs evenly over the pastry. Arrange the plums skin side down in the pastry shell in rows, fanning the quarters out and overlapping the plums slightly. (If using canned plums, arrange the halves hollow side down in concentric circles.) Sprinkle with the cinnamon sugar.

Set the tart on a baking sheet and bake in the lower third of the oven for 40 to 45 minutes, until the pastry is nicely browned and the filling bubbly. Before cutting, cool the tart to room temperature on a wire rack.

To serve: Carefully loosen and remove the tart tin sides, then transfer the tart (still on the pan bottom) to a round platter or cake stand. Cut into wedges at the table.

339

EXTRA DELICIOUS GRAPE TORTE
Feine Traubentorte

Annemarie Schätzel, whose family owns the Kapellenhof Weingut at Selzen, about an hour southwest of Frankfurt, sent us this recipe, which she obtained from the Hauswirtschaftliche Beratungsstelle *in Mainz, a civic organization not unlike our Agricultural Extension Service. It's where German women go for household tips, recipes, and solutions to cooking problems.*

Pastry:

1¼ cups unsifted all-purpose flour

8 tablespoons (1 stick) unsalted butter (no substitute), cut into bits

⅔ cup finely ground unblanched almonds

⅓ cup sugar

½ teaspoon ground cinnamon

1 extra-large egg yolk

3 tablespoons kirschwasser

Filling:

6 tablespoons unsalted butter or margarine, at room temperature

½ cup sugar

4 extra-large eggs, separated

2 tablespoons cornstarch

1 teaspoon finely grated lemon zest

⅛ teaspoon salt

1 pound seedless green grapes, rinsed and patted dry

Optional Topping:

1 tablespoon confectioners' sugar

Makes a 10-inch torte, 8 to 10 servings

For the pastry: Place the flour in a large mixing bowl, add the butter, and using a pastry blender, cut it in until the mixture resembles coarse meal. Stir in the almonds, sugar, and cinnamon. In a small bowl, whisk the egg yolk and kirschwasser to combine, drizzle evenly over the flour mixture, then fork briskly until the pastry just holds together.

EXTRA DELICIOUS
GRAPE TORTE

Shape the pastry into a ball, flatten slightly, wrap in wax paper, and refrigerate 30 minutes.

With a floured, stockinette-covered rolling pin, roll two thirds of the pastry on a well-floured pastry cloth into an 11-inch circle. Center the bottom of a 10-inch springform pan on the pastry circle and, with a well-floured sharp knife, trim the pastry so it is exactly ½ inch larger all around than the pan bottom. Gather the trimmings and add to the unrolled third of the pastry. Lift the pan bottom off the pastry circle, lay the rolling pin across the center of the pastry circle, carefully lop half the pastry over the pin, then transfer to and center on the pan bottom. Gently insert the pastry-covered pan bottom into the loosened springform sides. Tighten the springform sides and clamp shut.

Roll the remaining pastry into a strip 18 inches long and 5 inches wide. Using a ruler and a very sharp well-floured knife, square up the ragged edges so the strip measures 17½ x 4½ inches. Halve the pastry strip lengthwise into two 17½ x 2¼-inch strips. Next, halve each strip crosswise so you have four 8¾ x 2¼-inch pastry strips; reserve all trimmings. (The pastry is too fragile to apply a single long strip around the side of the springform pan, so it's best to fit it in in four sections.)

Lift one pastry strip and arrange it around the side of the springform pan, letting it overlap the pastry circle on the bottom by about ¼ inch. The upper edge of the pastry strip may lop over as you try to smooth it against the pan side; let it, then simply pinch the doubled-over portion together and press halfway up the side of the pan. Now press and fit a second pastry strip against the pan side the same way, letting one end of it overlap one end of the first pastry strip by about ½ inch; press all seams firmly to seal. Repeat with the remaining two pastry strips so that the side of the springform pan is lined with a continuous strip of pastry. Once again, press all seams well to seal, paying particular attention to the one where the side of the pastry shell meets the pastry circle on the bottom. Use any pastry trimmings to patch

341

continued on next page

cracks or skimpy areas – simply pinch off bits of pastry and press firmly into place. The pastry is now ready to fill and bake.

Preheat the oven to 375° F.

For the filling: Cream the butter in the small electric mixer bowl at high speed for 5 minutes, until light and fluffy. Reduce the mixer speed to medium and add ⅓ cup of the sugar, 2 tablespoons at a time. Continue beating 2 to 3 minutes at high mixer speed, until light. Beat in the egg yolks, one by one, then beat in the cornstarch and lemon zest. In the large electric mixer bowl (with washed and dried beaters), beat the egg whites with the salt at high speed until silvery. Add the remaining sugar, 1 tablespoon at a time, and continue beating the whites until they peak stiffly. Fold the whites into the yolk mixture and pour the batter into the pastry shell. Arrange the grapes in a single even layer on top of the batter, pushing them in slightly.

To bake: Bake the torte 1 to 1¼ hours, until puffed and golden. Let the torte cool in the pan to room temperature, then cover with plastic wrap and chill several hours.

To serve: Carefully loosen and remove the springform pan sides. For a festive touch, dust the top of the torte lightly with confectioners' sugar. Cut into slim wedges and serve.

342

ROSA WÜRZ'S QUARK PUDDING WITH CHERRIES

Quarkauflauf mit Kirschen von Rosa Würz

Germans are passionate about quark – a slightly sour, finely curded fresh cheese of the ricotta type. This unusual dessert (and its apple variation, which follows) is a snap to make once you've pitted the cherries (or peeled, cored, and sliced the apples). Hedy's mother would make the cherry version in summer when dark sweet cherries were available and at their peak of flavor, then use the apple variation the rest of the year.

1 pound dark sweet red cherries, stemmed and pitted, or 1½ (12-ounce) packages frozen, pitted, no-sugar-added, dark sweet cherries, thawed and drained as dry as possible

3 tablespoons freshly squeezed lemon juice

⅔ cup sugar

1 pound quark (see page 51), or 1 pound finely curded whole-milk ricotta puréed with 2 tablespoons crème fraîche or Devon cream or with 1 tablespoon sour cream, plain yogurt, buttermilk, or acidophilus milk

¼ cup quick-cooking semolina (unseasoned couscous; not a mix)

Finely grated zest of 1 large lemon

3 extra-large eggs, separated

1½ teaspoons baking powder

1 tablespoon unsalted butter or margarine, diced

Makes 6 servings

Preheat the oven to 375° F. Butter a 2½- to 3-quart soufflé dish and set aside.

Place the cherries in a large bowl, add the lemon juice and 2 tablespoons of the sugar, and toss well. Let stand at room temperature while you proceed with the recipe.

Place the quark in a food processor fitted with the metal chopping blade, add the remaining sugar, the semolina, and lemon zest and process 1 minute nonstop, scraping down the sides of the workbowl after 30 seconds. (If you have no food processor, force the quark through a fine sieve, transfer to the large electric mixer bowl, add the sugar, semolina, and lemon zest, and beat at highest mixer speed for 2 minutes.) Pulse (or beat) in the egg yolks, one by one, then beat in the baking powder. Beat the egg whites to stiff peaks and fold

343

continued on next page

ROSA WÜRZ'S QUARK PUDDING WITH CHERRIES (cont.)

into the yolk mixture gently but thoroughly. Fold in the cherries and all juice that has accumulated in the bottom of the bowl. Pour into the prepared soufflé dish and dot with the butter. Bake, uncovered, on the middle oven rack for 50 to 60 minutes, just until richly browned and set like custard. Cool 20 to 25 minutes before serving. The pudding will fall a bit on cooling, but this is as it should be.

Variation

Quark Pudding with Apples (Quarkauflauf mit Äpfeln): Substitute 1¼ pounds thinly sliced, peeled, and cored Rome Beauty, Golden Delicious, or McIntosh apples for the cherries. Sprinkle them with the lemon juice, 2 tablespoons of the sugar, and if you like, ¾ teaspoon ground cinnamon and ¼ teaspoon each ground allspice and freshly grated nutmeg. Toss well, then proceed as the recipe directs.

GRATIN OF QUARK AND PEACHES
Quark-Gratin mit Pfirsichen

344

At the Orangerie in Wiesbaden's Hotel Nassauer Hof, Chef Harald Schmitt, who honed his culinary skills at Munich's celebrated Restaurant Aubergine, among other places, prepares this dessert to order, one portion at a time, under the intense heat of a salamander. He also uses Germany's luscious little vineyard peaches, which grow among the vines. We've adapted the recipe for home cooks and for six portions with, we think, delicious results.

Peaches:

4 medium-size firm-ripe peaches (about 1½ pounds), peeled, pitted, and thinly sliced, or 1½ (12-ounce) packages frozen, no-sugar-added sliced peaches, thawed and drained of half their liquid

2 tablespoons freshly squeezed lemon juice

¼ cup Grand Marnier

Crumb Mixture:

4 tablespoons (½ stick) unsalted butter or margarine

3 cups moderately coarse brioche crumbs or firm-textured white bread crumbs (you'll need 4 to 5 brioches or 6 slices bread)

¼ cup sugar

Quark Mixture:

¾ pound quark (see page 51), or ¾ pound finely curded whole-milk ricotta puréed with 2 tablespoons crème

**GRATIN OF QUARK
AND PEACHES**

fraîche or Devon cream or with 1 tablespoon sour cream,
plain yogurt, buttermilk, or acidophilus milk

2 extra-large eggs

⅓ cup sugar

2 tablespoons cornstarch

2 teaspoons finely grated lemon zest

Topping:

1½ teaspoons confectioners' sugar

6 scoops pistachio or vanilla ice cream (optional)

Makes 6 servings

Preheat the oven to 400° F. Generously butter a shallow 2-
quart casserole (no more than 1¾ inches deep) or gratin dish
and set aside.

For the peaches: Place the peaches in a large mixing bowl,
sprinkle with the lemon juice and Grand Marnier, toss well,
cover, and set aside while you proceed with the recipe.

For the crumb mixture: Melt the butter in a heavy 12-inch
skillet over moderate heat, add the crumbs and sugar, and
sauté 2 to 3 minutes, tossing the crumbs constantly, until
richly amber. Set off the heat and reserve.

For the quark mixture: Blend all ingredients in a food
processor fitted with the metal chopping blade or in an electric blender at high speed for 15 seconds. Scrape down the
sides of the processor workbowl or blender cup and process
15 to 20 seconds longer, until smooth and creamy.

To assemble the gratin: Layer the brioche crumbs in the
bottom of the prepared casserole. Drain the peaches well,
reserving the liquid, then drizzle this liquid evenly over
the crumbs in the casserole. Cover with the quark mixture,
then arrange the peaches in rows on top as decoratively as
possible, overlapping the slices as needed.

345

continued on next page

GRATIN OF QUARK
AND PEACHES (cont.)

Bake, uncovered, 35 to 40 minutes, just until the quark mixture is softly set. Dust the casserole at once with the confectioners' sugar. Serve at table, topping each portion, if you like, with a scoop of pistachio (Chef Schmitt's preference) or vanilla ice cream.

QUARK CHEESECAKE
Käsekuchen

This cheesecake from the north of Germany is considerably lighter than its American counterparts because quark is made of milk, not cream. The thin shell of murbteig pastry remains surprisingly dry and flaky, even though it's filled, then baked.

Pastry:

1 recipe Sweet Murbteig Pastry (page 400)

Filling:

2 pounds quark (page 51), or 2 pounds finely curded whole-milk ricotta plus ¼ cup crème fraîche or sour cream

½ cup heavy cream

⅔ cup sugar

Finely grated zest of 1 large lemon

1½ teaspoons vanilla extract

4 extra-large eggs

Optional Topping:

1 recipe Red Berry Sauce (page 356)

Makes 12 servings

For the pastry: Prepare the pastry according to the recipe, then roll and fit into an ungreased 10-inch springform pan as directed. Set aside. Preheat the oven to 350° F.

For the filling: Place all ingredients in a food processor fitted with the metal chopping blade. Pulse 8 to 10 times, scrape down the sides of the workbowl, then process 30 seconds nonstop, until smooth and creamy. (If you don't have a food processor, beat all ingredients in the large electric mixer bowl at high speed for 1½ to 2 minutes, until creamy.) Pour

QUARK CHEESECAKE

the filling into the pastry shell. Bake for 1 hour to 1 hour and 10 minutes, until set and a toothpick inserted midway between the rim and the center comes out clean. Cool the cheesecake in the upright pan on a wire rack for 1 hour, then cover and refrigerate 4 to 6 hours before serving, or better yet, chill overnight. Serve as is or top, if you like, with Red Berry Sauce.

POOR KNIGHTS WITH FOAMY WINE SAUCE

Arme Ritter mit Weinschaumsauce

Fée Steifensand, whose husband Wilhelm's family owns the P.J. Valckenberg Winery at Worms, developed this light and airy version of a German classic. It's first cousin to the French pain perdu (and our French toast), and a better version you won't find. Although most people would serve Poor Knights as dessert, Hedy remembers that on Fridays, when she was growing up Catholic in Bavaria, her mother would put out heaping platters of these batter-dipped, butter-browned slices of toast. They were the main course and they were usually accompanied by a big bowl of homemade applesauce. Together they made a filling meatless meal. We also like Poor Knights with Red Wine Jelly à la Schätzel (page 393).

Poor Knights:

1 loaf (½ pound) French or Italian bread about 14 inches long and 3 inches wide

1 extra-large egg, lightly beaten

2 tablespoons sugar

⅛ teaspoon salt

1 teaspoon finely grated lemon zest

1 cup milk

3 tablespoons unsalted butter or margarine

Foamy Wine Sauce:

1 extra-large egg, separated

¼ cup sugar

1 teaspoon cornstarch

1 tablespoon freshly squeezed lemon juice

½ cup Sylvaner, Riesling, or other German white wine (not too dry)

Makes 4 to 6 servings

For the Poor Knights: Preheat the oven to 150° to 200° F. Remove the pointed ends from the bread, then slice the loaf

continued on next page

347

POOR KNIGHTS WITH
FOAMY WINE SAUCE
(cont.)

½ inch thick. Combine the egg, sugar, salt, lemon zest, and milk in a medium-size mixing bowl. Dip both sides of each slice of bread in the egg mixture and set on a wax-paper-covered surface. Melt the butter on a 10-inch-square griddle or in a heavy 12-inch skillet over moderate heat, then brown the bread in batches in the butter, allowing 2 minutes per side. As the bread browns, transfer to a baking sheet and set, uncovered, in the warm oven.

For the foamy sauce: Blend the egg yolk, sugar, and cornstarch in the top of a medium-size double boiler, then whisk in the lemon juice and wine. Set over simmering – not boiling – water and cook, beating with a hand electric mixer at low speed for 8 to 10 minutes, until pale, thick, and billowing; remove from the heat. Quickly beat the egg white to stiff peaks, blend in a little of the hot yolk mixture, then fold back into the yolk mixture. Set once again over simmering water and beat at high electric mixer speed for 1 minute.

Ladle the sauce over the Poor Knights and serve at once.

PUMPERNICKEL BAVARIAN CREAM WITH RASPBERRY PURÉE

Bayerische Creme mit Himbeermark

Turning pumpernickel into a silky dessert may seem ludicrous. But that's precisely what Josef Viehhauser, the innovative young chef at Hamburg's Le Canard Restaurant, has done – with stellar results. Our recipe is adapted from the restaurant original.

Bavarian Cream:

2⅓ cups fine dark pumpernickel crumbs

2 cups milk

½ cup sugar

2 tablespoons kirschwasser

1 envelope plain gelatin

1 vanilla bean, split lengthwise

3 extra-large egg yolks, lightly beaten

½ cup heavy cream, stiffly whipped

PUMPERNICKEL
BAVARIAN CREAM
WITH RASPBERRY
PURÉE

Raspberry Purée:

1 (12-ounce) package frozen unsweetened raspberries,
   thawed but not drained

¼ cup sugar

2 tablespoons red raspberry jam

1 teaspoon arrowroot

1 tablespoon freshly squeezed lemon juice

Optional Garnish:

1 pint fresh raspberries

6 sprigs mint, lemon geranium, or rose geranium

Makes 6 servings

Place the pumpernickel crumbs in a large heatproof bowl.
Bring 1 cup of the milk and ¼ cup of the sugar to a boil in an
uncovered small heavy saucepan over moderate heat. Pour
over the crumbs, add the kirschwasser, mix well, cover, and
let stand 2 hours at room temperature.

Pour the remaining milk into a second small heavy
saucepan, add the remaining sugar, sprinkle in the gelatin,
and let stand, uncovered, for 5 minutes. Drop in the vanilla
bean, set over moderately low heat, and cook, stirring often,
just until the mixture steams – about 5 minutes. Whisk a little of the hot milk mixture into the beaten yolks, stir back
into the pan, and cook, stirring constantly, over moderately
low heat about 5 minutes, to form a very thin custard. Scrape
the black seeds inside the vanilla bean into the custard, then
discard the pods. Remove the custard from the heat and
quick-chill 10 minutes in an ice bath, whisking briskly to
prevent a skin from forming. Blend the custard into the
pumpernickel mixture, then fold in the whipped cream.
Ladle into 6 (5-ounce) ramekins, cover, and chill for at least
8 hours or overnight.

continued on next page

**PUMPERNICKEL
BAVARIAN CREAM
WITH RASPBERRY
PURÉE** (cont.)

For the raspberry purée: Purée the raspberries with their juice, the sugar, and jam in a food processor for 30 seconds; push through a sieve to remove the seeds. Blend about ¼ cup of the purée with the arrowroot, combine with the remaining purée, and pour into a small heavy saucepan. Set over moderate heat and cook 2 to 3 minutes, stirring constantly, until the mixture bubbles up, thickens, and clears. Off heat, blend in the lemon juice. Cool to room temperature, cover, and refrigerate until ready to serve.

To serve: Puddle a little of the raspberry purée on each of 6 dessert plates and tilt from side to side until the well of each plate is evenly coated. Gently loosen each Bavarian Cream by dipping briefly in warm water and invert on a purée-coated plate. Garnish each portion, if you like, with 3 raspberries and a mint sprig. Pass any remaining purée.

RED BERRY DESSERT
Rote Grütze

Rote *means red. And* Grütze *is a kind of grain. So was this popular hot-weather dessert originally made with grain? No one knows for sure. As prepared in Germany today,* Rote Grütze *brims with the red berries and cherries of summer. We've turned it into a refreshing year-round dessert by calling for frozen berries and canned cherries (as an option).*
This dessert must chill 24 hours, so plan accordingly.

Red Berry Dessert:

2 (10-ounce) packages raspberries frozen in light syrup, thawed but not drained

1 (16-ounce) package strawberries frozen in light syrup, thawed, then puréed with their juice

1 pound dark, sweet red cherries, stemmed, pitted, and quartered, or 1 (1-pound) can dark, sweet, pitted cherries, drained and the juice reserved

1 quart (approximately) natural red grape juice or cranberry juice

¾ cup sugar

1 tablespoon finely grated lemon zest

¼ cup freshly squeezed lemon juice

⅔ cup unsifted cornstarch

1 cup dry red wine (preferably German)

RED BERRY DESSERT

Topping:

1 cup heavy cream

1 tablespoon Vanilla Sugar (page 400)

Makes 6 to 8 servings

For the red berry dessert: Combine the drained raspberry juice, the puréed strawberries, and, if using canned cherries, the cherry juice in a 1-quart measure. Add enough grape juice to total 1 quart, then pour this mixture into a large heavy saucepan (not aluminum) and add 2 additional cups grape juice. Stir in the sugar, lemon zest, and lemon juice and bring to a boil, uncovered, over moderate heat, stirring often.

Combine the cornstarch with the wine to make a thin smooth paste. As soon as the saucepan mixture boils, pour in the cornstarch paste, whisking vigorously. Immediately reduce the heat to low and cook and stir for 3 minutes – just until the mixture bubbles up once again, thickens, clears, and no raw starch flavor remains. Stir in the reserved raspberries and the cherries and heat and stir about 1 minute longer. Remove from the heat and cool to room temperature. Transfer to a large bowl, cover, and chill 24 hours.

For the topping: Shortly before serving, beat the cream with the vanilla sugar briefly, just until slightly thickened but still thin enough to pour. Spoon the *Rote Grütze* into stemmed goblets, top each portion with a generous ladling of the cream, and serve.

FRESH PLUM SORBET

Sorbet von frischen Zwetschgen

Not too tart, not too sweet, this velvety sorbet comes from the Black Forest, where markets brim with local strawberries, cherries, and plums. And where distillers in the little half-timbered town of Oberkirch turn cherries and plums into fruity firewaters.

1 envelope plain gelatin

½ cup cold water

¾ cup superfine sugar

3 pounds small blue-black plums (sold in many American markets as "Italian" plums), peeled and pitted (see note)

¼ cup freshly squeezed lime juice

⅓ cup light corn syrup

1 tablespoon zwetschgenwasser (plum eau-de-vie), kirschwasser, or Grand Marnier

Makes ½ gallon, 10 to 12 servings

Sprinkle the gelatin over ¼ cup of the water and set aside. Mix the remaining ¼ cup water and sugar in a small heavy saucepan, set over moderate heat, and cook about 2 minutes, stirring constantly, until the sugar dissolves and the mixture comes to a boil. Remove from the heat, add the softened gelatin, and stir until dissolved; set aside.

Place the plums, lime juice, corn syrup, and eau-de-vie in a food processor fitted with the metal chopping blade and purée for 30 seconds. Scrape down the sides of the workbowl and purée 30 seconds longer, until smooth. Add the gelatin mixture and pulse quickly to combine. Pour into a 9 x 5 x 3-inch loaf pan and freeze 3 to 3½ hours, until mushy.

Scoop the partially frozen sorbet into the food processor, once again fitted with the metal chopping blade, and process 30 seconds. Scrape down the sides of the workbowl and process 30 seconds longer, until light and fluffy. Or, if you prefer, beat the mixture in the large electric mixer bowl at highest speed about 2 minutes, until fluffy. Return the sorbet to the loaf pan and freeze 1½ to 2 hours, until soft-firm. If the sorbet becomes brick-hard – and leftovers will – simply soften 20 to 30 minutes before serving.

Note: The easiest way to peel plums is to blanch them for a minute or so in boiling water. The skins will then slip right off.

POPPY SEED ICE CREAM

Mohneis

In order for this ice cream to have the correct nutty flavor, you must use the freshest poppy seeds you can find. Some specialty food shops sell them already ground, the form this recipe requires. If you're unable to find ground poppy seeds, buy them whole, but again, accept nothing less than the very freshest (rancid ones will ruin the recipe). A little electric coffee grinder will reduce whole poppy seeds to the proper fine and feathery texture in 20 to 30 seconds. Our inspiration for this unusual ice cream was one we enjoyed at Die Ente vom Lehel Restaurant in Wiesbaden, where Chefs Hans-Peter Wodarz and Herbert Langendorf have a reputation for using popular German foods in inventive new ways.

3½ cups milk

1 cup heavy cream

2 vanilla beans, split lengthwise

⅔ cup sugar

¼ cup honey

⅓ cup freshly ground poppy seeds (if you grind them yourself, you'll need ¼ cup whole poppy seeds)

4 extra-large egg yolks, lightly beaten

Makes a generous quart, 6 to 8 servings

Heat 2 cups of the milk, the cream, vanilla beans, sugar, and honey in an uncovered large heavy saucepan over low heat for about ½ hour, just until the mixture steams. At the same time, heat the poppy seeds with the remaining 1½ cups milk in a small heavy saucepan over low heat for 10 minutes; remove from the heat and cool to room temperature.

Whisk a little of the hot honey-milk mixture into the beaten yolks, stir back into the pan, and cook over moderately low heat for about 5 minutes, stirring constantly, to form a very thin custard. Scrape the black seeds inside the vanilla beans into the custard, then discard the pods. Remove the custard from the heat, set in an ice bath, and cool 30 minutes, whisking often to keep a skin from forming on the surface. Pour the poppy seed-milk into the custard and stir well to combine. Pour into a 9 x 5 x 3-inch loaf pan and freeze until mushy – this will take 4 to 5 hours because of the richness of the mixture. Empty the partially frozen ice cream into the large electric mixer bowl and beat 1 to 2 minutes at highest speed, until fluffy. Pack into a ½-gallon plastic freezer container and freeze until soft-firm.

353

MARZIPAN ICE CREAM·
Marzipaneis

An unusual way to use marzipan. Serve the ice cream as is or top with sliced sun-ripened peaches, halved, pitted, dark sweet cherries, or chocolate or hot fudge sauce. For a refrigerator ice cream, this one is supremely creamy.

1 quart milk

2 cups heavy cream

2 vanilla beans, split lengthwise

½ cup sugar

6 extra-large egg yolks, lightly beaten

14 ounces marzipan, cut into small dice

Makes ½ gallon, 10 to 12 servings

Heat the milk, cream, vanilla beans, and sugar in an uncovered large heavy saucepan over low heat for about ½ hour, just until the mixture steams.

Whisk a little of the hot milk mixture into the beaten yolks, stir back into the pan, and cook, stirring constantly, over moderately low heat about 5 minutes, to form a very thin custard.

Scrape the black seeds inside the vanilla beans into the custard, then discard the pods. Remove the custard from the heat and cool 10 minutes.

Place the marzipan in a food processor fitted with the metal chopping blade. Add 1 cup of the warm custard and pulse 3 or 4 times to soften the marzipan. Add another cup of the warm custard, pulse quickly, then blend 1 minute, until the marzipan is completely smooth. Combine with the rest of the custard.

Pour the mixture into two 9 x 5 x 3-inch loaf pans and freeze until mushy – this will take 4 to 5 hours because of the richness of the mixture. Empty the partially frozen ice cream into the large electric mixer bowl and beat 1 to 2 minutes at highest speed, until fluffy. Pack into a ½-gallon plastic freezer container and freeze until soft-firm.

VANILLA SAUCE
Vanille-Sauce

This sauce – or either of its two variations – is superb ladled over Gratin of Quark and Peaches (page 344), Apple Pancakes (page 334), Red Currant Cake (page 367), and Eggnog Torte (page 368).

2½ cups milk

½ cup sugar

2 vanilla beans, split lengthwise

3 extra-large eggs, lightly beaten

Makes about 3 cups

Heat the milk, sugar, and vanilla beans in an uncovered medium-size heavy saucepan over moderately low heat for about 10 minutes, just until the mixture steams. Whisk a little of the hot milk mixture into the beaten eggs, stir back into the pan, and cook over moderately low heat for about 5 minutes, stirring constantly, to form a very thin custard. *Do not boil or the custard may curdle.* Scrape the black seeds inside the vanilla beans into the custard, then discard the pods. Pour the sauce through a fine sieve and serve hot or cold.

Variations

Lemon Sauce (Zitronen-Sauce): Prepare the Vanilla Sauce as directed but use only 1 vanilla bean. After sieving, mix in 1½ teaspoons finely grated lemon zest. Serve warm or cold.

Orange Sauce (Orangen-Sauce): Prepare the Vanilla Sauce as directed but use only 1 vanilla bean. After sieving, mix in 1½ teaspoons finely grated orange zest and, if you like, 1 tablespoon Grand Marnier. Serve warm or cold.

355

RED BERRY SAUCE I

Rote Beerensauce I

Ladle over Quark Cheesecake (page 346) or serve with sliced navel oranges, fresh berries, or tree-ripened peaches.

1½ cups fresh strawberries, hulled

1½ cups fresh raspberries

½ cup superfine sugar

½ cup red currant jelly

4 teaspoons cornstarch blended with 1 tablespoon each cold water and freshly squeezed lemon juice

1 tablespoon kirschwasser, Grand Marnier, or Cointreau

Makes about 2½ cups

In a food processor fitted with the metal chopping blade, purée the strawberries and raspberries with the sugar for 10 seconds. Press through a fine sieve set over a medium-size saucepan, extracting as much liquid as possible.

Blend in the jelly and cornstarch paste, set over moderate heat, and cook about 3 minutes, stirring constantly, until the mixture bubbles up and clears. Remove from the heat and cool, whisking often to prevent a skin from forming on the surface of the sauce. Stir in the kirschwasser and serve.

Variation

Red Berry Sauce II (Rote Beerensauce II): Prepare as directed, substituting 1 (12-ounce) package each thawed, frozen, unsweetened raspberries and strawberries (do not drain) for the fresh berries. Also increase the amount of cornstarch to 4½ teaspoons.

COOKIES AND CAKES
Kuchen und Gebäck

BLACK FOREST CHERRY TORTE
Schwarzwälder Kirschtorte

It's imperative that you grate the chocolate for this recipe very fine; otherwise it won't melt as the cake bakes and may sink to the bottom of the pan. The ground almonds, too, must be fine and feathery. The easiest way to obtain the proper texture is in the food processor. And here's a tip: Freeze the chocolate before you grate it so that the processor's heat won't melt it. The proper attachment to use for grating the chocolate and grinding the nuts is the metal chopping blade.

For Preparing the Pan:

1 tablespoon unsalted butter or margarine, at room temperature

2 tablespoons all-purpose flour

Torte:

¾ cup sifted cake flour

2 teaspoons baking powder

Pinch of salt

8 tablespoons (1 stick) unsalted butter (no substitute), at room temperature

½ cup plus 3 tablespoons sugar

½ teaspoon vanilla extract

¼ teaspoon almond extract

6 extra-large eggs, separated

4 (1-ounce) squares semisweet chocolate, very finely grated

½ cup very finely ground unblanched almonds

Filling:

6 tablespoons kirschwasser

1 (1-pound) jar whole cherry preserves

1 cup heavy cream, whipped to stiff peaks

Topping:

2 cups heavy cream

⅓ cup unsifted confectioners' sugar

357

continued on next page

BLACK FOREST CHERRY
TORTE (cont.)

2 (1-ounce) squares semisweet chocolate, shaved into curls
    with a swivel-bladed vegetable peeler

8 large maraschino cherries, patted dry on paper toweling

Makes a 9-inch, 3-layer cake, about 12 servings

For the Pan: Line the bottom of a 9-inch springform pan
with wax paper, butter the paper and the pan sides well, then
coat with flour, tapping out the excess. Set the pan aside.
Preheat the oven to 325° F.

For the torte: Sift the flour with the baking powder and salt
onto a piece of wax paper and set aside.

Cream the butter with the ½ cup sugar, vanilla, and almond
extract in the large electric mixer bowl by beating at high
speed for 2 to 3 minutes, until light and fluffy. Reduce the
mixer speed to low, add the egg yolks, and beat 1 minute.
By hand, fold in the grated chocolate, set aside.

Whip the egg whites to soft peaks with the remaining 3
tablespoons sugar. Fold 1 cup of the beaten whites into the
cake batter to lighten it, then gently but thoroughly fold in
the balance until no streaks of white or brown remain.

Sift about a fourth of the sifted dry ingredients over the batter and fold in gently; repeat until all the dry ingredients are
incorporated. Finally, fold in the ground almonds, using as
light a touch as possible. Spoon the batter into the prepared
pan, smooth the top, and bake for about 45 minutes, or until
the torte begins to pull from the sides of the pan and feels
springy to the touch.

Remove the torte from the oven and cool in the upright pan
on a wire rack for 10 minutes. Loosen the torte around the
edges with a spatula, then release and remove the springform pan sides. Cool the torte completely, remove the pan
bottom, and peel off the wax paper.

It will be easier to slice the torte into layers if you wrap it
snugly in plastic wrap and let it stand at room temperature
for at least 24 hours before proceeding. Using a serrated

BLACK FOREST CHERRY TORTE

knife, divide the torte horizontally into three layers of equal thickness. Place the bottom layer on a cut-to-fit cardboard circle and set on a cake plate or, better yet, a lazy Susan.

For the filling and torte assembly: Drizzle the bottom layer evenly with 2 tablespoons of the kirschwasser, spread with half the cherry preserves, then with half the whipped cream. Top with the middle torte layer, drizzle with 2 more tablespoons kirschwasser, then spread with the remaining cherry preserves and whipped cream. Set the top layer in place, pressing down lightly. Drizzle with the final 2 tablespoons kirschwasser.

For the topping: Whip the cream with the confectioners' sugar to fairly stiff peaks, then use to frost the top and sides of the torte, swirling it into peaks and valleys. Sprinkle the chocolate shavings on the top and sides of the torte, then decorate the top with the cherries, arranging them in a circle around the edge. Let the torte stand 2 to 3 hours (in the refrigerator if your kitchen is hot) before serving.

359

CAFÉ KRANZLER'S CHOCOLATE CAKE
Schokoladenkuchen à la Café Kranzler

Cakes, it's said, make the Konditorei *(pastry shop/café), which explains why Berlin's Café Kranzler is so beloved. In a place that specializes in cakes of drop-dead opulence, none is more popular than this dense, dark raspberry-filled torte. For all its glamour, it isn't difficult to make but does require time and patience. Our recipe, translated not only from the German but also from the metric and from institutional*

For the Pan:

1 tablespoon unsalted butter or margarine, at room temperature

2 tablespoons unsweetened Dutch process cocoa powder

Chocolate Cake:

2 cups sifted all-purpose flour

½ cup sifted unsweetened Dutch process cocoa powder

½ pound (2 sticks) plus 1 tablespoon unsalted butter (no substitute)

1 cup unsifted confectioners' sugar

1 cup granulated sugar

9 extra-large eggs, separated

continued on next page

*proportions, is as true to
the original as we could
make it. To simplify filling and frosting the
cake, you will need a
lazy Susan and a 10-
inch cardboard cake
disk. These are sold at
specialty food shops and
baker's supply houses,
but you can easily cut
one yourself from heavy
white poster or mat
board, using the spring-
form pan bottom as a
pattern.*

360

1 teaspoon freshly squeezed lemon juice

½ teaspoon ground cinnamon

¼ teaspoon salt

4 ounces top-quality bittersweet chocolate, melted
(see note)

Raspberry Layer:

¼ cup sieved and melted raspberry jam

Ganache:

1⅓ cups heavy cream

⅓ cup unsifted unsweetened Dutch process cocoa powder

6 tablespoons unsalted butter (no substitute)

10 ounces top-quality bittersweet chocolate, coarsely
chopped (see note)

Decoration:

2 (1-ounce) squares bittersweet chocolate (use everyday
American baking chocolate packaged in chunky squares)

1 teaspoon confectioners' sugar

Makes a 10-inch, 2-layer torte, about 16 servings

For the pan: Butter a 10-inch springform pan well, add the
cocoa, and tilt the pan first to one side, then to another, until
all surfaces are evenly coated with cocoa. Tap out any excess
cocoa and set the pan aside. Preheat the oven to 350° F.

For the chocolate cake: Sift the flour and cocoa together
twice and set aside. Cream the butter, confectioners' sugar,
½ cup of the granulated sugar, the egg yolks, lemon juice,
cinnamon, and salt in the large electric mixer bowl at highest speed for 5 minutes, until very light and fluffy. Beat in
the melted chocolate.

In a separate bowl and using a hand electric or rotary beater,
beat the egg whites until frothy, add the remaining ½ cup

CAFÉ KRANZLER'S
CHOCOLATE CAKE

granulated sugar, 1 tablespoon at a time, beating all the while, then continue beating until the meringue peaks stiffly.

Fold about one fourth of the meringue into the chocolate mixture to lighten it, then fold in the balance gently but thoroughly until no streaks of white or brown show. Sift one fourth of the flour mixture over the batter and fold in gently. Add the remaining flour mixture the same way in three batches. The batter will be very stiff, but you must fold the dry ingredients in with as light a touch as possible or the cake will be tough and the texture coarse.

Spoon the batter into the prepared pan and smooth the top. Rap the pan several times on the counter to release any large air bubbles, then bake 40 to 45 minutes, until the cake begins to pull from the sides of the pan, is springy to the touch, and a cake tester inserted in the middle comes out clean. Cool the cake in the upright pan on a wire rack for 15 minutes, then loosen it around the edge with a small spatula. Release and remove the springform pan sides and cool the cake, still on the pan bottom and cake rack, to room temperature.

Carefully run a large, thin-bladed spatula between the cake and the pan bottom. When the cake is loosened all around, invert on a second cake rack and lift off the pan bottom. Place a 10-inch cardboard disk on the cake and invert once again so the cake is right side up. If the top of the cake is humped, trim it with a sharp serrated knife until level. Place the cake, disk and all, on a lazy Susan and, using the serrated knife, carefully halve the cake horizontally. Slide one or more large thin-bladed spatulas between the two layers and gently transfer the top one to a cake rack, placing it right side up. This cake isn't very fragile, so it's not likely to break or crumble.

For the raspberry layer:

Brush any loose crumbs from the surface of the bottom cake layer, then, using a broad spatula, spread smoothly with the

361

continued on next page

CAFÉ KRANZLER'S
CHOCOLATE CAKE
(cont.)

raspberry jam, leaving a ½-inch margin all around. Let dry while you prepare the ganache.

For the ganache: Place the cream, cocoa, and butter in a medium-size heavy saucepan. Set, uncovered, over moderate heat and bring to a boil, stirring constantly. Reduce the heat at once to its lowest point, then add the chocolate, a handful at a time, stirring briskly the whole time. The instant all the chocolate has been added, remove the pan from the heat and whisk the ganache hard until smooth. Pour at once into a medium-size bowl (preferably metal) and cool for 45 minutes, whisking often to keep the ganache smooth. Set, uncovered, in the refrigerator and cool for 35 to 40 minutes, whisking every 10 minutes or so, until thick enough to spread.

To assemble the cake: Spread about one third of the ganache on top of the raspberry layer, leaving a ½-inch margin all around. Set the top layer into place, then frost the top and sides of the cake – smoothly but thinly – with the remaining ganache. Your aim is a slick finish, not a frosting full of peaks and valleys.

For the decoration: Run a swivel-bladed vegetable peeler over 1 square of the chocolate, letting the shavings fall directly onto the top of the cake. Repeat with the remaining chocolate square until the top of the cake is entirely covered, but work carefully so the shavings don't fall onto the sides of the cake. For the final touch, lightly dust the top of the cake with the confectioners' sugar.

Let the cake stand several hours, then, using the cardboard circle and two large spatulas for support, carefully transfer the cake to a cake plate. To serve, cut into slim wedges.

Note: The bittersweet chocolate you use for the ganache (butter cream filling and frosting) must be of top quality, Swiss or Belgian, otherwise it may not melt smoothly. It is also imperative that you don't overheat the chocolate because it may separate. Once that happens, there is no way to reconstitute it and you must begin again.

AUNT BETTY'S CHOCOLATE ROLL

Tante Bettys Schokoladenrolle

Hedy's mother's sister, who lives in Chicago, continues to prepare her beloved German recipes. This nearly flourless, soufflé-light chocolate roll twirled up with whipped cream is a particular favorite.

Cake:

6 extra-large eggs, separated

1 cup granulated sugar

3 tablespoons unsweetened Dutch process cocoa powder

2 tablespoons all-purpose flour

2 tablespoons confectioners' sugar (for dusting)

Filling:

1 cup well-chilled heavy cream

3 tablespoons confectioners' sugar

½ teaspoon vanilla extract

Topping:

2 tablespoons confectioners' sugar

Makes a 15½-inch roll, about 12 servings

363

Preheat the oven to 350° F. Butter a 15½ x 10½ x 1-inch jelly roll pan, line it with wax paper, letting the paper overhang the pan all around. Butter the wax paper and miter the corners so they are crisp and neat. Set the pan aside.

For the cake: Beat the egg yolks for 3 minutes in the small electric mixer bowl at high speed, until smooth and thick. With the mixer set at highest speed, add ¾ cup of the sugar, 2 tablespoons at a time. Continue beating at highest speed for 5 minutes, until the mixture forms ribbons that fold back on themselves when the beaters are withdrawn. Sift the cocoa and flour onto a piece of wax paper, add to the yolk mixture, and beat 1 minute at moderate speed.

Beat the egg whites at moderate speed in the large mixer bowl (with clean dry beaters) for about 1 minute, until silvery. With the motor still running, add the remaining

continued on next page

¼ cup sugar, 1 tablespoon at a time, then raise the speed to high and continue beating until the whites peak stiffly. Mix ¼ cup of the beaten whites into the chocolate mixture to lighten it, then fold in the balance, gently but thoroughly, until no streaks of white or brown remain.

Pour the batter into the prepared pan, spreading it smoothly to the corners, and bake 20 to 25 minutes, until springy to the touch and a toothpick inserted in the center comes out clean. Cool the cake in the upright pan on a wire rack for 5 minutes, cover with a dampened dish towel, and cool 15 minutes longer. Remove the dish towel, sift the confectioners' sugar evenly over the cake, cover with wax paper, then a baking sheet. Carefully invert the cake on the baking sheet and gently peel off the wax paper pan liner. Cover the cake with a fresh piece of wax paper and cool to room temperature.

For the filling: Whip the cream, sugar, and vanilla until stiff. Remove the wax paper covering the cake and spread the filling evenly over the cake, leaving a 1-inch border along one long side. Beginning with this long side, lift the wax paper so the cake rolls up on itself, jelly-roll style. Ease the roll onto a platter, seam side down, and dust with the 2 tablespoons confectioners' sugar. Cover loosely and chill until ready to serve. The cake keeps well in the refrigerator for about a day.

To serve: Using a sharp serrated knife, cut the roll, slightly on the diagonal, into generous 1-inch slices.

GUGELHUPF

Gugelhupf

To most Americans, gugelhupf is a sweet yeast bread baked in a Bundt pan. This one is a pound cake strewn with two kinds of raisins. It's a favorite of commercial German bakers, but this scaled-down recipe is typical of the gugelhupfs baked by home cooks throughout the country.

For the Bundt Pan:

Nonstick vegetable cooking spray or 1½ tablespoons unsalted butter or margarine

2 tablespoons all-purpose flour

Cake:

3 cups sifted all-purpose flour

½ cup seedless raisins

½ cup golden seedless raisins (sultanas)

1 teaspoon baking powder

½ teaspoon freshly grated nutmeg

¾ pound (3 sticks) unsalted butter (no substitute), at room temperature

2¼ cups granulated sugar

Finely grated zest of 1 large lemon

1½ teaspoons vanilla extract

1 teaspoon freshly squeezed lemon juice

5 extra-large eggs

1 extra-large egg yolk

⅓ cup finely ground blanched almonds

¾ cup milk

Topping:

1 tablespoon confectioners' sugar

Makes a 9-inch Bundt cake, about 16 servings

For the pan: Liberally spray or butter a 9-inch (12-cup) Bundt pan, add the 2 tablespoons flour, and tilt the pan first to one side, then to another, until all surfaces are evenly

continued on next page

365

GUGELHUPF (cont.)

coated with flour. Tap out any excess flour and set the pan aside. Preheat the oven to 300° F.

For the cake: Mix ¼ cup of the flour with the two kinds of raisins in a small bowl, toss well to coat, and set aside. Sift the remaining flour, baking powder, and nutmeg onto a piece of wax paper and set aside. Cream the butter, sugar, lemon zest, vanilla, and lemon juice in the large electric mixer bowl at highest speed for 5 minutes, until light and fluffy. Reduce the mixer speed to low and beat in the eggs, one at a time, then beat in the egg yolk and almonds. Add the sifted dry ingredients alternately with the milk, beginning and ending with the dry, and beating by hand after each addition only enough to incorporate. Finally, fold in the raisins and all dredging flour. Spoon the batter into the prepared pan and smooth the surface.

Bake about 1¾ hours, or until the cake has pulled from the sides of the pan, is springy to the touch, and a cake tester inserted midway between the rim of the pan and the central tube comes out clean. Cool the cake upright in the pan on a wire rack for 15 minutes. Loosen around the edge and around the central tube, turn out on the rack, and cool to room temperature.

For the topping: Set the cake, still on the rack, on a wax-paper-covered surface and sift the confectioners' sugar evenly over all. Cut the cake into slim wedges and serve.

RED CURRANT CAKE

Johannisbeerkuchen

Few fruits are more highly prized in Germany than red currants, maybe because their season is so short. These small, fragile, scarlet berries arrive in the dead of summer but are gone long before the weather turns crisp. Fresh currants are what give this cake its welcome tartness and moist, tender crumb. Do not substitute dried currants because the cake will not be the same. This cake batter is as stiff as cookie dough and you must be careful not to overmix it lest you toughen the cake.

For the Bundt Pan:

Nonstick vegetable cooking spray or 1½ tablespoons
   unsalted butter or margarine

2 tablespoons all-purpose flour

Cake:

5 cups sifted all-purpose flour

3 teaspoons baking powder

1 teaspoon baking soda

¼ teaspoon salt

½ pound (2 sticks) unsalted butter or margarine

1⅓ cups sugar

1½ teaspoons vanilla extract

Finely grated zest of 1 large navel orange

4 extra-large eggs

½ cup freshly squeezed orange juice

1 pint fresh red currants, washed, stemmed, and patted dry
   on paper toweling

Topping:

1 tablespoon confectioners' sugar

Makes a 9-inch Bundt cake, about 16 servings

For the pan: Liberally spray or butter a 9-inch (12-cup) Bundt pan, add the 2 tablespoons flour, and tilt the pan first to one side, then to another, until all surfaces are evenly coated with flour. Tap out any excess flour and set the pan aside. Preheat the oven to 350° F.

For the cake: Sift the flour, baking powder, soda, and salt onto a piece of wax paper and set aside. Cream the butter,

continued on next page

367

RED CURRANT CAKE
(cont.)

sugar, vanilla, and orange zest in the large electric mixer bowl at highest speed for 5 minutes, until light and fluffy. Reduce the mixer speed to low and beat in the eggs, one at a time. Add the sifted dry ingredients alternately with the orange juice, beginning and ending with the dry, and beating by hand after each addition only enough to incorporate. The batter is unsually stiff, but take care not to overbeat. Fold in the currants, spoon the batter into the prepared pan, and smooth the surface.

Bake about 1 hour, or until the cake has pulled from the sides of the pan, is springy to the touch, and a cake tester inserted midway between the rim of the pan and the central tube comes out clean. Cool the cake upright in the pan on a wire rack for 10 minutes. Loosen around the edge and around the central tube, turn out on the rack, and cool to room temperature.

For the topping: Set the cake, still on the rack, on a wax-paper-covered surface and sift the confectioners' sugar evenly over all. Cut the cake into slim wedges and serve as is or topped by Vanilla, Lemon, or Orange Sauce (page 355).

EGGNOG TORTE
Eierlikör-Torte

"A very delicious cake for a kaffeeklatsch," says Angelika Miebs of the Hesse region of Germany, whose recipe this is. "You can," she adds, "omit the hazelnuts." But we like the torte better with them. This is a high, single-layer torte, dense of texture but not too chocolaty. It's easy to make, but take care not to overbeat once you begin adding the flour.

Torte:

3 cups sifted all-purpose flour

2 teaspoons baking powder

¼ teaspoon salt

8 tablespoons (1 stick) unsalted butter or margarine

1½ cups sugar

1½ teaspoons vanilla extract

4 extra-large eggs

4 ounces bittersweet chocolate, melted

EGGNOG TORTE

The batter is very stiff and if you're too vigorous about mixing in the flour, you'll coarsen the torte's texture. To apply the eggnog, you'll need a plastic squirt bottle with a pointed tip – the kind used for ketchup and mustard.
We think that scattering chocolate sprinkles over the finished torte merely obscures the carefully piped-on spiral of eggnog. But if your spiral is less than perfect, the sprinkles are a dandy cover-up.

1⅓ cups (4 to 4½ ounces) finely ground unblanched hazelnuts (optional)

⅔ cup milk

Eggnog:

2 tablespoons sugar blended with 1 tablespoon all-purpose flour

½ cup milk

1 extra-large egg yolk, lightly beaten

1 teaspoon rum extract

Frosting:

1 cup heavy cream, whipped to stiff peaks

Optional Decoration:

1 to 2 tablespoons chocolate sprinkles

Makes a 10-inch torte, about 16 servings

Preheat the oven to 350° F. Liberally butter the bottom and sides of a 10-inch springform pan or spray with nonstick vegetable cooking spray and set aside.

For the torte: Sift the flour, baking powder, and salt together twice and set aside. Cream the butter, sugar, and vanilla in the large electric mixer bowl at highest speed for 5 minutes, until light and fluffy. Reduce the mixer speed to low and beat in the eggs, one by one. Beat in the melted chocolate and, if using, the hazelnuts. Add the sifted dry ingredients alternately with the milk, beginning and ending with the dry, and beating by hand after each addition only enough to incorporate. Spoon the batter into the prepared pan and smooth the top. Rap the pan several times on the counter to release any large air bubbles, then bake about 1 hour and 20 minutes, until the torte begins to pull from the sides of the pan, is springy to the touch, and a cake tester inserted in the middle comes out clean. Cool the torte in the upright pan on

continued on next page

EGGNOG TORTE (cont.)

a wire rack for 15 minutes, then loosen it around the edge with a small spatula. Release and remove the springform pan sides and cool the torte, still on the pan bottom and cake rack, to room temperature.

For the eggnog: Blend the sugar-flour mixture with the milk in a very small heavy saucepan. Set over moderate heat and cook, stirring constantly, about 3 minutes, until thickened and smooth. Whisk a little of the hot mixture into the beaten yolk, stir back into the pan, and cook and stir over moderately low heat for 2 minutes longer. Remove from the heat, mix in the rum extract, then pour the eggnog through a fine sieve into a small metal bowl. Set in an ice bath and chill 15 to 20 minutes, whisking often to prevent a skin from forming on the surface of the sauce. Pour the eggnog into a plastic squirt bottle with a pointed tip and an opening no more than ⅛ inch in diameter; refrigerate until ready to use.

To frost the torte: Set the torte, still on the springform pan bottom, on a lazy Susan and frost the top and sides smoothly and thinly with the whipped cream. Starting in the center of the torte and exerting steady but gentle pressure on the squirt bottle, apply the eggnog in a tight spiral on the top of the torte, spacing the lines about ½ inch apart. Scatter the chocolate sprinkles over the top of the torte, if you like, then transfer the torte, still on the springform pan bottom, to a cake plate and serve.

Note: Because the eggnog contains egg yolk, any leftover torte should be stored in the refrigerator, preferably on a covered cake plate so it doesn't absorb refrigerator odors.

370

AUNT BETTY'S HAZELNUT TORTE

Tante Bettys Haselnusstorte

This astonishing cake contains only four ingredients, yet it's moist and light. Nothing could be easier to prepare because flavored whipped cream both fills and frosts the torte. The recipe comes from Hedy's Aunt Babette (known to everyone as Betty), who grew up in the Bavarian village of Murnau. Hedy often makes the torte for parties because it's showy. To decorate it, she may arrange whole toasted hazelnuts in a circle on top of the torte or scatter with finely ground toasted hazelnuts.

For the Pans:

Nonstick vegetable cooking spray or 1½ tablespoons
   unsalted butter or margarine

3 tablespoons all-purpose flour

Hazelnut Torte:

10 extra-large eggs, separated

1½ cups sugar

4 cups finely ground unblanched hazelnuts (see note)

¼ teaspoon salt

Filling and Frosting:

2½ cups well-chilled heavy cream

2 tablespoons sugar

1 teaspoon vanilla extract

Decoration:

12 whole blanched and toasted hazelnuts, or ¼ cup finely
   ground, lightly toasted hazelnuts (see note)

Makes a 10-inch, 2-layer torte, about 12 servings

For the pans: Liberally spray or butter two 10-inch spring-form pans, add half the flour to each, and tilt the pans first to one side, then to the other, until all surfaces are evenly coated with flour. Tap out any excess flour and set the pans aside. Preheat the oven to 350° F.

For the hazelnut torte: Beat the egg yolks and sugar in the large electric mixer bowl at highest speed for 3 to 5 minutes, until the color and consistency of mayonnaise. Reduce the speed to low and mix in the hazelnuts (the mixture will be very thick). Beat the egg whites with the salt to stiff peaks. Fold about one fourth of the beaten whites into the hazelnut

371

continued on next page

mixture to lighten it, then gently but thoroughly fold in the balance until no streaks of white or tan show. Divide the batter evenly between the two prepared pans, smoothing the surface as much as possible. Bake in the lower third of the oven for 45 minutes. Remove the torte layers from the oven and cool upright in their pans on wire racks for 10 minutes. Loosen each layer around the edge with a spatula, then release and remove the springform pan sides. Very carefully loosen each torte from the pan bottom, lift the bottoms off, and cool the layers on wire racks to room temperature.

For the filling and frosting: Whip the cream with the sugar and vanilla to very stiff peaks. Place one torte layer upside down on a large cake plate and spread with half the whipped cream. Set the second layer on top, right side up, and frost with the remaining whipped cream. Do not frost the sides of the torte.

To decorate: Arrange the whole hazelnuts in a circle around the top of the torte or sprinkle the finely ground nuts evenly over the top. Let the torte stand at least 30 minutes before serving. When cutting, use a sharp serrated knife.

Note: To blanch and toast hazelnuts, spread the nuts in a baking pan and set in a 350-degree oven for 30 to 35 minutes. Cool 10 minutes, bundle in a clean tea towel, and rub briskly to remove the skins. Don't fret about any stubborn bits still clinging to the nuts. They will add color.

The easiest way to grind hazelnuts fine – either unblanched or blanched and toasted – is in a food processor fitted with the metal chopping blade. But proceed with caution lest you churn the nuts to paste. For this torte, they should be feathery.

TERRACES

Terrassen

These three-tiered cook-
ies are easy to make,
with a little patience
and the right cookie
cutters. You'll need three
fluted round cutters: 1¼
inches in diameter, 1¾
inches, and 2¼ inches.
Most good kitchen sup-
ply stores and specialty
food shops sell little tins
of nested, graduated
cutters, both the fluted
and the plain, that
range in diameter from
1¼ to 3¾ inches.

½ pound (2 sticks) plus 2 tablespoons unsalted butter (no substitute), at room temperature

⅔ cup granulated sugar

1 tablespoon plus 1 teaspoon dark rum

1 tablespoon vanilla extract

¼ teaspoon salt

1 extra-large egg yolk

Finely grated zest of 1 lemon

3¾ cups sifted all-purpose flour

½ cup red currant jelly

¼ cup unsifted confectioners' sugar (for dusting)

Makes about 4 dozen cookies

373

Cream the butter, granulated sugar, rum, vanilla, salt, egg yolk, and lemon zest in the large electric mixer bowl at high speed for 2 to 3 minutes, until light and fluffy. Reduce the mixer speed to low, add the flour, and beat just enough to incorporate – no longer or the cookies will be tough. Divide the dough into fourths; flatten each into a disk and wrap in plastic wrap. Refrigerate for at least 2 hours or, better yet, overnight.

When ready to proceed, preheat the oven to 350° F.

Roll one fourth of the dough to a thickness of ⅛ inch between sheets of lightly floured wax paper. Using lightly floured fluted round cutters in 1¼-, 1¾-, and 2¼-inch sizes, cut out an equal number of cookies of each size. Repeat with each piece of dough. Space the cookies 1 inch apart on lightly greased baking sheets, placing all the small cookies on a single sheet, all the medium size on a second sheet, and all the large on a third sheet (the smaller cookies will bake

continued on next page

TERRACES (cont.)

faster than the large ones, so it's best not to mix the sizes on the baking sheets).

Bake the cookies for 8 to 10 minutes, or until very lightly colored. Cool the cookies for 1 minute on the baking sheets, then transfer to wire racks and cool to room temperature.

To assemble the terraces: Spoon about ¼ teaspoon of the jelly onto the center of each large cookie. Top with a medium-size cookie, pressing down lightly to spread the jelly, but don't let it ooze out. Spoon a scant ¼ teaspoon of the jelly onto the center of each medium-size cookie, then top with the small cookies, again pressing lightly. Finally, lightly dust the cookies with the confectioners' sugar. Layer the terraces between sheets of wax paper and store in airtight containers. You may need to dust them again with confectioners' sugar before you serve them.

CHOCOLATE-ORANGE ROUNDS
Orangenplätzchen

Cookies:

8 tablespoons (1 stick) unsalted butter (no substitute), at room temperature

½ cup firmly packed light brown sugar

2 tablespoons finely grated orange zest

¼ teaspoon salt

1 extra-large egg

4 (1-ounce) squares semisweet chocolate, very finely chopped

1¾ cups sifted all-purpose flour

Glaze:

1½ cups unsifted confectioners' sugar

2 tablespoons freshly squeezed orange juice

4 teaspoons freshly squeezed lemon juice

CHOCOLATE-ORANGE
ROUNDS

Makes about 3 dozen cookies

For the cookies: Cream the butter, sugar, orange zest, and salt in the large electric mixer bowl at highest speed for 1 to 2 minutes, until light and fluffy. Add the egg and beat 1 minute at moderate speed. Add the chocolate and flour and beat at low speed just enough to combine. Divide the dough, flatten each half into a 6-inch circle, wrap in plastic wrap, and chill for at least 2 hours or, better yet, overnight.

When ready to proceed, preheat the oven to 375° F.

Roll each circle of dough, one at a time, between sheets of lightly floured wax paper until a scant ¼ inch thick, sprinkling with flour once during rolling. Carefully peel off the top piece of paper and, using a 2½-inch round cutter, cut the dough – still on the bottom sheet of wax paper – into rounds, but do not lift off the paper. Slide the paper of dough onto a baking sheet and set in the freezer for 5 minutes so the individual cookies will be easier to remove. Using a small spatula, carefully lift the cookies from the wax paper and space 1 inch apart on lightly greased baking sheets.

Bake the cookies in the middle of the oven for 8 to 10 minutes, or until lightly browned around the edges. Transfer at once to wire racks set over wax paper.

For the glaze: Whisk the confectioners' sugar with the orange and lemon juices in a small bowl until smooth and of good glazing consistency. Using a pastry brush, brush the glaze on the still-warm cookies.

As soon as the glaze hardens, layer the cookies between sheets of wax paper and store in airtight containers.

375

CINNAMON STARS

Zimtsterne

12 tablespoons (1½ sticks) unsalted butter (no substitute), at room temperature

⅔ cup granulated sugar

Finely grated zest of 1 lemon

1¼ teaspoons ground cinnamon

¼ teaspoon freshly grated nutmeg or ground mace

¼ teaspoon salt

2 extra-large egg yolks

1 cup finely ground blanched almonds

1 cup finely ground walnuts

1⅔ cups sifted all-purpose flour

1½ cups unsifted confectioners' sugar blended with 3 tablespoons freshly squeezed lemon juice (glaze)

Makes about 4 dozen cookies

Cream the butter, granulated sugar, lemon zest, cinnamon, nutmeg, and salt in the large electric mixer bowl at high speed for 2 to 3 minutes, until light and fluffy. Reduce the mixer speed to low, add the egg yolks, and beat for 1 minute. Add the almonds, walnuts, and flour and beat at lowest mixer speed just enough to combine.

Divide the dough in half, shape each half into a ball, then flatten into a 6-inch circle. Wrap in plastic wrap and chill for at least 2 hours or, better yet, overnight.

When ready to proceed, preheat the oven to 350° F.

Roll each half of the dough to a thickness of ⅛ inch between sheets of lightly floured wax paper. Slide the papers of dough onto a baking sheet, set in the freezer, and chill for 5 minutes, so that the dough will be easier to cut. Very gently peel

CINNAMON STARS

off the top sheet of wax paper. Using a lightly floured 2¾-inch star cutter, cut into cookies – right on the bottom sheet of wax paper – then, using a lightly floured spatula, carefully transfer the cookies to lightly greased baking sheets, spacing 1 inch apart.

Bake the cookies in the middle of the oven for 10 to 12 minutes, or until lightly browned around the edges. Cool the cookies on the baking sheets on wire racks for 3 minutes, then transfer the cookies to the racks and cool about 5 minutes longer.

To glaze the cookies: Using a pastry brush, brush the still-warm cookies with a thin wash of the glaze. Let the glaze harden and apply a second thin layer. Once the glaze has hardened, layer the cookies between sheets of wax paper and store in airtight containers.

ROLLED GINGER COOKIES
Lebkuchen

377

Lebkuchen, *the ginger-bread of Germany, is cut at Christmastime into fancy shapes – bells, stars, rocking horses, wreaths. It's also used to build gingerbread houses of awesome detail. Unlike our own shattery-crisp ginger wafers,* Lebkuchen *is hard and chewy, a real jaw-breaker. This cookie dough must chill overnight before it's rolled and cut.*

Lebkuchen:

8 tablespoons (1 stick) unsalted butter (no substitute), at room temperature

¾ cup honey

⅔ cup sugar

2 tablespoons unsweetened Dutch process cocoa powder

1 teaspoon ground cinnamon

1 teaspoon ground allspice

½ teaspoon ground ginger

½ teaspoon freshly grated nutmeg

½ teaspoon ground cloves

Pinch of salt

3¾ cups sifted all-purpose flour

2 teaspoons baking powder

continued on next page

ROLLED GINGER
COOKIES (cont.)

1 extra-large egg

1 extra-large egg yolk blended with 2 tablespoons cold water
(egg glaze)

Decorator Icing:

1½ cups unsifted confectioners' sugar

1 tablespoon egg-white powder (available at specialty food
shops and bakery supply stores)

1 tablespoon cold water

1 tablespoon freshly squeezed lemon juice

Makes about 3 dozen cookies

For the Lebkuchen: Combine the butter, honey, sugar, cocoa,
cinnamon, allspice, ginger, nutmeg, cloves, and salt in a
medium-size saucepan. Set, uncovered, over moderately low
heat and cook and stir about 5 minutes, until the mixture
boils and the sugar dissolves. Remove from the heat and
cool for 30 minutes.

Meanwhile, sift the flour and baking powder into a very large
bowl, make a well in the center, and set aside. Beat the egg
into the cooled honey mixture, pour all into the well in the
dry ingredients, then mix with a wooden spoon until no dry
flecks of flour remain. Divide the dough into 4 equal parts,
wrap each snugly in plastic wrap, and chill overnight.

When ready to proceed, preheat the oven to 350° F.

Roll each piece of the dough between lightly floured sheets
of wax paper into a circle 7½ inches across and ¼ inch thick.
Carefully peel off the top sheet of wax paper. Invert the dough
on a lightly floured pastry cloth and peel off the remaining
sheet of wax paper. Using 2- to 3-inch cookie cutters, cut
into stars, bells, wreaths, or other fancy shapes.

Space the cookies 1 inch apart on lightly greased baking
sheets and brush the tops lightly with the egg glaze. Bake 8

378

ROLLED GINGER
COOKIES

to 10 minutes, until the cookies are lightly golden. Remove at once to wire racks and cool to room temperature.

For the decorator icing: Combine the sugar, egg-white powder, water, and lemon juice in a small bowl, then beat with an electric mixer at high speed for 1 to 2 minutes, until stiff and glossy. Spoon the icing into a pastry bag fitted with a fine writing tip, then pipe double or single lines around the edge of each cookie and fill in the centers with stripes, cross-hatches, zigzag lines, or dots - let your imagination soar.

Once the icing hardens, store the cookies in single layers between sheets of wax paper in airtight containers.

ROSA'S CINNAMON-HAZELNUT LEBKUCHEN WITH CANDIED ORANGE RIND

Rosas Elisenlebkuchen

To most of us, Lebkuchen *are fancily cut and decorated ginger cookies.* Elisenlebkuchen, *the specialty of Nuremberg, are altogether different – a sort of cinnamony macaroon made of ground hazelnuts, confectioners' sugar, eggs, and finely chopped candied orange peel. They contain no flour and are thus difficult to remove from the baking sheet. A German cook's answer to this sticky problem is to use* Oblaten, *crisp, edible baking disks. They're available here at some German groceries, also at fancy food shops. If you should find them, by all means use them in the recipe that follows –*

Cookies:

5 extra-large eggs

1 pound unsifted confectioners' sugar

2 teaspoons ground cinnamon

1 teaspoon freshly grated nutmeg (do not use commercially ground nutmeg, which lacks the lemony fragrance of the freshly ground)

1 pound unblanched hazelnuts, ground very fine (the food processor does this to perfection)

¼ pound candied orange peel, moderately finely chopped

Finely grated zest of 2 large lemons

Chocolate Coating:

6 ounces bittersweet or semisweet chocolate

Makes about 10 dozen cookies

For the cookies: Preheat the oven to 350° F. Place 12 *Oblaten* or squares of foil (dull side up) on an ungreased baking sheet, spacing them about 2 inches apart.

continued on next page

379

ROSA'S CINNAMON-
HAZELNUT LEBKUCHEN
WITH CANDIED
ORANGE RIND (cont.)

380

*the 50 millimeter
Oblaten (about 2 inches
across) is a good size.
If you're unable to buy
Oblaten, you can substi-
tute communion wafers,
provided they're big
enough. Otherwise, cut
aluminum foil into 3-
inch squares (you'll need
120 of them, alas, but a
little time spent snipping
foil at the outset will
spare you grief later
when you try to remove
the cookies from the
baking sheet).
There are many
theories as to how
Elisenlebkuchen came
to be named, but the
most plausible is that
they are named for St.
Elisabeth, the patron
saint of bakers and
gingerbread makers
in Germany.
Don't make these cookies
in rainy or humid
weather because they
won't be crisp.*

Beat the eggs, sugar, cinnamon, and nutmeg in the large electric mixer bowl at highest speed until thick and lemony – 3 to 5 minutes. Fold in the hazelnuts, then the candied orange peel and lemon zest. Drop the batter by scant tea-spoonfuls onto the *Oblaten* or foil squares. If using the *Oblaten*, spread the batter almost to the edges all around.

Bake the cookies for 8 to 10 minutes, until lightly browned. Remove from the oven and let the cookies cool on the baking sheet for 2 to 3 minutes – just until they firm up slightly but are not yet brittle. If you have used the *Oblaten*, use a broad spatula to transfer the cookies to wire racks to cool (dipping the spatula in hot water helps loosen any recalcitrant areas where the cookies may have spread over onto the baking sheet). If you have dropped the cookies onto foil, merely peel the foil off. Continue baking batches of cookies the same way until all batter is gone.

For the chocolate coating: Melt the chocolate in a double boiler set over simmering water, then brush a thin wash of chocolate over each cookie. Set the cookies in a cool spot to harden the chocolate (you can also quick-chill the chocolate by setting a tray of cookies in the freezer).

As soon as the chocolate hardens, layer the cookies between sheets of wax paper and store in airtight containers.

PEPPERNUTS
Pfeffernüsse

These fruit-studded, whole wheat cookies are called peppernuts *because they're intensely spicy and look like unshelled walnuts. When first baked, Pfeffernüsse are as hard as rocks and must season for at least ten days in an airtight canister before they're glazed and eaten. The seasoning not only mellows the flavor of the Pfeffernüsse but also softens them considerably.*

¾ cup honey

¾ cup firmly packed light brown sugar

Finely grated zest of 1 lemon

14 tablespoons (1¾ sticks) unsalted butter (no substitute), at room temperature

3 cups unsifted whole wheat flour

1¼ cups sifted all-purpose flour

1 cup finely ground unblanched almonds

¾ cup finely chopped candied citron

¾ cup dried currants

2 teaspoons ground cinnamon

2 teaspoons ground allspice

½ teaspoon ground ginger

1 tablespoon baking powder

¼ teaspoon salt

1½ cups unsifted confectioners' sugar blended with 3 tablespoons freshly squeezed lemon juice (glaze)

Makes about 8 dozen cookies

Combine the honey, brown sugar, and lemon zest in a large saucepan. Set, uncovered, over moderate heat and cook about 5 minutes, stirring often, until the mixture boils and the sugar dissolves. Remove from the heat and add the butter; set aside for the moment.

Mix the whole wheat and all-purpose flours, the almonds, citron, currants, cinnamon, allspice, ginger, baking powder, and salt in a very large bowl and make a well in the center. Stir the honey mixture until well blended, then pour into

continued on next page

PEPPERNUTS (cont.)

the well in the dry ingredients. Stir together to make a stiff dough. Cover and let stand for 30 minutes.

Meanwhile, preheat the oven to 350° F.

Roll the cookie dough into ¾-inch balls and space 1 inch apart on ungreased baking sheets. Bake for 15 to 17 minutes, until firm to the touch and lightly browned on the bottom. Transfer at once to wire racks and cool to room temperature.

Layer the cookies between sheets of wax paper and store in airtight containers for at least 10 days to allow them to season and soften.

When ready to glaze the cookies, set wire racks on a wax-paper-covered counter. Dip each cookie into the glaze, then set on the rack to harden. Once the glaze has hardened on the cookies, store them in airtight containers.

HAZELNUT THUMBPRINT COOKIES

Husaren-Krapferln

14 tablespoons (1¾ sticks) unsalted butter (no substitute), at room temperature

½ cup granulated sugar

1 tablespoon vanilla extract

¼ teaspoon salt

2 extra-large egg yolks

1 cup finely ground unblanched hazelnuts

2¾ cups sifted all-purpose flour

¼ to ⅓ cup sieved raspberry jam

½ cup confectioners' sugar

Makes about 3½ dozen cookies

Preheat the oven to 375° F.

HAZELNUT
THUMBPRINT COOKIES

Cream the butter, granulated sugar, vanilla, and salt in the large electric mixer bowl at high speed for 2 to 3 minutes, until light and fluffy. Reduce the mixer speed to low, add the egg yolks, and beat 1 minute. With the mixer at lowest speed, mix in the hazelnuts, then the flour.

Divide the dough into 4 equal portions. Working with lightly floured hands, roll each portion on a lightly floured surface into a log 10 inches long. Cut the log into 1-inch lengths, then, using your hands, roll these into balls.

Space the balls 1 inch apart on lightly greased baking sheets. Using your thumb, press a little well into the center of each cookie, then spoon about ¼ teaspoon of the jam into each. Bake the cookies for 13 to 15 minutes, until pale tan. Transfer at once to wire racks set over wax paper and cool to room temperature.

Lightly dust the cookies with the confectioners' sugar. The cookies will be prettier if you let the jam centers show, but you must dust them one by one. Lift a cookie to a small rack, shield the jam center with a turned-upside-down measuring spoon approximately the same size as the center, and sift on the sugar. When all the cookies have been dusted with confectioners' sugar, layer between sheets of wax paper and store in airtight containers. Redust the cookies with confectioners' sugar, if needed, just before serving.

VANILLA CRESCENTS
Vanillekipferl

Guaranteed to melt in your mouth. This cookie dough must chill overnight before it's shaped and baked, so plan accordingly.

14 tablespoons (1¾ sticks) unsalted butter (no substitute), at room temperature

½ cup granulated sugar

2 extra-large egg yolks

1 tablespoon vanilla extract

Pinch of salt

1 cup finely ground blanched almonds

2⅔ cups sifted all-purpose flour

1 cup Vanilla 10X Sugar (page 400)

Makes about 4 dozen cookies

Cream the butter, granulated sugar, egg yolks, vanilla, and salt in the large electric mixer bowl at high speed for 2 to 3 minutes, until light and fluffy. Reduce the mixer speed to low and beat in the almonds and 1⅔ cups of the flour; mix in the remaining flour by hand. Divide the dough into 4 equal portions, wrap each in plastic wrap, and refrigerate overnight.

When ready to proceed, preheat the oven to 375° F.

Working with one fourth of the dough at a time, shape into ropes 12 inches long, then cut into 1-inch lengths. Roll each length of dough between your palms into a 3-inch log, tapering the ends to points. Bend into crescents and space 1 inch apart on lightly greased baking sheets.

Bake for 12 to 15 minutes, until very lightly golden. Transfer at once to wire racks and cool for 2 to 3 minutes. Roll the still-warm cookies in the vanilla 10X sugar until evenly coated, then transfer to wire racks set over wax paper. Sift any remaining vanilla 10X sugar over the cookies. Layer between sheets of wax paper and store in airtight canisters.

HONEY-ALMOND BARS
Honigkuchen

Bars:

1½ cups honey

¾ cup vegetable oil

1¼ cups sugar

6 cups sifted all-purpose flour

1 tablespoon baking powder

½ teaspoon ground cinnamon

½ teaspoon ground allspice

¼ teaspoon ground cloves

¼ teaspoon freshly grated nutmeg

¼ teaspoon salt

2 cups finely ground blanched almonds

½ cup finely chopped candied citron

½ cup finely chopped candied orange peel

3 extra-large eggs, lightly beaten

Decoration:

12 candied red cherries, halved

48 blanched whole almonds

48 pieces candied citron, cut into ½ x ⅜ x ⅛-inch wedges

Makes 2 dozen cookies

For the bars: Combine the honey, oil, and sugar in a large heavy saucepan over moderate heat. Cook, uncovered, for 10 to 15 minutes, stirring occasionally, until the mixture froths up and the sugar dissolves. Remove from the heat and cool 30 minutes.

continued on next page

HONEY-ALMOND BARS
(cont.)

Preheat the oven to 350° F. Butter a 15½ x 10½ x 1-inch jelly roll pan and set aside.

Mix the flour, baking powder, cinnamon, allspice, cloves, nutmeg, salt, almonds, citron, and orange peel in a large bowl and make a well in the center. Scrape the cooled honey mixture into the well in the dry ingredients. Add the eggs and stir into the mixture, then slowly incorporate the dry ingredients. The dough will be quite stiff. Spread in the prepared jelly roll pan, smoothing well into the corners and leveling the surface.

To decorate the bars: Score the top of the dough into 24 squares by dividing lengthwise into 6 strips and crosswise into 4 strips. Center a candied cherry half in each square, then arrange an almond at the 5 and 10 o'clock positions and a citron wedge at the 2 and 8 o'clock positions, letting them radiate out from the cherry like flower petals.

Bake the bars for 35 to 40 minutes, until a wooden pick inserted near the center of the pan comes out clean. Cool the bars in the upright pan on a wire rack to room temperature. Cut into squares, following the scored lines. Wrap airtight in plastic wrap to prevent the bars from drying.

BASIC RECIPES
Grundrezepte

FOREST MUSHROOM SAUCE
Waldpilzsauce

Serve over Semmelknödel *(page 226), boiled potatoes, or even rice.*

4 tablespoons (½ stick) unsalted butter or margarine

1 medium-size yellow onion, peeled and coarsely chopped

¾ pound chanterelles or boletus mushrooms (or cultivated white mushrooms), wiped clean with a damp cloth, stemmed, and thinly sliced

½ teaspoon dried leaf marjoram, crumbled

¼ teaspoon dried leaf thyme, crumbled

¼ teaspoon freshly grated nutmeg

4 tablespoons all-purpose flour

1 cup rich beef broth (preferably homemade)

1½ cups milk

½ cup heavy cream

¾ teaspoon salt

⅛ teaspoon freshly ground black pepper

Makes about 5 cups

Melt the butter in a heavy 12-inch skillet over moderate heat. Add the onion and sauté 5 minutes, stirring often, until limp and golden. Add the mushrooms, marjoram, thyme, and nutmeg and sauté 5 minutes, stirring often, until the mushrooms have released their juices and these have evaporated. Sprinkle the flour into the skillet and cook and stir 1 minute. Pour in the broth, milk, and cream and cook 5 minutes, stirring constantly, until thickened and no raw taste of flour remains. Mix in the salt and pepper, taste, and adjust as needed. Serve at once.

FRANKFURT GREEN SAUCE
Frankfurter Grüne Sauce

Prepare this with fresh herbs – dried herbs lack their summery bouquet. Green Sauce is particularly popular in the Frankfurt area and, adds Walter Carle, executive chef of the Hotel Gravenbruch Kempinski Frankfurt, whose recipe this is, "it is the traditional accompaniment for boiled beef and all manner of pâtés." We also like it with steamed lobster and poached salmon.

3 extra-large hard-cooked eggs, shelled, then the yolks sieved and the whites finely chopped

½ cup corn oil

1 teaspoon Dijon mustard

½ cup sour cream

½ cup plain yogurt (use the low-fat or non-fat, if you like)

½ cup finely chopped fresh chervil or tarragon

½ cup finely chopped watercress leaves

⅔ cup moderately finely snipped fresh chives

½ cup finely chopped sorrel leaves

½ cup finely chopped flat-leaf parsley

2 tablespoons freshly squeezed lemon juice

½ teaspoon salt

¼ teaspoon freshly ground black pepper

Makes about 3 cups

Blend the egg yolks, oil, and mustard in an electric blender at high speed or in a food processor fitted with the metal chopping blade for 1 minute, until smooth and thick. Add the sour cream, yogurt, chervil, watercress, chives, sorrel, parsley, lemon juice, salt, and pepper and blend for 30 seconds. Taste for salt and pepper and adjust as needed. By hand, mix in the chopped egg whites. Spoon into a medium-size bowl, cover with plastic wrap, and refrigerate until ready to serve. Stir well before serving.

WARM HORSERADISH SAUCE

Warme Meerrettichsauce

Serve with Pälzer Fleschknepp *(page 172), boiled beef, or tongue.*

3 tablespoons unsalted butter or margarine

5 tablespoons all-purpose flour

2 cups milk, at room temperature

2 tablespoons finely grated fresh horseradish, or ¼ cup prepared horseradish

1 tablespoon freshly squeezed lemon juice

¾ teaspoon salt

¼ teaspoon white pepper

Makes about 2½ cups

Melt the butter in a small heavy saucepan over moderate heat, blend in the flour, and cook and stir 1 minute. Add the milk and cook 3 minutes, whisking constantly, until thickened and smooth. Reduce the heat to its lowest point and mellow the sauce for 5 minutes, whisking often. Mix in the horseradish, lemon juice, salt, and pepper and serve.

APPLE-HORSERADISH SAUCE
Apfel-Meerrettichsauce

Just the sauce to accompany baked ham, boiled tongue, assorted wursts and cold cuts. Stored tightly covered in the refrigerator, it keeps well for about a week, although it may darken somewhat.

2 tablespoons unsalted butter or margarine

1½ pounds McIntosh, Cortland, or other cooking apples (not too tart), peeled, cored, and thinly sliced

2 tablespoons freshly squeezed lemon juice

1 tablespoon sugar

½ teaspoon freshly grated nutmeg

¼ cup heavy cream

1 teaspoon salt

¼ teaspoon freshly ground black pepper

¼ cup finely grated fresh horseradish, or ⅓ cup prepared horseradish

Makes about 2 cups

Melt the butter in a heavy 12-inch skillet over moderate heat. Add the apples, lemon juice, sugar, and nutmeg and toss well to mix. Sauté 5 minutes, stirring often, until the apples are golden. Reduce the heat to its lowest point, cover, and cook 15 minutes, until the apples are very soft. If there is a lot of skillet liquid, raise the heat to moderate and boil, uncovered, for 1 to 2 minutes, until the juices evaporate.

Transfer the skillet mixture to a food processor fitted with the metal chopping blade. Add the cream, salt, and pepper and purée 30 seconds, scraping down the sides of the workbowl at halftime. Add the horseradish and pulse 4 to 5 times to incorporate. Serve warm or cold.

APPLE-CHEESE SAUCE
(Apfel-Käsesauce)

Serve with Vintner's Fondue (page 164), roast beef, or pork. Also good with baked ham and pork chops. The recipe comes from Annemarie Schätzel, whose family owns the Kapellenhof Weingut in Selzen.

3½ ounces cream cheese, at room temperature

1 small, tart, red apple, cored and finely grated but not peeled

1 teaspoon freshly squeezed lemon juice

1 teaspoon finely grated fresh horseradish, or 2 teaspoons well-drained prepared horseradish

3 tablespoons Riesling or other dry white wine

½ cup heavy cream, whipped to stiff peaks

2 tablespoons finely minced parsley

2 tablespoons finely snipped fresh chives

2 tablespoons finely snipped fresh dill

2 tablespoons finely chopped fresh lemon verbena or lemon geranium

¼ teaspoon salt

Makes 2 cups

Combine the cream cheese, apple, lemon juice, horseradish, and wine in a medium-size bowl. Fold in the cream and all remaining ingredients. Serve as an accompaniment to meat.

RED CURRANT SAUCE
(Johannisbeersauce)

Serve with Vintner's Fondue (page 164), roast beef, venison, or pork.

5 tablespoons red currant jelly

2 tablespoons Dijon mustard

2 tablespoons dry red wine

1 teaspoon freshly squeezed lemon juice

¼ teaspoon salt

¼ teaspoon sugar

2 tablespoons olive or corn oil

Makes ⅔ cup

Whisk all ingredients in a small bowl until smooth and creamy. Cover and chill until ready to use.

RED WINE JELLY À LA SCHÄTZEL

(Rotweingelee à la Schätzel)

This unusual recipe comes from Annemarie Schätzel, whose family owns the Kapellenhof Weingut near Selzen. Frau Schätzel says this wine jelly tastes wonderful on waffles, cottage cheese, and on toast spread with butter or cream cheese. She also serves the jelly as a condiment for cold roast beef, turkey, ham, and smoked tongue; as a flavoring for red cabbage; to fill tortes, and to sandwich Christmas cookies together. In addition, Frau Schätzel uses Red Wine Jelly as the basis of her Red Wine Jelly Horseradish Sauce and Red Wine Jelly Curry Glaze, both of which follow. She even serves it as a dessert ladled on top of baked Camembert. Frau Schätzel would use Selzener-Osterberg, Dornfelder, or Portugieser Trocken for making Red Wine Jelly, German wines all, and none alas, easily available. So, if necessary, substitute any well-balanced red table wine that's not too tannic or dry.

1 envelope plain gelatin

½ cup sugar

½ cup water

1½ cups dry red wine (preferably German)

Makes 2¼ Cups

Combine the gelatin and sugar in a small heatproof bowl, add the water, and let stand 5 minutes.

Heat the wine in a small heavy saucepan over moderately low heat just until it steams and bubbles form around the edge. Pour the hot wine into the gelatin mixture and stir until the sugar and gelatin dissolve completely. Cover and refrigerate 1½ hours, or until set.

393

RED WINE JELLY HORSERADISH SAUCE À LA SCHÄTZEL
(Rotweingelee-Meerrettichsauce à la Schätzel)

Annemarie Schätzel serves this sauce with a variety of meats (beef, pork, ham, tongue, chicken, etc.). She also likes to use it as a spread for meat sandwiches.

½ cup heavy cream, stiffly whipped

2 tablespoons prepared horseradish

2 teaspoons freshly squeezed lemon juice

¼ cup Red Wine Jelly à la Schätzel (see preceding recipe)

Makes about ⅔ cup

Combine the whipped cream, horseradish, and lemon juice in a small bowl, then fold in the red wine jelly.

RED WINE JELLY CURRY GLAZE À LA SCHÄTZEL
(Rotweingelee-Curry Glasur à la Schätzel)

Another imaginative recipe from Annemarie Schätzel of Selzen. Brush this mixture on capon, chicken, chicken breasts, or game birds as they roast, broil, or grill. "You will never have a more juicy bird than this," promises Frau Schätzel.

4 teaspoons melted unsalted butter or margarine

2 tablespoons curry powder

¼ teaspoon salt

¼ teaspoon freshly ground white pepper

¼ cup Red Wine Jelly à la Schätzel (page 393)

Makes about ⅓ cup

Combine all ingredients. Brush frequently over poultry as it roasts, broils, or grills.

BAKED WINE-GLAZED APPLES STUFFED WITH MARZIPAN, CRANBERRIES, AND RAISINS

(Glasierte Bratäpfel, Gefüllt mit Marzipan, Preiselbeeren und Rosinen)

Use this edible garnish to trim a platter of Christmas Goose (page 191), a ham, or roast of pork.

8 large Rome Beauty apples, cored but not peeled

Juice of 1 large lemon

1 (7-ounce) package marzipan, at room temperature and finely diced

1 cup coarsely chopped fresh or unthawed frozen cranberries

½ cup coarsely chopped raisins

2 tablespoons minced toasted blanched almonds

1 teaspoon finely grated lemon zest

¼ teaspoon freshly grated nutmeg

⅔ cup dry red wine (preferably German)

⅓ cup sugar

⅓ cup honey

2 tablespoons unsalted butter or margarine

Makes 8 servings

Preheat the oven to 375° F. Peel the top third of each apple and brush lightly with lemon juice. Mix the remaining lemon juice with the marzipan, cranberries, raisins, almonds, lemon zest, and nutmeg and press the mixture firmly into the hollows of the apples. Stand the apples upright in an ungreased shallow baking dish just large enough to hold them comfortably (they should not touch one another or the sides of the dish).

Place the wine, sugar, honey, and butter in a small heavy saucepan. Set, uncovered, over high heat, bring to a boil, then boil, uncovered, about 10 minutes until syrupy. Spoon over the apples. Bake the apples, uncovered, 50 to 60 minutes, basting often with the wine mixture, until tender and nicely glazed. Serve at once.

GERTRUD SCHALLER'S RUM POT
(Gertrud Schallers Rumtopf)

This isn't so much a recipe as a technique of layering fresh fruits, sugar, and rum into a crock and letting the mixture "work" the better part of a year. Germans say that "a Rumtopf *that begins in May will be ready by Christmas." How do you use* Rumtopf? *As a dessert or dessert topping, as a filling for crepes and omelets, as an ingredient in drinks, even as a flaming sauce. Gertrud Schaller, a superlative home cook who lives and works in Munich, says that to make a proper* Rumtopf, *you need, first of all, a deep, 3- to 5-quart ceramic crock with a tight-fitting lid. Next, you need a cool, dark, dry spot to store the crock. Here, then, is how Gertrud makes* Rumtopf:

(Recipe too flexible for a specific yield)

1. Begin as soon as the first spring fruits ripen. In late April, May, and June, for example, put a layer of ripe strawberries – carefully stemmed, washed, and dried – in the crock and add an equal weight of sugar. Next, pour in enough dark rum to cover the berries by 1 inch. Cover the crock tightly and let it begin to "work."

Check now and again and if the rum has seeped into the fruit, add enough fresh rum to bring the level of it a full inch above the fruit. Also, stir the *Rumtopf* occasionally because the sugar tends to sink to the bottom. Don't worry if you mash the fruit while stirring – it's a sign the *Rumtopf* is "working" well.

2. In June and July when cherries come into season, add them to the *Rumtopf.* Stem (but do not pit) the cherries, wash well, pat dry, then add to the crock along with an equal weight of sugar and enough dark rum to cover the cherries by 1 inch. Once again, stir the fruits occasionally and if the level of rum falls below an inch, top it off. The rum should cover the fruits by 1 inch at all times.

3. Between June and August, add ripe apricots and peaches. They should be peeled, pitted, and halved or quartered, if large, then added to the *Rumtopf* along with an equal quantity of sugar and enough dark rum to cover them by 1 inch. For extra flavor, drop in a few cracked pits.

4. Between June and October, you can add as many or as few of the following as you like: ripe gooseberries, red or black currants, lingonberries, blueberries, blackberries, raspberries. But each time you add fruit you must also add an equal weight of sugar and enough dark rum to cover the combined fruits by 1 inch. Again, check the *Rumtopf* from time to time, stirring and adding more rum, if needed.

5. The time to add plums is between July and September – purple plums, the smaller Italian variety, and if available,

GERTRUD SCHALLER'S
RUM POT

the little golden Mirabelles. Add each in layers (stem but do not peel or pit). And, as before, add the requisite amounts of sugar and rum. You can also add grapes during the summer; choose seedless varieties and stem them but do not peel.

6. Between August and October, add apples and/or pears. Use only top-quality fruits, immerse them briefly in hot water, pat dry, peel, quarter, and core. As before, add an equal weight of sugar and enough dark rum to cover.

7. At any time you can add fresh pineapple that's been peeled, cored, and cut into 1-inch chunks, but you must also add the requisite amounts of sugar and rum.

Some people put citrus fruits in their *Rumtopf*, but Getrud never does. You must remember to check your *Rumtopf* every few weeks, stirring it and adding rum as needed to keep the fruits covered at all times by at least 1 inch.

Gertrud says it's traditional to let the family taste the *Rumtopf* at Advent, but that no one should actually begin eating it before Christmas. "A good *Rumtopf*," she adds, "takes seven months altogether."

How to Use Rumtopf

1. Take a large wine goblet, half fill with *Rumtopf*, and add an equal amount of whipped cream, sour cream, or crème fraîche. Mix well, then top with more whipped cream.

2. Use as a topping for any ice cream, yogurt, or pudding.

3. Drain off the excess liquid, coarsely chop the fruits, and use to fill crepes, pancakes, or dessert omelets.

4. Sieve, then serve warm or cold over peach Melba, vanilla ice cream, yellow or white cake, etc.

5. Warm carefully, blaze with a match, and spoon — still flaming — over ice cream, vanilla pudding, or cake.

6. Stir into a Christmas cocktail using about 1 part *Rumtopf* and 2½ parts well chilled dry Sekt (German sparkling wine) or Champagne.

MURBTEIG PASTRY
Mürbteig

1¼ cups sifted all-purpose flour

1 teaspoon baking powder

¼ teaspoon salt

5⅓ tablespoons well-chilled unsalted butter (no substitute), cut into small dice

1 extra-large egg

Makes enough to line a 9- or 10-inch springform pan or a 10- to 14-inch tart tin

Unlike standard American piecrusts, which tend to shatter or toughen when mishandled, murbteig *is altogether malleable and accommodating. It patches like a dream, takes a fair amount of abuse without toughening, and remains remarkably dry and flaky even with berry or cheesecake fillings. The proportion of fat to flour is relatively high and the only liquid ingredient is a single egg, which not only moistens the pastry, but also keeps it from crumbling as you work with it.* Murbteig *is as plastic as Pla-Doh and just as much fun to shape.*

Sift the flour, baking powder, and salt into a large mixing bowl. Scatter the bits of butter over the surface, then, using a pastry blender, cut the butter into the dry ingredients until the mixture resembles coarse meal. Break the egg into the bowl and fork briskly, mashing any still dry areas into the moistened ones to form a smooth soft pastry. Wrap the pastry in wax paper and let rest at room temperature for 30 minutes – this makes it easier to handle.

To line a 9- or 10-inch springform pan: Roll two thirds of the pastry on a well-floured pastry cloth with a floured, stockinette-covered rolling pin into a circle about 1 inch larger in diameter than the springform pan bottom. Center the pan bottom on the pastry circle and, with a well-floured sharp knife, trim the pastry so it is exactly ½ inch larger all around than the pan bottom. Gather the trimmings and add to the unrolled third of the pastry. Lift the pan bottom off the pastry circle, lay the rolling pin across the center of the pastry circle, carefully lop half the pastry over the pin, then transfer to and center on the pan bottom. Gently insert the pastry-covered pan bottom into the loosened springform sides. Tighten the springform sides and clamp shut.

Roll the remaining pastry into a strip 18 inches long and 5 inches wide. Using a ruler and a very sharp well-floured

MURBTEIG PASTRY

knife, square up the ragged edges so the strip measures 17½ x 4½ inches. Halve the pastry strip lengthwise into two 17½ x 2¼-inch strips. Next, halve each strip crosswise so you have four 8¾ x 2¼-inch pastry strips; reserve all trimmings. (The pastry is too fragile to apply a single long strip around the side of the springform pan, so it's best to fit it in four sections.)

Lift one pastry strip and arrange it around the side of the springform pan, letting it overlap the pastry circle on the bottom by about ¼ inch. The upper edge of the pastry strip will lop over as you try to smooth it against the pan side; let it, then simply pinch the doubled-over portion together and press halfway up the side of the pan. Now press and fit a second pastry strip against the pan side the same way, letting one end of it overlap one end of the first pastry strip by about ½ inch; press all seams firmly to seal. Repeat with the remaining two pastry strips so that the side of the spring-form pan is lined with a continuous strip of pastry. Once again, press all seams well to seal, paying particular atten-tion to the one where the side of the pastry shell meets the pastry circle on the bottom. Use any pastry trimmings to patch cracks or skimpy areas – simply pinch off bits of pastry and press firmly into place. The pastry is now ready to fill and bake.

To line a 10- to 14-inch tart tin: Roll the pastry on a well-floured pastry cloth with a floured, stockinette-covered rolling pin into a circle 2 inches larger than the diameter of the tart tin. Lay the rolling pin across the center of the pastry circle, carefully lop half the pastry over the pin, then ease the pastry into the tart tin. Gently press the pastry into the bottom and against the side of the tart tin, then trim off any overhang by running the rolling pin firmly across the sharp upper edge of the rim. If there are any cracked or skimpy spots, patch with the trimmings.

To bake an unfilled tart shell: Preheat the oven to 425° F. Prick the bottom of the tart shell well with a four-tined fork, place a large square of wax paper in the tart shell (use a

continued on next page

399

MURBTEIG PASTRY (cont.)

double thickness of paper for extra support), and fill with uncooked rice, dry beans, or pie weights. Bake the tart shell for 10 minutes, remove from the oven, and lift out the paper of rice. Return the tart shell to the oven and bake, uncovered, for 2 to 3 minutes longer, just until pale tan. Cool the tart shell to room temperature, then fill as individual recipes direct.

Variation

Sweet Murbteig Pastry (Süsser Mürbteig): Prepare Murbteig Pastry as directed, but omit the salt and add 2 tablespoons sugar, sifting it into the bowl along with the flour and baking powder. Roll and fit the pastry into a springform pan or tart tin according to the directions above. Also, for any tart shells that are to be baked before they're filled, proceed as directed above.

VANILLA SUGAR
Vanillezucker

Vanilla-flavored granulated sugar is sold in Germany in little packets much the way yeast and gelatin are here. Serious German cooks prefer to make their own supply by burying split vanilla beans in an airtight canister of sugar.

4 cups sugar

3 vanilla beans, split lengthwise

Makes 4 cups

Pour the sugar into a 1-quart preserving jar and thrust the vanilla beans down into the sugar, distributing them evenly. Screw the jar lid on tight, then let the sugar season for a week to 10 days before using. Use in any recipes calling for Vanilla Sugar.

Note: Whenever you dip into the jar of vanilla sugar, always replace the amount you remove with fresh sugar. And if the vanilla beans lose strength, insert fresh beans.

Variation

Vanilla 10X Sugar (Vanillepuderzucker): Prepare as directed above, but substitute 4 cups unsifted confectioners' (10X) sugar for the granulated. Use in any recipes calling for confectioners' sugar or Vanilla 10X Sugar.

ORANGE SUGAR

Orangenzucker

Wonderful to have on hand. Sprinkle over fruit pancakes, over cakes and cookies, over fresh berries or peaches, even over drifts of whipped cream. If you have a mini food processor, this is a snap to make. It can also be done in a large food processor or electric blender, but these aren't so efficient with such small amounts. Choose a dry day for making Orange Sugar. If the humidity's high, the sugar will become sticky, even syrupy.

½ cup sugar

Zest of ½ large navel orange, removed in strips with a
   swivel-bladed vegetable peeler

Makes about 1 cup

Place the sugar and strips of orange zest in a mini food processor and buzz 20 seconds. Scrape down the sides of the workbowl, then buzz 20 to 30 seconds longer, until the orange rind is finely grated. Spread the orange sugar out on a sheet of wax paper and allow to air-dry several hours. Store in an airtight jar in a cool dry spot. It keeps almost indefinitely. Use in any recipe calling for Orange Sugar.

Variation

Lemon Sugar (Zitronenzucker): Prepare as directed above, but substitute the zest of 1 large lemon for that of ½ orange. Store airtight. Use interchangeably with Orange Sugar.

401

BIBLIOGRAPHY

Bibliographie

Adam, Hans Karl. *Das Kochbuch vom Ober-rhein*. Münster: Wolfgang Hölker, 1975.

Allkemper, Gisela. *Das Kochbuch von der Mosel*. Münster: Wolfgang Hölker, 1978.

Allkemper, Gisela, and von der Haar, Anne-lene. *Das Kochbuch aus dem Münsterland*. Münster: Wolfgang Hölker, 1974.

————. *Bayerische Küchen-Schätze*. Münster: Wolfgang Hölker, 1982.

Ambrosi, Hans, and Stewart, Kerry. *Travellers Wine Guide: Germany*. New York: Sterling Publishing Co., Inc., 1990.

A Short Guide to German Wines. Mainz: Deutsches Weininstitut GmbH.

Aureden, Lilo. *Was Männern so gut schmeckt*. Munich: Paul List, 1961.

Baedeker's Germany. New York: Prentice Hall Press.

Baedeker's Munich. Stuttgart: Baedeker. English Edition, London: Jarrold and Sons Ltd., 1987.

Becker, Fritz. *Cookbook from Berlin*. English translation by Jacqueline Jeffers. Münster: Wolfgang Hölker, 1988.

Bentley, James. *Blue Guide Germany*. New York: W.W. Norton, 1987.

Berlitz German for Travellers, Second Revised Edition. Lausanne: Berlitz Publishing S.A., 1990.

Berlitz European Menu Reader. Lausanne: Editions Berlitz, 1982.

Berlitz Travellers Guide to Germany 1992, Alan Tucker, General Editor; John Dornberg, Editorial Consultant. New York: Berlitz Publishing Company, Inc., 1992.

Bianchini, Francesco; Corbetta, Francesco; and Pistoia, Marilena. *The Complete Book of Fruits & Vegetables*, English translation by Italia and Alberto Mancinelli. New York: Crown, 1976.

Bol, Bernard. *Frankforter, Ein Kochbuch für Frankfurter Fans*. Taufkirchen: Verlag Zabert Sandmann GmbH, 1991.

Brot mit Fantasie. Bonn: Centrale Marketing gesellschaft der Deutschen Agrarwirtschaft mbH.

Brot Zeiten. Bonn: Centrale Marketinggesell-schaft der Deutschen Agrarwirtschaft mbH.

Burger, Hannes, and Schuhbeck, Alfons. *Bayern mit Leib und Seele; die Menschen, die Landschaft, die Küche*. Taufkirchen: Zabert Sandmann GmbH, 1991.

Das grosse Weihnachtsbuch. Gütersloh: Mohndruck Reinhard Mohn OHG.

Davidson, Alan. *North Atlantic Seafood*. New York: Viking, 1979.

————. *Seafood, A Connoisseur's Guide and Cookbook*. New York: Simon & Schuster, 1989.

————. *Fruit: A Connoisseur's Guide and Cookbook*. New York: Simon & Schuster, 1991.

Deskins, Barbara B. *Everyone's Guide to Better Food and Nutrition*. Middle Village, New York: Jonathan David Publishers, Inc., 1975.

Die gute Küche: Kleingebäck. Munich: Mosaik Verlag, GmbH, 1987.

Deutschland. Karlsruhe: Michelin Reifenwerke KGaA, 1991.

Dr. Oetker Weihnachtliches Backen. Bielefeld: Ceres-Verlag, Rudolf-August Oetker KG, 1984.

Dowell, Philip, and Bailey, Adrian. *Cooks' Ingredients*. New York: William Morrow, 1980.

Duff, Gail. *A Book of Herbs & Spices: Recipes, Remedies, and Lore*. Topsfield, Massachusetts: Salem House Publishers, 1987.

Editors of *essen & trinken. Die schönsten Rezepte der deutschen Küche*. Cologne: Naumann & Göbel Verlagsgesellschaft.

Ellison, Al. *Ellison's German Menu Reader*. Miami: Ellison, 1977.

Essen Wie Gott in Deutschland. Hamburg: Zabert Sandmann, 1987.

Exporthandbuch für Süsswaren der Bundesrepublik Deutschland, 5e Edition. Bonn: Centrale Marketinggessellschaft der deutschen Agrarwirtschaft mbH., 1989/90.

Fitness und Lebensfreude mit Milch, Butter, Käse. Bonn: Centrale Marketinggesellschaft der Deutschen Agrarwirtschaft mbH.

Gabriel, Ingrid. *Herb Identifier & Handbook*, adapted from the German book, *Die farbige Kräuterfibel*, © 1970 by Falken-Verlag Erich Sicker KG, Wiesbaden. Translated by Manly Banister, adapted by E.W. Eagan. New York: Sterling Publishing Co., Inc., Fourth Printing, 1980.

Gayot, André. *André Gayot's The Best of Germany*. New York: Gault Millau, Prentice Hall Travel, 1991.

Gerhard, Frank. *Es weihnachtet sehr*. Künzelsau/Salzburg/Thalwil: Sigloch Edition, 1978.

German Foods and Beverages, US Product Information Catalog. CMA (Centrale Marketinggesellschaft der deutschen Agrarwirtschaft mbH). Bonn, 1989.

Germany: A Phaidon Cultural Guide. Englewood Cliffs, New Jersey: Prentice Hall, Inc., 1985.

Germany: West Germany and Berlin, Michelin, 7th ed. Harrow, England: Michelin Tyre Public Limited Company, Davy House, 1986.

Graff, Monika. *Pfeffernuss und Mandelkern*. Weil der Stadt: Walter Hädecke Verlag.

Grieve, M. *Culinary Herbs and Condiments*. New York: Dover Publications, Inc., 1971.

Grigson, Jane. *Jane Grigson's Book of European Cookery*. New York: Atheneum, 1983.

Guten Appetit! (Fifth Printing). New Braunfels, Texas: Sophienburg Museum, 1988.

Hale, William Harlan, and The Editors of *Horizon Magazine;* Wendy Buehr, Editor; Tatiana McKenna, Recipes Editor; Mimi Sheraton, Historical Foods Consultant. *The Horizon Cookbook and Illustrated History of Eating and Drinking through the Ages*. New York: American Heritage Publishing Co., distributed by Doubleday, 1968.

Harte, Ingeborg. *Gut essen ist mein Leibgericht*. Marbach/Neckar: Süd-West Verlags-und Vertriebs-GmbH, 1958.

Hazelton, Nika Standen, and the editors of Time-Life Books. *The Cooking of Germany*. New York: Time-Life Books, 1969.

Hofmann, Maria. *Bayerisches Kochbuch*. Munich: Birken-Verlag, 1972.

Howe, Robin. *German Cooking*. London: Granada, 1971.

Insight Guides: Germany, Director, Hans Höfer, APA Publications. Singapore: Hoefer Press Pte., Ltd.

Jackson, Michael. *Pocket Guide to Beer*. New York: Simon & Schuster, 1991.

Jamieson, Ian. *Pocket Guide to German Wines*. New York: Simon & Schuster, 1987.

Johnson, Hugh. *The Atlas of German Wines*. New York: Simon & Schuster, 1986.

———. *Hugh Johnson's Modern Encyclopedia of Wine* (Third Edition, Revised and Updated). New York: Simon & Schuster, 1991.

Kane, Robert S. *Germany at Its Best*. Lincolnwood, Illinois: Passport Books, 1988.

Kulinarische Streifzüge durch Baden. Künzelsau: Sigloch Edition, 1982/1987.

Lambley, Hanne. *The Home Book of German Cookery*. London: Faber and Faber, 1979.

Langenscheidts Enzyklopädisches Wörterbuch der englischen und deutschen Sprache, "Der Grosse Muret-Sanders," Deutsch-Englisch, 1. Band A-K, 2. Band L-Z, 5. Auflage 1990. Edited by Dr. Otto Springer. Berlin: Langenscheidt KG, 1974, 1975.

Langenscheidt Condensed Muret-Sanders German Dictionary: English-German, Edited by Helmut Willmann and Heinz Messinger and the Langenscheidt Editorial Staff. Berlin: Langenscheidt KG, 1985.

Leeb, Olli; English translation by Maria M. Rerrich. *Bavarian Cooking*. Munich: O. Leeb Kochbuch-Verlag, 1981.

Lichine, Alexis. *Alexis Lichine's Encyclopedia of Wines & Spirits.* New York: Knopf, 1967.

Loewenfeld, Claire, and Back, Philippa. *The Complete Book of Herbs & Spices.* North Pomfret, Vermont: David & Charles, 1978; New Edition, 1985.

Lukullischer Reiseführer: 45 Autoreisen durch Deutschland. Bonn: Centrale Marketinggesellschaft der Deutschen Agrarwirtschaft mbH. Bielefeld: Ceres-Verlag Rudolf-August Oetker KG.

McClane, A.J., photography by de Zanger, Arie. *The Encyclopedia of Fish Cookery.* New York: Holt, Rinehart and Winston, 1977.

Miller, Fulton. *Miller's German Cookbook.* Concord, California: Nitty Gritty Productions, 1972.

Müller, H.P. *Frankfurter Küch und Sprüch.* Frankfurt: Frohes Frankfurt, 1984.

Münster: Ein Spaziergang durch die Hauptstadt Westfalens. Münster: Helikon Verlag, 1986.

Nagel, Kurt, and Brommer, Ulrike. *Das Kochbuch aus dem Schwarzwald.* Münster: Wolfgang Hölker, 1978.

———. *Das Kochbuch aus Baden.* Münster: Wolfgang Hölker, 1982.

Neuner-Duttenhofer, Bernd. *Cookbook from Munich and Bavaria.* English translation by Jacqueline Jeffers. Münster: Wolfgang Hölker, 1982.

The Penguin Guide to Germany, Alan Tucker, General Editor; John Dornberg, Editorial Consultant. New York: Penguin Books, 1991.

Pigott, Stewart. *Great Wines of the Rhine & Mosel.* London: S.M. Pigott Books, 1990.

Rivkin, Bernard. *The Gourmet's Companion, Germany.* New York: John Wiley & Sons, Inc., 1991.

Root, Waverley. *Food.* New York: Simon & Schuster, 1980.

Scharfenberg, Horst. *The Cuisines of Germany: Regional Specialities and Traditional Home Cooking.* New York: Poseidon Press, 1989.

Schneider, Elizabeth. *Uncommon Fruits & Vegetables, A Commonsense Guide.* New York: Harper & Row, 1986.

Schnitzer, J.G. *Backen mit Vollkorn für Hausfrauen und Hobby-Bäcker.* St. Georgen im Schwarzwald: Schnitzer Verlag.

Schuhbeck, Alfons. *Das neue bayrische Kochbuch.* Steinhagen: Zabert Sandmann GmbH, 1990.

Sheraton, Mimi. *The German Cookbook.* New York: Random House, 1965.

Straub, Maria Elisabeth. *Grönen Aal und Rode Grütt, Von Tafelfreuden und Trinksitten an der Waterkant.* Hamburg: Ernst Kabel Verlag GmbH, 1971.

Sturtevant's Notes on Edible Plants, edited by U.P. Hedrick. Albany, New York: J.B. Lyon Company, 1919.

Tannahill, Reay. *Food in History: The New, Fully Revised, and Updated Edition.* New York: Crown, 1973, 1988.

Trager, James. *Foodbook.* New York: Grossman, 1970.

Ward, Artemus. *The Encyclopedia of Food.* New York: Artemus Ward, 1923.

Wason, Betty. *Cooks, Gluttons, and Gourmets.* Garden City, New York: Doubleday, 1962.

Witzigmann, Eckhart. *Das Tantris Kochbuch.* Munich: Mosaik Verlag GmbH, 1978.

———. *La Nouvelle Cuisine Allemande et Autrichienne.* Paris: Robert Laffont, 1984.

Wood, George. *The Visitor's Guide to Germany: Black Forest.* Edison, New Jersey: Hunter Publishing, Inc., 1990.

The World Atlas of Food, Jane Grigson, Contributing Editor. London: Mitchell Beazley Publishers, and New York: Simon & Schuster, 1974.

Younger, William. *Gods, Men, and Wine,* The Wine and Food Society. Cleveland: World, 1966.

405

ACKNOWLEDGMENTS
Danksagung

In Germany

Clemens Averbeck, chef, Restaurant Averbecks Giebelhof, Senden; Karen Baedeker, Munich; René Alexander Balin, managing director, Hotel Vier Jahreszeiten Kempinski, Munich; Helga Baumeister, Murnau; Philipp W. Bonnet, Weingut-Sektgut Alfred Bonnet, Friedelsheim; Brenner's Park-Hotel, Baden-Baden; Bernhard Breuer, Weingut Georg Breuer, Rüdesheim; Bristol Hotel Kempinski, Berlin; Michael Brodersen, press officer, Berlin Tourist Office; Willi Brunner family, Hotel-Restaurant Ritter, Durbach; Café Kranzler, Berlin; Walter Carle, executive chef, Hotel Gravenbruch Kempinski, Frankfurt; Horst-Dieter Ebert, formerly contributing editor, *Feinschmecker*, Hamburg; Wolfgang Engel, Hochheim; Ingrid Finger-Koester, public relations manager, Hotel Gravenbruch Kempinski, Frankfurt; Alice Fitz, Weingut Fitz-Ritter, Bad Dürkheim; Heide Gekeler, Hotel Nassauer Hof, Wiesbaden; Helmut J. Gentner, assistant to the general manager, Breidenbacher Hof, Düsseldorf; Ulrike Gerz, Kiedrich; Hanns Joachim Louis Guntrum, Weingut Louis Guntrum, Nierstein.

Also Annemarie Göbel, Garmisch-Partenkirchen; Grand Hotel Berlin; Birger R. Hansen, Deinhard & Co., Koblenz; Axel Henkel, chef, Le Délice, Hamburg; Frank Heppner, chef, Mark's Restaurant, Hotel Rafael, Munich; Gertrud Heinz, Deutsches Weininstitut GmbH, Mainz; Friedrich Hübner, Hochheim; Josef and Frau Huber, proprietors, Hotel Tonihof, Eschenlohe; Hildegard Jorek, Frankfurt; Christa Jüngling, Weingut Paulinshof, Kesten; Claus Köchling, chef de cuisine, Atlantic Hotel Kempinski, Hamburg; Kur-und Sporthotel Dollenberg, Bad Peterstal-Griesbach; Klaus Lauer, Hotel Römerbad, Badenweiler; Helmut Leyendecker, former director, Grand Hotel Sonnenbichel, Garmisch-Partenkirchen; Hedda Manhard, Munich; Angelika Miebs, Mainz; Joachim Möhringer, chef, Hotel Römerbad, Badenweiler; Edith Müllenbrock, Stuttgart;

Jörg Müller, chef, Landhaus Nösse, Sylt; Ilona Neufang, Ansbach; Parkhotel Adler, Hinterzarten; Hermann Pflaum, chef, Pflaums Posthotel, Pegnitz; Peter Ploog, editor, *essen & trinken*, Hamburg; Petra Pohl, Weinkellerei Peter Mertes KG, Bernkastel-Kues; the late Werner Pompl, Bamberg; Post-Hotel Partenkirchen, Garmisch-Partenkirchen; Herbert Pucher, chef, Krone, Assmannshausen; Elisabeth Riehemann, public relations manager, Hotel Vier Jahreszeiten Kempinski, Munich; Anne Roehnaldt, Hamburg; Doris Rüttinger, Heidelberg.

Also, Judith Schäfer from Weingut Michael Schäfer, Burg Layen; Dr. Verena Schäfer, Munich; Gertrud Schaller, Munich; Annemarie Schätzel, Weingut Kapellenhof ÖK. Rat. Schätzel Erben, Selzen; Günter Scherrer, chef, Victorien Restaurant, Düsseldorf; Beatrix Carolyn Schmitt, Weingut Hermann Franz Schmitt, Hermannshof, Nierstein; Harald Schmitt, chef, Orangerie, Hotel Nassauer Hof, Wiesbaden; Alfons Schuhbeck, chef-owner, Kurhaus Stüberl, Waging am See; Bernhard Schuster, chef, Hotel Breidenbacher Hof, Düsseldorf; Petra Schuster, Weingut Eduard Schuster, Kallstadt; Johannes and Barbara Selbach, Weingut Selbach-Oster, Zeltingen; Susanne Semmroth, director of public relations, Atlantic Hotel Kempinski, Hamburg; Cissy Spranger, Munich; Fée Steifensand, Weingut P.J. Valckenberg, Worms.

Vielen Dank, too, to Kerry Stewart, director of public relations, H. Sichel Söhne GmbH, Alzey, for gathering such a treasury of recipes from friends and vintners all over Germany; Martina Stock, Garmisch-Partenkirchen; Erika Stölzl, Murnau; Erika Wedell, Frankfurt; Peter Wehlauer, formerly chef-owner, Burg Windeck, Baden-Baden; Josef Viehauser, chef, Le Canard, Hamburg; Hanne Vogt, formerly German National Tourist Board, Frankfurt; Margot von Glasenapp, Pinneberg; Freifrau von Gleichenstein, Weingut Freiherr von Gleichenstein, Oberrotweil am Kaiserstuhl, Heinz Wehmann, chef, Landhaus Scherrer, Hamburg; Weingut Dr. Willkomm'sche Weingutsverwaltung, Bernkastel-Kues; Frau Reverchon, Weingut Edmund Reverchon, Konz-Filzen; Weingut Gustav Gessert, Nierstein; Weingut Schales, Flörsheim/Dalsheim; Weingut Selbach-Oster, Zeltingen; Paula Willibald, Geienhofen-Horb; Friedl Winkler, Munich; Heinz Winkler, chef-owner, Residenz Heinz Winkler, Aschau im Chiemgau; Herbert Winkler, Tourist Office, Munich; Eckhart Witzigmann, chef-owner, Restaurant Aubergine, Munich; Karl Uwe Woggon, Mainz; Harald Wohlfahrt, chef, Schwarzwaldstube, Baiersbronn-Tonbach; Hannelore Würz, Düsseldorf, and not least, Karl-Heinz Zimmermann, general manager, Hotel Rafael, Munich, for being a perfect host.

And in New York

To Helga Brenner, German National Tourist Office, for giving so freely of her time, translation talents, and recipe files; Ruth Buchan, for her deft hand with the tasting spoon and keen editorial eye; Monika Dorman, manager of tourism, The Hamburg North American Representation, for sharing her cookbook library and directing us to talented German home cooks now living in the U.S.; Dr. Lamar Elmore, formerly executive director, German Wine Information Bureau, for sounding the call for recipes throughout the German wine country, for writing the chapter on German wines and beers, and for answering a zillion questions with grace and alacrity; Marion Gorman for so generously sharing the names and numbers on her Rolodex, Linda E. Greco, for answering our call for recipes; Linda Gwinn, director, public relations, The Leading Hotels of the World, for providing dozens of recipes from a stellar roster of German hotel chefs, also for seeing that the pillows we laid our heads on during our many research trips to Germany were never less than the best; Lucille M. Hoshabjian, corporate communications manager, Lufthansa German Airlines, for ensuring that each of our trips to Germany was made in supreme comfort.

Thanks, too, to Peter Kump, president, The James Beard Foundation, for unflagging support and encouragement; Inke Littman, for sharing her knowledge of Hamburg cooking; Dr. and Mrs. Allen W. Mead, taste-testers extraordinaire; Sara Moulton, executive chef, *Gourmet*, for leading us to purveyors of unusual and out-of-season foods.

For a thousand and one assists, our deepest thanks to Brigitte U. Rothlisberger, director of marketing, German Agricultural Marketing Board, who opened doors and files, not to mention both her professional and personal libraries; to Susanne Rüttinger, too, German Information Center; and to Schaller & Weber, *ein wunderbarer* butcher, for helping us sort out the bewildering array of German wursts.

Also, many, many thanks to Peter M. F. Sichel, chairman, H. Sichel Söhne; to Carol Sullivan, executive director, German Wine Information Bureau, and her assistants, Cindy Krebs and Monica Neufang, for endless checking and rechecking plus a hundred and one other assists; to Dieter von Lehsten, Hamburg North American representative; Christa Willibald, German National Tourist Office, and Carol Zaiser, Gillies and Zaiser, for so generously sharing family recipes.

And finally…

A thousand thanks to Hedy's aunt, Betty Muller, Chicago, home baker without peer, for allowing us to print so many of her cherished recipes.

407

INDEX

411

416